It's Interpersonal

An Introduction to Relational Communication

It's
Interpersonal
An Introduction to Relational Communication

Bruce Punches

Kalamazoo Valley Community College

Leslie Ramos Salazar

West Texas A&M University

W. W. NORTON & COMPANY
Independent Publishers Since 1923

W. W. NORTON & COMPANY has been independent since its founding in 1923, when William Warder Norton and Mary D. Herter Norton first published lectures delivered at the People's Institute, the adult education division of New York City's Cooper Union. The firm soon expanded its program beyond the Institute, publishing books by celebrated academics from America and abroad. By midcentury, the two major pillars of Norton's publishing program—trade books and college texts—were firmly established. In the 1950s, the Norton family transferred control of the company to its employees, and today—with a staff of five hundred and hundreds of trade, college, and professional titles published each year—W. W. Norton & Company stands as the largest and oldest publishing house owned wholly by its employees.

Editor: Peter Simon
Senior Associate Editor: Gerra Goff
Associate Editor: Katie Pak
Editorial Assistant: Olivia Atmore
Manuscript Editor: Samantha Held
Project Editor: Linda Feldman
Production Managers: Elizabeth Marotta and Stephen Sajdak
Managing Editor, College: Marian Johnson
Managing Editor, College Digital Media: Kim Yi
Media Editor: Joy Cranshaw
Associate Media Editor: Katie Bolger
Media Project Editor: Cooper Wilhelm
Ebook Production Manager: Sophia Purut
Market Research and Strategy Manager, Communication & Media: Trevor Penland
Sales and Market Development Specialists, Humanities: Kim Bowers, Elizabeth Pieslor, and Emily Rowin
Design Director: Rubina Yeh
Designer: Lissi Sigillo
Photo Editor: Melinda Patelli
Photo Researcher: Lynn Gadson
Director of College Permissions: Megan Schindel
Permissions Researcher: Elizabeth Trammell
Composition/Illustrations: Graphic World
Manufacturing: TC Transcontinental, Interglobe

Permission to use copyrighted material is included in the credits section of this book, which begins on page C1.

Names: Punches, Bruce, author. | Ramos Salazar, Leslie, 1984- author.
Title: It's interpersonal : an introduction to relational communication / Bruce Punches
   & Leslie Ramos Salazar.
Description: First edition. | New York : W.W. Norton & Company, Inc., [2022] |
   Includes bibliographical references and index.
Identifiers: LCCN 2021013300 | **ISBN 9780393442014** (paperback) | ISBN 9780393442052 (epub)
Subjects: LCSH: Interpersonal communication.
Classification: LCC HM1166 .P86 2022 | DDC 158.2—dc23 LC record available at https://lccn.loc.
   gov/2021013300

W. W. Norton & Company, Inc., 500 Fifth Avenue, New York, NY 10110
wwnorton.com

W. W. Norton & Company Ltd., 15 Carlisle Street, London W1D 3BS

1 2 3 4 5 6 7 8 9 0

In loving memory of Beverly Ann Punches
(1940–2017)

brief contents

contents

I Introducing Interpersonal Communication 3

Chapter 2
The Process of Interpersonal Communication 30

II Foundations in Interpersonal Communication 59

Chapter 3
Perception and the Self 60

Chapter 5
Verbal Communication 118

Chapter 6
Nonverbal Communication 144

Chapter 7
Emotional Expression 170

Chapter 8
Relationship Dynamics 198

Chapter 9
Interpersonal Conflict 226

III Contemporary Topics in Interpersonal Communication 257

Chapter 10
Diversity and Inclusion 258

Chapter 11
Communication and Technology 286

Chapter 12
Ethics and Civility 310

about the authors

Bruce Punches teaches interpersonal communication and public speaking at Kalamazoo Valley Community College in Kalamazoo, Michigan. He earned a teaching degree in speech communications from Alma College, an MA in counseling psychology from Central Michigan University, and an MA in interpersonal communication from Western Michigan University. Bruce is also a licensed psychotherapist in private practice. His specialty is in relational communication and couples' therapy. As a professional speaker and consultant, Bruce presents workshops on interpersonal communication topics to companies large and small.

Leslie Ramos Salazar is a tenured associate and Abdullat professor at the Paul and Virginia Engler College of Business at West Texas A&M University. She earned a PhD in interpersonal communication at Arizona State University. She teaches interpersonal communication, business communication, health communication, and public speaking, and has published more than 30 articles and book chapters. She has presented more than 70 papers at communication conferences, and her research specialties include health communication, education, cyberbullying, and relationships.

preface

Prior to writing this textbook, we spent a considerable amount of time talking to students who were enrolled in introductory-level interpersonal communication courses. Most attend a high school, community college, or technical/vocational college and were taking the course as a general education requirement or elective. We also interviewed colleagues from diverse campuses who teach this course on a regular basis.

Based on feedback from these students and faculty, we concluded that students often lack the motivation to read and learn when they perceive their assigned reading material as dry, uninteresting, or not personally relevant. One of our colleagues stated: "I work hard to get my students fired up about the content in the textbook. I'd love to teach from a textbook that generates more student interest and engagement."

Along with reader disinterest, we also discovered that if an introductory interpersonal textbook is written for a different audience—for communication majors or scholars—students taking a general education introductory course may feel overwhelmed by lengthy chapters that cover a lot of content. As a result, students may put forth less effort to read assignments, which may reduce their learning potential.

It's Interpersonal: An Introduction to Relational Communication is meant to provide instructors and students with a topical textbook that emphasizes engagement, conciseness, and skill-building practicality. Our goal is to motivate students to read and learn from their textbook by making the content thought provoking, relevant, and fun to read.

We also committed ourselves to expressing the material in a clear, concrete, and succinct way. Compared to the current leading interpersonal textbooks, our text is composed of shorter chapters. Our emphasis is on the big concepts, theories, and techniques of interpersonal communication. Most students will read an entire chapter in less than an hour without experiencing information overload or reader fatigue.

It's Interpersonal is written in a lively manner using a relaxed, conversational tone. The authorial "voice" is often in the first person. Students have a strong presence in the writing—it is for and about them. We include narratives and personal examples from our own experiences and those provided to us by our students. We made an effort to include real-life scenarios, popular culture references, character dialogue, stimulating questions, and humor.

We wrote *It's Interpersonal* for the non-majors introductory course, but the response from dozens of instructors to draft versions of the chapters has made us realize—happily—that the book's practical, relevant, and engaging approach will be eagerly welcomed in interpersonal communication courses of all types and levels. We have been gratified by this early response and we look forward to hearing from both instructors and students in the years to come so that we can continue to improve the text's appeal and usefulness.

What's in the Book

It's Interpersonal covers all the major topics of a typical introductory interpersonal course in 12 chapters that are organized into three major parts: Introducing Interpersonal Communication (two chapters that establish the importance, relevance, and nature of interpersonal communication), Foundations in Interpersonal Communication (seven chapters that cover the most commonly taught topics in IPC), and Contemporary Topics in Interpersonal Communication (three chapters that focus on issues of diversity, technology, and communication ethics).

Each chapter in *It's Interpersonal* offers the following:

- **Opening Vignette.** We begin each chapter with a vignette that connects the theme of the chapter with a real-life scenario. These stories introduce the chapter content to students in a relatable and engaging way, and they demonstrate the ways skillful IPC can be used to create and enhance healthy relationships.

- **YouTube Features.** To illustrate the key concepts of interpersonal communication, each chapter presents multiple YouTube videos to prompt students to recognize and analyze what they've just learned.

- **Short Narratives.** Personal narratives inspired by our students are peppered throughout the text to provide engaging examples of core concepts. Readers are asked to identify ways in which they can relate to and interpret the communication behaviors of other students: *How have I experienced this before? Where did they go wrong (or right)?*

- **Marginal Key** Terms. In the margins of the text, abbreviated definitions of each key term recap important information as students read and provide a helpful study tool during review.

- **Section Reviews.** Each chapter is organized into three sections, each with its own review. Each section review contains a summary, list of key terms, and comprehension questions that ask students to define and explain the section's terms and concepts. In addition, an *Apply It!* feature asks students to apply what they've learned to their own lives or an imagined scenario and share with classmates.

- **End-of-chapter Assessment and Skill-building Exercises.** *It's Interpersonal* helps students incorporate what they've learned in each chapter into their daily lives through exercises that assess and build upon their IPC skills. Found at the end of every chapter, these exercises *assess* IPC skills such as *communication comprehension* and *nonverbal expressiveness* through quizzes and self-observations. To *build* IPC skills, *It's Interpersonal* provides exercises that teach students techniques such as *perception checking* and the affective use of *I-language*. The end-of-chapter material also includes a prompt to visit InQuizitive, Norton's adaptive learning tool.

What's Online for Students

Ebook. *It's Interpersonal* is available as an ebook—readable on all computers and mobile devices—and access is included with all new print copies of the text. Students can also quickly link to relevant pages of the ebook from within InQuizitive activities. Offered at less than half the price of the print book, the ebook provides an active reading experience, enabling students to take notes, bookmark, search, highlight, and read offline. Instructors can even add notes that students can see as they are reading the text.

InQuizitive. Norton's award-winning, easy-to-use adaptive learning tool personalizes the learning experience for students, helping them to master—and retain—key learning objectives. Premade activities for each of the major chapters in the book start with questions about key concepts, proceed to application questions, and even include questions about popular culture examples cited throughout the text. Offering a variety of question types, answer-specific feedback, and interactive, gamelike features, InQuizitive motivates students to carefully read and engage with course content. As a result, students arrive better prepared for class, giving instructors more time for lecture, discussion, and activities, and giving students a more solid foundation for advanced learning and success in the course.

A robust activity report makes it easy to identify challenging concepts and allows for just-in-time intervention when students are struggling, and the convenience of learning management system (LMS) integration saves you time by allowing InQuizitive scores to report directly to your LMS gradebook.

What's Available for Instructors

Norton Teaching Tools. Building on the practical, relevant, and engaging approach of the book, Norton Teaching Tools for *It's Interpersonal* provide support for teaching every chapter in the text, including chapter outlines, tips for tackling difficult concepts, PowerPoint lecture slides, additional pop culture examples for use in class and assignments, and suggested activities and assignments for both in-person and online classes. The Norton Teaching Tools site is searchable and sortable by chapter or by resource type, making it easy to find exactly what you need for your course.

Resources for Your Learning Management System. Digital resources provided by Norton—including InQuizitive—can be integrated with your online, hybrid, or lecture courses so that all activities can be accessed within your existing learning management system. You can also add customizable multiple-choice and short-answer questions to your LMS using Norton Testmaker.

Test Bank. Norton uses evidence-based models to deliver high-quality and pedagogically effective testing materials. The framework used to develop our test banks is the result of a collaboration with leading academic researchers and advisers. More than 700 questions for *It's Interpersonal* can be searched and filtered by chapter, type, difficulty, learning objective, and other criteria in Norton Testmaker, making it easy to construct tests and quizzes that are meaningful and diagnostic. Available online, without the need for specialized software, Testmaker allows easy export of tests to Microsoft Word or Common Cartridge files for the course LMS.

Your Norton representative can provide more information about all of these resources. Visit https://wwnorton.com/find-your-rep to find your representative.

acknowledgments

The late journalist George Matthew Adams once said, "There is no such thing as a self-made [person]. We are made up of thousands of others. Everyone who has ever done a kind deed for us, or spoken one word of encouragement to us, has entered into the make-up of our character and of our thoughts, as well as our success." We are deeply grateful to the following individuals who are part of our personal and professional growth. Their positive influence helped us complete this book and inspired its content.

Bruce's Acknowledgments

During my work on this book, my mother, Beverly Punches, passed away. I owe her my first and most heartfelt thanks. I get my passion for learning and teaching from her. And to her and my father, James Punches, thank you for opening so many doors of opportunity for me and for running with my passions.

Many thanks to my partner, Torrey, and my daughters, Kaitlin and Avery. When I had to focus on my deadlines, you made it easier for me. To my colleagues in the English department at Kalamazoo Valley Community, William Dedie and Carl Ross, thank you for your significant editorial support. Many friends offered ideas in the early stages of the textbook-writing process and along the way, and the book wouldn't be what it is without their input—thank you to Ken Barr Jr., Ray Hippolyte, Jedidiah Smith, Becky Noricks, Leelan N. M. Bhagwandeen, and Tony Cherette. And most important, thank you to my former and current students, who told me quite candidly what they wanted in a book and took such an interest in its content.

Leslie's Acknowledgments

To my loving parents, Jeffrey and Elvia, thank you for your commitment, time, and support, and for raising me to believe that great things are possible.

Many thanks to my colleagues and students at West Texas A&M, who enthusiastically supported the development and completion of this book. In particular, I am grateful to Olanike Ajayi, who provided valuable feedback to several early draft chapters.

We both wish to thank the amazing team at W. W. Norton. Their talents are evident . . . everywhere! We would especially like to thank two individuals who worked right alongside us, from beginning to end: our editor, Peter Simon, and senior associate editor, Gerra Goff. Your interest in our field of study added to our enthusiasm, making our work together very productive and fulfilling. Your editing prowess, steady patience, and diligence are greatly appreciated.

We'd also like to thank our tireless manuscript and project editors, Samantha Held and Linda Feldman, for the many enhancements they made to the text. A big thank you as well to Lissi Sigillo, who created the book's brilliant design.

We extend our thanks to the many communication scholars and content experts who reviewed draft material of *It's Interpersonal*, from the first proposal that we submitted to Norton through the last round of draft versions of chapters, and who contributed helpful ideas at just the right moment in the book's development:

Brent Adrian, *Central Community College*
Mike Alvarez, *University of Massachusetts, Amherst*
Christina Ballard, *Central Community College*
Cameron Basquiat, *College of Southern Nevada*
Brett Billman, *St. Ambrose University*
Shannon Bowden, *Mississippi Valley State University*
Erin Brummett, *Bloomsburg University*
Adele Caruso, *Niagara College*
John Christensen, *University of Connecticut*
Steven Cohen, *John Hopkins Carey Business School*
Marilyn Cristiano, *Paradise Community College*
Diana Crossman, *El Camino College*
Claire Crossman, *California State University Los Angeles*
Kathleen Czech, *San Diego State University*
Andrea Davis, *Western New England University*
Amanda Denes, *University of Connecticut*
Keith Forrest, *Atlantic Cape Community College*
Janene Frahm, *City College of San Francisco*
Sonya Hopkins Barnes, *Dallas College-North Lake Campus*
Jaclyn Gaule, *Wayne State University*
Michelle Givertz, *California State University, Chico*
Jenny Goshorn, *Trident Technical College*
Chris Gurrie, *The University of Tampa*
Danielle Harkins, *Germanna Community College*
Brittany Hochstaetter, *Wake Technical Community College*
John Hyatt, *Trident Technical College*
Mary Jackson, *Jefferson Community & Technical College*
Alexis Johnson, *Arkansas Tech University*
Pamela Henderson, *University of Kentucky*
Sara Kennedy, *Hudson Valley Community College*
Linda Levitt, *Stephen F. Austin State University*
Jenny Lewallen, *Fresno City College*
Allyn Lueders, *Wayne State College*

James McCoy, *College of Southern Nevada*

Laural Medhurst, *Baylor University*

Nathan Miczo, *Illinois University*

Kevin Mitchell, *College of Southern Nevada*

Carol Morgan, *Wright University*

Marcie Pachter, *Palm Beach State College*

Andrea Peck, *Cuyahoga CC, Western*

Josh Potter-Dineen, *Pierce College*

Rody Randon, *Phoenix College*

Rachel Reznik, *Elmhurst College*

Beth Ribarsky, *University of Illinois, Springfield*

Alex Rister, *Embry-Riddle Aeronatical University*

Lori Roe, *Ivy Tech Community College*

Traci Rowe, *Wake Technical Community College*

Bryan Rufener, *Wake Technical Community College*

Erting Sa, *University of Albany, SUNY*

Scott Sellnow-Richmond, *Columbus State University*

Laura Stafford, *Bowling Green State University*

Jamie Vega, *Valencia College*

Alice Veksler, *Christopher Newport University*

Beth Waisner, *Owens Community College*

Susan Ward, *Delaware Valley Community College*

Nakia Welch, *San Jacinto College*

Maureen Wieland, *Purdue University*

Your feedback and encouragement has been invaluable, and because of it, this book is as much yours as ours. We hope your students enjoy and benefit from this book as much as we have from your good advice and support. If you have suggestions about how we might make the book even more useful, please write to us at communication@wwnorton.com.

Thank you all.

Bruce Punches
Leslie Ramos Salazar

author's note

I n *It's Interpersonal: An Introduction to Relational Communication,* we include our experiences and the experiences of others in the form of examples, narratives, and quotes to illustrate key concepts and theories. This information is edited for content, and when others are referenced, we use first name pseudonyms. Any resemblance to a specific person is entirely coincidental. Some of this content represents a combination of real-life experiences from actual people we know or from conversations we've had with students, family, and friends. We include this content for the purpose of illustration only. Where first and last names are used, these are the names of individuals who have given their permission to be named in the book and/or have been the subject of public reports.

It's
Interpersonal
An Introduction to Relational
Communication

Introducing Interpersonal Communication

1

The Importance of Interpersonal Communication

learning objectives

Reading this chapter will help you:

- Understand the relationship between IPC needs, goals, and behaviors
- Appreciate how IPC affects your well-being, relationships, and career
- Describe the characteristics of IPC competence

New York Times bestselling author Megan McCafferty published an article about her whirlwind college romance with "Ben." Their relationship came to a screeching halt quite unexpectedly. For no apparent reason, Ben stopped returning Megan's calls and texts. When he saw her at a party, he'd disappear!

Megan couldn't figure it out. What happened? She had really connected with Ben and was convinced the feelings were mutual. Megan was heartbroken. The next semester, Ben transferred to another university, and she never saw him again.

Years later, Megan came across Ben's profile on a popular social media site. The uncertainty she had about their relationship still bothered her, so she decided to reach out again to get some answers. Her initial inquiries— "Remember me?" and "Why did you behave like that?"— netted a response from Ben a month later.

Ben gave Megan an interesting answer: In a "backward way," Ben replied, "the coldness of my exit was in direct proportion to the desire I felt for you." He went on to explain how, despite his feelings for her, he thought she was totally out of his league. His insecurity took over and he panicked. He broke it off in sort of an "I'll dump you before you have the chance to dump me" maneuver.

Ben apologized for his "childish behavior," and Megan thanked him for his candor. The mystery was solved! After giving each other an update on where life had taken them, their communication ended as quickly as it started.[1]

Interpersonal communication competence can improve your health, enhance the quality of your relationships, and bolster your career success. In this image, members of a support group rely on interpersonal communication to help each other cope with personal challenges in a healthy, productive way.

Have you ever been in a situation like this? Perhaps you can relate to Megan in some way. Someone you know may have left you wondering, *What was that all about? What's going on here?* Like Megan, you may rely on your ability to communicate to clear up what you don't know.

Megan's story is a reminder that we all need, at times, to reduce uncertainty in order to manage various emotions, like worry, vulnerability, curiosity, hurt, and bewilderment. In order to minimize these feelings, we may rely on the cooperation and support of others. And it's usually mutual: to lessen what's unknown to them, they may rely on you, too.

This interdependence is not limited to reducing uncertainty in relationships. There are other interpersonal needs, as you are about to learn, that are important to fulfill. How can you meet your needs—and help your relational partners satisfy theirs—using effective communication? This is a key question as we begin our study. In this chapter, we'll (1) explore the important relationship between interpersonal communication and your needs, goals, and behaviors, (2) examine how interpersonal communication affects your health, relationships, and career, and (3) explain what it takes to improve your skills.

1.1 Interpersonal communication is purposeful

In the story you just read, Megan didn't know why Ben behaved the way he did toward her. She had a need to know. Her goal was to get a straightforward answer. To accomplish her goal, Megan chose several communication behaviors: She contacted Ben using social media and asked him several direct questions.

Like Megan, your needs, goals, and behaviors play a role in your interpersonal communication. **Interpersonal communication (IPC)** is the process of assigning meaning to the messages you exchange with potential or established relational partners. A **relational partner** is someone you know and share a connection with on some level, such as a parent, sibling, relative, friend, coworker, or romantic partner.

Every time you communicate a message interpersonally—whether deliberately or accidentally—there's a conscious or subconscious motive behind it.

Section 1.1 will help you appreciate the important relationship between interpersonal communication and your needs, goals, and behaviors. We'll also explore why it's important to think about your communication choices and how they influence your relationships.

Interpersonal needs

A need is a necessity. For example, you need food, water, and shelter to survive. Some needs are not required for survival but are nonetheless important to your physical, psychological, and social health. An **interpersonal need** is an inner drive that is essential to your well-being and relational in nature. Sharing and receiving affection is one such interpersonal need. According to Dr. Gary Chapman, a *New York Times* bestselling author, we seek and express affection in five ways, which he calls the five love languages: acts of service, gifts, quality time, touch, and words of affirmation (TABLE 1.1).[2]

According to Chapman, we value all five of the love languages to some extent, but we each differ in our preferences; we may value some more than others. Chapman also believes we generally express affection the way we prefer to

interpersonal communication (IPC) The process of assigning meaning to the messages you share with potential and established relational partners.

relational partner Someone you know and share a connection with on some level.

interpersonal need An inner drive that is essential to your well-being and relational in nature.

table 1.1	Chapman's Five Love Languages
Acts of service	• Offering your friend a ride • Cooking a special meal for your sick aunt • Helping your roommate fix his computer
Gifts	• Crafting a handmade present for your mom • Surprising your grandfather with his favorite candy bar • Buying your coworkers lottery tickets for the company holiday party
Quality time	• Spending time and doing mutually enjoyable activities together, such as yoga, fishing, or tennis
Touch	• Hugs • Cuddling • Holding hands • Sexual intimacy
Words of affirmation	• Giving compliments • Expressing appreciation • Saying "I love you" • Sharing affectionate language, like terms of endearment and flattering nicknames

receive it. For example, you may really like hearing words of affirmation more than any other love language. Likewise, you're more likely to express affection with words of affirmation because that's the love language you like the most.

But what if a relational partner—your dad, for instance—prefers to receive affection in the form of quality time? Chapman predicts you'll meet his need for affection, and thus fill his "love tank" better, by spending more quality time with him.

Along with reducing uncertainty and sharing affection, other interpersonal needs include socializing and having fun, fitting in, influencing others, offering and receiving support, gaining the respect of others, and feeling understood. These interpersonal needs are essential to your physical, psychological, and social health. Your IPC needs are what drive your IPC goals and behaviors.

Interpersonal goals

An **interpersonal goal** is what you're striving to accomplish with your communication. An interpersonal goal helps you satisfy an interpersonal need. For example, let's say your goal is to get a few friends together to play beach volleyball. If your goal is met, it satisfies your need to feel close to your friends and have fun

interpersonal goal What you are striving to accomplish with your communication.

with them. According to communication scholars Ruth Anne Clark and Jesse Delia, you communicate to achieve one (or a combination) of three primary goals: practical, relational, and self-presentational.[3]

Practical goals

Practical goals help you meet the demands of daily living. For example, Scott shares the same car with his younger stepbrother, Dain, and they coordinate their schedules each day. Their goal is to get to their respective commitments on time. In another instance, Jordan and his wife, Claire, take time to talk about the unexpected Christmas bonus Claire received from her employer. Their goal is to put this money to good use.

Relational goals

Relational goals help you to initiate, develop, maintain, repair, and terminate relationships. For example, Rolanda and her partner, Jennifer, spend several hours planning for their three-year anniversary. Their aim is to make this special day very memorable. Likewise, Gordon, a busy professional and parent, wants to stay connected with his 17-year-old stepdaughter. He's not a fan of texting, but he makes a point to text her more often because it's her preferred way to communicate.

Self-presentational goals

Self-presentational goals help you appear socially attractive. For example, on a first date with Avery, Garrick casually mentions how much he enjoys watching Lake Michigan sunsets off his 43-foot sailboat. Why? Garrick really likes Avery and wants to continue dating her. He thinks this information will impress her. Sarah has a similar goal in mind when she posts flattering pictures of herself with friends on social media. She wants everyone to know how much fun she's having—and that she has a lot of friends!

Actress Kristen Bell reveals to talk show host Ellen DeGeneres what her boyfriend, Dax, did to surprise her on her birthday. Using the five love languages, describe how Dax communicated his affection to Kristen. What needs did he try to fulfill for himself? What were his goals? Incorporate Clark and Delia's primary goals in your answer. On YouTube, search using the keywords: "Kristen Bell's Sloth Meltdown." (3:43)

Interpersonal behaviors

An **interpersonal behavior** is what you say and/or do to convey a message. An interpersonal behavior is meant to help you achieve an interpersonal goal and satisfy an interpersonal need. Interpersonal behaviors can be spoken or unspoken. Examples are bragging, making a promise, raising your voice, extending a heartfelt apology, or staring longingly into someone's eyes.

interpersonal behavior
What you say and/or do to
convey a message.

Let's look at the communication behaviors of three of the individuals mentioned previously: Scott, Gordon, and Garrick. Scott bargains with his brother Dain to coordinate their shared use of a car, a practical goal, by saying: "I won't ask for the car on Friday if you let me have it today." Bargaining is an interpersonal behavior.

To connect more with his teenage stepdaughter, a relational goal, Gordon starts texting her more often. Texting is an interpersonal behavior. During his date, Garrick discloses he owns a boat. He hopes this information will make him more appealing to Avery—a self-presentational goal. Self-disclosure is an interpersonal behavior.

Let's take what you've read so far (summarized in **TABLE 1.2**) and compare it to a specific communication behavior. A friend of yours, Sebastian, posts this on social media: "I've seen it with my own eyes. All my tall, good-looking friends are getting the hottest women to go out with them, and I'm spending Saturday night sitting on the couch . . . alone." Within minutes, you notice he's flooded with comments like, "I'd date you in a heartbeat, boo!," "Move to Los Angeles," and over a half dozen other compliments and heart emojis.

Why did Sebastian post this? People put themselves down for various reasons, but in this case, it appears Sebastian *needed* to feel good about himself. His *goal* was to reel in some flattering remarks. We call his *behavior* "fishing for compliments."

Our social interactions have taught us that if we express self-criticism, our relational partners will say something nice to make us feel good about ourselves, especially in a face-to-face situation.

table 1.2	Interpersonal Needs, Goals, and Behaviors
Interpersonal need	An inner drive that is relational in nature
Interpersonal goal	What you're striving to accomplish with your communication
Interpersonal behavior	What you say and/or do to convey a message

IPC involves choices

Throughout this textbook, we'll encourage you to think about your interpersonal needs, goals, and behaviors and how they're interrelated. For example, how do your needs and goals influence your communication behaviors? How do your communication behaviors affect your ability to satisfy and achieve your needs and goals?

It's also important to consider how your communication choices affect your relationships. For example, let's take a look at the narrative provided by Kana. What need is she trying to fulfill? What is her goal? What are her behaviors? Fill in the blanks with the words that match what is described: *need*, *goal*, or *behavior*.

"I love getting flowers. They make me feel loved and appreciated (_____). To get my boyfriend to buy me flowers more often (_____), I started bringing home flowers I ordered for myself (_____). He'd ask who I got them from, and I'd casually mention clients who appreciate the work I do for them (_____). Sure enough, he started sending me flowers at work. He also stops by the office unexpectedly to take me out to lunch!" –Kana

Kana's communication behaviors worked! Her boyfriend, Drew, started showering her with romantic attention. However, is Kana communicating her needs in the best way? What if Drew finds out she deceived him? Will he feel manipulated and stop sending her flowers altogether? Drew may have other reasons for distrusting Kana. Will Kana's communication choices make Drew's trust issues worse? How will this affect their relationship?

Now let's consider another scenario. Bryce is studying for an exam and his 6-year-old brother, Arie, keeps barging into his bedroom. Bryce thinks, *Arie is purposely trying to irritate me.* So he yells at Arie and threatens to tell on him when their mother comes home. He pushes him out of the room and slams the door in his face.

Here's an alternative choice: Bryce takes a moment to think about what's motivating his brother's behavior. Is Arie trying to irritate Bryce? Or is he determined to distract Bryce from his homework (*goal*) by coming into his room repeatedly (*behavior*) to enjoy time with his big brother and get some attention (*needs*)?

Bryce could choose to respond by saying to Arie, "I know how much you love to play *Go Fish*. I can even show you how to play a new game called *Egyptian Ratscrew* this weekend, but I have to study for an important test tomorrow. If we play *Go Fish* for twenty minutes, will you let me study quietly by myself for the rest of the evening?"

Bryce's communication is an attempt to satisfy both of their needs. If Arie agrees, Bryce will have the time he needs to study uninterrupted, and Arie will enjoy time with his brother. Bryce's communication is both other-centered and relationship-centered.

other-centered communication When you consider your relational partner's needs and goals as much as your own.

Your communication is **other-centered** when you consider your relational partner's needs and goals as much as your own. Bryce pauses for a moment to think

In this scene from the reality show *Chrisley Knows Best,* Chase Chrisley tries to hide his new tattoo from his father, Todd. Todd confronts Chase in the family's living room. Describe their communication using the concepts of interpersonal needs, goals, and behaviors. Next, imagine they're seeking your advice on how to improve their communication. What would you say to them? Incorporate the concepts of other-centered and relationship-centered communication in your answer. On YouTube, search using the keywords: "Chrisley's Top 100: Chase Tries To Hide His Tattoo From Todd." (2:25)

about what's motivating Arie's behavior. He looks past Arie's actions—which he finds very annoying—and factors in the needs Arie is trying to satisfy in the moment. Bryce adjusts his communication accordingly without neglecting his own need to prepare for and do well on his exam.

Your communication is **relationship-centered** when you make communication choices that are good for your relationship. Bryce responds to Arie in a way that enhances their relationship and reflects how much he values it.[4]

Many positive relational outcomes are associated with other-centered and relationship-centered interpersonal communication, including increased support, trust, openness, closeness, commitment, liking, love, passion, productivity, relationship satisfaction, and cooperation.[5] Sometimes, however, we communicate with only our needs in mind, and overlook our partner's needs. This behavior may reduce levels of support and trust as well as the other positive qualities that strengthen relationships.[6]

relationship-centered communication When you make communication choices that are good for a relationship.

section review

1.1 **Interpersonal communication is purposeful**

Your needs, goals, and behaviors play an important role in your IPC. Interpersonal communication also involves choices. You're more likely to experience positive relational outcomes when your communication choices enable you to (1) express your needs and goals skillfully and (2) help your relational partners satisfy their needs and achieve their goals.

(continued)

Key Terms

interpersonal communication (IPC), *p. 6*

relational partner, *p. 6*

interpersonal need, *p. 6*

interpersonal goal, *p. 7*

interpersonal behavior, *p. 9*

other-centered communication, *p. 10*

relationship-centered communication, *p. 11*

Comprehend It?

1. Define each of the key terms in Section 1.1. To further your understanding of these terms, create examples to support your definitions.

2. Compare and contrast the following concepts:
   • Interpersonal needs, goals, and behaviors
   • Other-centered and relationship-centered communication

Apply It!

Create your own narrative to illustrate the relationship between an interpersonal need, goal, and behavior. Refer to Kana's story as an example. Your narrative may serve to illustrate what you think is an effective or ineffective approach. You may draw on your own communication experiences for this exercise.

1.2 Interpersonal communication is consequential

After a heated argument, two college roommates, Jared and Felix, stop talking to each other. Despite the awkwardness and stress it causes them, they continue giving each other the silent treatment for over a week. Just before going to bed one night, Jared realizes he needs help waking up at 6:00 a.m. to get ready for an 8:00 a.m. interview. Jared has a tendency to sleep through his alarm, and getting up this early is highly unusual for him. Felix, on the other hand, is an early riser.

If all goes well tomorrow, Jared will arrive for his interview on time and land a well-paying summer internship at a company he hopes to work for someday. However, he doesn't want to break his silence and ask Felix to wake him up. He's not about to lose to Felix in their stubborn standoff, so he writes on a sticky note: "Please wake me up at 6:00 a.m.—very important." He leaves it on Felix's pillow where Felix is sure to see it.

The next morning Jared wakes up and is shocked to see it's 8:00 a.m.! He slept through his alarm and missed the interview! Next to his head is a sticky note on his pillow from Felix. It reads: "It is 6:00 a.m., wake up!"

Interpersonal communication is consequential. Our communication choices, driven by our needs and goals, may affect us positively, or in the case of Jared and Felix, negatively. Let's elaborate more on the relationship between interpersonal communication and your well-being, relationships, and career.

IPC and well-being

Satisfying social interactions and close relationships are major sources of happiness. Whether it's a quick pick-me-up when you're feeling down or some tough love to keep you out of trouble, your communication with friends, family members, coworkers, and romantic partners affects your physical and emotional health.[7] One of our students, Dante, had this to say: "Friends and family. You just gotta have them. They're great for eating next to, dancing with, second opinions, inside jokes, bear hugs, reality checks, and inspiration."

Research suggests that relationships are particularly beneficial and gratifying if the communication you have with a relational partner is positive, healthy, meaningful, and supportive.[8] For example, in one study, female subjects participated in a conversation meant to foster closeness. Researchers took saliva samples from the participants before and after the conversation. Tests on the saliva sampled after the conversation measured higher levels of progesterone, a hormone linked to elevated mood.[9]

Interpersonal communication enhances well-being in other ways.[10] For example, people frequently smile and laugh during pleasant conversations. Studies have found that sustained smiling and laughing increase the immune response, decrease the release of the stress hormone cortisol, and reduce pain perception and stress.[11]

Here are some notable findings from other studies:

- Adolescents who frequently share meals with their parents score better on a range of well-being indicators, including measures of mental health, substance use, and delinquency.[12]
- Police officers who talk about on-the-job stress with helpful colleagues are healthier physically and mentally compared to colleagues who don't.[13]
- Expectant mothers with little or no social support experience higher rates of medical complications compared with those who have support.[14] Expectant mothers with social support are also less likely to experience postpartum depression.[15]

While interpersonal communication affects well-being in positive ways, it can also do just the opposite. On which three days of the year are heart attacks most often reported? The answer: Christmas Day, the day after Christmas, and New Year's Day.[16] Why? It may have a lot to do with stress.

Deciding what gifts to buy and what you can afford, making travel plans, preparing for gatherings, dealing with family squabbles, and accommodating guests who overstay their welcome are all sources of stress. Stress affects heart health and the immune system's ability to fight off infections.[17]

We have a much greater chance of managing stressful situations with effective communication, but when loved ones don't agree on the best way to handle holiday demands, it's a source of conflict. **Interpersonal conflict** is a perceived struggle or tension between two or more relational partners. Incompatible goals, strongly held differences of opinion, and unmet needs are common sources of interpersonal conflict.[18]

When you're unwilling or unable to resolve a disagreement successfully, what might happen? Unsettled conflicts may linger or multiply, fueling ongoing

interpersonal conflict A perceived struggle or tension between two or more relational partners.

Marcus McArthur was feeling very discouraged after he received a job rejection letter in the mail. See what happens when he rips it up in front of his 8-month-old son, Micah. How might a simple social interaction like this contribute to your well-being? On YouTube, search using the keywords: "Baby Laughing Hysterically at Ripping Paper." (1:44)

resentment, anger, and frustration. Given its relationship to stress, conflict can aggravate health problems, including insomnia, nausea, headaches, high blood pressure, and anxiety.[19] By communicating effectively, however, you have a greater chance of avoiding conflict altogether, or at least managing it much better—and the stress that comes with it.

IPC and relationships

A **strong tie** is a relationship that is significant to you. It has a stronger influence on your thoughts, feelings, and behaviors than your other relationships do. A strong tie may include someone you've known for a long time, like a best friend, a godparent, or a cousin, but it can also involve someone you're just getting to know, such as a new roommate, stepsibling, or romantic interest.[20]

Most relationships, however, are considered weak ties. A **weak tie** is a relationship that is less developed or influential compared to a strong tie. For example, you may get to know some of your classmates at school, but as soon as the semester is over, you may never see or talk to them again.

Weak ties are not significant relationships, but they are important. They may make work tasks and social interactions light, fun, and meaningful. Weak ties can help enhance your creativity, increase your productivity, and extend your network of contacts and social resources. They provide added social support too, which is important to your well-being.[21]

We've established that your ability to share and experience love, companionship, and community with strong and weak ties is vital to your well-being. But have you ever felt stifled or emotionally troubled by a relationship? In general, any kind of relationship has the potential to influence you in many ways.

Let's explore the importance of IPC in four types of relationships: family relationships, friendships, work relationships, and romantic relationships.

strong tie A relationship that is significant to you.

weak tie A relationship that is less developed or influential compared to a strong tie.

Family relationships

When you were a child, did your adult caregivers admit to their mistakes? Did you witness family members relying on manipulation, yelling, or threats to meet their needs? Were disagreements discussed in a calm, rational manner? Was love withheld from you as a form of punishment? When you made a mistake and apologized for it, was it never brought up again?

During your formative years, members of your family, especially your adult caregivers, taught you how to interact. On a conscious and subconscious level, you've probably adopted many of their communication behaviors and attitudes.

Communication scholars suggest that there are two types of conversation orientations within a family. As you read about each one, consider which conversation orientation best describes your family.

Families with a **high conversation orientation** talk frequently, openly, and spontaneously about a wide range of topics. They view conversations as a positive way to express affection, experience pleasure, and relax. Such families also tend to include all family members in conversations about important decisions, encourage the sharing of feelings and needs, and address conflict productively by finding solutions that work for everyone.[22] Research suggests that if you grow up in a family with a high conversation orientation, you are more likely to develop a greater range of interpersonal skills and find interpersonal interactions rewarding.[23]

In contrast, families with a **low conversation orientation** interact less frequently and openly. They place more restrictions on the topics they'll discuss. They tend to derive little pleasure from their conversations and are guarded in sharing personal information. Decisions are left to one or two adults with very little or no input from others. Family members tend to keep secrets and hold grudges. If you grew up in this kind of environment, you are more likely to perceive honest and spontaneous communication as problematic.[24]

Along with your own family, you may, at some point, form significant relationships with a romantic partner's family. Relationships with them can be satisfying and supportive or unpleasant and taxing. How are you able to relate to Renata's experience? Should she keep her thoughts to herself, or should she say something to her mother-in-law? If Renata decides to confront her, how can she do so in a manner that is other-centered and relationship-centered?

high conversation orientation Family communication in which members interact frequently, speak more candidly, and talk spontaneously about a wide range of topics.

low conversation orientation Family communication in which members interact infrequently, speak less candidly, and with more restrictions on conversation topics.

"I was trying to get my 3-year-old son to sit still during the pastor's sermon. My mother-in-law sat behind us and kept tapping my son on the shoulder, causing him to get restless. At home, when he pouts, she immediately hands him a cookie to make him happy. It works, but it also teaches him how to get what he wants. I could go on and on. I sometimes wonder if she's trying to sabotage my efforts to parent effectively. How do I tell her how I feel? She tends to get defensive and overly sensitive when anyone critiques her, but not saying anything is causing me to really resent her." –Renata

Friendships

The word *friend* encompasses a lot of different relationships: a childhood play-mate, a college buddy, a lifelong best friend, a sorority sister, to name a few. Some of our friendships are mostly or exclusively maintained online; others exist because we live as roommates or next-door neighbors. Some friends are very close to us—we would do just about anything for them; other friends are loosely tied to us—in our lives more out of association, convenience, or obliga-tion. Some friendships last a lifetime; others are short term. Some are platonic or nonsexual; others may come "with benefits," or some level of sexual activity.

Changes in our society are making friendships increasingly important. A Gallup survey indicated that 52% of people ages 18–29 were single in 2004, yet the per-centage jumped to 64% in 2014.[25] Many single people say they enjoy time with friends more than going on dates.[26]

Friendships are special. They give us something our other relationships do not. For example, what if no one in your family shares your passion for disc golf? You may turn to a friend—or start a friendship with someone who enjoys the game.

Friendships are also influential. Being around a strong-willed or highly disciplined friend may help you break a bad habit, such as eating junk food.[27] Research has shown that you're five times more likely to eat healthy foods if you know a close friend is committed to a healthy diet.[28] In addition, the alcohol consumption of your close friends, compared to the alcohol consumption of your peers or the general public, is a solid predictor of whether you drink alcohol and how much.[29]

Your desire to initiate, develop, and maintain friendships has a lot to do with interpersonal communication. A student of ours, Holland, shared how she was growing increasingly distant from a relatively new friend, Ann, due to Ann's "self-absorbed long-windedness." Holland said, "To give you an example, I was telling her about my weekend in Chicago yesterday, and true to form, Ann inter-rupted me mid-sentence to talk on and on about her recent trip there. Argh!"

Ann's tendency to dominate their conversations left Holland feeling increas-ingly frustrated and dissatisfied with the relationship. If you were Holland, and you wanted to give this friendship a chance, how would you communicate your feelings in an other-centered and relationship-centered way?

Work relationships

Close work relationships are messy. You should keep your work and non-work life very separate. These statements reflect a prominent view in the workplace. Many companies discourage relationships between employees outside the office—especially romantic entanglements between subordinates and members of man-agement. Some have firm policies and disciplinary plans in place, including the use of 1-800 numbers to anonymously report colleagues who spend time together outside of work.

Tom Rath, a Gallup researcher and author of *Vital Friends,* believes companies should scrap non-fraternization policies and encourage workplace friendships.

He says companies do need, however, to provide training on how to maintain professional standards and appropriate boundaries. Rath is convinced that having a best friend at work, or several good friends, is one of the strongest predictors of **workplace engagement**—the degree to which people are happy with, committed to, and energized by their jobs.[30]

According to Rath, 30% of employees have a best friend at work, and they are seven times more likely to report high levels of workplace engagement. A close friend at work increases job satisfaction by nearly 50%. Those who have at least three close friends at work were 96% more likely to describe themselves as extremely satisfied with life. For people who report no close relationships at work, the odds of feeling engaged are only 1 in 12.[31]

While close, meaningful work relationships are potentially beneficial, the undesirable behaviors and difficult personalities of people who work with you 8 hours a day, 5 days a week, are bound to test your nerves. A coworker may slack off or waste your time talking about his personal life. Another may have a bad attitude, criticizing colleagues or complaining about work conditions but doing nothing to make things better.

Organizational psychologist Ken West has found that a bad relationship with a direct supervisor greatly diminishes job satisfaction and motivation. When bosses play favorites—heaping praise and opportunities on some employees while ignoring others—and when they exclude some workers from decisions that relate to their work, employees will understandably feel discontent and underappreciated. Employees will also find their work unrewarding if they don't know what is expected of them or how their work contributes to the organization's mission.[32]

Your relationships at work also affect your relationships outside of work. Let's say at the end of a day, your boss says enthusiastically, "You did a great job handling the supplier's concerns this afternoon. I observed the whole thing. I know who I can turn to when situations like this come up." How would you feel? Chances are, her compliment would give you quite a lift. The positive feelings you have may carry into your evening or weekend with friends and family. Just the opposite can happen, too. Criticism at work can negatively affect your time with friends and family after the workday is done. Either scenario is referred to as a **spillover effect**.[33]

Romantic relationships

In the music video for his hit song *Just the Way You Are*, Bruno Mars tells his love interest she's the bright spot in his life, and he loves what he sees in her. When she smiles, "The whole world stops and stares for a while."

In the TV comedy *Brooklyn Nine-Nine*, detectives Jake (Andy Samberg) and Amy (Melissa Fumero) go from being coworkers to a married couple over the course of five seasons. In the early stages of their office romance, the lines between professional and personal blur, causing many uncomfortable (and funny) moments. What are your views on workplace romance? Does this scene support your perspective? Why or why not? On YouTube, search using the keywords: "Brooklyn Nine-Nine: Amy confronts Jake." (1:09)

workplace engagement
The degree to which you are happy with, committed to, and energized by your job.

spillover effect Carrying feelings that originate at work to people and situations outside the workplace.

Why are so many song lyrics inspired by romance? The great philosopher Aristotle once described romantic love as "a single soul inhabiting two bodies." Romantic relationships embody the feeling of completeness and inspire the deepest levels of physical, emotional, and sexual intimacy. In many cultures, romantic relationships are associated with passion.

Studies indicate that interpersonal communication has the clear potential to increase satisfaction within romantic relationships:

- Effective, appropriate use of nonverbal communication behaviors, such as touching, smiling, and making eye contact, correlates with longer and happier romantic relationships.[34]
- People who say their romantic partners are effective communicators also report more positive feelings about their relationship.[35]
- Most heterosexual women say their partner's ability to express his thoughts, needs, and feelings is more important to them than his financial success.[36]

While effective interpersonal communication can naturally enhance romantic relationships, ineffective communication is considered by many to be the main cause of disagreement and conflict. Poor communication is a bigger problem than any other issue, including money, in-laws, parenting, extramarital relationships, and sex.[37]

One of our students, Belen, agrees. She explained how her husband, Alejandro, wanted Belen to express her opinions and feelings with him more: "So, to make him happy, I tried to open up. When I told him things he apparently didn't want to hear, he'd get quiet for a period of time or withhold affection from me. It's like I'm getting punished for the very thing he's asking me to do. I clam up now more than ever, which drives him—both of us—crazy."

IPC and career success

Interpersonal communication skills are essential for on-the-job effectiveness. According to Bill Gates, cofounder and former chairman of Microsoft:

Communication skills and the ability to work well with different types of people are very important. . . . Software innovation, like almost every other kind of innovation, requires the ability to collaborate and share ideas with other people. . . to sit down and talk with customers, get their feedback, and understand their needs.[38]

Interpersonal communication skills are highly correlated with securing job offers. Personnel managers representing a wide range of companies were asked to rank the top ten qualities they look for in job candidates:[39]

1. Leadership skills
2. Teamwork
3. Writing skills

4. Problem-solving skills
5. Oral communication skills
6. Strong work ethic
7. Initiative
8. Analytical skills
9. Flexibility
10. Technical skills

As you read over the list again, what's the one thing the top five qualities have in common? They all incorporate the ability to communicate interpersonally!

Along with getting hired, IPC plays a prominent role in career advancement. One of your authors, Bruce, heard a speaker at a conference describe what happened to a newly hired product design specialist at a technology company. One day, she left a quality improvement meeting thinking: *My God, I've ruined my career! I just told someone four levels above me that he was wrong.*

As it turned out, the executive was looking for new managerial talent. Impressed by her assertiveness and ability to communicate disagreement in a tactful, professional manner, he encouraged the product design specialist to interview for a high-level position, which she did. She was promoted to general manager of one of eight regional divisions; she was given a corner office, more perks, and a substantial raise.

IPC skills often outrank technical competence, work experience, and academic background as a factor in awarding promotions. Even in the highly technical field of engineering, communication skills are considered very important for career advancement. In one study, researchers discovered that engineers spend more than half of their day communicating with others.[40]

"Nah, work related stress isn't a problem – I've never taken a job seriously enough for it to bother me!"

Since you'll be relying on the help of colleagues to achieve your career and financial goals, another important element associated with career success is work climate. You can influence the atmosphere at work—making it more or less positive and supportive—with your interpersonal communication.

Job satisfaction increases when employees witness and practice effective communication.[41] In a survey of American and British employees, 80% said that workplace communication affects their desire to keep or leave their job, with one-third saying it was a "big influence."[42] Interestingly, the 200 most-admired companies spend more than three times what the 200 least-admired companies do on training programs for employee communication.[43]

1.2 Interpersonal communication is consequential

Interpersonal communication affects your well-being, which is a state of happiness, health, and life satisfaction. IPC may help you cultivate positive, close, and supportive relationships and reduce unnecessary conflict. Along with helping you secure job offers and advance your career, interpersonal communication plays a major role in your job satisfaction and productivity.

Key Terms

interpersonal conflict, *p. 13*

high conversation orientation, *p. 15*

workplace engagement, *p. 17*

strong tie, *p. 14*

low conversation orientation, *p. 15*

spillover effect, *p. 17*

weak tie, *p. 14*

Comprehend It?

1. Define each of the key terms in Section 1.2. To further your understanding of these terms, create examples to support your definitions.

2. Explain why interpersonal communication is important to your well-being, relationships, and career.

Apply It!

Create a table with two vertical columns. Label one column *Plus* and the other column *Minus*. Next, with a classmate or discussion group, brainstorm and make a list of specific communication behaviors and practices you associate with satisfying, positive, and supportive relationships. Put them in the *Plus* column. List those that challenge relationships or make them less satisfying, positive, and supportive in the *Minus* column. Which behaviors, positive or negative, are universal, meaning they influence all kinds of relationships? Could any of the communication behaviors or practices affect a particular type of relationship more or less than others?

1.3 Interpersonal communication is skills-based

One of our students, Brenda, shared that she was having problems communicating with her son: "Brandon has a hard time remembering to do his chores and homework. If I remind him too much, then I'm nagging him and he complains. If I don't remind him, I'm at fault for neglecting to tell him anything! We are really getting on each other's nerves!"

Their relationship took a positive turn when they tried a different approach. Brenda created a daily chart on a whiteboard in their kitchen. Now, Brandon sees what he has to do when he comes home from school every day. He checks off each item on his To Do list when it's completed. When he's done, he lets his mother know and she inspects his work. His daily performance is tied to a reward system. This new method of communication gives Brandon the information he needs, and Brenda no longer feels like she's hounding him. The communication between Brenda and her son has had a positive effect on their relationship.

Our interactions with relational partners can often be difficult and frustrating, but we have the potential to adopt new and better ways of communicating. With these skills, our relationships improve, along with our own well-being. To help you understand how to strengthen your IPC, we'll explore *IPC competence* and subjectivity, the four stages of skill development, and the role of self-monitoring in communication growth.

What is IPC competence?

Communication scholars Brian Spitzberg and William Cupach define **interpersonal communication competence** as the ability to communicate effectively and appropriately on a relational level.[44] Along with being effective and appropriate, competent interpersonal communication is associated with accommodation and ethics.

Interpersonal communication effectiveness

Let's describe interpersonal communication competence by analyzing a conversation between Ahmad and his younger cousin Callie. Ahmad listens intently as Callie describes a problem she's having with her best friend, Hamida. He doesn't interrupt, and he asks her relevant questions only when he needs to clarify what she's telling him. He stops himself before offering Callie advice because he has learned in his IPC class that giving advice is not generally well received unless someone asks for it.[45]

Ahmad wants to be there for his cousin and help her through this tough time. His communication is meeting this need. Callie is responding positively because she needs to feel listened to and understood. Ahmad's communication is helping her satisfy her own need. Ahmad's communication is considered competent because it's effective—both of them are benefiting from their communication.

Interpersonal communication appropriateness

When you communicate in a manner that is appropriate, you're aware of the expectations and needs your relational partners have in a given situation. Timing is an important aspect, too. In addition to saying the right thing at the right moment, it's just as important to know when *not* saying the *wrong* thing is the best approach.

With tears streaming down her face, Callie tells Ahmad about the mean-spirited things Hamida said about her at school. Callie also just learned that Hamida has excluded her from a preplanned spring break trip. Ahmad told Callie months ago that he didn't think highly of Hamida and even encouraged her to find a better friend. He's about to blurt out, "What did I tell you about her?" but he catches himself and doesn't say it.

Callie is clearly upset and already feels bad, so hearing Ahmad say something like "I told you so" would only make her feel worse. Ahmad puts his arm around her instead and comforts her in silence. When she looks up at him, he says, "I'm sorry this is happening to you. Can I do anything to help you feel better?" Ahmad's awareness of what is appropriate in this situation makes his interpersonal communication competent.

Interpersonal communication and accommodation

Moments before meeting up with Callie, Ahmad is very upbeat. He's just received an acceptance letter from West Point and is eager to tell Callie, but as he approaches her, he sees she's visibly upset. He sits down next to her to find out what's wrong. He sets his news and his feelings aside, choosing to focus on her instead. This is an example of accommodation.

According to Howard Giles's **communication accommodation theory (CAT)**, a relational partner may perceive your communication as effective and appropriate when you alter your communication to reflect your relational partner's communication style and emotional state. Modifying your speech rate, vocal inflection, choice of words, and physical expressiveness in this manner can make a conversation feel more in sync and comfortable.[46]

By being silent, speaking softly and slowly, and putting his arm around his cousin, Ahmad is adjusting his communication in a way that is very accommodating and mirrors Callie's communication style and emotional state in an effective and appropriate way.

An important aspect of accommodation is **empathy**, the ability to understand, appreciate, and value what someone else is feeling. As he listens, Ahmad imagines being in Callie's situation. His empathy causes his demeanor and body language to shift, reflecting the emotions they are now feeling together.

Interpersonal communication ethics

Later in the day, Ahmad is approached by Nasrin, one of Callie's friends, who says, "I saw you consoling Callie outside the campus library this morning. What's going on?" Ahmad says softly, "Yeah, she's dealing with something. If you're concerned, feel free to ask her, but I'm not at liberty to say."

In this instance, Ahmad makes a communication choice based on his ethics. Callie hasn't given him permission to tell others what she's going through, and he didn't ask if it was okay to tell anyone. He is respecting Callie's privacy and doesn't want to potentially start a rumor. Respecting someone's privacy is considered an ethical communication choice.

Interpersonal communication ethics are your beliefs about the communication behaviors you consider right (good or moral) or wrong (bad or immoral) within a relationship. You judge what others say or do based on your interpersonal ethics. Similarly, others judge your communication behavior according to their interpersonal ethics.

A desire to adhere to a strong set of ethics and the ability to think critically when ethical situations present themselves may affect how others perceive your

communication accommodation theory (CAT) The idea that a relational partner may perceive your communication as effective and appropriate when you alter your communication to reflect your partner's communication style and emotional state.

empathy The ability to understand, appreciate, and value what someone else is feeling.

interpersonal communication ethics The beliefs, values, and principles that guide communication behaviors within a relationship.

communication competence. The foundation in all relation-ships is trust. You establish trust when your communication is perceived as consistently fair, truthful, respectful, and reli-able. Trust adds to your credibility and makes what you say and do believable. It can also expand your sphere of influence and leadership potential.[47]

IPC competence is subjective

While communication scholars explain what it means to be a competent communicator in fairly similar ways, it's important to remember that IPC competence is a **subjective evaluation**—that is, an evaluation based on one's own perceptions, feelings, tastes, and opinions. Your communication competence is not just determined through a self-evaluation; it also involves how others view your skill level.

Let's say one of your roommates sampled your expensive nutritional supplements without asking. You confront him about it. Afterward, you think to yourself: *That went well, I communicated very competently.* Your roommate may com-pletely agree—or he might disagree with you. He may not like being confronted regardless of the approach you use, but he'll have an opinion—positive or negative—about the way you conveyed your message.

Your own perception of how you communicate can be described as either congruent (similar) or incongruent (dis-similar) with the way others perceive your communication. **Congruence** is the degree to which two or more people share similar perceptions, expectations, or opinions about a communication expe-rience. **Incongruence**, on the other hand, is the degree to which they don't. An example of incongruence occurs when you think you've communicated effec-tively, but the other person doesn't.

In a study focusing on the interpersonal communication skills of doctors, 75% of orthopedic surgeons believed they communicated effectively with their patients, but only 21% of their patients agreed![48] These findings illustrate how our self-perceptions may differ from how others perceive us. Do you overestimate your ability to communicate? Is it also possible that you underestimate your commu-nication skills? Research suggests you can both overestimate and underestimate your skills.[49]

The four stages of skill development

Are some people just naturally better at communicating than others? Research does suggest that social composure, wit, attentiveness, assertiveness, extrover-sion, and language acquisition skills are at least partly linked to heredity.[50] Even

On the reality TV series *The Hills*, Lauren accuses Heidi's boyfriend, Spencer, of spreading nasty rumors about her. Heidi is trying to be loyal to both Spencer and Lau-ren, so she's walking a fine line. Compare Heidi's communication with Lauren's. Who seems to be communicating more compe-tently? In what ways are Heidi and Lauren's communication more or less competent? Join a discussion group and have everyone share their critiques. Does everyone agree with each other? Relate this activity to the subjective nature of IPC competence and the concepts of congruence and incongruence. On YouTube, search using the keywords: "'Forgive and Forget' Official Throwback Clip - The Hills." (3:32)

subjective evaluation A judgment based on your own perceptions, feelings, tastes, and opinions.

congruence The degree to which two or more people share similar perceptions about a communication experience.

incongruence The degree to which two or more people share dissimilar perceptions, expectations, or opinions about a communication experience.

though genetics may give some people an edge, the single biggest difference between people who communicate competently and those who don't is the desire to improve and the willingness to practice.

To improve your IPC skills, you can do what Jada describes in her narrative: Observe people who communicate effectively, and incorporate their methods. Think of a time when you were impressed after observing someone's interpersonal communication. What was the situation? Which communication behaviors did you observe?

"I grew up in a family business. I watched how my parents read their customers' body language, listened carefully to what they said, handled their questions, and overcame initial objections to close the sale. Those observations taught me a lot and have helped me succeed in my business today." –Jada

You can also ask relational partners who are competent communicators to critique you. Throughout this textbook, you'll have many opportunities to assess your own IPC. This may include asking others who know you to give you helpful feedback.

In addition to observing and getting feedback from competent communicators, you can take IPC courses. Research indicates that students of all academic abilities benefit from the various techniques taught in introductory and advanced communication courses, including students who struggle with stuttering, autism, Asperger's syndrome, and aphasia.[51]

Numerous resources are available in print and digitally, and there are self-improvement books, too, such as *Getting to YES: Negotiating Agreement Without Giving In* by Roger Fisher and William Ury, and *That's Not What I Meant! How Conversation Style Makes or Breaks Relationships* by Deborah Tannen. They offer valuable insights and practical tips for strengthening communication and relationships.

IPC skill development involves a four-stage growth process (**FIGURE 1.1**). The stages are awareness, awkwardness, skillfulness, and integration.[52]

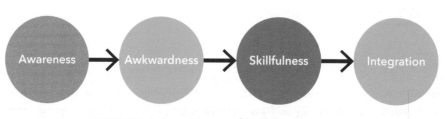

FIGURE 1.1 **Four Stages of Skill Development**

Stage 1: Awareness

Awareness is the state of knowing or having knowledge. IPC awareness includes knowing what your communication options are in a given situation and recognizing why some may work better than others.

Stage 2: Awkwardness

Awkwardness is often experienced when you apply something you learn for the first time. As you try out some of the skills and approaches in this textbook, you may hesitate or falter a bit. If you find yourself thinking: *This isn't me* or *I don't talk like this*, try not to brush aside a new communication technique simply because it's unfamiliar and doesn't feel natural to you. With time and effort, you will get used to the techniques and incorporate them using your own style of communicating.

Stage 3: Skillfulness

You achieve *skillfulness* once you become aware of a technique and have practiced it enough to move beyond the awkwardness stage. You'll also know how to move smoothly from one technique to another. For example, if you have to confront an employee at work about an undesirable behavior, your awareness and application of two skills may kick in: *perception checking* and *I-language*. (We'll explain both of these skills fully in later chapters.)

You may approach an employee who takes a long break with a perception check, such as, "I noticed you returned from break later than the 15 minutes allowed. Am I right?" If your perception is correct, you state what you want from the employee using I-language: "I need you to return from your breaks on time so we have adequate coverage on the floor. Our success depends on the way we treat our customers, and that includes providing them with prompt service. Can I count on you to do this?"

Before jumping to conclusions, you are checking to see if your perception of the employee's extended break is accurate. Next, you communicate a clear and assertive message using I-language, focusing on the specific behavior you expect and why. You also ask the employee to make a commitment to the behavior you want.

Stage 4: Integration

Integration means that a skill is applied on an unconscious level. For example, once perception checking and I-language are integrated into your communication skill set, you will use these techniques often because you know they work. At this stage in skill development, the successful techniques are ingrained—done without any forethought or preparation.

Growth requires self-monitoring

Self-monitoring is the process of thinking about and analyzing your communication with others. Self-monitoring can increase self-awareness and lead to self-growth. By boosting self-awareness, you can consciously change and improve aspects of your interpersonal communication.[53]

self-monitoring Thinking about and analyzing your communication with others.

SON, YOUR TEACHER TOLD ME THAT YOU'RE HAVING TROUBLE FOCUSING, AND OTHER THINGS THAT I ZONED OUT ON.

12/29   STAHLER.

©Jeff Stahler/Distributed by Universal Uclick for UFS via CartoonStock.com

A good time to self-monitor is right after you finish a conversation, while it's fresh in your mind. For example, as soon as you get off the phone with someone, before you move on to the next task, pause and ask yourself: *How did I communicate just now? What would this person say about me? What did I do well? How can I communicate better next time?*

Earlier in this chapter, you learned about the relationship between interpersonal needs, goals, and behaviors. Right after your phone conversation, you can also ask yourself: *Which needs did I try to fulfill? What were my communication goals? How did my relational partner respond to my communication behaviors? Were my behaviors other-centered and relationship-centered?*

In addition, consider these same questions in reverse. Analyze someone's communication with you. For example, if you spoke on the phone with a friend earlier in the day, ask yourself: *Which needs did she try to fulfill? What were her goals? Which communication behaviors did she choose? How did I react to them? Were her behaviors other-centered and relationship-centered?*

Here are some other questions to stimulate self-monitoring:

- How often did I interrupt?
- Were my directions clear and to the point?
- Did I dominate the conversation or listen intently?
- Did I show an interest in what the speaker said?
- Did I express appreciation for the feedback I received?
- Did I avoid giving unsolicited advice?
- Did I pick the right time and place to communicate my message?
- Did I respond hastily before clarifying what was said?
- Did I stay calm? If not, what can I do next time to keep a cool head?

You can also self-monitor by asking people what they think about your communication. For example, you may ask your spouse, "Did I listen to you better this time?" or "Did I seem impatient with your mom yesterday?" or "When you say I'm indecisive, what do you mean?" A willingness to receive and consider information about your IPC is associated with greater self-awareness and increased competence.

Keep in mind that self-monitoring is best done in moderation. Analyzing your interpersonal exchanges too often—by yourself or with the help of others—may lead to unnecessary social anxiety or self-criticism. Your goal is to be mindful, not overly self-conscious or paranoid.

mindfulness The ability to notice new things in your surroundings, within yourself, and in others.

Self-monitoring is closely associated with what social psychologist Ellen Langer calls **mindfulness**—the ability to notice new things in your surroundings, within yourself, and in others. Mindfulness is also the ability to recognize other possibilities. Langer states that we often make communication choices as if we're on "auto-pilot," without thinking, and without considering other available options.[54]

section review

1.3 Interpersonal communication is skills-based

IPC competence is effective and appropriate communication. Competence is also associated with accommodation and ethical standards. Competence is a subjective evaluation. Learning to improve your interpersonal communication skills involves four stages: awareness, awkwardness, skillfulness, and integration. Effective communication habits are strengthened with self-monitoring and mindfulness.

Key Terms

interpersonal communication competence, *p. 21*

communication accommodation theory (CAT), *p. 22*

empathy, *p. 22*

interpersonal communication ethics, *p. 22*

subjective evaluation, *p. 23*

congruence, *p. 23*

incongruence, *p. 23*

self-monitoring, *p. 25*

mindfulness, *p. 26*

Comprehend It?

1. Define each of the key terms in Section 1.3. To further your understanding of these terms, create examples to support your definitions.

2. Compare and contrast the following as they relate to IPC competence:
   - Effective, appropriate, accommodating, and ethical.
   - Congruence and incongruence.
   - Self-monitoring and mindfulness.

3. Explain the four stages of skill development: awareness, awkwardness, skillfulness, and integration.

4. Describe why self-monitoring is important, and explain how it is done.

Apply It!

To assess your IPC competence and practice self-monitoring, complete the two exercises that follow.

What are your communication strengths? Which areas need improvement?

chapter exercises

Building Your IPC Skills: Self-Monitoring

Purpose: To practice self-monitoring, I'll ask the significant people in my life to share with me how they perceive my IPC competence.

Directions: Ask three people who know you well to read the statements in the *Assessing Your IPC* exercise. Have them rate your ability to communicate in these sixteen areas. Look over the scores. To help you understand why you were given a high, medium, or low score, ask questions such as: "Why do you think I am skilled in this area?" or "What can I do to get a higher rating?"

Ask for honest responses and demonstrate receptivity and mindfulness—be open to feedback without getting defensive. Listen appreciatively and accept criticism positively. Don't debate what you hear, just say something like, "This is good to know. I will use this information to improve. Thank you." Stay focused on your self-improvement and avoid critiquing your relational partner's communication during the exercise.

You may find it very enlightening if you recruit a variety of individuals to evaluate your communication skills. Select those who represent the various types of relationships you have, including friends, coworkers, roommates, family members, and romantic partners (past and present). Include people you've known a long time, as well as those you're just getting to know.

You can download copies of the assessment to give to participants by going to https://digital.wwnorton.com/interpersonal on the Digital Landing Page. After you receive their feedback, think about the following questions:

1. What are my strengths?

2. What do I need to work on?

Assessing Your IPC: Competence

Purpose: To assess some of my IPC strengths and weaknesses, I'll have various relational partners evaluate me.

Directions: Read each statement and circle the number that best represents this person's skill level in each area.

	1	2	3
	Needs improvement	Good at this	Very good at this

1. Enlists the help of others to get things done when needed.   1   2   3
2. Seeks and applies constructive feedback from others.   1   2   3
3. Clearly expresses thoughts and feelings.   1   2   3
4. Expresses thoughts and feelings in a timely manner.   1   2   3
5. Asks for and appears to value my opinions.   1   2   3
6. Remembers important things I say.   1   2   3
7. Is honest and transparent about intentions.   1   2   3
8. Accepts responsibility for faults or mistakes.   1   2   3
9. Allows me to finish my thoughts without interrupting.   1   2   3
10. Shows a genuine interest in what I have to say.   1   2   3
11. Expresses negative feelings without saying hurtful things.   1   2   3
12. Makes me feel like our relationship is important.   1   2   3
13. Compliments, praises, and encourages me at appropriate times.   1   2   3
14. Respects my privacy and keeps what I say confidential.   1   2   3
15. Handles tense situations with patience and tact.   1   2   3
16. Shows initiative by making plans and following through.   1   2   3

Want to earn a better grade on your test? Go to INQUIZITIVE to practice actively with this chapter's content and get personalized feedback along the way.

2

The Process of Interpersonal Communication

learning objectives

Reading this chapter will help you:

- Describe the seven elements of the IPC process
- Explain eight foundational principles of IPC
- Apply seven strategies for improving your IPC

Zeeland High School students and alumni will never forget their social studies teacher, Bruce Struik. According to newspaper columnist Tom Rademacher, Mr. Struik made sure every student received a personalized cupcake on their birthday. Students with summer birthdays received a cupcake on the last day of school.

One student fought back tears when Mr. Struik surprised him with his cupcake. His parents were in the midst of a tumultuous divorce and were seemingly unaware of their son's birthday. Another student received her cupcake on the day her father was admitted to the hospital for cancer treatment.

Many students, especially those who were facing challenges outside of school, later recalled Mr. Struik's kindness and the impact it had on their lives. Haleigh Heveveld, a high school junior, described it this way: "It made you feel . . . blessed."

Over the course of his career, Mr. Struik never missed a student's birthday. Having delivered over four thousand cupcakes, he earned the honorary title of Cupcake Man at his retirement.[1]

The father in this photo is introducing his son to the joys of baking. This process involves a series of progressive steps while combining several key ingredients. Interpersonal communication is also a process. It's quite a bit more dynamic and complex but, similar to baking, entails certain interdependent elements.

This sweet story introduces us to the process of interpersonal communication. In Chapter 1 you learned that interpersonal communication (IPC) is the process of assigning meaning to the messages you share with potential, new, and existing relational partners.

In this chapter, we'll (1) describe the seven elements involved in the IPC process, (2) explain eight foundational principles of IPC, and (3) highlight seven strategies for improving your IPC skills.

2.1 Seven elements of IPC

Imagine it's your birthday and you are one of Mr. Struik's students. He hands you a brightly colored box with a personalized cupcake inside. Mr. Struik starts out as a *sender*. His *message* is: "Today is special because it's your birthday!" He uses a cupcake, his voice (when he sings "Happy Birthday"), and his body (to smile and clap) as *channels*. You start out as the intended *receiver*, and you become a sender the moment you respond to his gesture. This is referred to as *feedback*.

Mr. Struik is strategic about the *context* of his communication. To make your birthday special, he delivers it at a time when there are plenty of students around to witness the celebration and participate.

Mr. Struik's thoughtfulness might catch you off guard. This, combined with the sudden attention you receive, may leave you feeling speechless or tongue-tied—a result of *noise*. If you are going through the same thing as the young man whose parents forgot his birthday, you too might be moved to tears by Mr. Struik's gesture because of your *frame of reference*.

The italicized words in the preceding paragraphs make up the interpersonal communication process. FIGURE 2.1 illustrates the IPC process. Notice how both communicators are labeled sender and receiver. In face-to-face and voice-to-voice interactions, you're able to send and receive messages at the same time. For example, as Mr. Struik wishes you happy birthday, you receive his message, but you also send him a message as you laugh, smile, or nod your head approvingly as he is singing to you.

In Section 2.1, we'll explore the significance of the key elements of the IPC communication process in greater detail.

Sender/Receiver

A **sender** encodes a message and transmits it. **Encoding** is the mental process of creating and sending a message. A **receiver** decodes a message. **Decoding** is the mental process of interpreting or attaching meaning to a message. Many factors influence how you encode and decode messages.

A few of these factors are readily apparent in a scene from the hit TV series *The Big Bang Theory*. Leonard Hofstadter and Sheldon Cooper are close friends, roommates, and physicists who work at Caltech. Their relationship is often challenged by Sheldon's self-absorbed, eccentric ways. In one episode, two separate

sender A person who encodes a message and transmits it.

encoding The mental process of creating and sending a message.

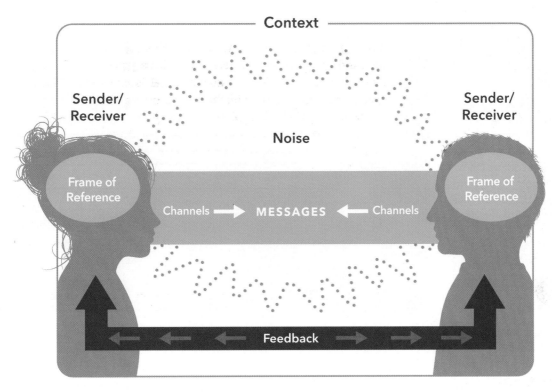

FIGURE 2.1 **The Interpersonal Communication Process**

issues trouble Leonard and Sheldon. During their conversation, Leonard suddenly realizes they're talking completely past each other:

> **Leonard:** Is it possible we're having two different conversations?
> **Sheldon:** How would I know? I'm not listening to you.

Sheldon's faulty listening and Leonard's feelings of frustration influence their communication as senders and receivers.

Message

A **message** is the meaning communicators assign to a symbol. A **symbol** is anything that stands for a thought, person, object, feeling, or idea. There are two types of symbols: verbal and nonverbal. **Verbal symbols** are the letters or words of a particular language. Verbal symbols are spoken, handwritten, typed, signed, or read. **Verbal communication** is the use of words to convey meaning.

Nonverbal symbols convey meaning without the use of letters or words. They include visual representations (for example, colors, photos, graphics, and objects) and specific hand gestures, facial expressions, and vocalizations, like snorting, sighing, or laughing. Sending and receiving messages without the use of language is **nonverbal communication**.

There are times when a message is conveyed using just one type of symbol. For example, if you reach for your cell phone during a church service, your mom

receiver A person who decodes a message.

decoding The mental process of interpreting a message.

message The meaning communicators assign to a symbol.

symbol Anything that stands for a thought, person, object, feeling, or idea.

verbal symbol Any of the letters or words of a particular language.

verbal communication The use of words to convey meaning.

nonverbal symbol Anything that conveys meaning separate from a letter or word.

nonverbal communication Sending and receiving messages without the use of language.

Leonard (Johnny Galecki) uses a chess clock hoping it will make his conversation with Sheldon (Jim Parsons), his roommate, more productive and satisfying. Was it a good idea? Why or why not? Use this scene to describe the concepts of sender, receiver, encoding, and decoding. On You-Tube, search using the keywords: "Leonard and Sheldon talked about their problems." (3:01)

may give you the death stare. Her look is a nonverbal symbol. No words are needed! There are also times when a message is sent using a combination of verbal and nonverbal symbols. You might send a text to your romantic partner using the words "love you boo" (verbal symbols) along with an emoji (a nonverbal symbol) such as the universal blowing-a-kiss face.

Channel

A **channel** is the medium through which a message passes from sender to receiver. When talking to someone face-to-face or on the phone, you rely on your vocal cords, which produce sound waves. Your body allows you to send messages with your face, eyes, and hands. Your vocal cords and body are major channels. The Internet is an electronic channel. Electronic channels also include laptops, fax machines, and cell phones.

Later in the chapter, we'll explain how your choice of a communication channel can make it easier or harder to send a clear, effective, and timely message. Here's an example. Post office employees at a Pennsylvania university found an unopened letter addressed to someone named Clark Moore, postmarked February 20, 1958—64 years ago! They had no idea why it never made it out of the campus post office. When they couldn't locate Clark Moore, they opened the letter hoping to identify the writer. A woman had signed it, "Love forever, Vonnie." She had a romantic interest in Clark. Her last words were: "I still miss you as much as ever and love you a thousand times more. Please write me back soon."[2] Even though Vonnie's handwritten message didn't reach Clark, the letter and the U.S. Postal Service were her channels.

channel The medium through which a message passes from sender to receiver.

Feedback

Feedback is a verbal and/or nonverbal response to a message. Feedback may consist of a smile, a nod of the head, a hearty laugh, or a question, such as "What makes you say that?" Silence on the phone is a form of feedback. Feedback may occur instantaneously, or it can be delayed for seconds, minutes, hours, days, months, and even years. Feedback lets you know how your message is interpreted.

The following is a journal entry by one of our students, Sadie, who writes of the trouble she's having with her husband, John:

> *John will not talk about things that worry him . . . everything is just fine. There is no touching in our marriage . . . no romance. I think he believes as long as he is there and provides for us he's doing a great job. But, I need more. I can't remember the last time we just talked, really talked. I'm not sure what to say to him without sounding hypercritical. In the past I've bottled up my feelings and ended up saying something very harsh at the worst possible moment. I then feel terrible and try to sugarcoat everything, telling him he's doing great. I'm right back to where I started.*

As Sadie's entry suggests, no feedback, not enough feedback, too much feedback, poorly timed feedback, or feedback that is too kind or too harsh may affect a relationship significantly.

Context

Context is the environment or setting—where and when communication takes place and the people involved. The physical dimensions of a given context include the size, setup, and design elements of a meeting place; the room

feedback A response to a message.

context The environment or setting in which communication takes place and the people involved.

During an episode of *Will & Grace*, Will (Eric McCormack) expresses some assumptions he has about his best friend, Jack (Sean Hayes). Jack responds by giving Will "a good dose of reality." See if you can identify examples of feedback in this scene. Next, use this scene to describe feedback and its potential to influence your relationships. On YouTube, search using the keywords: "Will & Grace—Jack Drops a Truth Bomb." (4:12)

temperature and lighting; extraneous sounds; and whether participants share the same space or communicate at a distance using cell phone or internet technology.

A particular context also has social and psychological dimensions. These include the emotional state participants are in at the time (relaxed or rushed), the activities they're doing together (eating at a restaurant or conducting a meeting at the office), and the social behaviors they expect from one another (behaving professionally or partying).

Context has the potential to influence interpersonal communication significantly. Stephen Fried, author of an article titled "Confessions of a Naked Man," writes about the things men talk about while sweating in the sauna. He shares some of his conversations, or "chest hair dialogues," with his wife, and she feels left out. He sympathizes and recognizes he could open up to her more, and yet he also relishes the intimate conversations he has with the guys. Some of their talks are rich and revealing. He's heard men talk about serious regrets, personal triumphs, private struggles, and lofty dreams. Fried writes, "They've told me wonderfully moving things about themselves, their wives and families—things they may not have said to anyone else."[3] Fried says the candor between men in saunas is unique to this context: an intimate space where they see each other frequently and forge friendships over time.

Noise

Noise is anything that makes clear and effective communication challenging. One of our students, Nick, shared this example. He was out one night partying at a pub with friends and had too much to drink. Glassy-eyed, he stared longingly into his girlfriend's eyes. She leaned in and kissed him, and without thinking he whispered, "Will you marry me?" Astonished but delighted, his girlfriend immediately screamed, "Yes! Yes! Oh, yes!" She had taken his proposal seriously, as had Nick's friends who were sitting with them at the table! They bought several rounds of drinks in celebration, and strangers came up to congratulate the couple.

Nick hadn't really meant to propose to his girlfriend, but he didn't have the guts to fix the mess he'd made, so he played along for the rest of the night. On their ride back to their apartment, he told his girlfriend he hadn't really intended to propose, and though she didn't break up with him, their relationship definitely took a hit.

We may say and do things we later regret because of alcohol. Noise is anything—like alcohol—that interferes with our ability to encode and decode messages. There are three types of noise: internal, external, and semantic.

Internal noise

Internal noise occurs within the mind (psychologically) or body (physically). Anxiety, pain, daydreaming, a headache, stress, illness, and hunger are examples of internal noise. It's possible to experience several sources of internal noise at the

noise Anything that makes clear and effective communication challenging.

internal noise Noise that occurs within your mind or body.

same time. For instance, feeling fatigued (physical noise) may make you highly irritable (psychological noise).

External noise

External noise occurs in the environment—outside the mind and body. Have you ever found yourself wanting to cut off a conversation to get away from someone's cigarette smoke or excessive application of cologne? A strong odor is an example of external noise, along with yelling and poor cell phone reception. Behaviors such as repetitive throat clearing, gum smacking, speaking with a monotone voice, or mumbling are also potential sources of external noise.

Semantic noise

Semantic noise occurs when language affects your ability to understand some-one. For example, if Lance knows how to speak English but knows very little Spanish, he may have a tough time understanding Alejandro, who only speaks Spanish.

Specialized vocabulary, too, has the potential to create semantic noise. Suppose a theater major describes an upcoming stage production he's working on to a friend who majors in physics. As he speaks he uses technical words such as *fly space, wings,* and *scrim*. Due to her lack of experience with theater production, the physics major may not understand what he's saying. She might say some-thing like, "I don't get what you're talking about. What's a scrim?"

Is it possible to experience more than one type of noise at the same time? The answer is yes, and Abbie describes this in her narrative. Which types of noise—internal, external, and semantic—influenced the communication between her and Caleb?

> "I had serious doubts about passing my driver's license road test. To help me practice, my boyfriend, Caleb, put me behind the wheel of his car and told me to drive around the block. No problem, right? Try driving for the first time using a manual transmission! I didn't even know what a clutch was. His car lurched back and forth violently, and I hit the curb. I was so nervous that I kept interrupting him while he was trying to tell me what to do. He became very impatient with me, which only made things worse." –Abbie

Frame of reference

Frame of reference is the perspective you bring to a conversation or interaction. It's what you know about yourself, other people, and life in general. Your frame of reference is like an inner filter. It colors and shapes your perceptions, values, and beliefs.

What you deem important or unimportant, appropriate or inappropriate, right or wrong, and desirable or undesirable is intricately intertwined with your life experiences and what you've learned from them. Life experiences include how

external noise Noise that occurs in the environment—outside your mind and body.

semantic noise Noise that occurs when language affects your ability to understand someone.

frame of reference The perspective you bring to a conversation or interaction.

you were raised, your exposure to other cultures, and your educational background. You'll experience life differently because of your race, ethnicity, gender, and sexual orientation.

Your communication choices are influenced greatly by your frame of reference. Let's assume you are single and interested in dating. Your friend Scott says he'd like to set you up on a blind date. Maybe you've gone on a few blind dates before and they were pleasant experiences. Or, perhaps all the blind dates you've had in the past were disastrous. Either way, your prior experiences with blind dating make up your frame of reference and will influence how you respond to Scott's offer. You might express an interest, or you might simply say, "Dude, not at all interested. Nope, don't even want to hear about it!"

In addition, you may feel more or less inclined to entertain Scott's idea if you know that his dating standards and tastes are similar or dissimilar to yours. What you know about Scott—a result of your past interactions with him—is a part of your frame of reference.

section review

2.1 Seven elements of IPC

The seven elements of the IPC process include senders and receivers who exchange messages using verbal and nonverbal symbols. Messages are transmitted through various channels. Feedback occurs when senders and receivers respond to each other's messages. Interpersonal communication takes place in various contexts. Noise (internal, external, and semantic) makes it harder to communicate effectively. Everything that has happened to you up until now, along with what you know about yourself, others, and life in general, shapes your frame of reference.

Key Terms

sender, *p. 32*	symbol, *p. 33*	channel, *p. 34*	external noise, *p. 37*
encoding, *p. 32*	verbal symbol, *p. 33*	feedback, *p. 35*	semantic noise, *p. 37*
receiver, *p. 33*	verbal communication, *p. 33*	context, *p. 35*	frame of reference, *p. 37*
decoding, *p. 33*	nonverbal symbol, *p. 33*	noise, *p. 36*	
message, *p. 33*	nonverbal communication, *p. 33*	internal noise, *p. 36*	

Comprehend It?

1. Define each of the key terms in Section 2.1. To further your understanding of these terms, create examples to support your definitions.

2. Compare and contrast the following concepts:
   - Encoding and decoding
   - Verbal and nonverbal symbols
   - Verbal and nonverbal communication
   - Internal, external, and semantic noise

(continued)

Apply It!

Think back to your most recent significant conversation. Next, use the key terms to help you describe and break down your interaction. Identify the senders and receivers, the messages expressed (including the verbal and nonverbal symbols used), the channels, the type of feedback given, and the communication context. Did noise and frame of reference affect the conversation in any way? If so, how?

2.2 **Eight principles of IPC**

In the reality TV series *The Pickup Artist*, eight socially awkward men tackle their greatest fear: dating. These diehard masters of courting disasters are selected to live together for the purpose of gaining social sophistication. Helping them in this process is Mystery, a self-proclaimed dating coach.

Mystery observes a cast member, Alvaro, talking to a woman at the bar. He advises Alvaro to curtail how often he strokes and adjusts his tie, a nervous habit Alvaro was totally unaware of. Another member, Joe, uses the line "Hello, let's be friends" as a conversation starter. Women respond well to this, but Joseph can't get past the "friend zone." Mystery tells him to ditch the "let's be friends" line.

Fortified with this information, Mystery's protégées practice their dating skills at clubs, shopping malls, and coffee houses. It appears Mystery's methods work— that is, if what we see as viewers represents reality and not biased editing.

Do the men ever experience rejection using Mystery's "proven" techniques? Are there times when the men receive positive reactions even when their approach is "lame," as Mystery would say? Can we always count on certain interpersonal communication tactics to work the same way every time?

The answer to this question is, simply, no. Specific strategies may yield fairly predictable results, but the dynamic, complex nature of interpersonal communication makes it difficult to gauge and predict with absolute certainty. This is an important foundational principle to keep in mind, one of many.

In Section 2.2 we'll examine eight additional principles. They'll help you navigate the IPC process with greater understanding and skill.

IPC is systemic

A *system* is made up of components or parts that function together as a whole. For example, the human body is made up of several systems—the nervous system, circulatory system, the digestive system, and so on. And each of these systems is made of different parts. The circulatory system is made up of the heart, blood, and blood vessels; the digestive system includes the stomach and intestinal tract; and the nervous system consists of the brain, spinal cord, and nerves.

When we share a relationship with someone, we communicate as parts of an interpersonal system. An **interpersonal system** is composed of two or more interdependent individuals. Relational partners are *interdependent* if they coordinate their efforts and rely on each other to accomplish both individual and shared goals. They also have the capacity to influence each other directly.

An interpersonal system may consist of two people, called a *dyad*, such as a professional golfer and her personal caddie. An interpersonal system may also consist of a *small group* of three or more individuals, such as a NASCAR driver and her racing team.

You undoubtedly belong to many interpersonal systems. For example, if you're in a romantic relationship, rent a house with three other people, and work part-time at a clothing store, you and your romantic partner, roommates, and coworkers all belong to separate interpersonal systems. There are layers to systems, too. For instance, your immediate family is a *subsystem* or smaller system within a larger *suprasystem*—your extended family, which includes aunts, uncles, grandparents, and cousins.

It's important to think critically about your communication within an interpersonal system. Your interactions with relational partners in one system may affect relational partners in another smaller or larger interrelated system, with unexpected and unwanted consequences.[4]

For example, during a therapy session, one of Bruce's clients, "Cassie," shared that she had caught her husband, "Jared," having explicit online conversations with another woman. Cassie felt very betrayed. Cassie chose to confide in a trusted friend who was far removed from their close circle of friends and family. Cassie also sought the private help of a therapist. Why did Cassie handle things this way?

Perhaps her understanding of the systems perspective influenced her choices. In case she were to work things out with Jared (the two of them make up a dyadic interpersonal system), she didn't want to say things out of hurt or anger to her parents and siblings or their close mutual friends—members of several interconnected suprasystems. Divulging this information could damage the relationships Jared had with them, particularly her family. If they found out, would they judge Jared or treat him differently? Would Jared distance himself from her family out of embarrassment or shame, which might happen if she told them?

Do you agree with the choices Cassie made? Why or why not? What would you do? Which choices are more other-centered or relationship-centered, and why?

IPC systems create culture, roles, rules, and norms

Our interactions within interpersonal systems play a major role in the formation of communication patterns and expectations, including culture, roles, rules, and norms.[5]

Culture

Culture refers to the shared language, beliefs, interests, values, and customs of an interpersonal system or society. Let's say you're a bank employee and are transferred to a different branch. Even though you work for the same company, you notice that the staff at the new branch dress more casually, go out together for lunch a lot, and bring snacks to share on Fridays. Unlike the branch you came from, they participate in betting pools for the Oscars and March Madness. Their meetings rarely start on time and they refer to each other using funny nicknames. Two distinct interpersonal cultures exist at each branch, resulting from a history of social interactions between the employees and their supervisors.

Roles

When your group of friends relies on you to organize get-togethers, you're performing the role of "social planner." When your family turns to you for humor in tense moments, you're the "family jokester." In this context, a **role** is a specific pattern of behavior a person is expected to perform within an interpersonal system. When you fail to perform your role, your friends may say something about it, like "When are we getting together next?" Or a family member might look to you for a joke when a conversation gets heated.

Rules

Rules are guidelines for what you can or cannot do from a communication standpoint within an interpersonal system. Rules are established explicitly or implicitly. An **explicit rule** is communicated in a clear, direct, and obvious manner. As children, whenever you bumped into someone, wanted something, or received a compliment, an adult caregiver probably reminded you to say "Excuse me," "Please," and "Thank you."

Implicit rules, on the other hand, are expressed in an indirect way. You may not bring up a certain topic with your romantic partner because he's gotten quiet or quickly changed the subject when you've talked about it in the past. These behaviors let you know he's thinking, if not saying: *I don't want to talk about it.* It's a rule you follow by putting two and two together.

When you violate a rule, you might receive a **sanction**, a verbal and/or nonverbal reprimand. A sanction could be a stern rebuke from your roommate: "Stop acting like you own this place! I pay just as much rent as you do." It might be a disapproving look from your father when you crack a joke he doesn't think is appropriate.

Norms

Norms are the customary ways of behaving and interacting within social settings. Norms are established right along with an IPC system's culture, roles, and rules. For example, if you've gone to the same family doctor ever since you were little, you expect certain things to happen when you visit her office.

Let's say you're waiting in one of the examining rooms. Your doctor strolls in wearing jeans and a t-shirt. She's sporting big pink wireless headphones—and

culture The shared language, beliefs, interests, values, and customs of an interpersonal system or society.

role A specific pattern of behavior you are expected to perform.

rules Behavioral guidelines for communication within an interpersonal system.

explicit rule A rule that is communicated in a clear, direct, and obvious manner.

implicit rule A rule that is communicated in an indirect, subtle manner.

sanction A reprimand for breaking a communication rule.

norms Common ways of communicating and behaving in social settings.

In this scene from the film *On the Basis of Sex*, Ruth Bader Ginsburg (Felicity Jones) attends a welcome dinner hosted by Dean Griswold (Sam Waterston) as one of a few women accepted into Harvard Law School in 1956. Identify examples of culture, roles, rules, and norms in the clip. On YouTube, search using the keywords: "On the Basis of Sex Movie Clip—More Patient and Understanding Wife." (2:17)

she's singing and dancing to a pop song and tries to get you to sing along using her stethoscope as a microphone. How would you react?

You may laugh and think it's hilarious, or you may find it very troubling. Regardless, her behavior does not reflect a norm—what you'd expect in this particular social context—and it's known as an expectancy violation. According to the **expectancy violations theory**, originated by interpersonal communication professor Judee Burgoon, you'll have an emotional reaction to your doctor's behavior because it isn't customary.[6] Several factors can influence your emotional response, including your mood at the time, sense of humor, and openness to new experiences and unexpected events.

IPC is synchronous and asynchronous

Interpersonal communication occurs in one of two ways: it is either synchronous or asynchronous. Suppose you're telling your friend Jorge, "I took a 20-mile bike ride Saturday. Halfway into it, a bee flew into my mouth and stung my lip." As you are describing the remainder of your trek with "a swollen lip flapping in the wind," Jorge is smiling, shaking his head, and laughing. This manner of communication is synchronous (SIHN-kruh-nuhs). **Synchronous communication** is communication in which two or more people send and receive messages simultaneously—influencing each other's communication in "real time."

Now suppose you've just sent a text to a friend to tell her how much you enjoyed playing mini golf with her earlier in the day. In your text, you attach a funny picture of her hunched over a bush trying—unsuccessfully—to retrieve her golf ball, which ricocheted wildly off a small windmill.

You'll receive no feedback from her until she views your text and decides to respond. This delay may take seconds, minutes, hours, or days. You'll have no

expectancy violations theory A communication theory that explains your reactions to behaviors that contradict social expectations.

synchronous communication Sending and receiving messages simultaneously.

table 2.1	Synchronous and Asynchronous Communication	
Approach	**Characteristics**	**Contexts**
Synchronous	• Message exchange is simultaneous. • Communicators influence each other's communication in the moment.	• Talking face-to face • Talking on the phone • Video chatting or conferencing
Asynchronous	• Message exchange is delayed. • Communicators can't influence each other's communication in the moment.	• Sending emails, texts, cards, or letters • Leaving a voice mail • Posting a photo on social media

way of knowing how she reacted to your text. You also can't influence her communication with you while you wait for her response. This kind of **asynchronous communication** occurs in a back-and-forth manner, with a delay in the exchange of feedback.[7] **TABLE 2.1** summarizes the differences between synchronous and asynchronous (A-sihn-kruh-nuhs) communication in terms of characteristics and contexts.

There are times when communicating using a synchronous approach is a better choice. For example, to fire up your work team about a new sales promotion, a face-to-face meeting allows you to deliver information to everyone at the same time, brainstorm ideas, and make decisions with no delays. You can answer questions, gauge reactions, and build excitement right then and there.

On the other hand, if you are planning a launch party to promote your new pet grooming business, your goal is to get all the event details to friends and family fast and efficiently. An email invitation—an asynchronous approach—is a good choice. It takes a lot of time to call or meet up face-to-face with everyone individually to share information. This approach allows invitees to reread the event details and respond to your invitation when it's convenient for them.

Using both approaches is ideal at times. In the second scenario, you could follow up your invitation (an asynchronous approach) with a few phone calls to key individuals (a synchronous approach) to get them involved. You could also talk to friends and associates at parties, luncheons, and committee meetings leading up to your launch party to build enthusiasm and spread the word.

Take a look at the following interpersonal communication goals. Which approach (synchronous or asynchronous) is best, assuming you want to communicate effectively and net the best results? Would both approaches work well with any of these goals?

- I want there to be a paper trail or documentation as evidence.
- I want to say everything I need to say, without getting interrupted or sidetracked.

asynchronous communication
Sending and receiving messages back and forth with a delay in feedback.

In this scene from *Crazy Rich Asians*, Rachel (Constance Wu) confronts her boyfriend's mother, Eleanor (Michelle Yeoh), who won't welcome Rachel into the family because of cultural and socioeconomic differences. Rachel uses a synchronous approach to convey her message. In a situation such as this one, what are the advantages of communicating synchronously as opposed to asynchronously? On YouTube, search using the keywords: "Crazy Rich Asians- Mahjong Scene." (4:48)

- I want to know if someone is honest with me about something.
- I want to come across as very sincere and emotionally available.
- I want to deliver a message without getting into a long conversation.
- I need to send routine information fast and efficiently.
- I need to work out a relationship issue or solve a problem with someone.

IPC is irreversible and unrepeatable

Interpersonal communication is irreversible. You can't take back or rewind the messages you send, nor reverse the effect your words and actions have on people. Memories of your conversations, both good and bad, stay with you and your relational partners—sometimes for a lifetime.

Prudence Kohl, author of *Hole in the Garden Wall*, shares a story about a father who tries to help his son manage his anger and understand the consequences of losing his temper. Each time his son said something hurtful out of anger, the father had his son hammer a nail in the fence that encircled their backyard. The first day, the boy hammered five nails. The next day, he hammered eight. Over the course of the first week, he hammered twenty-five nails.

This continued for a while, but as the son learned how to control his anger, he pounded fewer nails as time passed. One day, he didn't lose his temper at all. Each day he successfully controlled his anger, his father would praise him and tell him to pull out one of the nails.

Eventually all the nails were removed. The father took his son by the hand to the fence. He said, "I am proud of you for removing the nails. But look at the fence. Even though you've taken out the nails, the holes remain. The fence will never be the same." The father made his point: Just like nails hammered into a fence, angry words and actions leave behind holes or wounds that never quite heal.[8] They are *irreversible*.

Interpersonal communication is also unrepeatable. Every interaction or behavior—what you say or do in any given moment—is unique and different. It's impossible to duplicate a moment in time. You can't repeat an interaction in exactly the same way or expect to get the exact same results. Jamal aptly notes this in his narrative. Has something like this ever happened to you?

> **"While interviewing for a job, I made a few comments that made the interviewer laugh. She seemed impressed with my sharp wit and offered me a position on the spot. Thinking I had struck gold, I made the same comments in the same way during an interview later at another company. This particular manager took exception to my sense of humor and clearly wasn't amused." –Jamal**

IPC has content meaning and relational meaning

Two dimensions of meaning exist in any interpersonal communication: *content meaning* and *relational meaning*.[9] When Karen asks her roommate, "Jacob, did our singing around the bonfire last night keep you up?" the content meaning is what's explicitly stated; Karen wants to know if her noise last night kept Jacob up. The relational meaning is what her question suggests about the nature of their friendship: *I care about you, and I hope we didn't cause you to lose any sleep.*

If your boss at work says, "I want this report finished and on my desk by 9:00 a.m. sharp tomorrow," the content meaning is clear (and identical to the words he spoke). The relational meaning, however, is this: *I am your boss. You work for me, and I can tell you what to do.*

If a friend says, "I haven't seen you in a while," the content meaning is: *A significant amount of time has passed since I last saw you.* What's the potential relational meaning?

There are also content and relational dimensions to your communication even when words are not exchanged. For example, you may see your cousin walking on the other side of a busy downtown street. You let out a shrill whistle. Your cousin turns in your direction. You smile and wave enthusiastically. The content meaning is: *Hi! I see you.* The relational meaning is: *I'm excited to see you, and I'm going out of my way to tell you.*

Your ability to detect the relational meaning of messages may influence your interpersonal communication. For example, you may focus too much on the content meaning of a message and not pick up on the subtle yet significant nuance of a relational message like "I haven't seen you in a while." What you

say or do in response can send a strong message to a relational partner that you either value the relationship or you don't. How often do you overlook the relational meaning of messages? How might your ability to do so effectively enhance your relationships? Can hyperfocusing on relational meanings negatively affect your IPC?

IPC is impersonal and personal

Along with its content and relational meanings, any instance of interpersonal communication can range from impersonal to personal. When IPC is task-oriented, superficial, or done mostly out of necessity or politeness, it's considered impersonal. It serves a purpose, but it's uneventful from a relationship-building standpoint.

For example, if you pass by Boyd, someone you know casually on campus, and say, "Hey, how's it going?" but neither of you stops to hear each other's answer, this message is basically impersonal. Although it's a friendly gesture, it's mostly a matter of politeness. But if you sit next to Boyd in the food court and say, "Hey, how's it going?" and you listen to his answer with genuine interest, your communication is more personal. Just like swapping stories with family members or sharing a secret with a trusted friend, personal exchanges indicate a relationship exists—one you value—or one you'd like to have with someone.

IPC with a significant individual can be both impersonal and personal. Impersonal communication with a romantic partner may include discussing what you want for dinner, whether the cable bill was paid, and whose turn it is to command the TV remote—routine task-oriented interactions. In addition, asking, "How was your day?" is impersonal if it's done out of habit and without much care.

In contrast, a couple may laugh about something funny that happened during a game night they hosted over the weekend, or they might work out a conflict during a nature walk. These exchanges, along with conversations in which they share their hopes and dreams, fears, personal regrets, and intimate desires, are clearly personal.

Personal communication helps you build and deepen significant relationships, but when is it better to communicate less personally? And what if your communication becomes too impersonal—how might this affect your relationships?

IPC is not always intentional

Unintentional communication occurs when you send a message you don't mean or wish to send. One of your authors, Leslie, heard a speaker share an anecdote about a successful businesswoman who invited her boss and several members of her management team to her home for a fancy dinner. Her 4-year-old stared at the boss for the longest time. She couldn't keep her

In this intense scene from the TV drama *This Is Us,* Rebecca Pearson (Mandy Moore) confronts her mother Janet (Elizabeth Perkins) about the way she talks to and treats her two twins and adopted son, Randall (Lonnie Chavis). How is this scene a good example of unintentional communication? Was this situation avoidable in any way? If so, how? On YouTube, search using the keywords: "This Is Us—You're Racist, Mom." (3:57)

eyes off of him. The boss checked his tie, felt his face for food, patted his hair in place, but nothing stopped her from staring.

The boss started getting very self-conscious. Finally, it was too much for him and he asked her, "Sweetheart, why are you staring at me?" The table went silent. The little girl answered, "My mom says you drink like a fish, and I don't want to miss it!"

There are times like this when you know you've just sent an unintentional message—your child overhears a phone conversation you've had with a coworker about the boss's drinking habits, and she makes it known to him in the worst possible way! There are also times when you send unintentional messages unknowingly—for instance, when a romantic partner hears you talk in your sleep or reads a private text message on your cell phone.

No matter how hard you try to control your communication, you're not always going to succeed. If you're sitting at the dinner table during a family reunion and suddenly the discussion gets heated, you may shift uncomfortably in your seat or stare at your dinner plate. You're not consciously trying to communicate a message in this instance, but others can observe your behaviors and assign meaning to them. It's really impossible *not* to communicate in the presence of others—whether verbally or nonverbally.

IPC is problematic at times

A student of ours, Sara, related a frustrating situation she has with her sister:

When my sister and I fight, I tend to want to keep talking and try to fix things, but she just wants to be left alone to cool off. I'm the type of person who can't stand the anxiety of a fight and wants things fixed right away! So I keep trying to communicate my feelings to her, which only makes things worse.

Poor listening, harsh accusations, unnecessary ultimatums, and not allowing someone a pause or a time out are a few of the many ways interpersonal communication can cause problems. The act of confronting a person might even make an existing disagreement worse, for instance. In a study involving college students, researchers discovered that college roommates sometimes created more relational problems by trying to talk out things that were bothering them.[10]

Addressing a problem using the best practices and techniques can backfire. Suppose you approach a colleague, Ladell, and with a smile say, "Hey Ladell, you did a great job opening the meeting today and going over the agenda to get us focused. Just so you know, Mr. Turner is accustomed to making a few remarks before we launch into new business. I figured you'd want to know. Oh, and thanks also for thinking ahead and ordering everyone new folders. They arrived just in time!"

In this instance, you used what is called the **sandwich approach**: presenting a constructive suggestion in the middle of two positive or complimentary statements (see also Chapter 5). The sandwich approach is intended to deliver corrective information in a softer, gentler way.[11] In addition, you spoke privately to your colleague, and your tone of voice was friendly and your body language relaxed.

The sandwich approach, generally speaking, works well, but Ladell could still get upset and say, defensively, "You know, the last person I worked with was always telling me what I should or shouldn't do." He may storm off or even give you the cold shoulder for a while.

sandwich approach
Presenting a constructive suggestion between two positive, complimentary statements.

Despite your best efforts, effective communication won't always make things better, and problems may continue or get worse. Your relational partners might not want to hear what you have to say or appreciate your good intentions.

section review

2.2 Eight principles of IPC

Eight principles will help you navigate the interpersonal communication process with greater insight and skill. IPC is systemic, and IPC systems create culture, roles, rules, and norms. IPC involves synchronous and asynchronous approaches, is irreversible and unrepeatable, and has content meaning and

(continued)

relational meaning. IPC is impersonal and personal, not always intentional, and despite your best efforts, it will sometimes cause problems and won't always solve them.

Key Terms

interpersonal system, *p. 40*

culture, *p. 41*

role, *p. 41*

rules, *p. 41*

explicit rule, *p. 41*

implicit rule, *p. 41*

sanction, *p. 41*

norms, *p. 41*

expectancy violations theory, *p. 42*

synchronous communication, *p. 42*

asynchronous communication, *p. 43*

sandwich approach, *p. 48*

Comprehend It?

1. Define each of the key terms in Section 2.2. To further your understanding of these terms, create examples to support your definitions.

2. List and summarize each of the eight principles of IPC.

3. Compare and contrast the following concepts:
   - Interpersonal system, subsystem, and suprasystem
   - Interpersonal culture, roles, rules, and norms
   - Synchronous and asynchronous communication
   - Irreversible and unrepeatable communication
   - Content meaning and relational meaning
   - Impersonal and personal communication

Apply It!

Imagine your close friend starts dating your recent ex without talking to you about it. How would you feel? What would you do? Let's say you wanted to date your friend's recent ex. How would you approach the situation? Watch the hosts of the talk show *The Real* discuss this issue and compare their opinions with yours. Which of the principles of IPC relate to this scenario, and how might they guide you? On YouTube, search using the keywords: "Can a Friend Date Your Ex?" (1:52)

2.3 Seven strategies for improving IPC

To become an effective communicator, you must understand the process of interpersonal communication. Expanding your repertoire of interpersonal skills is also essential.

In Section 2.3, we'll learn about seven specific approaches for strengthening your communication skills. Each approach involves applying one of the elements of the IPC process in an effective way.

Send and receive messages strategically

How often do you conduct a conversation when the timing isn't right? Make a commitment prematurely? Or regret saying something hurtful in the heat of the moment? Making it a habit to think before you speak—or hit send—is a wise choice.

Taking a few seconds, minutes, or hours allows you to reflect on the other person's communication needs and goals, sort out your feelings, carefully

mixed message
Communication in which verbal and nonverbal messages contradict each other.

choose your words, and anticipate where a conversation may go based on your responses. You can also practice or rehearse what you're going to say and how to say it in a competent way.

One way to think before you speak involves two steps: (1) state why you need to postpone your response, and (2) invite the other person to help you identify a mutually convenient time to continue the conversation. Here are some examples:

- "I need to give it some more thought. I'll call you back in twenty minutes, is that okay?"

- "I'm not sure how to respond to what you just said [or did]. I need some time to process this. When is a good time tomorrow for you to talk?"

- "Before I commit, I'd like to look at my calendar and make sure I don't have any other obligations. When would you like me to get back to you?"

Clarify mixed messages

If you run into your friend, Drake, and say "Let's get together sometime" or "I'll give you a call, and we'll catch up"—but then you never do—you're probably giving Drake the impression you're not actually interested in hanging out with him. Your verbal message and your subsequent behavior are not in sync.

A **mixed message** occurs when your verbal and nonverbal messages contradict each other in some way. Research suggests that receivers believe the nonverbal aspects of a mixed message more than the verbal ones—"actions speak louder than words."[12] For example, if you say you're not angry but your voice is raised, or if you tell a friend you're too busy to hang out with her tonight but she can see you're on social media pretty much the entire evening, you are sending a mixed message. Your actions, rather than your words, reveal your true message.

If you frequently send mixed messages, others may perceive you as unreliable, indecisive, insincere, or dishonest. As you read the following anecdote from Tobin, identify the mixed message. Think of a time you received a mixed message. What was the situation? How did you respond?

"For Christmas this year my sister gave me a yellow mug, and it looked awfully familiar. I thought about it and realized this gift was the very one I had given her two years ago for Christmas! She said she really liked it when I gave it to her. Her regifting suggests otherwise." –Tobin

Mixed messages may seem harmless or insignificant, and sending them can even seem funny at times. But they can also undermine clear communication and damage relationships. You can address mixed messages in two ways. First, you can clarify your own mixed messages. For example, you could say to your cousin Greg, "I know I just said I'd go with you to the club, but I realize I was slow to answer you for a reason. I'm tired and would rather go home and crash."

Second, you can clarify a mixed message when you receive one. Before you overreact or jump to conclusions, a tactful clarification using an objective observational I-statement can help. A specific type of I-language, **observational I-statements** focus on a person's observed behavior, starting with the first-person pronoun I, as in "I recall," "I sense," "I notice," "I heard," and "I see." After making an observational I-statement, you can ask a question to clarify the mixed message. Here are some examples:

- "<u>I heard</u> you say you're not disappointed I wasn't at your show, but <u>I also notice</u> that you're not speaking to me. (Observational I-statement) Is it safe to say you're feeling at least some disappointment? (Question)"

- "<u>I remember</u> hearing you praise my idea last week. <u>I also heard</u> someone say you were critical of it in yesterday's meeting after I left. (Observational I-statement) Have your thoughts changed? (Question)"

An observational I-statement is less intimidating and confrontational than a blaming you-statement, such as "You're ignoring me again" or "You're trying to undermine me."[13] Observational I-statements are more effective if your voice is calm and your body language is relaxed. The person you're speaking to may respond defensively if your voice sounds angry or condescending or if you stand with your arms crossed authoritatively.

Replace lean channels with rich channels

A manager sends an email alerting employees about a new workplace ban on social media use. Some employees are upset because the email comes across as dictatorial and accusatory. This wasn't the manager's intention. She has no idea anyone is upset about her email until her administrative assistant alerts her days later. Did she choose the best medium to convey her message?

Email is considered a lean communication channel. A **lean channel** provides a small amount of sensory information (in this case, just words) to convey meaning. When reading emails or texts, it's easy for the receiver to attach an unintended meaning to the sender's words. There are no vocal cues, such as tone of voice, word emphasis,

observational I-statement A statement that focuses on an observed behavior, starting with the pronoun *I*.

lean channel A communication medium that provides few sources of sensory information to convey meaning.

"It's not easy. He'll tweet one thing, then text another. I'm getting mixed messages."

rich channel
A communication medium that provides many sources of sensory information to convey meaning.

metacommunication
Communicating about communication.

inflection, or pauses. Without these vocal cues, certain emotions and sarcasm are very difficult to convey and interpret.[14]

While lean channels are useful in certain communication situations, your ability to understand a message is often enhanced when messages are conveyed using a rich communication channel. A **rich channel** provides a large amount of sensory information, thereby minimizing the possibility of miscommunication.[15] For example, unlike a text or email, video chat enables you to capture what's going on around you, including the reactions of others. You can send and receive messages with your voice and body (using, for example, facial expressions and gestures). Research has shown that when negotiators communicate using video chat or face-to-face channels, they exchange three times more information than they do with email.[16]

Seek and provide helpful feedback

When relational partners talk about their past, present, or future communication, they're engaged in **metacommunication**—communicating about communication. You can harness metacommunication as a form of feedback. Consider the following scenario.

Dante is getting quite annoyed with his girlfriend's friend Tiana. He'd like Tiana to cut back on her frequent surprise visits to their house and numerous daily calls to his girlfriend, Ashanti. He feels like he has to compete with Tiana for Ashanti's time and attention.

While they're getting supper ready one evening, Dante says to Ashanti, "I want to tell you something, but I don't want you to get upset." Ashanti replies, "Okay, what's on your mind?" Dante says, "Promise you'll hear me out completely before you say anything." Ashanti assures him, "I will. Let's go sit down on the couch."

Asking Ashanti to hear him out before saying anything is an example of metacommunication. Ashanti's suggestion that they sit on the couch is also a form of metacommunication. It means they're going to have a significant conversation—one that follows several communication rules they've established, such as listening to each other without interrupting.

Metacommunication has the potential to improve your communication and relationships, but the way in which you do it is important.[17] If Dante and Ashanti use effective approaches such as active listening, validating each other's views, staying calm, and focusing on solutions, their metacommunication could lead to several positive outcomes, including mutual understanding, closeness, and relationship satisfaction.

Conversely, Dante may say that Ashanti allows Tiana to take up too much of their "together" time in a way that is critical, insensitive, or hurtful. The couple's metacommunication, in this instance, is off to a bad start. It may even turn

Recent challenges have put a strain on a couple, Ben (Jason Winston George) and Miranda (Chandra Wilson) of *Grey's Anatomy*. Ben wants to put their relationship back on track and has an important message to convey to Miranda. In this scene, you'll notice several instances of metacommunication. See if you can identify them. Then critique Ben's effort to metacommunicate with Miranda. Is his approach effective? Why or why not? On YouTube, search using the keywords: "Bailey's Treehouse–Grey's Anatomy, Season 15, Episode 12." (1:50)

into yelling, threatening, accusing, blaming, ignoring, or name calling. Dante might interrupt Ashanti and say, "Forget it! I knew you would get defensive." And Ashanti may respond, "*I'm* defensive? You aren't even listening to me!"

The following list of statements and questions includes examples of metacommunication. As you read each example, think about its purpose and potential benefits:

- "I'd like it if you looked at me when I'm speaking to you."
- "How can we avoid this argument next time?"
- "I really appreciate how you include me in our team discussions."
- "I love it when you say things like that to me."
- "Let's keep this between the two of us—okay?"
- "Can we shut off our cell phones when we go out on our date tonight?"
- "How do you want me to handle this next time?"
- "You really kept your cool when. . . ."
- "That didn't come out right, let me say it better."
- "Thanks for asking!"
- "I don't want you to take this as a criticism, just a helpful observation."

Optimize the context

One of our students, Logan, asked members of the class for some pointers on how to end a 3-month romantic relationship that wasn't going anywhere. He then described to the class what happened the following week. He took Gracie to a nice restaurant and had reserved a table in a corner to give them as much privacy as possible. After they had eaten and Logan had picked up the bill, he shared his feelings with her. Gracie wasn't completely surprised. She expressed some of her doubts about their relationship as well, and though neither was happy about it, they decided to call things off and separate amicably.

Logan felt that his efforts to optimize aspects of the communication context made a difficult conversation a little easier. And optimizing the context made his communication with Gracie feel more mature, considerate, and respectful as well.

Altering the context may support your communication objectives. For example, if you're leading a meeting and your goal is to get your employees to speak up more, you can change the arrangement of chairs. Research suggests we feel more comfortable participating in a group discussion when everyone is seated in a circle or horseshoe configuration.[18]

You can also promote effective interpersonal communication by eliminating possible distractions in your environment, approaching people at the right time and place, and not inviting certain people to a social event who don't get along.

Recognize and eliminate noise

How skilled are you at recognizing noise and eliminating it when possible? You might say, for instance, to someone on the phone, "Hey, I'm getting a bad signal, let me call you right back." Or: "Is it feeling too warm in here? Let me lower the thermostat." Or: "I'm starting to get really upset, let me cool off. Can we continue this conversation when I see you tonight?"

To avoid unwanted noise during a conversation, one helpful strategy is to find out whether a relational partner is experiencing noise using this two-step technique: (1) State what you'd like to talk about briefly, and (2) ask if your conversational partner is willing to discuss it. Here are a couple of examples:

- "I'd like to talk about what we're going to say at our team meeting tomorrow. Is this a good time?"

- "I took a look at our credit card statement, and the amount we owe is way over budget. Can we take a few minutes to talk about some solutions?"

At times, you'll use this approach and discover the other person is too busy, stressed out, or not prepared to talk, or you'll sense internal or external noise is present. Postponing the conversation until a time that works for both of you may improve the communication process and what happens as a result.

It's also important to think about how your IPC choices create your own noise. For example, if you keep accepting drinks at a bar from a generous friend, how might this affect your ability to communicate the rest of the evening? Or, if you choose not to prepare for a job interview, what effect will this have on your communication anxiety before and during the interview?

Consider a person's frame of reference

One of our students, Laural, shared what she wrote in her journal:

> *In my family affection wasn't shown to us. We never hugged or rarely said 'I love you.' As I matured, I found it hard being affectionate even with my close friends. When I moved to the United States, it felt awkward to hug people at church. My fiancé often questioned my feelings for him because 'I love you' wasn't something I said much, nor did I like to cuddle. He asked me why on a few occasions, but I didn't really give him much of an answer. I could tell he felt hurt by my behavior more and more as time went by. I sat down with him one evening and really explained my upbringing. I think it helped him understand that my cold demeanor has little to do with him. I'm trying to show more affection and express my love outwardly to break this cycle.*

Laural made a point of explaining her past to her fiancé. This expanded his frame of reference. He was able to interpret her behavior more accurately as a result.

To better understand your relational partners, it is helpful to consider how their frame of reference influences their communication. If you're not sure, ask more questions and listen carefully to the answers you receive. One question in particular may help:

- "Is there something I'm not aware of that is influencing how you see this situation or how you feel about it?"

You may also find it helpful to speak in hypothetical terms when you're not sure how a relational partner may respond to an idea. For example, you might say to a housemate, "What would you say about having someone live with us and help us lower our rent?" Or to a romantic partner you may inquire, "How would you feel about us sleeping in different beds during the week because of our sleep schedules?" Speaking hypothetically is a tentative way to broach a topic before you state a strong opinion or make a decision.

section review

- -

2.3 Seven strategies for improving IPC

There are various strategies to help you effectively leverage the elements of the IPC process. This includes sending and receiving messages strategically, avoiding and clarifying mixed messages, replacing lean channels with rich channels, seeking and providing feedback using effective metacommunication, optimizing the context, recognizing and eliminating noise, and considering a person's frame of reference.

(continued)

Key Terms

mixed message, *p. 50*   lean channel, *p. 51*   metacommunication, *p. 52*

observational I-statement, *p. 51*   rich channel, *p. 52*

Comprehend It?

1. Define each of the key terms in Section 2.3.
   To further your understanding of these terms, create
   examples to support your definitions.

2. Explain how you can improve your IPC by using the
   following approaches:

   - Send and receive messages strategically.
   - Clarify mixed messages.

- Choose the best communication channel
  (lean or rich).
- Seek and provide helpful feedback.
- Optimize the context.
- Recognize and eliminate noise.
- Consider a person's frame of reference.

Apply It!

To continue your efforts at self-improvement, complete the *Assessing Your IPC* and *Building Your IPC Skills* exercises at the end of the chapter. They'll provide you with an opportunity to engage in metacommunication with a significant person in your life and establish some communication goals.

---

② chapter exercises

Assessing Your IPC: Self-Monitoring

Purpose: To gauge my IPC competence.

Directions: Self-monitoring is the mental process of analyzing your communication (see Chapter 1). Read over the list below. These are your communication goals—what you are striving to do with your communication during the metacommunication exercise.

After completing the *Building Your IPC Skills* exercise, convert these goals into self-monitoring questions, such as "Did I pick a quiet, comfortable place to talk?"

Were you able to answer yes to each question? Was the feedback you received helpful? How? Were you at all surprised by any of the feedback you received? Why or why not?

Did I

1. Pick a quiet, comfortable place to talk.

2. Listen without interrupting.

3. Encourage honest feedback.

4. Listen intently without getting defensive or argumentative.

5. Agree with my conversational partner's input at appropriate times.

6. Communicate a willingness to change aspects of myself.

7. Refrain from using this exercise to critique my conversational partner.

8. Receive constructive feedback without justifying my behavior.

Building Your IPC Skills: Metacommunication

Purpose: To practice self-monitoring, I'll ask the significant people in my life to share with me how they perceive my IPC competence.

Directions: Ask someone you know quite well to participate in this metacommunication exercise with you. The goal of this conversation is to receive honest feedback about your communication competence. Commit yourself to being open and receptive–practice mindfulness (see Chapter 1). Even if you don't agree with everything you hear, say with genuine gratitude, "Thank you. I appreciate this information. I will definitely think about what you're telling me and use it to improve how I communicate." Avoid critiquing your partner's communication in any way.

If you're not sure about something you've heard, ask, "To help me understand what you are saying better, can you give me an example?" Use the following questions to initiate metacommunication:

1. Name a topic you and I have a tough time talking about. Why do you think this is difficult for us? What might I do to make communicating about the topic easier?

2. When we have a conflict, what can I do to help us work through it better?

3. Think of a recent conversation you had with me. What went well? What could have been better? How could I have made it better?

4. In terms of how I communicate, what would you like to see more from me? What would you like to see less from me?

Want to earn a better grade on your test? Go to INQUIZITIVE to practice actively with this chapter's content and get personalized feedback along the way.

II

Foundations in Interpersonal Communication

Perception and the Self

learning objectives

Reading this chapter will help you:

- Comprehend the perception process and its influence on IPC
- Understand the relationship between self-perception and IPC
- Improve your perceptual accuracy

They each control one arm and one leg. Both have their own heart and set of lungs. Their spines connect at the pelvis, but one rib cage protects all of their vital organs. Abby and Brittany Hensel are conjoined twins.

Even though they share the same body, Abby and Brittany perceive themselves as two distinct individuals. Both completed separate road tests to get their own driver's licenses. They take up a single seat at the movie theater, but they purchase two tickets.

Abby considers herself the feisty and stubborn twin, while Brittany is quick-witted and easygoing. Despite their personality differences, they function with amazing synchronicity. They can play the piano or type out a text message together, with each twin controlling one hand, intuitively.

Everything they do—deciding what to wear, what they'll eat for dinner, who they'll spend time with—involves coordinated effort. "When it comes to decisions, there are compromises we have to make," says Abby. "We take turns. We want to work it so each of us is happy."

It's not always easy though. When Brittany was very sick and bedridden for several days, Abby complained that she wished she had her own body so she could go out with friends. Brittany started to cry. Abby put her hand to her sister's face and reassured her lovingly that she was sorry.

The twins' way of life is normal for them, but when Abby and Brittany leave the closeness and

Members of a dance crew rely on perception to synchronize their movements. Hours of interactive practice go into perfecting the choreography and creating a performance that reflects the group's identity.

familiarity of their community, people gawk at them—a lot. Complete strangers have taken pictures of them without asking. Notwithstanding the challenges, Abby and Brittany appear happy and well adjusted.[1]

To get to know the twins better, you can search "Abby and Brittany Hensel: The Conjoined Teachers!" (2:47) on YouTube. How are they similar to you? What makes them different from

you? To answer these questions, you'll rely on your perception to formulate impressions and opinions. Your perception may also cause you to feel something—perhaps amazed or inspired.

In this chapter, we'll (1) explore the perception process and how it can influence interpersonal communication, (2) examine the role self-perception plays in your IPC, and (3) identify strategies to improve your perceptual accuracy.

3.1 The perception process

What would cause you to question a friend's honesty, make you think that a coworker is stressed, or give you the impression that a professor is playing favorites with students in your class?

Your ability to sense things, otherwise known as perception, can help you answer these questions. **Perception** is the mental process of receiving and interpreting sensory information—what you taste, touch, smell, see, and hear. Perception helps you make sense of the messages you receive, and it can also help you understand how the messages you send affect other people.

After striking up a conversation with a classmate for the first time, you may think, *She's friendly*, or *He's standoffish*. The process of perception, whether within the context of a single interaction or many interactions over time, leads you to form thoughts about and develop feelings toward your conversation and relational partners.

Perception also affects your communication choices. You may, for example, choose to make a greater effort to get to know someone who seems friendly than someone who appears standoffish.

Section 3.1 will help you understand the process of perception and a number of factors that influence it.

The process of perception

The stages of the perception process include selecting, organizing, interpreting, storing, and recalling. Each stage is shown in **FIGURE 3.1**. Perception is a sequential and cyclical process. The stages flow from one to the other almost simultaneously, often within fractions of a second. During a conversation, this cycle repeats itself over and over.

Let's follow the perception process with Josie. She's with her friend at a trendy bar in downtown Chicago on a bustling Friday night.

Selecting

Josie and her friend, Ruben, are sitting at the bar talking. Ruben, an avid fan of professional basketball, offers to get Josie a ticket for an upcoming Chicago Bulls game, but Josie is distracted. She's focusing her attention on a specific stimulus—someone sitting across the bar who she finds particularly attractive.

Selecting is focusing your attention on a particular stimulus using one or more of your five senses. Since there's a lot happening at a crowded bar, Josie may choose to focus her attention on what stands out, what she has on her mind, or her needs at the time.

perception The mental process of receiving and interpreting sensory information.

selecting Focusing your attention on a particular stimulus using one or more of your five senses.

Selective attention is your tendency to pay attention to what interests you the most at a given moment and tune out what doesn't. Research suggests that Josie's selective attention may affect her ability to listen to Ruben and notice other things going on around her.[2]

Organizing

The man who has Josie's attention is about her age and height. He has long, dark hair and a strong jaw. He is with two women and one man, all professionally dressed. Josie will soon find out his name is Marcel.

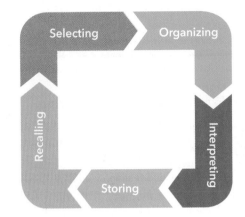

FIGURE 3.1 Perception Process

Josie looks at Marcel and smiles. He returns her smile and continues his conversation with his friends, but he repeatedly sends friendly glances her way. After a few moments, Josie makes eye contact with him again. This time she nods at him and Marcel smiles and tips his glass in her direction.

Josie is connecting the dots, or organizing what she's sensing. **Organizing** is arranging sensory information in a meaningful way. Josie is doing this by comparing what she is sensing to her schemas.

Schemas (SKEE-mahs) are the clusters of knowledge or structured thoughts you have about certain events and experiences. Figuratively speaking, Josie's mind grabs a file out of a cabinet marked "bar flirting." In the file are sticky notes, each with a behavior that Josie associates with flirting at bars—what she's witnessed or experienced firsthand and what she's seen on television and in the movies.

Included in her schemas are scripts. A **script** is a sequence of behaviors you associate with an event or experience. In fact, if you were to ask Josie, "What is bar flirting?" she may describe it as though she's narrating a scene from a movie: "Bar flirting starts with two people making back-and-forth eye contact. Person A smiles, and Person B smiles back. Person A approaches Person B and initiates a conversation with a compliment or a witty comment. This is followed by an offer to purchase Person B a drink."

Josie thus organizes the sensory information she's receiving using her schemas, or clustered knowledge, of bar flirting, including the script that she uses to recognize and later interpret her experience.[3]

Interpreting

Interpreting is assigning meaning to sensory information. As Josie focuses her attention on Marcel and organizes the behaviors she's seeing, her mind interprets: *I think he's looking at me. Am I right? Wait. Yes, he is looking and ... I think he's interested! This is cool!* Are Josie's interpretations accurate? Maybe. Marcel might be flirting with her or with Ruben, her handsome friend who is standing right next to her.

selective attention The tendency to pay attention to what interests you the most at a given moment and tune out what doesn't.

organizing Arranging sensory information in a meaningful way.

schemas The clusters of knowledge or structured thoughts you have about certain events and experiences.

script The sequence of behaviors you associate with an event or experience.

interpreting Assigning meaning to a message using sensory information.

selective perception
Seeing what you want to see or hearing what you want to hear.

storing Sorting sensory information—putting some into memory, and discarding the rest.

recalling Retrieving or remembering a message or sensory information.

selective memory Remembering what you want to remember.

memory reconstruction When you alter aspects of a memory.

Josie may interpret Marcel's behaviors in a certain way because she really wants him to take an interest in her. **Selective perception** is seeing what you want to see or hearing what you want to hear. It occurs when your wants, needs, or beliefs influence how you interpret sensory information.

Storing

Josie approaches Marcel and introduces herself. As she chats with him, Josie continues to select, organize, and interpret what Marcel says, does, and looks like—the shape and color of his eyes and the way he smells, among other things. Josie's brain records these impressions. It can store only a certain amount of information at a time, though, so it also filters out or discards some of what she is receiving. **Storing** is this process of sorting sensory information—putting some into memory, and discarding the rest.

Recalling

Recalling is retrieving or remembering sensory information. During their conversation, Marcel tells Josie he manages a law firm and loves sushi. Josie makes a point to remember these facts about Marcel so she can bring them up again later in the conversation. When the conversation ends and Marcel gets up to leave, Josie hands him her business card and quips, "I know of a great sushi bar we could go to sometime that caters to lawyers. It's called *Sosumi*." The two share a laugh, and Marcel says, "That's a good one!"

The next day, while having lunch with her sister, Josie tells her about her chance encounter with Marcel. Josie has no problem remembering what happened in great detail because her conversation with Marcel was ... well ... exciting!

Like Josie, your ability to retrieve memories is influenced by many factors. You may recall with greater clarity what happens during an interaction (before and after, too) if it evoked a strong emotion: excitement, joy, fear, anger, or sadness.[4] You also tend to remember what's important to you and anything that affects you directly. **Selective memory** or *selective recall* is remembering what you want to remember. Conversely, your brain may distort or block uncomfortable or painful memories.

You may even "remember" things that didn't actually happen. **Memory reconstruction** occurs when you alter aspects of a memory. You may reconstruct a memory to feel better about it, or you might remember it in a way that justifies or alters your feelings. For example, Josie may "remember" Marcel saying he loves going to auto shows, when in reality, he said that he checked out an auto show once and liked it. Josie's interest in him and her love of cars may distort her memory.

As we mentioned at the start of this section, the stages of perception flow from one to the other in a rapid-fire, continuous manner. From the time Josie first notices Marcel until the moment she watches him walk away with her phone number, she is *selecting*, *organizing*, *interpreting*, *storing*, and *recalling* sensory information.

The significance of attributions

attribution A reason you come up with to explain someone's communication behavior.

Josie eagerly awaits a call from Marcel. One day passes, then two. She figures that Marcel doesn't want to appear too eager. Another day goes by—no call. She tells herself he must be extremely busy; he did say he was organizing a conference this weekend for his law firm.

A week later and there's still no word from Marcel. Disappointed, Josie comes up with yet another reason: *I bet he wants to date me, but he's not completely single. He's probably half in and half out of a relationship right now.*

To make sense of her perceptions, Josie is coming up with **attributions** or reasons to explain Marcel's communication behavior. Josie's attributions help reduce her uncertainty and possibly soothe a bruised ego.[5]

Like Josie, you may make an attribution when you perceive that a friend has not returned your text message in a timely manner. You might tell yourself: *She must be very busy and hasn't checked her phone yet.* On the other hand, you might think: *I bet she's ignoring me again.*

Are attributions always correct? No. If Marcel never called Josie because he misplaced her number or just wasn't that interested, Josie's attributions would

On the reality show *Project Runway*, fashion expert Tim Gunn meets with one of the show's contestants, Swapnil, who has been commissioned to design a dress for a client. Describe how Tim's perceptions of Swapnil's verbal and nonverbal communication influence his reaction to Swapnil's work. Do you think the communication behaviors of Tim's client also influenced Tim's perception? If so, how? Incorporate the stages of the perception process and the concept of attributions in your analysis. On YouTube, search using the keywords: "Project Runway: Season 14, Episode 10: Tim Yells at Swapnil." (1:49)

be inaccurate. We'll explore ways to try to reduce attribution errors in the last section of this chapter.

Factors that play a role in perception

You may have heard the adage "perception is reality." What you perceive is usually what you believe; however, it may not represent reality as it is in fact.

For example, time intervals seem longer when you're impatient. If you're in a hurry to get somewhere, and you're parked outside of a pharmacy waiting for your brother, the 10 minutes it takes for him to return to the car may seem like an eternity.

None of us perceive interpersonal communication in the exact same way for a number of reasons.[6] In this section, we'll discuss a few factors that may affect the perception process: culture, first impressions, frame of reference, physiological differences, and stereotypes.

Culture

Does extended silence in the company of others seem odd to you? Do you interpret it as a sign of discomfort or unfriendliness? Generally speaking, Western culture places a high value on talking; chattiness is a marker of sociability. Some Asian and Native American cultures tend to view silence differently. Within these cultures, silence is very common in many social contexts and may enhance a person's credibility and authority.[7]

During parent-teacher conferences, American educators may perceive parents of Asian cultural backgrounds as very quiet or reserved, and they may attribute the parents' lack of verbal responsiveness to indifference. However, one Japanese student said that he and his parents communicate a lot without saying anything: "With a glance, we understand enough."[8]

Along with silence, culture may play a role in how you perceive someone's communication. Let's say you're waiting in line with friends at a movie theater. A male friend joins you and puts his arm around a female friend as they laugh about something. You may not perceive it as anything out of the ordinary. In some cultures, however, it is considered very inappropriate for a man to touch, or even tap on the shoulder, a woman who is not a relative.[9]

These examples remind us that people from different cultures vary in how they communicate and how they perceive communication. Keep this in mind as you interact with others. Increasing your awareness of other cultures will help you perceive things more accurately. We will discuss this topic in more detail in Chapter 10 on diversity and inclusion.

First impressions

We place a lot of emphasis on first impressions in all kinds of communication contexts, and research suggests that they may influence our future interactions.[10] For example, people who participate in speed dating rely on very brief interactions to screen prospective dates.

Initial impressions may occur even before you meet someone. For example, in the MTV show *Room Raiders*, contestants inspect the bedrooms of three potential dates and select the person they'd like to go out with based on their observations. To make their choice, contestants examine everything from the clothes hanging in the closets to the posters, trophies, books, knick-knacks, and photos that decorate the shelves and walls. Research suggests you're able to make reasonably accurate judgments about people after a quick examination of their physical space.[11]

While it helps to make a good first impression, if you don't, you can still change how someone perceives you; it may just take another interaction or two. If the bad impression was quite bad, though, it may take multiple interactions over a period of time.[12]

First impressions may cause you to focus your perception on communication behaviors that confirm what you've perceived in the past. This is referred to as **confirmation bias**. For example, if your initial impressions of a neighbor cause you to perceive her as odd, you may focus on the behaviors that come across to you as odd the next time you interact with her. If someone shares information with you about your neighbor that conflicts with your bias, you may discount or even ignore it.[13]

confirmation bias When you focus your perception on communication behaviors that confirm what you've perceived in the past.

Frame of reference

In Chapter 2, you learned that your *frame of reference* is the perspective you bring to an interaction. This includes what you know about yourself, others, and life in general. One aspect of your frame of reference is your relational history with someone—how you have interacted in the past and what has been happening between the two of you up until now. Brianna's narrative is an excellent example of how your frame of reference may affect your perception. Has your frame of reference ever led you to question a relational partner's actions?

"My sister-in-law, Amelia, and I have always been close, but we've been arguing about carpooling recently. Last week, I saw her and my nephews in the grocery store and waved. She pretended that she didn't even see me and kept her gaze on the cart and the boys. Later, at a graduation party, I confronted her: 'To pretend you didn't see me just to avoid saying hello is a bit rude, don't you think?' Amelia said she didn't see me, but I'm not convinced." –Brianna

Brianna made an attribution based on her frame of reference. A string of recent disagreements with Amelia have put a strain on their relationship. When Amelia didn't acknowledge her at the store (a perception), Brianna assumed Amelia was still mad at her and didn't want to be cordial (an attribution).

When relational partners are not getting along they're more inclined to think badly about each other. This may include assigning reasons or attributions to each other's behavior that are negative. Conversely, if Amelia and Brianna were getting along, Brianna may have attributed Amelia's behavior to something more neutral: *Amelia must not have seen me. She did look like she was in a hurry.*

Physiological differences

Many physiological factors influence the perception process. None of us hear, see, touch, smell, or taste things the exact same way. Our bodies regulate heat differently. Even differences in skin sensitivity, height, and hormones affect perception.

For example, research suggests that, generally speaking, women are more sensitive to odors; they can detect and distinguish them faster than men can. A recent study appears to explain why. When scientists compared the postmortem brains of men and women, they discovered that the women's brains had an average of 43% more cells and 50% more neurons in their olfactory centers.[14]

One of our students, Jasmine, can attest to this. She complained that her brother, Scott, leaves his smelly laundry out for too long and applies way too much cologne at times. She says, "He just seems oblivious to it."

Stereotypes

Our perceptions are also affected by stereotypes.[15] A **stereotype** is an overly simplistic, preconceived impression or assumption you have about a group of individuals. In other words, stereotyping is assuming something about people based solely on their group affiliation.

Sometimes there is a thread of truth to a stereotype. However, we can't assume that a stereotype applies to all members of a group because all individuals have unique identities. To assume you know something about a stranger, or even a friend, based on a stereotype will often make you look foolish, and it's likely to offend or hurt the other person.

A stereotype may be positive or negative. For example, if your neighbor exclaims she's excited that a gay couple bought the house next door because the previous owners didn't take care of it, her reaction to the news is based on a positive stereotype. Popular opinion and even research suggests that when LGBTQ families move into an area, generally speaking, property values go up because LGBTQ homeowners tend to invest in and take care of their homes, yards, and gardens.[16] However, this particular couple may or may not fit this stereotype.

stereotype An overly simplistic, preconceived impression or assumption you have about a group of individuals.

In this sketch from *Saturday Night Live*, a software engineer from Indiana (John Mulaney) accompanies his girlfriend (Ego Nwodim) to her cousin's wedding. He notices immediately that he's quite different from everyone and feels out of place. How does his communication reflect and contradict his initial perceptions? In what ways are stereotypes humorously depicted in the clip? On Youtube search using the words: "Cha Cha Slide-SNL." (4:16)

Negative stereotypes exist too. For example, during conversations about American politics, you may have heard Democrats call Republicans uneducated, backward thinking, or heartless, while Republicans stereotype Democrats as elitist, radical, or oversensitive.

A stereotype—positive or negative—may lead you to perceive others differently, which could affect the way you communicate with them. For instance, you may focus your perception on behaviors that reinforce the stereotype, or you may allow a stereotype to change the way you relate to someone.

section review

3.1 **The perception process**

Perception is the mental process of receiving and interpreting sensory information—what you taste, touch, smell, see, and hear. Perception is a five-stage process that involves selecting, organizing, interpreting, storing, and recalling sensory information. Attributions are an important corollary of the process, and there are many factors that affect perception.

Key Terms

perception, *p. 62*

selecting, *p. 62*

selective attention, *p. 63*

organizing, *p. 63*

schemas, *p. 63*

script, *p. 63*

interpreting, *p. 63*

selective perception, *p. 64*

storing, *p. 64*

recalling, *p. 64*

selective memory, *p. 64*

memory reconstruction, *p. 64*

attribution, *p. 65*

confirmation bias, *p. 67*

stereotype, *p. 68*

(continued)

Comprehend It?

1. Define each of the key terms in Section 3.1. To further your understanding of these terms, create examples to support your definitions.

2. Compare and contrast the five stages of the perception process: selecting, organizing, interpreting, storing, and recalling.

3. What is the difference between schemas and scripts?

4. Explain the role of attributions in the perception process.

5. Describe some of the factors that influence perception.

Apply It!

Subjects in a study listened to an audio recording of conversations between men and women. During the recording, a man states, "I am a gorilla" several times. 90% of the subjects who were told to pay attention to the male voices heard "I am a gorilla." Only 30% who were told to focus on the female voices heard it.[17]

To experience a visual version of this study on YouTube,[18] search using the keywords: "Test Your Awareness: Do The Test" (1:09) and follow the instructions. How did the process of selecting, organizing, interpreting, storing, and recalling influence your perception? Use this experiment to explain how perception is not always accurate.

3.2 Self-perception and IPC

Rachel Pappas joined Delta Zeta sorority at DePauw University because of its reputation as a fun, welcoming chapter composed of accomplished women. The sorority's national organization, however, didn't see it that way. When Delta Zeta representatives visited the campus, ostensibly to investigate the DePauw chapter's declining membership, they undertook efforts to improve the sorority's image. This included sending members to workshops emphasizing fashion and makeup. One of the representatives running the workshops was quoted as saying, "You need to be more sexually appealing; you need to make the guys want you."[19]

When the national representatives staged a recruiting event at the sorority house soon after, members of the sorority deemed the most attractive were asked to participate, while the other sisters, including Rachel, were told their help was not needed. The sisters who were asked to leave were understandably very upset. One was so hurt and offended that she crashed the social and skipped around the house wearing a big wig and a pair of John Lennon rose-colored glasses, shocking the national representatives. She states that one of them looked at her as if "I'd run over her puppy with my car."

Soon after this event, 23 out of the 35 sisters who lived at the house received a letter from the national Delta Zeta office. Their membership status had been changed from active to alumna because they had not helped sufficiently with recruitment, according to the sorority. Rachel believes all 23 sisters who were demoted had one thing in common: they were the least conventionally attractive in the house. Every member who was Korean or Vietnamese was also asked to leave. After an investigation by university officials, DePauw University closed its chapter of Delta Zeta.

After this humiliating experience, Rachel was left feeling increasingly self-conscious about her looks and body weight. Her other qualities and contributions had seemed unimportant to the people she looked up to.[20]

The messages you receive and internalize from others may influence the perceptions you have of yourself. Your sense of self is your private, inner world. It consists of three intricately interrelated elements: self-concept, self-esteem, and self-confidence (see **FIGURE 3.2**).

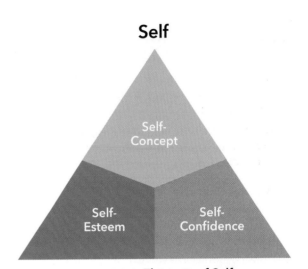

FIGURE 3.2 **Elements of Self**

To make sense of and improve your interpersonal communication, it helps to understand how you perceive yourself. Your self-perception is the focus of Section 3.2.

Self-concept

How would you describe yourself? What comes to mind when you ask yourself the question "Who am I?" Your **self-concept** (also referred to as your *self-image* or *perceived self*) is how you see yourself as a person. It's composed of the relatively stable, multifaceted perceptions you have of yourself. It can also change over time and in short spurts.

Take a moment to look over the descriptive words listed under the various categories in the box "Self-Concept: I am (a, an)" on page 72. Which words describe how you see yourself today? Which words represent the person you were in the past? Which words match the person you are striving to become? Are there words you'd use to describe yourself that are not listed?

Your answers to these questions represent your self-concept. Over the course of your life, your social interactions with parents, family members, friends, romantic partners, and acquaintances shape your self-concept as you become increasingly aware of your strengths and weaknesses, social roles, beliefs, interests, aspirations, and worldview.

And as **TABLE 3.1** on page 73 illustrates, the verbal and nonverbal messages you receive will lead you to conclude some things about yourself, perhaps giving rise to an emerging self-concept.

self-concept How you perceive yourself.

Self-Concept: I am (a, an)

Beliefs
Wiccan, Buddhist, Taoist, Catholic, Muslim, agnostic, atheist, liberal, conservative, libertarian, Republican, Democrat, socialist, naturalist, environmentalist, secular humanist, feminist, evolutionist, realist, idealist, minimalist, vegetarian

Gender Characteristics/Sexuality
Female, male, gender nonconforming, transgender, masculine, feminine, androgynous, gay, lesbian, heterosexual, bisexual, asexual, monogamous, polyamorous, pansexual, flirtatious

Intellect/Psyche
Logical, creative, inquisitive, open-minded, techy, street smart, book smart, intuitive, scientific, confident, insecure, suspicious, cooperative, trusting, impatient, spontaneous, organized, pessimistic, optimistic, mellow, anxious, philosophical, hands-on

Physicality/Health/Age
Beautiful, ugly, stocky, tall, well proportioned, thin, curvy, overweight, muscular, athletic, bald, hairy, blonde, freckled, dark skinned, diabetic, cancer survivor, youthful, old, middle aged, disabled, lethargic, energetic, healthy

Roles
Father, mother, son, daughter, sister, brother, aunt, uncle, grandparent, accountant, Marine, police officer, dental hygienist, accountant, club officer, Sunday school teacher, union representative, bartender, volunteer, coach, mentor, student, friend, partner, boyfriend, girlfriend

Social Characteristics
Clumsy, unconventional, candid, guarded, disagreeable, tactful, quiet, talkative, humorous, family oriented, loyal, team player, shy, flamboyant, friendly, generous, thoughtful, touchy-feely, cultured, ladylike, gentlemanly, bossy, persuasive, charismatic

Class/Race/Culture/Ethnicity
African American, Black, White, Jewish, Hispanic, Asian, Italian, Middle Eastern, Greek, Haitian, Pacific Islander, Native American, brown skinned, mixed race, rural, first-generation immigrant, upper class, blue collar, middle class, working class, poor

Talents/Interests
Musical, rapper, theatrical, writer, contortionist, comical, fashion savvy, dancer, triathlete, basketball player, biker, builder, mechanical, outdoorsy, camper, gamer, movie buff, card shark, skilled conversationalist, sports enthusiast, avid reader

Values
Loyal, trustworthy, kind, honest, fair, modest, respectful of others, an advocate for equality, cooperative, selfish, frugal, generous, revengeful, forgiving, peaceful, responsible, service oriented, compassionate, materialistic

Unfortunately, we don't always receive messages that reinforce a positive self-concept. For example, nine-time Grammy winner and R&B artist Mary J. Blige had a very difficult childhood that affected how she saw herself, and the decisions she made, for many years.

After Mary's father abandoned her family when she was a little girl, her mother moved with Mary and her siblings to a public housing project near New York City. Her mother worked long hours and often left the children with neighbors. Mary, like nearly every woman she knew, was abused—a few of her neighbors physically and verbally abused her, she was molested at the age of five, and she had a series of abusive boyfriends. One even put a gun to her head.

She credits an intervention by a friend, Kendu Isaacs, for helping her change how she saw herself. He challenged her to stop drinking, form healthy relationships,

table 3.1	Social Interactions Shape Self-Concept
Verbal Messages	**Emerging Self-Concept**
"Thanks for always having my back."	I am loyal.
"I know I can count on you."	I am reliable.
Nonverbal Messages	**Emerging Self-Concept**
People laugh at my jokes.	I am funny.
People listen to me intently.	I am respected.

and believe in herself, and these healthy decisions fed her positive self-image. When she began a romantic relationship with Kendu, at first, she was guarded. It felt foreign to have someone treat her with such positive regard and respect. Mary says, "I never experienced real love before . . . it seemed too good to be true."[21]

Mary rejected her unhealthy friendships and sought out new ones with those who supported her self-growth, even though it wasn't easy for her. Research suggests that this rings true for all of us—we tend to gravitate to and maintain relationships with people who reinforce how we see ourselves.[22] To form a more positive self-concept, it's important to seek out and create relationships with those who build you up. As you do, try to tune out or reject the harsh, negative messages you receive from others and focus on the messages that are kind and loving.

You can also entertain affirming messages through *self-talk* or **intrapersonal communication**. Intrapersonal communication is the communication you have with yourself. It includes the silent thoughts you have, the things you may write or type in private to yourself, or what you say when you talk to yourself out loud—a very normal thing to do![23]

You may use intrapersonal communication to plan out your day, rehearse for an important conversation or job interview, or simply sort out your thoughts and feelings. Your inner dialogue has the potential to influence your self-concept and your attitudes, emotions, motivation, task achievement, and coping skills.[24]

You can *commonly focus* your self-talk on your failures and shortcomings as well as your successes and strengths. As you continue reading, you'll learn that your intrapersonal communication can affect your self-esteem and self-confidence both positively and negatively. The following narrative from Alessandra is a good example of how intrapersonal communication can reinforce a positive self-concept. Have you ever talked to yourself in a similar manner?

intrapersonal communication The communication you have with yourself, also called self-talk.

"When I was 17 years old, I gave birth to my son, whose ethnicity is Egyptian, Eritrean, and Italian. I was feeling pretty bad about myself for having a child out of wedlock, and I felt like a bit of an outcast from my family—many are very religious and a few are outright racist. During a family get-together, my aunt said, 'Your son is so adorable. He makes me smile every time I look at him. What a gift!' She really lifted my spirits. She affirmed that my son is a part of me and we are both deserving of love and respect. I'm not totally comfortable with how he came into this world, but I tell myself every day that I'm blessed to have him and that I'm a very good mother." –Alessandra

Another way your self-concept may change is through social comparison. **Social comparison** occurs when you use your perception to determine how you measure up to others, whether in the context of appearance, performance, or life circumstances. If you perceive that you are equal to or greater than another person in some way, you may think more positively about yourself. If you perceive that you are less than another person in some way, and you make this comparison important to you, you may think negatively about yourself.[25] Focusing your thoughts on how you don't measure up to some kind of ideal may adversely affect your self-concept. This is particularly true if you compare yourself to unreasonable or unrealistic standards.[26]

Social comparison can motivate you to make changes if you believe you can, with effort, get closer to your ideal self. For example, you may strive harder to become more well liked at work if you (1) admire how popular a coworker is, (2) identify the qualities that people seem to like about her, (3) believe you can develop these same qualities in yourself, and (4) make the effort to do so.

It's important to keep in mind that you may adopt self-perceptions that others do not share: Self-concept is subjective. As we learned in Chapter 1, psychologists use the term *incongruence* to describe the extent to which relational partners perceive something or each other differently. Your self-perception may be incongruent with the perceptions others have of you.[27]

For example, you may view yourself negatively when others don't, as in Mike's case. Mike's team at work thinks he has lots of leadership potential. He listens well, offers sound advice, and organizes all his projects effortlessly. Mike, however, doesn't see himself as a leader. His self-perceptions are therefore incongruent with those of his coworkers. His interpersonal communication behavior mirrors his self-concept, and so he is hesitant to volunteer for leadership roles.

Alternatively, you may view yourself more positively than others do. For instance, Mike may think his ability to get along with others and resolve staff conflict is admirable, but some of his coworkers perceive his ability less glowingly.

One probable cause of this discrepancy is **self-delusion**—the act or state of deceiving oneself. Self-delusion may occur if you are unwilling to accept accurate and

social comparison When you use your perception to determine how you measure up to others.

self-delusion The act or state of deceiving oneself.

constructive feedback about yourself from others. If you've been fed false praise or no one has confronted you about your behavior before, this may contribute to your self-delusion.

Self-esteem

Self-concept is a cognitive appraisal: what you *think* about yourself. **Self-esteem** is how you *feel* about yourself as a result. It is an emotional evaluation. Like self-concept, your self-esteem is relatively stable, but it too can fluctuate in short spurts or over a period of time.

If you have moderate to high self-esteem, you mostly feel good about yourself—you like, respect, and value yourself. If you have low self-esteem, you generally don't feel good about yourself. You may dislike yourself or seriously question your worth as an individual. If you have high self-esteem, you're more likely to communicate positively—that is, say nice, complimentary things—about others. You're also more apt to express your needs assertively, expect others to accept and like you, and stand up for yourself and others against harsh comments or unfair treatment.[28]

TABLE 3.2 lists the findings of several studies that focused on the interpersonal communication behaviors of subjects with high self-esteem. Using a "Y" for yes or "N" for no, indicate whether each research finding describes your own communication behavior. Are there aspects of your self-esteem and interpersonal communication you'd like to improve?

self-esteem How you feel about yourself as a result of how you perceive yourself.

table 3.2	Self-Esteem and IPC

Compared to those with low self-esteem, people with high self-esteem are more:

- outgoing and willing to communicate.[29]
- likely to initiate and pursue new relationships.[30]
- willing to work harder to master a task after a failed attempt.[31]
- accepting of other people's expressions of love.[32]
- likely to end a dissatisfying relationship.[33]
- skilled at recognizing and managing their emotions.[34]
- accepting (less judgmental) of others who are different.[35]
- generous with praise and compliments versus speaking poorly (critically) of others.[36]
- certain they control what happens to them in life.[37]
- inclined to express their feelings of affection toward others.[38]

High self-esteem is generally associated with positive outcomes, including optimism, a more productive life, and the ability to cope better with challenges and negative feedback. However, high self-esteem doesn't always translate into desirable qualities. According to one study, aggressive people are more likely to have high self-esteem.[39] Another study argues that teenagers with high self-esteem are not any less likely to use alcohol or other drugs.[40]

Adults with high self-esteem may have inflated, inaccurate self-perceptions. For example, one study found that these individuals rated their ability to get along with others and resolve conflict as high; however, others who rated them were more likely to describe them as rude, antagonistic, and less likable.[41]

Self-confidence

Self-confidence is the degree to which you believe in your abilities and judgment. Like self-concept and self-esteem, your self-confidence is relatively stable but may go up or down for various reasons. In particular, your expectations about how communication will go in a given situation can affect your self-confidence. If, for example, you believe you are well rehearsed and prepared for a job interview, you'll expect it to go well. Your positive expectations lead you to behave in ways that increase the likelihood the interview will be a success.

You tend to live up to what you think you can or cannot do. A **self-fulfilling prophecy** is a prediction that comes true because the prediction itself causes you to act in ways that make it come true. It is the very result of what you expect will happen. For example, research suggests that if you anticipate social rejection, you're more apt to behave in ways that invite it.[42]

Let's say you doubt your ability to do well in a job interview. Your uncertainty may influence your performance. You may fumble over your words, limit your eye contact, or answer questions too briefly. Your behaviors may cause the interviewer to respond less favorably to you—the very result you anticipated.

Along with your own expectations, the expectations of others may influence a self-fulfilling prophecy. For example, in one study, teachers at an elementary school were brought into a meeting and given the names of students who scored unusually high on an achievement test. The teachers were told to expect the best from these "gifted" youngsters. Unbeknownst to the teachers, these students were actually randomly selected and represented a wide range of academic skill levels. At the end of the school year, the "gifted" students had the greatest gains on standardized tests compared to the other students. Why did they emerge as high achievers? The researchers speculate that the teachers expected more from these students and communicated their expectations in various ways. Perhaps they praised the "gifted" students' work and called on them more frequently or gave them more opportunities to read out loud or lead classroom activities?[43]

This study suggests that your interpersonal communication can affect the self-fulfilling prophecies others create for themselves. Think of the influence

self-confidence The degree to which you believe in your abilities and judgment.

self-fulfilling prophecy A prediction that comes true because the prediction itself causes you to act in ways that make it come true.

you have. What might you say or do to build the confidence of a younger sibling struggling to stand up to a bully at school, or a friend trying to muster the courage to end an abusive romantic relationship?

In addition to being closely associated with self and other-imposed prophecies, self-confidence is correlated with communication apprehension. **Communication apprehension (CA)** is the anxiety or nervousness you feel in a social situation. If you doubt your ability to communicate effectively, this may increase your CA. Your apprehension may in turn feed your doubts, causing you to communicate poorly or avoid communication situations altogether. Approximately 10–20% of college students suffer from high levels of CA.[44]

Research conducted by communication scholar James McCroskey suggests that if you have high CA you are less likely to ask for help in social situations, pursue new job opportunities, go on a blind date, or date in general. You're more likely to feel dissatisfied with your job, have your thoughts and opinions overlooked, and struggle academically. You're also more apt to get married straight out of college versus taking more time to date or explore other romantic relationships.[45]

The Personal Report of Communication Apprehension (PRCA-24) is an assessment to help you measure your level of communication apprehension in four major contexts: interpersonal communication, small group settings, formal work-related meetings, and public speaking.[46] To find out if you have low, moderate, or high CA, complete the *Assessing Your IPC* exercise at the end of this chapter. What do the results suggest about your level of communication apprehension?

The elements of self are interconnected

If one aspect of your self changes, such as your self-concept, it will likely affect the other aspects of your self—your self-esteem and self-confidence. The following example can help explain how self-concept, self-esteem, and self-confidence are interconnected and can influence your interpersonal communication.

Dwight initiates a conversation with Joel, a student who lives several doors down from him in his dorm. Joel seems aloof and cuts off the conversation abruptly. If Dwight lacks self-esteem, he may assume that Joel doesn't like him for some reason. His self-esteem influences the attribution he assigns to Joel's behavior.[47]

As a result of this experience, and perhaps a few others like it, Dwight's self-confidence is a little shaky; he's reluctant to initiate conversations with other people because he doesn't want to experience repeated social rejection. His confidence mirrors his self-concept. The verbal and nonverbal messages he's received in interactions with others have caused Dwight to see himself as "socially awkward" and "not likeable." As a result, he has feelings of low self-esteem.

Dwight's sense of self perpetuates a continuous self-fulfilling prophecy. He avoids social risks and doesn't give himself the chance to experience new

communication apprehension (CA) The anxiety or nervousness you feel in a social situation.

In this scene from the TV show *Superstore*, Jonah (Ben Feldman) decides to confess a long-standing secret to his parents—he's not studying to be a doctor as they had hoped. Instead, he's working at a department store as a floor clerk. Use this scene to describe how the messages we receive from relational partners influence the elements of self: self-concept, self-esteem, and self-confidence. On YouTube, search using the keywords: "Jonah Tells His Parents his Secret - Superstore." (1:44)

relationships because he expects rejection and wants to avoid it. This may also explain why Dwight experiences high communication apprehension whenever a new social opportunity presents itself.

In a nutshell: Dwight doesn't see himself as likeable and socially attractive (self-concept). He doesn't feel good about himself as a result (self-esteem), and his belief in his ability to socialize successfully with others (self-confidence) plummets. The three components of self are all working against him.

The good news is that Dwight can change his sense of self by getting educated on how to do it and putting forth the effort to do so. Therapists can be helpful in this regard, and there are numerous self-help books written by scholars and mental health professionals that provide helpful guidance on how to improve your self-concept, self-esteem, and self-confidence.

Public image, impression management, and saving face

A businessman opened the doors of his beautiful new office. To project an image of success, he decorated it lavishly and furnished it with antiques. He placed his numerous diplomas on a wall for all to see. He caught a glimpse of a potential client standing in the reception area and waved him in. Wanting to appear savvy and successful, he picked up the phone and pretended he had a big deal in the works. He bounced around big figures and made impressive claims. He sealed the deal, smiled, and hung up. He then addressed the visitor, "May I help you?" The man said, "Yeah, I think so. I'm with the phone company. I'm here to activate your phone lines."

Can you think of everyday problems you may encounter in your relationships if you try too hard to impress other people? To make a good impression, is it best to "just be yourself" or "be real"? When is it wise to try to be the "the best version of yourself" or "fake it till you make it"? Consider these questions as you read about public image, impression management, and saving face.

Public face

You have a private face. This is your self-concept or how you see yourself as a person. You also have a public face that you wish for others to see.[48] Your **public face** (also referred to as *public image* or *presenting self*) is how you want to appear to others. This face includes what you want others to know or not know about you.

You may see certain qualities in yourself that you want others to see. For example, you may see yourself as a skilled nurse (private face). You also want to appear skilled to your patients (public face). Alternatively, your private face may not match your public face. You may not see yourself as a great cook (private face), but you want your date to think you are (public face).

Impression management

In order to satisfy your IPC needs and achieve your IPC goals, you have learned that it helps, and in some cases it's imperative, to have people perceive you in a certain way. **Impression management** (also referred to as *facework*) is what you say or do to influence how others perceive you. For example, it benefits you at work to appear cooperative and friendly. This makes your interactions with coworkers and managers pleasant and productive. To give this impression, you may withhold critical comments and show an interest in your manager's stories about her weekend.

Impression management is something we all do to some extent. It's a social lubricant that helps us fulfill our interpersonal needs—to express and experience love, acceptance, respect, and belonging. It's also how we let people know we're ethical and trustworthy. We engage in impression management to spread goodwill, establish our credibility, and cultivate civility.[49] Positive social behaviors, such as being polite to our neighbors, on time to work, and kind to friends, are all examples of impression management.

Other impression management behaviors have more to do with self-promotion, such as embellishing aspects of a story to make it (and you) a little more exciting, hanging out with people who are popular, taking credit for things you didn't do, and posting flattering selfies. To appear as if you have it all together (public face), you may avoid situations where you come across as uninformed or incompetent (impression management).

Sometimes, however, we place too much emphasis on our public face, and our attempts at impression management come across as fake, deceptive, or insincere. This could possibly damage a relationship when deceptions or exaggerations are revealed. Have you ever gone to great lengths to impress someone?

public face How you want to appear to others.

impression management What you say or do to influence how others perceive you.

One of our students, Dayne, has. Dayne told us, "I really wanted this woman to like me. She asked me to stop by and pick her up for our third date. Knowing she loves cats—and has several of her own—I wanted her to think I'm great with cats (*public face*) so I rubbed catnip on my pants (*impression management*). When I sat down in her living room, her cats all jumped up on my lap and took an interest in me. She said, 'Wow, my cats really love you.'"

Dayne's attempt at impression management worked! His love interest perceived it very positively. However, could Dayne's attempt at impression management possibly have backfired? What are some potential risks?

Saving Face

Imagine that a friend is telling you about a Halloween party that his roommate is throwing this weekend, and he asks you what costume you're planning to wear. How would it look if you said you didn't know about the party because you weren't invited? You may not care one way or another, but if you did, what might you say or do? Would you act like you weren't interested in going, or would you make up an excuse as to why you couldn't go?

saving face The effort you make to protect or repair your public face when it's threatened.

Saving face (also referred to as *corrective facework*) is your effort to protect or repair your public face. In order to avoid social humiliation or maintain your positive social standing, you may employ a number of face-saving tactics (forms

Seinfeld creator Larry David and comedic actor Ted Danson play fictionalized versions of themselves in the TV show *Curb Your Enthusiasm*. In one scene, Larry confronts Ted when he learns that Ted is the "anonymous" donor for a major public exhibit. As you observe Larry and Ted's communication, note how their motivations and behaviors exemplify public face, impression management, and saving face. On YouTube, search using the keywords: "Curb Your Enthusiasm - Anonymous Donor Pt2." (3:22)

of impression management). You may dodge a question, deny responsibility, lie to cover up a behavior, or justify your actions by blaming someone else. This includes such excuses as, "I wouldn't have eaten all the chocolate chip cookies if you hadn't left them out," or face-saving statements like, "I was going to break up with her anyway."

For some people, the need to save face may also arise in order to maintain their independence. Many older adults who begin to experience the early onset of Alzheimer's disease or dementia may try to hide or mask their symptoms from loved ones for as long as they can, make excuses for their forgetfulness, avoid activities that may make the symptoms of their disease evident to others, or try to cover up mistakes caused by lapses in memory.[50]

section review

3.2 Self-perception and IPC

Your sense of self is composed of three interrelated elements—self-concept, self-esteem, and self-confidence—all of which influence your interpersonal communication. Your public face is how you want others to see you. Impression management involves all of the things you say and do to influence how others perceive you. Saving face is the act of protecting and repairing your public face.

Key Terms

self-concept, *p. 71*

intrapersonal communication, *p. 73*

social comparison, *p. 74*

self-delusion, *p. 74*

self-esteem, *p. 75*

self-confidence, *p. 76*

self-fulfilling prophecy, *p. 76*

communication apprehension (CA), *p. 77*

public face, *p. 79*

impression management, *p. 79*

saving face, *p. 80*

Comprehend It?

1. Define each of the key terms in Section 3.2. To further your understanding of these terms, create examples to support your definitions.

2. Compare and contrast the following concepts:
   - Self-concept, self-esteem, and self-confidence

   - Public face, impression management, and saving face

3. Create your own example to explain how the elements of self (self-concept, self-esteem, and self-confidence) are interrelated and influence your interpersonal communication.

Apply It!

Using the box "Self-Concept: I am (a, an)" on page 72, ask a friend or classmate to write down the words they associate with you under each category. Compare their choices with the words you associate with yourself. Were you surprised by any of the feedback you received? What are the similarities and differences between how you see yourself and how others see you? Share what you've discovered with a classmate or discussion group.

3.3 Improving perceptual accuracy

One of our students, Lamont, shared that his girlfriend, Claire, invited him over one evening to eat pizza and watch a movie. He was very tired and not feeling well, so he declined the invitation but promised to spend time with Claire later in the week. On his way home from work, he stopped by his friend Jessie's apartment to pick up his coat—he had left it there during a party two days before.

Meanwhile, Claire had decided to hang out with her friend Jasmine that evening since Lamont wasn't available. Claire and Jasmine happened to be walking past Jessie's apartment, and Claire noticed Lamont's car parked in the driveway. Claire could see from the sidewalk that Lamont was standing near the window talking to a woman she didn't know, so she called him on her phone.

Lamont pulled his phone out of his pocket, looked at it, and placed it back in his pocket; he was planning on calling Claire as soon as he left. Claire couldn't believe Lamont was ignoring her call and was at another woman's apartment when he was "too tired" and "too sick" to spend time with her.

She knocked angrily on the door, and when Lamont answered it, she accused him of lying to her. Lamont, embarrassed and angered by her behavior, shouted, "I can't believe you followed me here! You've got a problem, a serious problem." This led to a heated argument, and the two didn't speak to each other for a week.

Claire perceived Lamont's behavior and consequently made the attribution: *He deceived me and is up to no good.* Her attribution sparked feelings of anger, jealousy, and distrust—which in turn influenced her communication choices. Lamont perceived Claire's behavior and attributed it to unjustified paranoia, which left him feeling hurt and defensive.

Claire and Lamont's perceptions and attributions influenced their communication with each other quite negatively. What could they have done differently from a perceptual and communication standpoint?

An important part of communicating effectively is learning to perceive accurately. Section 3.3 includes several strategies that might have helped Claire and Lamont, and they can help you build your IPC skills, too.

Guard against attribution errors

Claire and Lamont's communication took a nosedive because they didn't stop to think about other possible attributions—or reasons—to explain each other's behaviors. To guard against attribution errors, try to give your relational partners the benefit of the doubt—assume the best about them and their behaviors first.

It also helps to express your perceptions tentatively and seek more information before jumping to conclusions. For example, Claire could have said at the door, "Hey Lamont! I'm surprised to see you here! Did your plans change? I just called you. Did you see that I called?" Lamont could have said, "I'm surprised to see you too. What brings you here?"

By asking more questions and listening to each other, Claire and Lamont would have realized that their assumptions weren't supported by the information they were lacking. It's usually very helpful to have as much information as possible before a communication choice is made.

You may communicate more effectively if you're also mindful of the tendency for certain perceptual biases to affect your communication. Chief among these is the fundamental attribution error. A **fundamental attribution error** occurs when you attribute a person's behavior to internal factors without considering external factors. For example, if a friend is late to a meeting, you might attribute her behavior to her chronic tardiness (a well-known trait of hers), when in reality she was held up for a legitimate reason.

"IT'S THE POOR ARTIST WHO BLAMES HIS CRAYONS."

While making a fundamental attribution error is something you may do to explain the behavior of others, self-serving bias pertains to your own behaviors. **Self-serving bias** is your tendency to attribute a positive outcome to your own inner qualities and attribute a negative outcome to outside factors. For example, if you talk your professor into giving your group more time to finish a project, you might say to your groupmates, "Teachers just love me," when in reality your professor is always generous with extensions. Or, if you and a friend aren't getting along, you might say to someone, "She is being so unreasonable and demanding," without acknowledging how your behavior plays a role in the conflict.

Check your perceptions

Perception checking is the way in which you test the accuracy of your perceptions. A simple question such as, "Are you mad at me?" is a perception check. Observing someone's behavior is another. To determine if others share your perceptions, you may ask things like, "What are your impressions of her so far?" or "Does he normally act like that?" You may even Google someone to test the accuracy of your perceptions.

Imagine you're having lunch with a friend. You casually glance at the menu and complain about the expensive prices. Your friend rolls his eyes and says, "You're so cheap." You're very sensitive to this kind of label, so you start to get defensive. Before you respond hastily, you maintain your composure and casually say:

> **You: I heard** you say just now that I'm cheap. (Observation)
> What makes you say that? (Question for clarification)

fundamental attribution error When you attribute a person's behavior to internal factors without considering external factors.

self-serving bias Attributing a positive outcome to your own inner qualities and attributing a negative outcome to outside factors.

perception checking The way in which you test the accuracy of your perceptions.

Your friend tells you that when the two of you go out you often complain about the cost. He also mentions, "By the way, the last three times we've gone out to lunch, I've paid the bill." You think about it for a moment and realize he's correct. Now that you know where he's coming from, your response is appropriate and effective: "You're right. I get why you'd think I'm cheap. I'll pay the bill this time and the next two to catch up."

In this interaction, you used a two-step perception check. With a **two-step perception check**, you vocalize what you are sensing using an *observational I-statement* (as explained in Chapter 2) followed by a question for clarification. The observational I-statement is a sentence that usually starts with: "I sense," "I noticed," "I heard," "I saw," "I observed," "I get the feeling," or "I wonder." Here are some additional examples of two-step perception checks:

- "**I noticed** you left quickly when Emily came into the room.

  Were you uncomfortable for some reason?"

- "**I see** the shirt I bought you is still in the bag with the tag on it.

  Would you like me to give you the receipt so you can buy a shirt you like better?"

- "**I heard** you introduce me without saying I'm your boyfriend.

  Is there a reason why?"

- "**I sensed** you snatched the diaper out of my hand just now.

  Do you need a break from the baby for a while?"

The language used is tentative; it shows that you're not jumping to conclusions. The observational I-statements focus on observable behaviors, a fairly neutral, less antagonistic alternative to an assumption like, "Why are you so intimidated by Emily?" or "You never seem to like the gifts I give you."

Use the two-step perception method to gain a more accurate picture of what you're sensing. Keep in mind a well-stated perception check doesn't mean the person you are talking to will be honest with you or respond in a positive, receptive manner. However, a perception check is generally an effective technique to add to your repertoire of communication skills.

Also, keep in mind that *how* you communicate a two-step perception check is important, too. Be sure your voice is soft, calm, and matter-of-fact. A perception check can sound sarcastic or demeaning depending on how you use your voice. Your nonverbal communication (facial expressions, posture, and gestures) should match your voice: casual, relaxed, and neutral.

Take into consideration personality differences

Have you ever wondered why you get along so well with certain people while others irritate you to no end? How often do you entertain thoughts such as, *If only he could be less difficult, I could possibly like him,* or *Why are we butting heads so often over the littlest things?* When you assign attributions to the communication behaviors of others, you may overlook personality differences. This may cause you to perceive behaviors with less understanding.

Your **personality** consists of the stable psychological characteristics or traits unique to you, including how you prefer to think, behave, and relate to people. Your personality is formed by your past social interactions with other people, life experiences, age, and genetics.[51]

When personalities complement each other, it's easier to get along. Clashes may occur when personality types are extremely similar or worlds apart. Someone with a very pronounced personality trait may also test your nerves.

There are many personality traits we could explore, but we'll focus on five in particular (see TABLE 3.3 on page 86). A personality assessment called the Five-Factor Model of Personality will let you know if you score "high," "moderate," or "low" in openness, conscientiousness, extraversion, agreeableness, and neuroticism.[52] "Moderate" means you tend to weave between both ends of the spectrum depending on the social situation.

Using the information and scales from the table, describe your personality to someone in class. Now, how do your self-perceptions compare to the results of the actual instrument? To find out, we encourage you to complete a modified version of this assessment in the *Apply It!* exercise at the end of this section.

Personality differences may cause you to perceive the communication of others positively or negatively. For example, Erica and Loren co-own an interior design firm specializing in urban residential remodeling projects. Erica scores high in openness. She loves to generate fresh ideas and think in inventive, creative ways. Loren scores high in conscientiousness. She may not be the first to come up with a novel idea, but if an idea has merit, she loves to critique it and approach it in a methodical, analytical way. This energizes her.

Erica often gets frustrated with Loren. She says, "I come up with an idea, and before I can fully articulate it, Loren will ask something like, 'So how would that work if it's three inches from an air vent?' Her way of thinking stifles my creative energy." On the other hand, Loren complains that Erica brushes her questions aside, leaving her feeling undervalued as a business partner. The differences in Erica and Loren's personalities lead them each to perceive the other's communication as demotivating and disrespectful.

After analyzing their personality test results, Erica and Loren understand each other better. Erica needs Loren to critique her ideas at some point if she wants to turn her visions into workable realities. So, when Loren does, Erica now perceives it as a compliment. Loren is actually excited about Erica's ideas, which brings out the conscientiousness in her. Loren now understands that when Erica first shares an idea, she should bask in the excitement initially and just "run with it" without analyzing it. This brings out the best in Erica's openness.

personality The stable psychological characteristics or traits unique to you.

table 3.3 Five-Factor Personality Dimensions

Openness

← ——— High ——— Moderate ——— Low ———→

High	Low
You like to cultivate a broad range of interests. You're curious, creative, and less conventional in your actions and beliefs.	You prefer consistency (stick with what is comfortable or familiar) and a smaller range of interests. You're more conventional or traditional in your thinking.

Conscientiousness

← ——— High ——— Moderate ——— Low ———→

High	Low
You prefer to plan things out, be on time, follow rules, and stick with agendas. You're methodical, neat, organized, precise, and analytical.	You prefer flexibility. You're relaxed with time and schedules. You're more in the moment, spontaneous, and receptive to sudden changes and disruptions.

Extraversion

← ——— High ——— Moderate ——— Low ———→

High	Low
You're easily excited, talkative, social, expressive, and assertive. You like being the center of attention. You enjoy small talk and networking.	You are socially reserved, reflective, and low key. You prefer to think and listen more and talk less. You prefer one-on-one conversations, and small, intimate get-togethers, and enjoy more alone time.

Agreeableness

← ——— High ——— Moderate ——— Low ———→

High	Low
You prefer to seek harmony over conflict. You're very accommodating, compromising, team spirited, self-sacrificing, compassionate, and trusting.	You prefer to compete. You like to be in control and do things on your own. You're strong willed, direct, critical, and comfortable with conflict. You're less likely to trust others.

Neuroticism

← ——— High ——— Moderate ——— Low ———→

High	Low
You tend to experience and express more negative emotions such as irritability, sadness, moodiness, anxiety, and vulnerability. You're generally pessimistic with a low stress tolerance.	You tend to experience more emotional stability and exercise control over your emotional reactions. You're content and happy most of the time, calm, more resilient, and better able to weather life's storms.

A student of ours, Noah, scored low on agreeableness. People who are less agreeable thrive on measuring their performance against the performance of others, so Noah is a perfect match for his job in sales. He's in charge of his own work, and he loves to compete against members of his sales team and even fires them up with new challenges and contests. However, he describes what happened when he was with his wife, enjoying a game night, and his personality became a problem. Have you ever been in a similar situation?

Emily's perceptions and attributions were tempered by the knowledge she's gained about Noah's personality. Noah's low agreeableness—his tendency to take charge of a situation and his spirited competitiveness—are not acts of hostility or disrespect toward her. It's how he is, and what he does best. She addressed Noah's behavior with this in mind. Noah accordingly modified his behavior, making their time together more enjoyable.

> "Emily and I were playing against another couple in a game of foosball. The score was close, and I kept telling her what to do and my intensity stressed her out. In the middle of the game, Emily said, 'Would you excuse us?' She took me by the hand and led me out of the room. She held both my hands in front of her, took a deep breath, smiled, looked me in the eyes, and said, 'I know you thrive on being in control and winning, but it's getting out of hand.' We came right back; she smiled at everyone and said, 'I think we are ready to play now.' I made sure to keep my cool the rest of the night." –Noah

Imagine if we all communicated with the significant individuals in our lives like this. Perhaps this is why many couples, families, and work teams complete personality assessments like the Five Factor Model. They want to understand themselves and each other better and perceive their differences in a more positive, productive, and shall we say, patient way.

section review

3.3 Improving perceptual accuracy

Making sure our perceptions are accurate can help us communicate more effectively. We can accomplish this by guarding against attribution errors, using more perception checks like the two-step method, and factoring a person's personality into our communication.

Key Terms

fundamental attribution error, *p. 83*

self-serving bias, *p. 83*

perception checking, *p. 83*

two-step perception check, *p. 84*

personality, *p. 85*

(continued)

Comprehend It?

1. Define each of the key terms in Section 3.3. To further your understanding of these terms, create examples to support your definitions.

2. Explain the two-step perception check method. Create your own example as a part of your explanation. Complete the perception checking exercise at the end of this chapter for additional practice.

3. Compare and contrast high and low openness, conscientiousness, extraversion, agreeableness, and neuroticism.

Apply It!

To determine your personality traits using a modified version of the Five-Factor Model of Personality, go to the Open-Source Psychometrics Project's website. Click on "Big Five Personality Test." What do the results suggest about your personality? Once you get your results, compare them to someone you're close to. How might your personality similarities and differences affect your perceptions of each other's communication?

chapter exercises

Assessing Your IPC: Communication Apprehension

Purpose: To determine my overall level of communication apprehension in certain communication contexts.

Directions: This assessment is tied to the material you read in Section 3.2 regarding communication apprehension. Indicate the degree to which each statement applies to you by marking whether you:

1	2	3	4	5
Strongly Disagree	Disagree	Neutral	Agree	Strongly Agree

_____ 1. I dislike participating in group discussions.

_____ 2. Generally, I am comfortable while participating in group discussions.

_____ 3. I am tense and nervous while participating in group discussions.

_____ 4. I like to get involved in group discussions.

_____ 5. Engaging in a group discussion with new people makes me tense and nervous.

_____ 6. I am calm and relaxed while participating in group discussions.

_____ 7. Generally, I am nervous when I have to participate in a meeting.

_____ 8. Usually, I am comfortable when I have to participate in a meeting.

_____ 9. I am very calm and relaxed when I am called upon to express an opinion at a meeting.

_____ **10.** I am afraid to express myself at meetings.

_____ **11.** Communicating at meetings usually makes me uncomfortable.

_____ **12.** I am very relaxed when answering questions at a meeting.

_____ **13.** While participating in a conversation with a new acquaintance, I feel very nervous.

_____ **14.** I have no fear of speaking up in conversations.

_____ **15.** Ordinarily I am very tense and nervous in conversations.

_____ **16.** Ordinarily I am very calm and relaxed in conversations.

_____ **17.** While conversing with a new acquaintance, I feel very relaxed.

_____ **18.** I'm afraid to speak up in conversations.

_____ **19.** I have no fear of giving a speech.

_____ **20.** Certain parts of my body feel very tense and rigid while giving a speech.

_____ **21.** I feel relaxed while giving a speech.

_____ **22.** My thoughts become confused and jumbled when I am giving a speech.

_____ **23.** I face the prospect of giving a speech with confidence.

_____ **24.** While giving a speech, I get so nervous I forget facts I really know.

Source: McCroskey, J. C. (1978). Validity of the PRCA as an index of oral communication apprehension. _Communication Monographs, 45_(3), 192–203.

PRCA-24 Interpretation

Directions: To find out your level of communication apprehension in each context, compute your score by adding the scores for the first three items. Next, add the scores for the next three items and subtract this total from the total you have for the first three items. Add 18 to your score and place the final number in the third column.

Communication Context	Scoring Formula	Score (Score +18)
Group Discussion	Items 2, 4, 6 minus 1, 3, 5	_____
Meetings	Items 8, 9, 12 minus 7, 10, 11	_____
One-on-One	Items 14, 16, 17 minus 13, 15, 18	_____
Public Speaking	Items 19, 21, 23 minus 20, 22, 24	_____

Scores on the four contexts (groups, meetings, interpersonal conversations, and public speaking) can range from a low of 6 to a high of 30. Any score above 18 indicates some degree of apprehension.

To determine your overall CA score, add together all four context scores: Your score should range between 24 and 120. If your score is below 24 or above 120, you have made a mistake in computing the score. Scores between 83 and 120 indicate a high level of communication apprehension. Scores between 55 and 83 indicate a moderate level of communication apprehension. Scores between 24 and 55 indicate a low level of communication apprehension.

Building Your IPC Skills: Perception Checking

Purpose: To improve my perceptual accuracy and IPC.

Directions: Write a two-step perception check for the following scenarios. Focus only on the behavior and address it without critical or accusatory language.

Use observational I-statements: "I noticed...," "I sensed...," "I heard...," "I saw...," "I get the feeling..."

> **Example:** You and your roommate just finished eating a dinner you made. You notice he leaves soon after and returns 20 minutes later with an empty Taco Bell bag.
>
> **Observation:** "I noticed you left and came back with an empty Taco Bell bag."
>
> **Question(s):** "Did you go get something more to eat? Is there something I could have done to make dinner more enjoyable?"

1. Your parents are gone for the weekend and your brother tells you he plans to stay at a friend's house over the weekend, too. You were glad to hear this because you want some time alone. It is late Saturday and he hasn't left yet. How can you ask about this without sounding rude or mean?

   Observation:_____

   Question: _____

2. Just as you say something, your friend rolls his eyes at you. Before you react negatively to it, you do a perception check.

   Observation:_____

   Question: _____

3. You notice that every time you and a close friend embrace, the hug and casual kiss is getting longer and stronger.

   Observation:_____

   Question: _____

4. Your closest friend has not returned your phone call in over a week. You call her again and this time she picks up.

   Observation:_____

   Question: _____

Want to earn a better grade on your test? Go to INQUIZITIVE to practice actively with this chapter's content and get personalized feedback along the way.

4

Listening and Responding

learning objectives

Reading this chapter will help you:

- Understand the process of listening
- Explain what makes listening difficult
- Identify techniques to improve your listening and responding skills

One of your authors, Bruce, was glued to his favorite TV show when his wife, Kimberly, asked him if it was okay to order an outdoor play set from a catalog for their two young daughters. Distracted by a tense, grisly scene from *The Walking Dead*, and without really listening to Kimberly's question, Bruce answered, "Yeah, sure babe."

Bruce was shocked when he arrived home from work several days later to find his driveway blocked by a Mount Everest–sized pile of lumber, plastic parts, canopies, sandbags, and metal poles for a massive, four-level play set. Bruce couldn't believe it. He thought, *What on earth is going on? Where did this all come from?*

When Kimberly reminded Bruce he had agreed to the purchase, reality set in. They now faced a frightening credit card bill, and Bruce had to take five days off of work and spend two weekends working with a professional carpenter to build the theme park–like attraction, which became the envy of all the neighborhood children.

Have you ever found yourself in an uncomfortable or difficult situation because you didn't listen effectively? Perhaps you've felt embarrassed after missing important social cues in conversation with friends. Maybe you've been reprimanded by your boss for not following the instructions you were given. If so, you know how important listening is to the communication process.

Effective listening plays an important role in the communication process because it helps you understand the thoughts, feelings, and needs of your relational partners. This kind of understanding is strongly correlated with relationship satisfaction; in fact, the inability or unwillingness to grasp another person's

Sometimes we're unable to be fully present when listening to our relational partners. But if we want to become skilled communicators and foster healthy relationships, we need to engage in active listening.

perspective is one of the most common communication problems that relationship therapists address with their clients.[1]

Research has confirmed that relationships, even superficial ones, benefit from skilled listening. In a recent study, communication scholar Harry Weger and his team paired each of 115 subjects with one of ten individuals trained to listen in different ways.

Those who were paired with a very skilled listener were more satisfied with the conversation. They also described the conversational partner as more relatable and socially attractive.[2]

In this chapter, we'll (1) discuss the process of listening, (2) examine the challenges associated with listening, and (3) identify various strategies to help you listen and respond competently.

4.1 Listening as a process

It's safe to say that Bruce and Kimberly could have avoided their miscommunication over the play set. What if Bruce had paused the show he was watching to give Kimberly's question his full attention? What if Kimberly had waited to ask her question until later, when Bruce wasn't so absorbed in the show? To determine what went wrong, it would help to pinpoint the exact moment a failure occurred in the listening process.

Section 4.1 will introduce you to the steps in this process and, most importantly, explain the crucial difference between hearing and listening.

Hearing versus listening

Hearing is the physiological process of receiving and recognizing sounds. Your ears capture sound waves and transmit them to your brain, and unless you are asleep, ill, have suffered an injury, have hearing loss, or wear ear plugs, you can't help but hear. Just like you don't consciously think to breathe, you don't consciously think to hear. Listening, however, is both a physiological *and* a psychological process.

Listening is hearing that is focused and intentional. Imagine you're chatting with a few friends as you give them a ride home from class, and you turn on the car stereo. You are aware of the music—you can *hear* it—but you're not really paying attention to it because you're engaged in a conversation—you're *listening* to your friends. If you begin to tune out your friends to appreciate the lyrics of your favorite song, you are now listening to the music even though you still hear the voices of your friends.

Is it possible to listen to the song lyrics and your friends' conversation at the same time? Yes—up to a point. If you attempt to listen actively to two things at once, you usually end up listening passively to one or the other—or both.

hearing The physiological process of receiving and recognizing sounds.

listening Hearing that is focused and intentional.

active listening Listening with a lot of mental focus and engagement.

passive listening Listening half-heartedly—tuning in and out.

Active listening occurs when you make a concerted effort to listen and respond. It occurs when you block out distractions and give someone your full, undivided attention, with the goal of processing their message accurately and responding appropriately. **Passive listening** occurs when you listen half-heartedly or tune in and out. Your lack of engagement makes you very susceptible to distractions.

In Khalil's narrative, he describes his experience with passive listening. Have there been times in your life when passive listening has negatively affected your communication? What happened as a result?

"Frankly, I've never given listening a lot of thought. Which isn't so good because I'd say 80% of my work involves listening to others. I'm a floor manager at a large retail store, and for a while, I felt like I didn't have time to really listen to my coworkers' complaints or questions. Things started to get really tense, and we weren't working well as a team. I now realize many of the troubles I had were the result of passive listening." –Khalil

Stages of the listening process

Now that you know the difference between hearing and listening, let's explore listening as a process. The listening process includes five overlapping sensory stages: *receiving, attending, interpreting, responding,* and *recalling*.[3] (It may help to remember the stages using the acronym R.A.I.R.R.; see **FIGURE 4.1**). When you listen, you cycle through these stages repeatedly, in rapid succession. Let's use a scenario to illustrate this process.

Receiving is gaining a sensory awareness of a speaker's message. For example, Joe is out to dinner with a friend, Aisha. Joe is focused on what Aisha is telling him, but as she's speaking, he sees his friends Jansen and Cara come in and sit at a booth nearby. His awareness of their presence is a part of the perception process.

Attending is focusing your attention on a particular message or conversation. When Aisha gets up from the table to grab her food order, Joe's attention turns to Jansen and Cara. They are speaking loud enough that Joe can attend to what they're saying because he is no longer attending to his conversation with Aisha.

Interpreting is making sense of or comprehending a message using sensory information. Joe determines that Jansen and Cara are talking about Jansen's stepbrother, Isaac, who is visiting for the holidays and is testing their nerves. As he attempts to interpret what he hears, he'll also evaluate it—form thoughts, opinions, and judgments based on his own knowledge and experiences. Joe may, for example, interpret Jansen and Cara's frustrations as completely justifiable, because he can imagine how difficult it would be to host a guest in their small, one-bedroom apartment. Or, he might interpret what they're saying as inhospitable, because he knows that Isaac is a considerate guy who is only staying with them for two days and bought groceries for all of them to share.[4]

Responding to a message involves some sort of reaction. In this situation, Joe may smile or frown. He might also turn to Jansen and Cara and join in on their conversation—or pretend he's not listening at all.

receiving Gaining awareness of a speaker's message.

attending Focusing your attention on a particular message.

interpreting Assigning meaning to a message using sensory information.

responding Reacting verbally and/or nonverbally to a message.

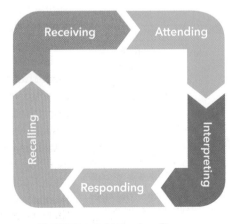

FIGURE 4.1 Listening Process

In this clip from the TV comedy *Black-ish*, Earl (Laurence Fishburne) explains how he met his new fiancée, Lynette (Loretta Devine). Describe how the listening process helped Earl initiate a relationship with Lynette. How does Earl's son Andre (Anthony Anderson) rely on this same process to reduce his uncertainty regarding Lynette and Earl's whirlwind engagement? On YouTube, search using the keywords "Pops Has a New Fiancee – black-ish." (2:38)

Recalling is the process of retrieving or remembering sensory information. Joe may recall, for example, some of the things he heard Jansen and Cara complain about and relay them to Aisha when she returns.

Back-channel cues

The responses that you make as part of the listening process are a form of *feedback* (see Chapter 2). They are called **back-channel cues**. For example, you may ask a thoughtful question during a pause in the conversation or laugh at a witty remark. These are back-channel cues.

Nonverbal back-channel cues are listening responses that do not involve language. Examples include focused eye contact, nodding your head to show approval or understanding, and frowning. **Verbal back-channel cues** are listening responses that involve the use of language. For instance, when someone is speaking to you on the phone, you might blurt out something or finish a person's sentence. While this may convey excitement or interest, it could also signal that you're getting impatient with someone's long-windedness. Either way, it's probably best to use this back-channel cue sparingly.[5]

It is not uncommon for listeners to respond using nonverbal and verbal back-channel cues simultaneously. For example, if a coworker whispers something to you, you may lean forward and nod your head (nonverbal) as you say, "Isn't that the truth?" (verbal). Users of American Sign Language "listen" to hand signals that represent letters and words (verbal) while also focusing on each other's eye movements, facial expressions, and posture (nonverbal).

When you are the one speaking, you look to the back-channel cues you're receiving to assess how your conversational partner is responding to your message. As a listener, the frequent and appropriate use of back-channel cues may help you listen more actively and effectively.[6]

recalling Retrieving or remembering a message or sensory information.

back-channel cues Verbal and nonverbal listening responses.

nonverbal back-channel cues Listening responses that do not involve language.

verbal back-channel cues Listening responses that use language.

Consciously consider the messages your back-channel cues convey to others. Try to use positive cues and avoid negative cues as much as possible.[7] Let's start by identifying positive back-channel cues.

Positive nonverbal back-channel cues

- Leaning slightly toward the speaker
- Listening without interrupting
- Showing interest with animated facial expressions
- Placing your hand on the speaker's arm or shoulder to convey concern or warmth
- Making vocal sounds to express engagement: "Uh-huh." "Hmm." "Ahah!" "Oh."

Positive verbal back-channel cues

- Reactions of surprise or excitement: "Wait a minute!" "No way!" "Yikes!"
- Expressions of understanding: "I see." "Yes!" "Exactly." "That's interesting."
- Questions or invitations for the speaker to elaborate or continue talking: "Go on." "What happened next?"
- Restatements of what you just heard: "So, you're feeling frustrated."

When positive listening responses occur at appropriate times, they're generally well received, but certain back-channel cues may not go over as well. They may also interfere with your ability to listen. Here are some common negative back-channel cues.

Negative nonverbal back-channel cues

- Checking your cell phone while someone is talking
- Sighing as if you're exasperated or put off
- Rolling your eyes
- Hanging up on someone in the middle of a phone conversation
- Giving someone a look of disgust or annoyance

Negative verbal back-channel cues

- Dismissive language: "Whatever!" or "You're crazy."
- Interrupting with a lot of questions
- Putting someone's ideas down: "That's totally wrong." "You're ridiculous."
- Threatening not to listen anymore: "I'm done listening." "This conversation is over!"
- Talking over someone who is speaking

Can you think of other positive and negative verbal and nonverbal back-channel cues? Which of these listening responses occur most often in your interpersonal communication?

Switched at Birth is a TV drama featuring hearing-impaired and deaf actors. Identify examples of positive and negative back-channel cues in this tense scene between Emmett (Sean Berdy), his brother Travis (Ryan Lane), and Emmett's mother, Melody (Marlee Matlin). How do their back-channel cues (verbal from signing and nonverbal from eye contact and body movements) affect the way they come across and listen to each other? Which back-channel cues are negative and which are positive? On YouTube, search using the keywords: "Season 5, Episode 7: Travis and Emmett Argue Over Dinner." (2:49)

Conversational turn-taking

Back-channel cues serve another important purpose: to regulate how people take turns speaking and listening. **Conversational turn-taking** is the method by which you alternate between being a speaker and a listener.[8] For example, when you want to encourage someone to speak, you may ask a question, put your hand out with your palm up to gesture *go ahead*, or pause and nod your head as if to say, *go on*. These are **turn-yielding signals**, or behaviors you use to encourage someone to speak.

When another person wishes to speak, but you're not finished talking, your voice may get louder and you may talk over the other person. You may hold your index finger up in the air to communicate *I'm still talking*, or say, "Just a minute, I'm not finished." These are **turn-denying signals**, or behaviors you use to deny someone the opportunity to speak.

You use **turn-requesting signals** if you want someone to stop talking so you can speak. You may open your mouth as if you are about to say something, hold your hand out to pause the conversation, or interrupt with "Let me respond to that," or "Now listen here," to assume the speaking role.

An example of conversational turn-taking is found in a video featuring 3-year-old Mateo and his mother, Linda. Linda has explained to Mateo that he can't have cupcakes for dinner, so Mateo shifts strategies and goes to his grandmother and tries to convince her to give him a cupcake, despite being told "no"

conversational turn-taking
Verbal and nonverbal behaviors you use to alternate between being a speaker and a listener.

turn-yielding signals
Verbal and nonverbal behaviors you use to encourage someone to speak.

turn-denying signals
Verbal and nonverbal behaviors you use to deny someone the opportunity to speak.

turn-requesting signals
Verbal and nonverbal behaviors you use to get someone to stop talking.

by Linda. When Linda confronts Mateo about this, he holds up his hands and interrupts his mother, repeating, "Linda, honey, just listen" (turn-requesting signals). He closes his eyes and lifts his chin (turn-denying signals), and he asks questions with his arms spread (turn-yielding signals). To view the clip on YouTube, search using the keywords: "My 3 year old must argue and debate everything!" (2:36)

Listening styles

Your **listening style** is your preferred way of making sense of spoken messages. Your attitudes, beliefs, goals, interests, gender, and personality may influence your listening preferences.[9]

Communication scholars describe and measure the different types of listening styles using various labels and scales, but five styles that are particularly common include *action-oriented*, *time-oriented*, *relational-oriented*, *content-oriented*, and *analysis-oriented* listening (see **TABLE 4.1**).[10] You may have a preference for one or more of these styles, or you may alter your listening style depending on the situation, whom you are talking to, and your communication goals. As you read each one, ask yourself if the description matches the way you prefer to listen.

Your relationship partners may perceive your listening style positively or negatively based on their needs at the time. For example, if a person wants to

> **listening style** Your preferred way of making sense of messages as you listen.

table 4.1	Listening Styles
Action-oriented	Action-oriented listeners focus on the parts of a message that help them make decisions, solve problems, or take appropriate action. Someone with this listening style will really appreciate facts, clear explanations, and accurate messages.
Time-oriented	Time-oriented listeners value concise messages that get straight to the point. They pay close attention to schedules, dates, and deadlines. Someone with this listening style may get impatient if your thoughts wander or if you become long-winded.
Relational-oriented	Relational-oriented listeners like in-depth, unrushed conversations that promote relationship closeness. They are eager to find commonalities and offer emotional support. Someone with this listening style is very inquisitive and will encourage you to share your personal stories and feelings.
Content-oriented	Content-oriented listeners are eager to learn. They're curious about ideas, facts, concepts, events, scientific explanations, and inferences. Someone with this listening style will want to understand what you're saying completely and is likely to ask a lot of clarifying and follow-up questions.
Analysis-oriented	Analysis-oriented listeners prefer to evaluate ideas in an investigative, critical, and logical way. They love to have hypothetical discussions, play the devil's advocate, and debate for the sake of debate. Someone with this listening style will likely point out inconsistencies or inaccuracies in what you say or remind you that your opinion is "not a fact."

connect with you on an emotional level or needs an empathetic ear, a relational-oriented listening style will go over much better than a time-oriented or analysis-oriented style will.

Tailoring your listening style to your particular social situation can help in professional scenarios, as well.[11] For example, if you're attending a conference for work, and your boss expects you to share what you learn with your coworkers when you return to the office, a content-oriented listening style would be most appropriate.

section review

4.1 Listening as a process

Hearing, the physiological process of receiving and recognizing sounds, is distinct from listening, which is both a physiological and a psychological process. Listening involves five stages: receiving, attending, interpreting, responding, and recalling. Your use of nonverbal and verbal back-channel cues, as well as your listening style, may enhance or hinder your interpersonal communication.

Key Terms

hearing, *p. 94*	interpreting, *p. 95*	conversational turn-taking, *p. 98*
listening, *p. 94*	responding, *p. 95*	turn-yielding signals, *p. 98*
active listening, *p. 94*	recalling, *p. 96*	turn-denying signals, *p. 98*
passive listening, *p. 94*	back-channel cues, *p. 96*	turn-requesting signals, *p. 98*
receiving, *p. 95*	nonverbal back-channel cues, *p. 96*	listening style, *p. 99*
attending, *p. 95*	verbal back-channel cues, *p. 96*	

Comprehend It?

1. Define each of the key terms in Section 4.1. To further your understanding of these terms, create examples to support your definitions.
2. Compare and contrast the following:
   - Hearing and listening
   - Active and passive listening
   - The five stages of the listening process
   - Verbal and nonverbal back-channel cues
   - Action-oriented, time-oriented, relational-oriented, content-oriented, and analysis-oriented listening
3. What are the differences between turn-yielding, turn-denying, and turn-requesting signals?

Apply It!

Imagine you are the director of human resources at a large corporation, and you're leading a training session on how to improve workplace listening skills. You begin the session by listing and describing the five stages of the listening process. Next, you give your trainees an example of a conversation, and as you do, you explain how the stages of the listening process are involved. Describe what you plan to say.

4.2 The challenges of listening

On average, listening consumes five or more hours in a typical day.[12] Based on studies of college students, communication researchers Kathryn Dindia and Bonnie Kennedy estimate that, on average, people spend 50% of their waking hours listening, 20% speaking, 13% reading, and 12% writing—that's more time spent listening than the other three activities combined.[13]

Listening, then, appears to dominate our interpersonal communication. But does listening a lot make us good at it? In one study, 94% of corporate managers surveyed rated themselves as "good" or "very good" at listening, and no managers rated themselves poorly. However, employees who worked for these same managers generally rated their listening skills in less glowing terms.[14]

Studies like this reveal that we may not be the good listeners that we think we are. Learning when and how listening can go wrong, however, can help us improve our skills. Section 4.2 will identify some listening challenges that inhibit effective interpersonal communication.

Listening fatigue

Listening fatigue occurs when listening becomes mentally tiresome. For example, you may grow weary of listening when someone speaks with a monotone voice, mumbles, or goes off on tangents.

Ongoing internal and external noise may also contribute to listening fatigue. As you learned in Chapter 2, *noise* is anything that distorts messages or makes clear and effective communication challenging; *internal noise* is any psychological or physical distraction, and *external noise* occurs in your environment. For example, your ability to stay focused on a message may diminish if internally you're preoccupied by personal concerns, or if externally there is constant background noise in your environment.

A speaker who talks too slow can also cause listening fatigue. The average person can comprehend up to 600 words per minute, but most people speak in the range of 100 to 150 words per minute. If someone is speaking to you too slowly, your brain tends to drift off.[15] The difference between the rate at which a person speaks and your ability to process spoken messages is called the **speech-thought differential**.

On the other hand, receiving too much sensory information can also lead to listening fatigue. **Sensory overload** (also referred to as *message overload*) occurs when sensory stimulation exceeds what your nervous system can handle. This may occur when you receive messages from too many sources or attempt to do several tasks (multi-task) at the same time. For example, perhaps you're trying to listen to a friend on the phone while you're ordering dinner online.

listening fatigue When listening becomes mentally tiresome.

speech-thought differential The difference between the rate at which a person speaks and your ability to mentally process the words.

sensory overload When sensory stimulation exceeds what your nervous system can handle.

selective listening
Focusing your attention on the messages you find interesting, unique, or important and tuning out those you don't.

insulating Blocking out or ignoring what you're hearing.

pseudolistening Acting like you're listening when your attention is focused elsewhere.

Your brain reaches its sensory-processing limit, and your listening suffers as a result.

Selective listening

How often do you surf TV channels or mindlessly scroll through newsfeeds on your cell phone? If you're like your authors, you may, at times, just sit on the couch or lay in bed flipping and swiping until something piques your interest.

In Chapter 3, you learned that *selective attention* is your tendency to pay attention to what interests you the most at a given moment and tune out what doesn't. For example, you may focus your attention on a smell that you love or a visual you find stimulating (e.g., when you are eating a delicious meal or when you are people watching). Selective listening is a form of selective attention specific to a conversation.

Selective listening occurs when you focus your attention on the spoken messages you find interesting, unique, or important and tune out those you don't. You tend to pay greater attention to messages that reinforce your existing beliefs; your desire to listen diminishes when information isn't essential to your objectives and desires.

Sometimes we don't want to hear certain messages. In situations where we'd rather not acknowledge or have to deal with something, we purposely **insulate** or block out what we're hearing. Other times, we want to hear a certain message badly enough that we selectively focus on the parts of the message we like and insulate the parts of a message we don't.

Below, Terrell describes an example of selective listening. His boyfriend, Jamal, uses a particular tactic to get his attention. Can you relate to what Terrell describes in any way? Do you use any tricks like this to get others to listen to you?

"I'm a die-hard Notre Dame fan. When Jamal senses I've lost interest in what he's talking about, he'll mutter, 'Notre Dame' in the middle of a sentence to catch my ear. I'll say, 'What? What did you say?' It gets my attention, but I can tell it bothers him that he has to resort to this to get me to listen." –Terrell

Pseudolistening

When you're talking with someone, it's generally considered rude to give them less than your complete attention. Even when you're not really listening, you may maintain the conversation with positive, encouraging back-channel cues to avoid offending your conversational partner. **Pseudolistening** is pretending to listen or acting like you're listening. For example, you may nod your head and make direct eye contact as if you're understanding or following along—even though you're thinking about something else. You may pseudolisten on the phone by setting the receiver down for a moment to do something and coming back seconds (or minutes) later, acting as if you never left the conversation.

Purportedly, this behavior so annoyed President Franklin Delano Roosevelt that he decided one evening to pull a prank on some of his guests at the White House. After greeting each guest and exchanging a few pleasantries, he said quite casually, "I murdered my grandmother this morning." Several guests pretended they were listening. They nodded, smiled, and said such things as "Thank you," "Mr. President, it's a pleasure to be here," "how kind of you," or "I couldn't agree with you more, a lovely evening." Finally, one guest seemed to actually listen to the president and laughed as he replied, "I'm sure she had it coming to her."[16]

Defensive listening

Defensive listening is listening for the purpose of winning an argument or proving that your conversational partner is wrong. When you listen defensively, you focus on the parts of someone's message you can attack, weaken, or refute. It's the kind of listening you'd expect in a debate tournament.

Defensive listening also occurs when you interpret innocent comments as personal attacks. You may misconstrue what someone says because of your insecurities. You can see this in the following dialogue between Drew and his stressed-out single father, Bob.

> **Drew:** Hey Dad, why don't you buy that frozen lasagna again this week since you're too busy to cook.
> **Bob:** (*defensively*) Sure, and while I do that, how about you try standing on your feet for 45 hours a week at the nursery, taking evening grad classes, and squeezing in time to cook, clean, and fold my laundry while you're at it.

Drew simply wanted to help his dad save some time by suggesting an easy-to-cook, prepackaged dinner they enjoyed the previous week. Bob feels guilty that he's not often around to do the things that make him feel like a good parent, and he accordingly interprets his son's suggestion as a critique of his parenting.

Narcissistic listening

Narcissistic listening is characterized by self-absorption—listening primarily to meet your needs and stroke your ego. Narcissistic listeners are not genuinely interested in what others have to say unless it benefits them in some way. Communication scholars argue that one of the common characteristics of narcissistic listeners is that they love to listen—to the sound of their own voices. They talk, "glibly, smoothly, confidently, and virtually nonstop about themselves."[17]

There are several behaviors associated with narcissistic listening. One is **stage-hogging**, which happens when you repeatedly shift the conversational spotlight back to yourself. For example, your friend, Amir, is sharing what he

defensive listening Listening for the purpose of winning an argument.

narcissistic listening Characterized by self-absorption; listening primarily to meet your needs and stroke your ego.

stage-hogging Making yourself the focus of conversation.

In the film *Before Sunset,* Jesse (Ethan Hawke) and Celine (Julie Delpy) reunite nine years after they shared a romantic interlude. They spend part of a day together while Jesse promotes a book about their experience. How would you describe Celine's listening behavior in this scene? Compare your answers to the concept of narcissistic listening and the behaviors of stage-hogging and monopolizing. On YouTube, search using the keywords, "Before Sunset (7/10) Movie CLIP – Stop the Car (2004)." (3:09)

did over the weekend in Sacramento, but before he has a chance to finish, you chime in to talk about your recent trip there.

Monopolizing, another characteristic of narcissistic listening, occurs when you talk too much and don't give others a chance to speak. If, after diverting the conversation away from Amir's trip to yours, you go on and on about it to such a degree that Amir can't jump back in, you are monopolizing the conversation.

A third behavior associated with narcissistic listening is **one-upping**. You may know people who will take what you say, no matter what you've experienced, and respond with how they've had it better—or worse. If Amir complains that he was stuck in traffic for three hours on his way back from Sacramento, and you jump in to say, "That's nothing! It takes me five hours every time I go there," you are one-upping.

Close-mindedness

Has anyone ever accused you of being stubborn, unyielding, or uncompromising? If so, close-mindedness may influence your listening. **Close-mindedness** occurs when you are unwilling to appreciate or consider another person's thoughts, ideas, or opinions. A close-minded listener might say things like:

- "It doesn't matter what you say."
- "I've heard this all before."
- "I don't have time for this."
- "My mind is made up . . . period!"
- "You're entitled to your opinion."

Close-minded listening can make communication in a relationship especially challenging. When you convince yourself you're right and your relationship

monopolizing Talking too much and not giving others a chance to speak.

one-upping Responding by saying how you have it better or worse.

close-mindedness When you are unwilling to consider another person's thoughts, feelings, or needs.

partner is wrong—with no room for flexibility—this leaves the other person with few options other than to shut down or fight harder. To listen effectively, it's important to readily admit your mistakes and acknowledge the possibility that your relationship partners could have more accurate recollections and perceptions than you do.

Close-minded listening often occurs when you refuse to appreciate the merits of an alternative point of view. For example, you may remove yourself from a conversation with a colleague when she starts to talk politics, because you know she is a liberal Democrat and you're a conservative Republican.

Interrupting

It's easier for us to communicate effectively with others if we take turns listening and speaking without interruption. **Interrupting** occurs when you say something before someone has finished speaking. You prioritize your own thoughts and take control of the conversation.

One form of interrupting is gap-filling. **Gap-filling** occurs when you interrupt to finish a person's thoughts or story, perhaps because you think you can say it better or more quickly. Gap-filling also occurs when you interrupt to add details to a speaker's story or to correct the speaker's recollections. You may think you are being helpful, but this behavior is usually not appreciated unless your conversational partner prompts you to fill in.

A major reason why people interrupt is to control a conversation and steer it in a favorable direction. You may employ certain communication tactics, such as interrupting, to redirect and restrain the communication efforts of another person.[18] Your goal may be to get the upper hand in an argument or to change the subject when it's making you feel uncomfortable.

Research suggests that most people find excessive interrupting frustrating and perceive it to be discourteous and unprofessional.[19] For example, communication researchers Karen McComb and Fredric Jablin found that interviewers viewed job applicants less favorably if they interrupted the interviewer during the interview.[20]

But is interrupting always a bad thing? There are a few situations in which interrupting can help us listen better. As you will learn in Section 4.3, interrupting can be a part of *paraphrasing*—a behavior that helps us listen more effectively. If, for example, someone is overwhelming you with a lot of unnecessary details, you may respectfully interrupt using a paraphrase such as, "So, you didn't see this coming," to help the speaker get to the point.

In addition, interrupting at just the right moment may help you gain clarity when you get lost in a story or need to verify whether you're decoding a message accurately. Interjecting a question such as, "I'm a bit confused. Who are you mad at? Is it me?" can prompt the speaker to clarify if necessary.

interrupting Saying something before someone has finished speaking.

gap-filling Interrupting to finish a person's thoughts or story or add details to a story.

Listening bias

A **listening bias** is a set of preconceived ideas or beliefs that affect how you listen to others. A gender bias, for example, may cause you to doubt a person's knowledge about a topic based on their gender.

As a part of a study by Stanford linguistics scholars Meghan Sumner and Ed King, subjects wrote down the first thing they thought of after hearing a word expressed by either a male or female voice. When a male voice said the word "academy," subjects were more likely to associate it with a military or sports-oriented school or training program. With the female voice, subjects were more likely to associate the word with the Academy Awards. This study suggests that we may unconsciously associate a male and a female voice with certain levels of authority or with specific events and activities.[21]

You may also listen to speakers differently if they speak with an accent or dialect. You may have an **accent** if you are speaking a language that is not your first language—that is, the language you were taught from birth. For example, someone who grew up speaking Spanish but later learned to speak English may pronounce English words differently than native English speakers do, though some multilingual people can lose their accents with enough study or early exposure. A **dialect**, by contrast, is a distinct way of speaking your first language. For example, English sounds different if you visit Great Britain, Australia, South Africa, or various regions of the United States.

Subjects in a study conducted by communication scholar Jesse Delia listened to voice recordings of speakers with various dialects and were then asked to share their impressions. Delia's results suggested that people may perceive others who do not speak with the same dialect less favorably. For example, subjects who were from the northeastern part of the United States were likely to describe a speaker with a southern American dialect as "less educated."[22] In another study, subjects living in the United States listened to voice recordings and rated speakers with a southern dialect lower in social status but higher in friendliness than speakers with a midwestern dialect.[23]

In these types of studies, subjects are often surprised or unaware of their biased associations and attitudes. Such *unconscious biases* may affect your listening even if you're not consciously aware of it.[24]

Hearing impairment

Hearing loss can occur suddenly as a result of an accident, deafening noise, or illness. For most of us, hearing loss occurs slowly, almost imperceptibly, as we age. However, 20% of American teenagers already suffer from some level of hearing loss—a 31% surge since the 1990s.[25]

"Just because the preacher is from Alabama doesn't mean he's speaking in tongues!"

Audiologists now routinely see levels of hearing loss in patients in their 30s and 40s that they are accustomed to treating in patients between the ages of 50 and 60. What's causing this sharp increase in hearing loss? The World Health Organization warns that the use of personal audio devices may be a contributing factor.[26] In one study, 189 college students listening to a personal listening device were stopped by researchers at a campus in New York. They were asked to surrender their headphones for a moment so that the volume could be measured using a calibrated sound meter. More than 58% were listening at volumes that exceed the recommended levels.[27]

Audiologists recommend that you replace your earbuds or ear speakers that go in the ear with smaller muff-type headphones that are placed outside the ear and limit your exposure to less than one hour a day. In addition, they recommend that you reduce the volume level below 60% on your device to protect your hearing.[28]

If you suffer from hearing loss, speech sounds garbled or muffled. Since it takes greater effort to understand what you hear, you may experience listening fatigue. Over time, your listening becomes more passive and lazy, and the hearing centers of your brain begin to atrophy. Research suggests that the longer adults go without hearing aids to correct for hearing loss, the greater their chances of developing memory disorders such as dementia and Alzheimer's disease.[29]

section review

4.2 The challenges of listening

Listening fatigue, selective listening, pseudolistening, defensive listening, narcissistic listening, close-mindedness, interrupting, listening biases, and hearing impairment can all interfere with your ability to listen and communicate effectively. Your effort to identify and manage these challenges will improve your interpersonal communication and relationships.

Key Terms

listening fatigue, *p. 101*

speech-thought differential, *p. 101*

sensory overload, *p. 101*

selective listening, *p. 102*

insulating, *p. 102*

pseudolistening, *p. 102*

defensive listening, *p. 103*

narcissistic listening, *p. 103*

stage-hogging, *p. 103*

monopolizing, *p. 104*

one-upping, *p. 104*

close-mindedness, *p. 104*

interrupting, *p. 105*

gap-filling, *p. 105*

listening bias, *p. 106*

accent, *p. 106*

dialect, *p. 106*

Comprehend It?

1. Define each of the key terms in Section 4.2. To further your understanding of these terms, create examples to support your definitions.

2. What is the difference between selective listening, insulating, and pseudolistening?

3. How can interrupting both inhibit and help your IPC?

(continued)

Apply It!

The next time you watch a TV show or movie, try to spot the listening challenges we've discussed in this section. When characters engage in interrupting or defensive listening, for example, what influence does this seem to have on the communication process and outcome? You can also do this the next time you are conversing in a small group. Observe how often these listening challenges appear. How do people respond to them?

4.3 Ways to improve listening and responding skills

Stephen Covey's top-selling self-help book, *The 7 Habits of Highly Effective People*, claims that listening well can greatly improve your life and relationships. One of the seven habits is to "seek first to understand, then to be understood"—that is, to approach every conversation with a desire to understand your conversational partner fully before expressing your own thoughts. This would involve not interrupting, of course, and using the positive verbal and nonverbal back-channel cues you read about earlier in the chapter.[30]

If you give your conversational partners as much time as they need to communicate what's on their minds, it also gives you more time to decode and form a comprehensive understanding of the information they provide. You also give yourself more time to encode an appropriate response. This may have a very positive effect on the conversation's direction and outcome.

Section 4.3 will introduce you to several other strategies that can similarly help you listen and respond effectively.

Postpone effectively

Sarah loves her mom. She enjoys having conversations with her—most of the time. However, sometimes Sarah isn't in the mood to talk, and when she feels noncommunicative, certain aspects of her mom's communication really get on her nerves. What does she do to solve this problem? She lets some of her mom's phone calls go to voicemail and waits to call her back until she's in a better mood. Screening her calls is a form of *postponement*, a strategy that helps her manage how well she listens.

In moments like this, **postponement**—delaying a conversation until you're ready to communicate effectively—is a good listening strategy. However, while postponement is generally a wise option, there are times when your conversational partner doesn't want to wait. Perhaps you've used an approach similar to the one Huang describes in his narrative. What kind of response did you get?

If this kind of approach to postponement hasn't worked well for you either, these four steps may help you delay a conversation and leave all parties

postponement Delaying a conversation until you are ready to communicate effectively.

> "Sometimes I'll argue with my fiancée and say, 'Forget it. I'm done. I'm not talking about this anymore.' She'll say, 'Well I'm *not* done. And we *will* keep talking about this!' I try to walk away, and she'll follow me around the house and try to get me to engage with her. Sometimes she even grabs my car keys so I can't leave the house. I need to come up with a better way to postpone." –Huang

feeling okay about the wait: (1) state the reason for postponement, (2) recognize the person's need to communicate, (3) agree on a time to reconvene, and (4) follow through.

Let's take a look at these four steps in action. Tahani has just finished her student teaching term and is actively seeking a full-time job. Her exhaustive efforts yield no offers until she receives a call from a school system in Australia. She calls her best friend, Mike, to share the good news:

> **Tahani**: I can't believe it. I was just offered an interview by a school in Sydney, Australia. What should I do?
>
> **Mike**: No way! This is great! Hey, I'm about to step into my manager's office for a meeting and need to prep for it. I know this is really important, and I can't wait to hear all the details. Can we talk about this during my break at 10:00 a.m.?

State the reason for postponement

Mike tells Tahani he's about to step into his manager's office and needs to prepare himself. This lets Tahani know why it's not a good time for Mike to listen.

Recognize the person's need to communicate

By saying, "Wow! This is great! I know this is really important, and I can't wait to hear all the details," Mike acknowledges Tahani's excitement and the importance of her call.

Agree on a time to reconvene

Mike asks, "Can we talk about this during my break at 10:00 a.m.?" By giving Tahani a chance to agree or disagree, Mike gives her a say (shared conversational control) in terms of an established time. Mike could also have said, "When is a good time later today?" or "How about as soon as I get home tonight?"

Follow through

If Mike calls Tahani during his morning break at 10:00 a.m., he demonstrates consistency and reliability. If Mike doesn't follow through, Tahani may feel dismissed or perceive his lack of follow-through as indifference. Or worse, she could think he's trying to avoid the conversation altogether.

If Mike gives Tahani a valid reason to postpone, recognizes her need to talk, and includes her in the decision to communicate later, Tahani is more likely to accept and respect Mike's need to postpone.

paraphrasing Briefly restating in your own words what you heard someone say.

Paraphrase

Another technique that may enhance your listening and responding skills is **paraphrasing**: briefly restating in your own words what you heard someone say in an attempt to capture the essence of their message.

Imagine your friend Rafiah shares how unhappy she is with her dad. You respond by paraphrasing: "So, you feel like he doesn't seem as interested in you now that he's married to your stepmom." A paraphrase like this not only sums up what you just heard but also communicates to Rafiah that you understand what she's saying without offering judgment or critique.

Paraphrases often begin with sentence starters like: "So," "Sounds like," "What I heard you say was," or "In other words. . . ." A paraphrase may consist of a statement, a question, or both. Here is an example of a paraphrase between two classmates, Adina and Mi-Kyung:

> **Adina:** (*sighs, frowning*) I'm supposed to paint an abstract picture, but I can only use one of the four techniques we learned in class. I'm limited to three colors, and I have to include seven glazes.
> **Mi-Kyung:** Sounds like you're not thrilled with these requirements. Are they stifling your creativity?

"So, to paraphrase... Damn."

Mi-Kyung's paraphrase encapsulates what she's seeing and hearing from Adina. She then asks a question based on how she interpreted Adina's message. Mi-Kyung's paraphrase is a confirming form of communication. It lets Adina know she is listening actively and cares about her thoughts. In fact, one communication study found that listeners who incorporate paraphrases in their listening responses are perceived as more relatable and relationally attractive.[31]

Did Mi-Kyung decode Adina's message correctly? If not, her paraphrase gives Adina the feedback she needs to correct Mi-Kyung if necessary. Mi-Kyung's paraphrase is also a helpful form of feedback for Adina; it allows Adina to hear what she is saying and how she's coming across—to process it—and then confirm or clarify her original message. This technique thus helps Mi-Kyung and Adina understand each other better.

When you listen and paraphrase, you communicate to your relationship partners: *I hear you, and this is what I understand.* They will likely reciprocate: *I feel understood; now I'm ready to listen to and understand you.* You'll have a chance to practice this important technique at the end of the chapter.

Metacommunicate

In Chapter 2, you learned about *metacommunication*—that is, communicating about communication. In the context of listening, two metacommunication behaviors are especially relevant. First, you can assess listening readiness, or check to see if the receiver is ready to listen. Second, you can confirm listening accuracy, or ask the receiver to paraphrase you.

Check to see if the receiver is ready to listen

Salina wants to talk about a new procedure at work with her coworker, Rosa. Unbeknownst to Salina, Rosa is juggling a lot of duties at the moment (*external noise*) and is feeling a bit stressed (*internal noise*). If Salina wants her conversation to go well, she should check to see if Rosa is receptive. **Receptivity** is a person's willingness to receive a message or engage in a conversation. Salina can mention what she would like to talk about and ask Rosa if this is a good time for her:

> **Salina:** I was wondering if we could talk about how the shifts were assigned this month. Is this a good time for you? Do you have five minutes?

Salina gives Rosa a general idea of the conversation topic, asks if it's a good time for Rosa to talk, and estimates how long the conversation will take. If Rosa is distracted or says it is not a good time, it's better to not force the conversation. The two can postpone the conversation and mutually decide on a later time.

Ask the receiver to paraphrase you

Asking your listener to paraphrase you is also an effective way to ensure your message gets across. Here are two examples, one from Kungawo, who is talking to a subordinate at work, and the other from Dex, who is speaking to his two teenage daughters:

> **Kungawo:** I'm not sure what I said made complete sense. Would you mind telling me what you heard?

> **Dex:** Kate and Avery, just so I know you understand, what three things did I say you need to do before you can sit down and watch *Riverdale*?

If you demand, "Tell me what I just said, now!" your relational partners are not likely to respond well. Asking politely and in a calm tone, "Would you please repeat my instructions?" may go over much better. You may also say, "Let's be sure we're on the same page. What have we decided?"

Mirror your conversational partner

In a study conducted by a research team at University College London, adults registered similar brain activity on MRI scans when they heard a baby's laugh and when they laughed out loud themselves.[32] This suggests we are wired to mimic the expressions and emotions of others. **Mirroring** occurs when you consciously and subconsciously imitate or reflect a speaker's emotional state and communication behaviors, such as vocal tones, speech patterns, gestures, and facial expressions.

receptivity Your willingness to receive a message or engage in a conversation.

mirroring When you consciously and subconsciously imitate or reflect a speaker's emotional state and communication behaviors.

In this clip from *Bachelor in Paradise,* Demi Burnett speaks to her former girlfriend Kristian Haggerty about her inner conflict and ultimate realization. Notice the mirroring behaviors in their interaction. What were they? What effect did her behaviors appear to have on their conversation? On YouTube, search using the keywords: "Demi's Girlfriend Kristian Arrives!" (6:34)

You can mirror your conversational partners by returning their eye contact, smiling when they smile at you, leaning forward to listen to them as they lean forward to listen to you, and shaking their hands as they reach out with their own. Mirroring may make the conversation feel more engaging and comfortable. This, in turn, may enhance your listening skills.[33]

You can also use mirroring to improve listening by exhibiting the listening behavior you want to see from your conversational partner. Imagine your angry brother comes toward you talking loud, fast, and aggressively. Rather than stepping forward confrontationally in response, you step back or even sit down, which is a less antagonistic posture. You invite him to sit down next to you. You may say, "I know you're upset. Let's work this out. I'm going to let you talk." You listen without interruption. When it's your turn to say something, you speak evenly, softly, and slowly. Your brother will likely calm down and reflect back what he is seeing and hearing from you.

Practice with recall tests

How often do you walk away from a conversation and realize minutes later that what you heard went in one ear and out the other? A technique called the **recall test**—checking to see if you remember what you've been told—may help you improve your ability to listen actively. Taking time to recall and process the information others share with you trains you to focus and concentrate.

Try a recall test the next time you have a phone conversation. After you end the call, but before you make another call or move on to your next task, ask yourself: *What did my conversational partner share with me?* Try recalling the main points first. Next, see which details you remember. If you can't remember much, this is a wakeup call! Did you allow distractions to interfere with your listening?

recall test Checking to see if you remember what you've been told.

Recall tests help you process what you hear and store the information in your long-term memory.[34] Sharpening your memory can also improve your conversational skills. People love it when you show an interest in them and remember the things they've shared with you in earlier conversations. Take Reggie and Tara. It's been a couple of weeks since they last talked, but Tara brings up a topic she remembers from their last phone call:

> **Reggie:** Hi Tara!
>
> **Tara:** What's up, Reggie? How was New York? Did you land tickets to the *Soul Train* anniversary gala?
>
> **Reggie:** (*Impressed she remembers this bit of information*) Girl, you know it!

Can you think of other interpersonal situations, such as a sequence of job interviews or your first few dates with someone new, where the consistent application of recall tests would enhance future conversations?

Besides trying to recall what a relationship partner said in a conversation, you can also ask yourself: *What did my conversational partner not say?* Paying close attention to the subtle and not-so-subtle messages conveyed by the omission of certain information can yield valuable insights. For example, perhaps you can tell that your date is avoiding questions about their family. You may want to stay clear of that subject until your relationship has progressed. Can you think of other reasons why it's important to pay attention to the information people leave out?

Listen and respond empathetically

Empathetic listening occurs when you listen in order to identify with and share the feelings of another person. Communication scholar Jon Hayes states that when you demonstrate empathetic listening, you let people "know they have been understood from within their own frame of reference, and that [you] can see their world as they see it while remaining separate from it."[35]

It's easier to identify with the excitement, joy, and success of others. It may not be as easy when someone you care about is in the midst of something painful, such as a major setback, loss, or illness. You may not know what to say or worry you'll say the wrong thing.[36]

Empathetic listening can also be difficult when you have a strong instinct to offer unsolicited advice—that is, advice you're not asked to give. Humorist Andy Rooney once said, "I've learned it's best to give advice in only two circumstances: when it is requested and when it is a life-threatening situation!" There is a lot of wisdom here. While our advice is usually well intentioned, research suggests we offer it a little too freely; it isn't usually as welcomed as we may think.[37]

To listen empathetically, it can help to think about what your own goals are when you share a personal struggle with someone. Is it usually your goal to

empathetic listening
Listening in order to identify with and share the feelings of another person.

How often do you privately resent being told how you should think or what you should do? Receiving advice isn't what we usually want, as illustrated in this humorous video. How would you describe the empathetic listening behavior of the guy sitting on the couch? On YouTube, search using the keywords "It's Not About The Nail." (1:42)

vent or explore what your thoughts mean to you? Do you simply want to feel heard and understood, or do you want to be told what you should do? Most of the time, reaching out to another person is a request for support and validation, and a listener who offers unsolicited advice is not providing helpful or desired feedback.[38]

If you are prone to giving advice too freely, it may make your relationship partners feel less confident in their ability to solve their own problems. Those who are closest to you may feel reluctant to seek you out for intimate dialogue if they think all you'll do is tell them what *you* would do in their shoes.

Unsolicited advice isn't the only mistake we make when we are in a position to offer an empathetic ear. Finding the right response can be difficult, but TABLE 4.2 can help guide you as you listen to others.[39] Ask yourself how you would respond to each statement or behavior below, and why.

Psychologist and author Camille Wortman states that while it's important to give our relational partners space and privacy during tough times, it's also helpful to continue to show an interest in them and concern for their well-being without being too pushy.[40] We can periodically reach out to see how they're doing and invite them to go for walks, go shopping, work out, see a movie—activities they normally enjoy—and always be ready to listen!

table 4.2	Empathetic Listening
Responses that are not generally well received	**Examples**
Telling a person how he or she should feel	• "You should be more upset about this!" • "You need to stop holding it all in. Just let it out." • "Stop worrying about it."
Stating your religious beliefs without knowing the other person's faith perspective	• "God needed him more than you did." • "She's with Jesus now." • "You just need to pray harder."
Minimizing the person's experience	• "You'll get over it." • "It could be worse." • "You can always have another baby." • "Well, that's nothing, you should meet my family."

(continued)

Assuming you know what a situation is like	• "I know exactly how you feel." • "I had the exact same thing happen to me. Here's what you should do . . ."
Offering your interpretation as if it's an absolute fact	• "The reason you keep breaking up is . . ." • "You'd get the promotions you deserve if you would just . . ." • "The problem started when you let him . . ."
Responses that are generally well received	**Examples**
Talking less and listening more	• Allowing for silence and maintaining a supportive presence • Paraphrasing back what the person is saying (sparingly) • Offering to hold a person's hand in silence or give a hug
Letting the person know you are available to help out	• "I am here for you." • "What do you need from me?" • "Can I offer you a ride to your next appointment?"
Sharing your collective feelings	• "I am feeling really sad right now. I can only imagine how you feel." • "I was so eager to see you get the promotion. We were all rooting for you." • "I'm thinking about your test results. I'm hoping for the best. Any word yet?"
Asking a few questions to show interest in the person's state of mind	• "How are you doing?" • "How is the therapy going?"
Asking questions that may help a person identify coping strategies	• "What is helping you get through this?" • "Is there someone you feel really comfortable talking to about this?"

section review

4.3 **Ways to improve listening and responding skills**

You can improve your listening and responding skills using various strategies and techniques, including postponement, paraphrasing, metacommunication about listening, mirroring, recall tests, and empathetic responses.

Key Terms

postponement, *p. 108*

paraphrasing, *p. 110*

receptivity, *p. 111*

mirroring, *p. 111*

recall test, *p. 112*

empathetic listening, *p. 113*

(continued)

Comprehend It?

1. Define each of the key terms in Section 4.3. To further your understanding of these terms, create examples to support your definitions.

2. Describe to a classmate the benefits and processes involved for each of the following listening strategies:
   - Postponement
   - Paraphrasing

   - Metacommunication
   - Mirroring
   - Recall tests
   - Listening and responding empathetically

Apply It!

Think of a communication situation where postponing a conversation would promote better listening. Create a dialogue like the one you read in the postponement section between Mike and Tahani, incorporating the first three steps of postponement.

chapter exercises

Assessing Your IPC: Listening and Concentration

Purpose: To improve my listening accuracy and concentration.

Directions: Improve your listening skills with auditory recall tests from Randall's ESL Cyber Listening Lab. First, go to "Randall's ESL Cyber Listening Lab" at www.esl-lab.com. Next, scroll down to the "General Listening Quizzes" section and choose the "difficult" category. Click on the following conversation topics. On your own or with a group, listen carefully and see if you can correctly answer the questions. Strive for a score of 80% or higher.

72-Hour Emergency Kit	Car Accidents
Divorce Lawyers	Dating Problems
Movie Review	Security Systems

Try doing one test per day for the next 21 days. You'll appreciate the effort needed to listen actively while the tests train you to concentrate and tune out distractions!

Building Your IPC Skills: Paraphrasing

Purpose: To practice paraphrasing.

Directions: Paraphrasing is a brief restatement of your conversational partner's thoughts in your own words. You can also paraphrase the emotions associated with a speaker's words. See the two examples below. Person A says something in the left column, and Person B responds with a paraphrase on the right.

Person A

"Devon acted so out of character last night. I can't believe he made those derogatory comments about women."

"My parents had a major blowup again. They were screaming at each other."

Person B

"This is not a behavior you'd expect from him."

"Another fight? I'm sorry to hear."

For items 1–4, write down what you think is an effective paraphrase. Be prepared to share your examples with a classmate.

1. "He just left. Not even a goodbye. I'm thinking everything is going great. One fight and he leaves without a word. He even had the nerve to take that expensive necklace he bought me in Venice."

   _____
   _____
   _____
   _____

2. "I'd like you to work this Saturday morning because we are short staffed. Sunday I could really use more coverage in the afternoon or evening."

   _____
   _____
   _____
   _____

3. "He's drawing marijuana leaves on his textbook covers. He has an unusual craving for cheese curls. His bedroom door is locked a lot, and I found a rolled up towel at the bottom of his door."

   _____
   _____
   _____
   _____

4. "I'm not sure if my boss is dismissing my ideas in particular, or if this is how he treats all of the new hires."

   _____
   _____
   _____
   _____

Want to earn a better grade on your test? Go to INQUIZITIVE to practice actively with this chapter's content and get personalized feedback along the way.

5

Verbal Communication

Adam Lowsir has always been self-conscious about his last name: "My last name is spelled *Lowsir*, but pronounced 'Loser.' When classmates found out my uncle was in the Air Force, someone snickered, 'Is he a major? Like a major loser?'" And at a party someone teased, "I know just the name for you if you have a daughter: Anita, as in, 'I needa loser.'" Adam faced this kind of teasing nonstop from kindergarten to college.

His discomfort with his name followed him into his professional life as well. "Not too long ago, I wanted to sell a diversity training program to a professional auto racing organization and realized they might not want to work with me if I introduced myself as Adam 'Loser.' At age 33, I've decided to legally change my last name."

A student of ours, Etain, shared with the class: "Names are something we truly own. They make us unique. People identify and remember us by our names. It's the first thing we share when we introduce ourselves. Before we're born, our parents often spend months deciding on which name to give us."

The men in this photo are collaborating on important work documents. Choosing the right words to convey a message is an important skill for effective communicators, especially in a professional setting. The success of a project could rely on the words these men use in their documents, and in their interactions with each other.

Names matter to us. Without language, however, names wouldn't exist. Names—and the meanings we attach to them—are part of the larger fabric of language that we use to communicate. In this chapter, we'll help you (1) appreciate the significance of language in interpersonal communication, (2) understand how ambiguous language can affect IPC, and (3) explore ways to enhance your verbal communication, with a focus on improving your relationships.

5.1 The significance of language

In the movie *A Thousand Words*, Jack McCall (played by Eddie Murphy) is cursed. If Jack speaks or writes a word, a leaf falls from the tree in his backyard. If the tree loses all of its leaves, Jack will lose his life! In one scene, Jack stops at a coffee shop. To avoid losing any leaves, he limits his communication to facial expressions and gestures and finds it very difficult to order something as simple as a cup of coffee. To watch this scene on YouTube, search using the keywords: "A Thousand Words (2012) - Triple Shot, No Assassinations Scene." (2:23)

Take a moment to think about the past 24 hours. Who did you spend time with? What did you say and do? How did language make this possible? Now, imagine spending the next 24 hours without speaking or writing, like Eddie Murphy's character, Jack. If you couldn't communicate using words, what obstacles might you encounter?

Language makes it possible to convey meaning quickly, efficiently— and often effortlessly. **Language** is a system of words that are collectively understood to have meaning. When you communicate verbally, you're using words to speak, write, and send electronic messages. **Verbal communication** is the use of words to convey meaning.

In Section 5.1, we'll examine what language is and what it can help you achieve in your IPC.

Language is influential

Mary Jane Mapes, a corporate speaker on workplace culture, often shares the story of the challenges her daughter faced as an aspiring actress. Despite her training at a prestigious acting school, Mary Jane's daughter struggled to find work after numerous auditions. Concerned that her daughter, now a starving artist, might take questionable roles that compromised her values, Mary Jane sent her an email of encouragement. "Honey," she wrote, "when your career takes off, I want you to look back and know you took quality roles that you can feel proud of." Her daughter wrote back, "I love your email! Thank you so much for believing in me! I feel very empowered right now! You said, '*when* my career takes off'—you didn't say '*if*.'"[1] A single word like "when" can really boost a person's confidence!

Words are influential. They have the power to affect our thoughts, feelings, and behaviors.[2] Let's say your friend Porter is throwing a party, and he's invited you to it. You're talking with him on the phone and he's describing some of his friends whom you'll meet for the first time. Porter mentions his friend Sanjay: "Yeah, he's really into weightlifting. He's on roids" (that is, steroids). What image

---

language A system of words that are collectively understood to have meaning.

verbal communication The use of words to convey meaning.

comes to mind when Porter says "on roids"? Now, imagine that Porter instead describes Sanjay as "chiseled." How does this change your image of Sanjay?

Porter also tells you something about another friend, Colette. He tells you that Colette is "energetic," though he could have said "hyper." Or, he may refer to her as "reserved," or "standoffish." The words he uses to describe Sanjay and Colette may influence your perceptions and opinions of them—and how you interact with them at the party.[3] Porter's choice of words may also affect how you perceive him, whether he's aware of it or not.

When Porter talks about his friends, his choice of words reveals his attitudes about his friends and their behaviors. This is referred to as **emotive language**. For example, if Porter describes Sanjay as "chiseled," you can assume he admires and respects Sanjay's hard work at the gym. You may assume that's not the case if Porter says instead that Sanjay is "on roids," with a hint of disapproval in his voice.

Verbal communication can be influential in other ways. For instance, say your cousin, Liz, needs money and asks you for a small loan, but you're reluctant to give it to her. She tries to persuade you by saying, "I know you've counted on me in the past to help you out financially. I'm really hoping you can help me out this time." This communication strategy is a **reciprocity appeal**: a way of saying that it's time to return a favor. Appeals like this may be hard to say no to because we're all socialized to return favors. As the old saying goes, "I'll scratch your back, if you scratch mine."

Similarly, if Liz wants you to sponsor her in a charitable bike-a-thon, she may use a social validation appeal. A **social validation appeal** is a persuasive technique used to convince you to do something because other people you know and like are doing the same thing. For example, Liz shoots you a message: "Hey, I wonder if you'd like to join Stasha, Caleb, and Emmanuel in their support of my bike-a-thon for St. Jude's Children's Hospital. I can't do it without ya!" For added pressure, she may even post the appeal on social media for you and your friends to see. It's harder to say no when the friends you like and admire have all said yes.

Language is affectionate

Affectionate language (AL) is the language you use to express positive feelings you have toward someone. Examples of AL include words of encouragement and appreciation: "You're going to do great tonight, I can't wait to see you perform"; "Thank you for always being there for me"; "I'm really glad we're friends." Loving thoughts, praise, and compliments are also considered AL: "I thought about you today"; "Your laugh cracks me up"; "I know who to call when I need a great idea."

AL can take the form of kindhearted or flattering nicknames and words of endearment such as "BFF," "bro," "bae," and "cuddlebug." A couple of unsuspecting audience members on the *Graham Norton Show*—Gerard and his partner,

emotive language Language that both describes something and reveals the speaker's attitude about what is being described.

reciprocity appeal An attempt to persuade someone by implying that it is time to return a favor.

social validation appeal A persuasive technique used to convince you to do something because other people you know and like are doing the same thing.

affectionate language (AL) The language you use to express the positive feelings you have toward someone.

During a pivotal moment in a Little League World Series game, a camera captures the conversation between a pitcher and his coach. After watching this scene, think of a time when you received a message like this from someone. What effect did it have on your thoughts, feelings, and behaviors? How would you relate this clip to the use of affectionate language? On YouTube, search using the keywords: "Dad Tells Son He Loves Him During Little League World Series." (1:24)

Jon—provide a funny example of this type of AL. Graham asks Gerard to hand over his cell phone, and he then proceeds to read out loud a series of text messages between Gerard and Jon. To the delight of the audience, Graham points out the affectionate language they use with each other, such as "angel" and "honeypuff." Another nickname also sparked good-natured laughs from the audience. To see what it was, on YouTube, search using the keywords: "Cute Gay Couple With Graham Norton." (2:46)

Research suggests that AL does more than help us express positive emotions; it reflects and fortifies relationship satisfaction. When AL is expressed sincerely—and well received—it increases fondness, closeness, and amiability within friendships, romantic relationships, and work and family relationships. AL also has a constructive effect on more casual relationships, such as those between doctors and patients, teachers and students, and coaches and athletes.[4]

AL can make relationships stronger and help them last longer.[5] According to one study of 168 couples, newlyweds who express greater verbal affection during the first 2 years of marriage are more likely to remain married 13 years later.[6]

Language structures thought

Anthropologist Edward Sapir and linguist Benjamin Lee Whorf devoted their careers to studying the way language shapes how people think about things. Two major ideas emerged from their work, sometimes grouped under a theoretical perspective called the Sapir-Whorf hypothesis. The first, **linguistic determinism**, suggests that we can't conceptualize something without a word for it. According to this hypothesis, language literally defines the boundaries of human thought.[7]

linguistic determinism
The idea that language determines people's ability to perceive and think.

Imagine you were never taught that there is a word for the feeling of jealousy. If a friend was jealous of a new friendship you made, you might sense something is wrong, but you'd attribute his behavior to something else. If you confronted him, you might say, "You don't seem to like my new friend for some reason." Without a word for jealousy, according to linguistic determinism, you would not be able to recognize it or even consider it as a possibility if you saw it.

The second, a more widely accepted view, is linguistic relativism. **Linguistic relativism** is the idea that language doesn't determine one's reality, as linguistic determinism suggests, but it does influence it.[8] Surfers, for example, may perceive and describe ocean waves differently than would those of us who are not surfers. The waves they encounter inspire them to create words that capture their unique interaction with the ocean; "perfect barrel," for instance, describes the hollow channel formed inside a good wave when it breaks and curls over. The language surfers create and use allows them to live their experiences together.[9]

linguistic relativism The idea that language may not determine one's reality, but it does influence it.

Tobin's narrative demonstrates how language can influence your social reality. Can you relate to Tobin's example in any way?

> "I'm a big fisherman. My girlfriend joined me and a few of my fishing buddies one day for lunch. Just as we sat down, I cracked a joke: 'What do you get when you cross a fishing lure with a gym sock? A hook, line, and stinker!' My friends laughed uproariously. My girlfriend, who has never fished and probably doesn't know what a lure is, kind of got it, but her reaction was delayed and subdued." –Tobin

According to linguistic relativism, language may affect the structure of your thoughts. We can see how this might work through the lens of verb tense. The use of future tense is common in English, Russian, and Korean. For example, if you say, "I *will* take a crowbar cardio class," it suggests that you plan to do so in the future. Japanese, Mandarin, and German languages, however, are less focused on the future tense. In Mandarin, rather than saying "I *will* take a crowbar cardio class," you would say the equivalent of "I take a crowbar cardio class." As opposed to "I plan to go to college," you would say "I go to college."

Things are more in motion with these languages; there's less of a distinction between now and later. Scholars wonder if this difference in language affects how speakers think about, talk about, and plan for the future. In one study, subjects who spoke a language with future tense verbs were 30% less likely to save for retirement compared to speakers of a language without future tenses. Perhaps speakers who talk as if plans or goals are in motion, rather than in the future, are less likely to put things off.[10]

Language has layers of meaning

When Liam's girlfriend, Sierra, says to him, "We need to talk," these four simple words convey layers of meaning. Sierra doesn't just want to have a conversation with Liam. She wants to have it right now. It's important. There's a problem, and Liam is (part of) the problem.

denotation The literal or dictionary meaning assigned to a word.

connotation The subjective or personal meaning attached to a word.

Sierra's words have both content and relational meaning. In Chapter 2, you learned that *content meaning* is literal: *We need to talk about something.* But there is another layer of meaning embedded in Sierra's message—its *relational meaning*—that suggests something about the nature of her relationship with Liam: *There is something happening between us that I don't like, and I would like to change it.*

Along with content and relational meaning, words have both denotative and connotative meanings. **Denotation** (dee-noh-TA-shuhn) is the literal or dictionary meaning assigned to a word. **Connotation** (kah-nah-TA-shuhn) is the subjective or personal meaning attached to a word. Connotative meanings of a word will vary from person to person because of differences in each person's frame of reference.[11] As explained in Chapter 2, your *frame of reference* is the perspective you bring to a conversation or interaction. This perspective includes your collective life experiences and what you know about yourself, about other people, and about life in general.

Consider this example involving one of your authors, Bruce, and his persistent daughter, Kaitlin. The denotative meaning for "No," according to several dictionaries, is "an expression of denial or refusal." When Kaitlin asks Bruce for extra allowance money, and he says "no," the denotative meaning is therefore: *I will not give you the money.* For Kaitlin, this should mean the same thing. However, because Bruce has said "no" in past interactions with Kaitlin, only to later give in to her persuasion, "no" to Kaitlin means something else. Its connotative meaning is: *I don't want to give you the money, but you could convince me.* Bruce needs to keep consistency in mind if he wants Kaitlin to interpret *no* to mean *no.*

Finally, we often create layers of meaning with metacommunication. As you learned in Chapter 2, *metacommunication* is communicating about communication. The layers of meaning we create using metacommunication may improve our interpersonal interactions.

One of our students, Elysia, shared how she and her girlfriend Francis will often ask each other, "Who's driving?" before they head out on a date. The answer to this question doesn't just determine who will drive the car. They talked about it and decided that when one of them asks who's driving, it means that the driver also gets to pick the restaurant and movie that evening. Elysia and Francis's metacommunication about what they want their words to mean in the future has made their date night decisions simple and easy. Their metacommunication has led them to attach their own connotative meaning to this message. "Who's driving?" is also an example of an interpersonal idiom, which you'll learn about in Section 5.2.

"*Test* has such a negative connotation. I prefer to call them *character building opportunities.*"

Language is interpretive

Verbal communication does not end with what you intend to say; how others interpret your message is just as important. The words you say may mean one thing to you, but they may mean something entirely different to someone else.[12] We may choose the wrong words to convey a message, or we may misinterpret the words we receive. Many unfortunate outcomes can occur when we misunderstand each other.

To help communicators interpret messages more consistently and accurately, every language has certain rules for its users to follow. When these rules are overlooked, the clarity and quality of verbal communication diminishes. Four sets of linguistic rules—phonological, syntactic, semantic, and pragmatic—are important to keep in mind.

Phonological rules (fah-nah-LAH-jih-kuhl) establish how a word is said or pronounced. Phonetic clues are provided in a standard dictionary, though there are some variations in how people pronounce words. Some commonly mispronounced words are: "mihs-CHEE-vee-uhs" for mischievous, and "AHR-tihk" for arctic. The correct pronunciations are "MIHS-chuh-vuhs," and "AHRK-tihk."

Syntactic rules (sin-TAK-tihk) govern the order in which words appear in a sentence. In English you would arrange a sentence like this: "Did you bring your phone?" In German, however, the correct order would be something like: "Did you your phone bring?" If you used German syntax when speaking with someone in English, your conversational partner would likely be very confused.

Semantic rules establish what a word means in a certain language. Like phonological rules, the meanings of English words are found in any standard print or online dictionary. If you say to someone, "I still want to go *irregardless*," you're breaking a semantic rule because *irregardless* is not commonly considered a word. The correct word is *regardless*.

Pragmatic rules influence word choice and interpretation based on social norms and expectations. For example, if you sneeze, what do you expect someone to say? Most likely, you wouldn't be surprised if someone said, "Bless you." What if someone said, "Cheese?" You'd probably think it was an odd response to a sneeze because it breaks a pragmatic rule.

Of the four rules, pragmatic rules are the least clear-cut and the hardest to navigate.[13] For example, if your supervisor at work notices that you're wearing a new item of clothing and says, "That looks great on you," do you interpret the comment as an innocent compliment or as a form of sexual harassment? A number of factors would play a role in your interpretation: what the supervisor is referring to (a piece of jewelry or your pants), where you were at the time (at a bar or at work), how the supervisor said it (in a matter-of-fact manner or a suggestive one), the kind of relationship you have with your supervisor (casual

phonological rules Rules that establish how a word is said or pronounced.

syntactic rules Rules that govern the order in which words appear in a sentence.

semantic rules Rules that establish what a word means in a certain language.

pragmatic rules Rules that influence word choice and interpretation based on social norms and expectations.

Film director James Cameron hired University of Southern California communications professor Paul Frommer to create an entirely new language for Na'vi society at the heart of the science fiction movie *Avatar*. The Na'vi language now exceeds 1,000 words. Fans of the movie have formed online communities dedicated to learning and using the Na'vi language. In this video, see if you can identify one or more of the linguistic rules described in this chapter. On You-Tube, search using the keywords: "Paul Frommer: The Secret Life of Scientists and Engineers" (3:49)

or strictly professional), and the frequency of such comments (often or rarely). Your supervisor's gender and sexual orientation and your own gender and sexual orientation may also affect how you interpret the message.

Culture also influences pragmatic rules. Language is tied to the norms, beliefs, and values of a given culture. From an interpersonal perspective, linguistic studies suggest that people who are multilingual will interact with others differently depending on the language they are using at a given time. For example, an American student who spent some time teaching in Mexico wrote about something she discovered. When she spoke in English, the male students treated her with more respect. When she spoke in Spanish, the interaction changed. They joked around with her more and seemed a bit flirtatious. This may have something to do with how Mexican men and women interact with each other within their own culture.[14]

section review

5.1 The significance of language

Language plays a prominent role in interpersonal communication. Language is influential, reflects and reinforces affection, structures thought, has layers of meaning, and is interpretive.

Key Terms

language, *p. 120*

verbal communication, *p. 120*

emotive language, *p. 121*

reciprocity appeal, *p. 121*

social validation appeal, *p. 121*

affectionate language (AL), *p. 121*

(continued)

Comprehend It?

1. Define each of the key terms in Section 5.1. To further your understanding of these terms, create examples to support your definitions.

2. Explain the following statements:
   - Language is influential.
   - Language is affectionate.

   - Language structures thought.
   - Language has layers of meaning.
   - Language is interpretive.

3. Compare and contrast:
   - Linguistic determinism and relativism
   - Denotative and connotative meaning

Apply It!

With a partner, jot down the following word: clique. Look up the dictionary or denotative meaning. Next, think of all of the possible connotative meanings for the word. Why might these connotative meanings exist?

5.2 Understanding language ambiguity

Whenever you communicate a verbal message, the words you choose (or choose to leave out) are always open to interpretation. If you say, for instance: "I'm delighted to say I used to work with Johanna," what does this mean exactly? Are you glad you had the chance to work with Johanna, or are you glad you no longer have to? The range of possible meanings associated with any verbal message means that, often, people will assign meanings that you don't intend for them to assign.

When word choice creates ambiguity, misunderstandings—and their consequences—may occur. For example, when a shift officer of a Massachusetts fire department was told to assemble his team of firefighters "at the corner of Harrison and Cleveland avenues" for a training session, he assumed that the empty house on the corner had been set aside for the firefighters to run through practice exercises. Using sledgehammers and saws, the firefighters smashed windows, knocked down walls, and sliced gaping holes in the roof of the Victorian home, just as they would have if they were fighting a serious fire. The department's training was considered a major success—until they learned they'd destroyed the wrong house. "Harrison and Cleveland" had just been the designated meeting point; the house they were supposed to demolish was two blocks away.[15]

In Section 5.2, we'll examine how to achieve clarity in your verbal communication so you can avoid similarly consequential miscommunications.

Concrete versus abstract language

In general, the more *concrete* language is, the less ambiguous it is. **Concrete language** refers to things in the physical world that are easily identifiable or measurable using one or more of the five senses—what you can see, hear,

concrete language
Language that refers to things in the physical world that are easily identifiable or measurable using one or more of the five senses.

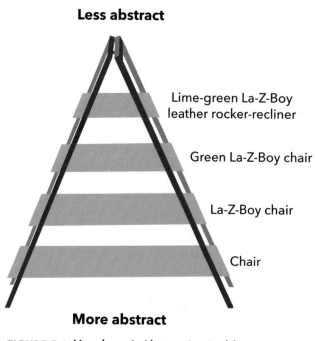

Less abstract

Lime-green La-Z-Boy leather rocker-recliner

Green La-Z-Boy chair

La-Z-Boy chair

Chair

More abstract

FIGURE 5.1 **Hayakawa's Abstraction Ladder**

smell, taste, and touch. People are more likely to agree on the meaning of words that are concrete. For example, the meanings of words like *tarantula*, *truck driver*, and *tuba* are not easily confused.

Abstract language, or language that refers to intangible concepts and ideas, is more open to interpretation. The meanings that people attach to abstract words, such as *charity*, *culture*, and *chauvinism*, generally vary more from person to person.

Samuel Hayakawa, a linguist and professor of English, developed a model called the *abstraction ladder* to illustrate the relationship between concrete language and abstract language (see **FIGURE 5.1**).[16] Hayakawa's abstraction ladder shows how you can make the meaning of a verbal message clearer by using more concrete, descriptive language. For example, even a concrete word like *chair* has a certain degree of ambiguity because there are many different types of chairs. If you say to your interior designer that you want "a comfortable living room chair" for your apartment, the designer will still have lots of chairs to choose from. However, if you say, "I want a green La-Z-Boy chair," he'll have a clearer picture. If you say, "I want a lime-green, La-Z-Boy, leather rocker-recliner that swivels," this helps him visualize and comprehend what you are saying even better.

Using detailed, descriptive language is important if you want someone to change a behavior. Let's say you are a manager at a health food store, and you say to one of your employees, Audrey, "I want you to use your downtime more productively." The words "downtime" and "productively" may mean something different to you than they do to Audrey. However, if your communication is clear and specific—"When there are no customers in the store, I would like you to line up the stock in aisles one and three and wipe down the displays like I showed you last week"—your words leave less room for misinterpretation, and Audrey will know exactly what you expect her to do.

abstract language
Language that refers to intangible concepts and ideas.

dating information
Information that specifies when something took place or will take place.

You can also add accuracy and precision to your messages by using **dating information** that specifies when something took place or will take place. When you use dating information, you acknowledge that people, behaviors, emotions, and attitudes change over time. For example, in response to the question, "How is Nicolai doing?" you might say, "When I saw Nicolai last Thursday, he was doing well." By using dating information—specifying the time you last saw Nicolai—you provide a more accurate response than if you had said, "Nicolai seems to be doing well lately." Unless you see Nicolai frequently, it's less accurate to generalize based on a single interaction.

Contrast the following statements: "Sales are up in our Mediterranean markets," and, "According to a report compiled by Camila two days ago, we saw a 7% increase in sales in our Mediterranean markets during the last quarter." Which statement is clearer to you? In the second statement, details and dating information specify when Camila drafted her report and what timeframe she used for her sales analysis.

Using more detailed, descriptive language and dating information may make what you say clearer and more accurate and reduce the frequency of miscommunication. This, in turn, may save you time, improve your productivity, and reduce unnecessary stress. It may also prevent unnecessary conflict.

Types of ambiguous language

Ambiguous language can take many forms, and it can impact your interpersonal communication in both positive and negative ways depending on how and when it is used. It's important to understand different types of ambiguous language and to know when or when not to use each type. In this section, we'll consider idioms, slang, jargon, equivocation, euphemisms, and convoluted language.

Idioms

Cultural idioms or *colloquialisms* are words or phrases whose meanings are unique to people who live in a certain geographic region or society. For example, many American idioms are related to sports. As a teacher hands a graded exam back, she might say to one student, "You really hit this one out of the park." She doesn't mean that the student literally hit a home run; she means the student scored well on the exam. Had the student not scored well, she might have said, "You struck out this time." An international student may not understand what her teacher is saying if she's not familiar with baseball.

People in close relationships also create words or phrases whose meanings only they understand, which we call **interpersonal idioms**. When one of your authors, Bruce, was around 10 years old, he was fighting with his older sister, Cheryl. They were yelling and driving their mom crazy, despite their mom's repeated warnings. Out of sheer frustration, Bruce's mom grabbed a plastic bottle of Magic Shell—the liquid chocolate that hardens on ice cream—and hurled it at them. It broke open, splattering chocolate all over the hallway. It took four hours for Bruce and Cheryl to clean up the white walls and carpets. From that point on, whenever it seemed like their mom was starting to get upset, either Bruce or Cheryl would whisper, "Magic Shell," and both would start behaving. "Magic Shell" had a special meaning only Bruce and Cheryl understood.

cultural idiom A word or phrase whose meaning is unique to people who live in a certain geographic region or society.

interpersonal idiom A word or phrase whose meaning is unique to two or more individuals who share a relationship.

The actors of *Grey's Anatomy* want to sound like real doctors. It takes a great deal of memorization and practice to do so. Identify five examples of medical jargon in this video. Have you ever had to learn jargon or slang in order to accomplish a task or interact successfully with members of a group? On YouTube, search using the keywords: "Grey's Anatomy: How Well Does the Cast Know Medical Jargon?" (2:20)

Cultural and interpersonal idioms give speakers a sense of shared identity, experience, purpose, and understanding. They're also used to exchange humor and engage in affectionate, light-hearted dialogue. The use of idioms, however, may confuse or cause *semantic noise* (see Chapter 2) for others who aren't familiar with the idioms.

Slang and jargon

Slang is informal language or words whose meaning is understood by members of a given social group. Slang is often associated with the vernacular of young people and people who belong to certain social groups or subcultures. For example, skateboarders may say that they "slaughtered" a move when they execute it perfectly. Cyclists may say that someone who isn't fit to compete but has the most expensive bike and accessories is "all show and no go."

Thanks to the Internet, new slang words emerge and spread at incredible speeds. Take, for example, the word *bae*: an abbreviation of the word *babe*, used as a term of endearment for a romantic partner. While its origins are not entirely clear, *bae* first became popular within Black communities and spread on Twitter and Instagram in the form of hashtags such as #cookingforbae and #baelove. It found its way into the mainstream after singer and rapper Pharrell Williams released the song "Come Get It Bae," and *Time* magazine published an article about the origins of the word.[17]

A form of ambiguous language similar to slang is jargon. Often referred to as *shop talk*, **jargon** is nonstandard language used by members of a particular profession, trade, or academic community. Jargon is useful for many reasons. For example, it often serves as shorthand that allows colleagues to communicate quickly. In an emergency room, for example, a health care worker might say something like, "we have a GSW arriving in ten minutes by medi." *GSW* is an abbreviation for gunshot wound. *Medi* is short for medevac, a medical transport helicopter.

Like cultural and interpersonal idioms, slang and jargon have many positive applications; they give individuals and groups a language of shared experience, connectivity, and identity.[18] They may cause others, however, to feel like outsiders or left out of a conversation. In some settings the use of slang may be seen as improper, disrespectful, or unprofessional. Likewise, the use of jargon out of context might be seen as elitist.

Equivocation

Equivocation (also referred to as *doublespeak*) is the intentional use of vague language in order to avoid saying what you really think or feel. Imagine, for

slang Informal language or words whose meaning is understood by members of a particular social group or subculture.

jargon Nonstandard language used by members of a particular profession, trade, or academic community.

equivocation The intentional use of vague language in order to avoid saying what you really think or feel.

example, that your good friend Gia has asked you to serve as a reference for a job she's pursuing. You agree to do this, but you don't really want to. While Gia is bubbly, funny, and the life of the party, she isn't very reliable. She rarely shows up on time for anything, and she's completely flaked on your plans more than once.

So when Gia's prospective employer calls you and asks whether Gia is reliable, you don't feel comfortable lying and saying, "Yes, absolutely." You may say instead, "Yes, she can be reliable," or, "I can think of several times when she was reliable. Just last week, she. . ."

In the first statement, you answer affirmatively without saying that Gia is consistently reliable. In the second statement, you equivocate by pointing to a specific (and isolated) instance when Gia's actions exemplified reliability. Rather than say what you really think and hurt Gia's chances of getting a job, your words skirt the truth.

You may also equivocate to protect someone's feelings. Let's say your aunt gifts your sister a hand-knitted Christmas sweater that's not really her style. When your aunt asks your sister if she loves it, she may say, "Oh, I love sweaters. You can never have enough!" Or she might reply, "Wow. It looks like you spent a lot of time on it. I bet it will keep me warm on a very cold day. Thank you." You may notice that your sister didn't *really* answer the question. Equivocation helps you avoid saying things that make a difficult or awkward situation even more difficult or awkward.

Can you think of other instances where equivocation is a better communication choice than straightforward and direct language? For example, research suggests that when you encounter a relational challenge at work, equivocal messages may help you maintain a positive atmosphere and avoid unnecessary conflict.[19] On the flip side, your attempt at equivocation may stand out in a negative way as evasive or crafty. If your equivocal language leads your coworkers to question your truthfulness, it may make what you say in the future less believable and tarnish your credibility.

Euphemisms

Euphemisms or *kind speech* are words a speaker uses that are easier on the ears or on the heart. For example, the word "dead" has strong, negative connotations. In a conversation with a friend you would say, "I'm so sorry your dog passed away" rather than "I'm so sorry your dog is dead."

Euphemisms help us convey harsh or disagreeable messages discreetly and sensitively.[20] As Quentin Crisp, author of *Manners from Heaven: A Divine Guide to Good Behavior*, writes, "Euphemisms are unpleasant truths wearing diplomatic cologne." So, for instance, rather than say a person is "old," we may say he's a "senior citizen." A real estate agent may say to a client, "This house is a tiny fixer-upper with good bones," or, "It just needs some love and attention," instead of, "This house is a total money pit."[21]

euphemism A kinder word or phrase that a speaker uses in place of a less agreeable one. Also called *kind speech*.

convoluted language
Complex words or phrases that are rarely used in everyday life.

Euphemisms can also be funny in a good-natured way. When referring to a buddy who was short and wide, Garrison Keillor, former host of the radio show *A Prairie Home Companion*, described him as "anatomically compact." Keillor referred to another friend's big beer belly as a "generous liquid grain-storage container."[22]

Putting a positive spin on things is warranted at times, but when you try too hard to make something seem more pleasant than it is, someone may call you out on it. Have you ever been accused of being misleading or of not taking something seriously because you used a euphemism?

Convoluted words

We may make our messages more ambiguous whenever we use **convoluted language**: complex words or phrases that are rarely used in everyday life. They're usually polysyllabic (more than three syllables), and/or difficult to pronounce. Speakers may use complex language to sound more intelligent or knowledgeable.

For example, when Umbro sportswear designer David Blanch presented a new uniform to the players of England's national soccer team, he boasted that the shirts had "intelligent ventilation points" and "tailored shoulder darts specifically designed to accommodate the biodynamics of the shoulder." He could have described the shirts as having larger-than-normal armholes and unique shoulder seams, but those words just don't sound as exciting.[23] While Blanch's use of convoluted language may have impressed some players, he ran the risk of sounding showy or ostentatious.

On the other hand, speakers with extensive vocabularies are often able to strengthen their messages with variety and description, which may make them more interesting, funny, and memorable. A higher vocabulary is also associated with greater intelligence.[24]

In the narrative below, Erica, a personal trainer and nutritionist, describes how she tries to use simple words so her clients can understand and appreciate what's in the supplements they're taking. What does Erica's narrative tell you about the benefits of straightforward language?

"I try to simplify the product labels of body building supplements for my clients. It's like the manufacturers want us to think there is something very scientific or revolutionary about their 'whey or milk protein.' The labels have explanations like: 'upregulates multiple genetic signaling pathways' or 'uses microsorb amino technology to enhance anabolism.' My clients often say they appreciate that I clarify this kind of stuff for them." –Erica

section review

- -

5.2 Understanding language ambiguity

Using more concrete, descriptive language can help you reduce language ambiguity and the problems associated with miscommunication. There are several types of ambiguous language, including idioms, slang, jargon, equivocation, euphemisms, and convoluted language.

Key Terms

concrete language, *p. 127*

abstract language, *p. 128*

dating information, *p. 128*

cultural idiom, *p. 129*

interpersonal idiom, *p. 129*

slang, *p. 130*

jargon, *p. 130*

equivocation, *p. 130*

euphemism, *p. 131*

convoluted language, *p. 132*

Comprehend It?

1. Define each of the key terms in Section 5.2. To further your understanding of these terms, create examples to support your definitions.

2. Compare and contrast:
   - Concrete language and abstract language
   - Idioms, slang, equivocation, euphemisms, and convoluted language

Apply It!

Create your own abstraction ladder (like Samuel Hayakawa's abstraction ladder) to demonstrate how an abstract word, phrase, or sentence becomes less ambiguous as you add more concrete, descriptive language.

5.3 Ways to improve verbal communication

When they first met on the set of *The Bachelor*, Jake Pavelka and Vienna Girardi were smitten. Vienna outlasted all the other contestants on the show, and the season ended with Jake and Vienna's engagement. Seven months later, the couple broke up. In an interview about their split, Jake and Vienna's language seemed to reflect and perpetuate their negative feelings for each other:

> **Jake:** I'm so mad at you. I'm disgusted with you.
> **Vienna:** You are a fame w**** is what you are . . . my impression was that you were a pilot, and we were going to go back to Florida . . . [to] live a normal life. Instead we're in L.A., and you're pursuing a career in acting.
> **Jake:** At least I am pursuing a career in something.

When the interviewer asked them who broke up with whom, they replied:

> **Vienna:** I called you and broke up with you over the phone.
> **Jake:** She's like a tabloid. You get 40% of the truth from her.
> **Vienna:** He was always mean to me and treated me like I was a child.
> **Jake:** She breaks me down, undermines me, she's mean. This is it right there.

This conversation between Vienna and Jake shows that when you address another person with dismissive, defensive, or hostile words, you can often expect to receive dismissive, defensive, or hostile words. Whether you're seeking understanding, sympathy, validation, an honest answer, a commitment, an apology, or a changed behavior, the response you get hinges a lot on your choice of words.

In this section, we'll explore seven strategies for using language that can help you create more satisfying and productive conversations—and benefit your relationships.

Use language strategically

Direct language communicates a message in a very straightforward and obvious way. For example, Lin tells her assistant, Dato, that she'd like him to draft a presentation that she can share with their company's board of directors by the end of the week. Dato thinks Lin's proposal is unrealistic and likely to cause him a lot of stress. If he wanted to use direct language to address this issue, he might say, "Lin, that's unrealistic given how much time we have between now and Friday. We are in the midst of two other major projects. Let's reconsider your timeline."

Indirect language, on the other hand, communicates a message in a subtle or suggestive way. It hints at something, rather than expressing it outright. Because Lin is Dato's boss, and because Dato knows Lin can be touchy, he decides that he would be better off using indirect language to respond to her idea. He asks, "Lin, are you suggesting that we present your proposal to the board and get the two other projects we're working on now completed by Friday?" Lin realizes it's not plausible and replies, "Well, I guess that timeline is a little unrealistic." By using indirect language in the form of a question, Dato gets Lin to realize that her plans are unrealistic without telling her that she's being impractical. Indirect language allows him to make a point without overstepping the boundaries of their working relationship.

If you want something from someone, and it's important to you, it's best to use direct language. This kind of language is harder to misread or overlook. However, if your language is too direct, it may come across as blunt or rude. For example, if you say to someone, "Your breath really stinks," this may be too direct. You might instead choose an indirect (and less embarrassing) message such as, "Would you care for a breath mint?" In general, a less direct approach is more harmonic and face-saving.[25]

In some situations, it may work best to try indirect language first. If it doesn't get your point across, you can follow up with direct language. For example, Jermaine wants his housemate, Red, to clean up their basement. He starts with an indirect message: "It took me three hours this morning to clean the upstairs from last night's party. I haven't even touched the basement yet!" Red will likely get the hint that he should help Jermaine out. However, suppose he answers noncommittally: "Don't worry, we can tackle it later." If Jermaine wants the basement cleaned up as soon as possible, he should say something more direct: "Yeah, we could, but since I've cleaned up the upstairs, I'd like you to tackle the downstairs before my parents visit tomorrow at 5:00 p.m."

As you read the scenarios below, consider the pros and cons of responding with indirect and direct language. Would you change the way you'd express any of these messages to make them more clear or tactful? Are there specific circumstances that would make a direct or indirect approach more appropriate?

You don't like how a coworker addressed a problem at the office.

- ■ **Indirect:** "How do you think that went?"
- ■ **Direct:** "I think that could have been handled better."

You want to spend time with a friend.

- ■ **Indirect:** "Do you have any plans for the weekend?"
- ■ **Direct:** "I'd enjoy spending Saturday evening with you. Are you free?"

You don't want a family member to cook for you.

- ■ **Indirect:** "I have taste buds that are very difficult to please."
- ■ **Direct:** "I don't enjoy your cooking."

"I also just want to be friends, but with someone else."

Monitor your use of powerless language

Powerless language is speech that makes the sender of a message sound less confident, convincing, resolute, or assertive. Imagine that you're trying to get some sleep in your dorm room, and your roommate starts playing his guitar. Which of the following statements sounds more firm?

- ■ **A:** "Um, would you mind holding off on playing your guitar? Maybe go to the lobby to play instead? Uh . . . I'm kinda having a hard time getting to sleep. Would that be a problem?"
- ■ **B:** "I'm trying hard to sleep so I am rested for my exam this evening. I need it completely quiet in here for the next hour. This is a good time to play your guitar in the lobby if you'd like. Thanks. I really appreciate it."

Powerless language is reflected in statement A. Rather than comply, your roommate may try to cajole you into letting him play or make light of your request. He may underestimate your resolve or even dismiss what you're saying entirely. Powerful language, on the other hand, is fluent, direct, and straightforward. People perceive those who use more authoritative language as more competent, credible, persuasive, and attractive.[26]

Powerless language is often characterized by *hedges, hesitations, disclaimers,* and *tag questions.*[27] These speech habits are defined and described in the *Assessing Your IPC* exercise at the end of the chapter. Go to the activity now and complete the survey. Which of these forms of powerless language surface in your communication the most?

Watch the "we" and replace the "but"

Using the pronoun *we* may encourage feelings of unity and togetherness among your relational partners.[28] If you say, "We did a great job," it's a compliment to everyone. If you are a manager and a problem arises at work that requires

powerless language
Speech that makes a speaker sound less confident, resolute, or assertive.

everyone's effort or participation, it's appropriate to say, "We have an opportunity to work together to create a more productive work environment."

However, using the pronoun *we* may not always go over well, especially if you follow *we* with a criticism.[29] Suppose you say to your team at work, "We can do better with our sales." An employee who is having a lot of personal success may feel unfairly chastised. If you say, "We need to work on starting our shifts on time," those who are punctual may think, *Hey, I'm on time every day!*

To avoid offending anyone, you could instead draw attention to the positive performance standards you'd like everyone to meet: "I really like it when I see employees start their shifts on time. It helps us meet and exceed our production goals. Thank you for making the effort." This statement avoids criticizing those who are punctual, and it reminds those who aren't to step up their efforts. If you are in a managerial position and a few individuals are not meeting your expectations, it's more effective to address your concerns privately with each person as opposed to collectively with the whole group.

If you are an employee and you see a problem happening at work, it's also important to use the pronoun *we* mindfully. If you speak up at a meeting as if you represent everyone or imply that everyone shares your thoughts and feelings, this may not go over well. Rather than say, "We are concerned about the payroll process," it may be more accurate to say, "I am concerned about the payroll process." Others will speak up to agree with you if they're concerned, too. You may even ask, "Is anyone else concerned about the payroll process?" It's generally safest to speak only for yourself unless you've been asked to speak for the group.

Skillfully using *we* language according to these guidelines is usually well received. It's an important interpersonal communication tactic worth mastering. Sheree agrees, yet in her narrative below, she provides one example of when using *we* backfired. How can you relate to her experience?

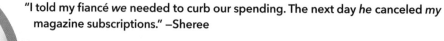

"I told my fiancé *we* needed to curb our spending. The next day *he* canceled *my* magazine subscriptions." —Sheree

Now, let's turn to the conjunction *but*, a contrast word that can be used to join two statements. *But* can be problematic when it joins a positive statement with a negative one. Examples include: "You're right, I could have said it better, but . . ."; "I think your intentions were good, but . . ."; "I'm not racist, but . . ."

When you hear someone use the conjunction *but* between two thoughts, which thought do you focus on more? Most likely, you focus on the thought that comes after *but*. Usually the second clause diminishes the impact or negates the meaning of the preceding clause. Imagine, for example, that you slip up one night and say something really offensive to one of your friends. You text her the next morning to apologize: "I'm sorry I said that, but I was drunk." The conjunction *but* is followed by an excuse that draws attention away from your apology, making it sound less genuine. It also sounds like you aren't taking much responsibility for your communication.

To avoid coming across as flippant or insincere, try to deliver your central idea without using *but*. You might say instead, "I'm sorry I said that. What I said was hurtful." This statement acknowledges the effect your words had on your friend, and it shows that you're taking ownership of your behavior.

Imagine that you are a supervisor and you need to provide a subordinate with some feedback. Take a look at the following statements. Both include a positive comment followed by a critical one. Statement A includes the word *but* and a criticism. In statement B, the conjunction is replaced with a period and a more constructive statement. How do the sentences sound to you? How would you respond to each?

- **A:** "Your report looks visually appealing, but it's missing timelines for several work tasks."

- **B:** "Your report looks visually appealing. Let's add timelines to the work tasks, too."

Like the examples given here, you can practice this technique by coming up with a message that includes the conjunction *but*. Then, rewrite the message so that the *but* is replaced by the conjunction *and* or a period. Notice how big a difference this small change can make.

Avoid put-downs

Put-downs are words that are demeaning or hurtful; they suggest that someone is inferior, bad, or flawed in some way. Negative labels, criticisms, and name-calling are all types of put-downs, as are statements that attack a person's thoughts, feelings, needs, or personhood. In TABLE 5.1, you'll see several statements in the left-hand column. Jot down what you think the meaning is in the right-hand column. What does it imply about the person being spoken to and why does it constitute a put-down?

Like put-downs, messages that use trigger words also imply something negative about their recipient, and they may provoke hostile responses.[30] **Trigger words** are known to spark negative emotional reactions (such as anger and

put-down Language that is demeaning or hurtful.

trigger words Language that sparks negative emotional reactions and intensifies arguments.

table 5.1	Put-Down Statements
Statement	**Meaning?**
Here you go again.	_____
You just don't get it.	_____
You should talk!	_____
Why are you so...	_____

defensiveness) and intensify arguments. Examples include: "You have issues," "What's your problem?" "You're crazy," "You people," and "Whatever."

It's always best to avoid put-downs in your interpersonal communication; they're often powerful enough to damage relationships. Rarely are put-downs used when relational partners speak to each other in a kind, patient, loving, and respectful way.

Apply you-language effectively

You-language is a statement or question that starts with the pronoun *you*. When *you* precedes a genuine compliment, the message is generally received very positively. Examples include: "You were hilarious last night," "You are so thoughtful and considerate," and "You are very observant."

Conversely, when *you* is followed by an accusation, a negative blanket statement, or an uncomplimentary comparison, it often provokes a defensive or retaliatory response from the receiver. Take a look at TABLE 5.2. If you were on the receiving end of one of these you-statements, how would you feel? How might you react?

Accusations

"You forgot our anniversary" is an accusation. An **accusation** implies that your communication partner did something bad or failed to do something important. Examples include: "You left me hanging," "You're ignoring my calls," and "You did that on purpose."

Accusations are often based on assumptions. *Perception checks*, which you learned about in Chapter 3, can help you determine if your assumptions are accurate and prevent you from making false accusations. First you make an observation using the pronoun I followed by one of these words: remember, sense, saw, heard, or noticed. Next, you ask a question for clarification.

> **You:** I notice you haven't mentioned anything about our anniversary yet. (Observation). Do you have some plans in mind? (Question for clarification)

Perception checks are generally better received than accusations. In the example above, you'll get an answer that may confirm or disprove your assumption;

table 5.2	You-Statements
Verbal Behavior	**Example**
Accusation	"You forgot our anniversary."
Negative blanket statement	"You always forget our anniversary."
Uncomplimentary comparison	"You could be a lot more like your brother. He really knows how to make their anniversary special."

either way, your romantic partner will likely appreciate being given the benefit of the doubt.

Negative blanket statements

"You always forget our anniversary" is a negative blanket statement. A **negative blanket statement** (often referred to as a *static evaluation* or an *overgeneralization*) implies that a person's feelings or behavior occur all the time or are unchanging. This particular statement suggests that your partner has never valued your anniversary or always dismisses it. But, forgetting your anniversary this one time or once in a while doesn't necessarily mean that your partner hasn't made you feel important in other ways or has never done anything special for your anniversary.

Words like *never*, *ever*, *always*, and *anything* tend to overgeneralize a person's behavior. For example, if you say, "You *never* apologize," "You don't *ever* want to talk about this," "You *always* say that," or, "You don't understand *anything* I'm saying," the receiver will likely think of an exception and want to argue the point with you. As a result, negative blanket statements are usually very unproductive.

Uncomplimentary comparisons

An **uncomplimentary comparison**—such as, "You could be a lot more like your brother. He really knows how to make their anniversary special"—is a statement that compares the person on the receiving end of the message to someone else in an unflattering way. It suggests that the receiver is lacking in some area or not performing up to par. Uncomplimentary comparisons can also take the form of questions, such as: "Why can't you get good grades like your sister?" While uncomplimentary comparisons are often meant to motivate and change the receiver's behavior, in reality, they usually trigger resentment and hostility.

Apply I-language effectively

A positive alternative to an accusation, negative blanket statement, or uncomplimentary comparison is **I-language** that focuses on the behavior or outcome you want from your relational partner. I-language—a statement or question that starts with the pronoun *I*—can help you convey a message without making the receiver feel personally attacked.[31] I-language often begins with phrases like, "I appreciate," "I need," "I like," or "I value."

Receivers are more likely to listen to and consider these messages, especially if your tone of voice is sincere and calm rather than sarcastic and angry. For example, instead of saying, "You are so unromantic," you could say, "I love it when you're romantic, especially on our anniversary," or "I'd like to talk about how we can make our anniversary more special. What are your thoughts?" Notice how the last two statements focus on the behavior or outcome you want, not on the problem as you see it.

Compare the following you-statements and I-statements. How do they sound to you? How would you respond to them?

negative blanket statement A statement or question that implies that a person's feelings or behavior occur all the time or are unchanging.

uncomplimentary comparison A statement or question that compares the receiver to someone else in an unflattering way.

I-language A statement or question that starts with the pronoun *I*.

In a scene from *Kourtney & Khloé Take the Hamptons*, Kourtney confronts her sisters Khloé and Kim for drinking and leaving alcohol out when her partner, Scott, is trying to maintain his sobriety. Pick out examples of you-language in their conversation. Which statements are accusations, negative blanket statements, and uncomplimentary comparisons? Write a new dialogue showing how Kourtney could express her feelings effectively using I-language. On YouTube, search using the keywords: "Kourtney Kardashian Rips Sisters for Alcohol Mishap." (2:38)

- **A:** "You're wrong! You don't know what you're talking about."
- **B:** "I have some information I'd like you to consider."
- **A:** "You always forget to fill up the gas tank after using my car."
- **B:** "I really like it when you remember to fill up the gas tank after using my car."
- **A:** "You haven't bothered to ask me about my new job."
- **B:** "I'd love it if you were more curious about my new job."

The you-statements (statement B in each pair) are free of accusations, blanket statements, and uncomplimentary comparisons. Rather than focus on what the person is doing wrong, these messages focus on the behavior the speaker wants to encourage. For added practice, we encourage you to complete the *Building Your IPC Skills* exercise at the end of this chapter.

Use the sandwich approach

Delivering an unpleasant or critical message without offending the recipient can be tricky; the last thing you want is for the recipient to feel hurt or get defensive. One way to convey a critique with sensitivity and tact is to use the **sandwich approach**: saying something positive about your conversation partner before and after delivering a suggestion (see also Chapter 2). This approach is intended to present constructive feedback in a softer, unaggressive way.[32]

For example, if you need to point out to a colleague, Mel, that she is doing something wrong, you may approach her privately, smile, ask how her day is going, and then say:

Hey Mel, your agendas look sharp! Your use of graphics and color—top notch! Just so you know, Ms. Turner is accustomed to making opening remarks at board meetings, so you may want to put her on the agenda first next time. She said something to me about it yesterday, and I figured you would want to know. Oh, and thanks also for thinking ahead and ordering everyone new folders and name tags. They came in just in time.

In this instance, you sandwiched a suggestion between two compliments. In addition, you spoke privately to your colleague, and your tone of voice and body language appropriately conveyed the message.

Expressing constructive criticism using the sandwich approach may take some advance thought. It also helps to rehearse or practice out loud what you want to say ahead of time so your delivery is smooth and polished. The more you use this technique, the better you'll get at it. Here are a few additional examples:

sandwich approach
Presenting a constructive suggestion between two positive or complimentary statements in order to deliver corrective information in a softer, gentler way.

A Professor to Her Student:	
"Candice, I see you really improved the organization and structure in your second essay."	Positive
"I'm still seeing quite a few spelling errors, however."	Constructive
"If you focus on this in your next paper, you'll see a significant improvement in your grade. I also like how you incorporated more recent research to support your first main idea. Keep it up!"	Positive

A Sibling to His Brother:	
"It was fun hanging out with you last night. My friends thought so too."	Positive
"You may want to tone it down a little when you joke about Scott's height. He's sensitive about that."	Constructive
"Other than that, your humor was a hit. You had everyone in stitches with some of your golf swing imitations."	Positive

section review

5.3 Ways to improve verbal communication

There are many ways to improve your verbal communication: you can use direct and indirect language strategically, monitor your use of powerless language, watch the "we" and replace the "but," avoid the use of put-downs, apply you-language effectively, replace negative you-language with positive I-language, and use the sandwich approach.

Key Terms

direct language, *p. 134*   put-down, *p. 137*   accusation, *p. 138*   I-language, *p. 139*

indirect language, *p. 134*   trigger words, *p. 137*   negative blanket statement, *p. 139*   sandwich approach, *p. 140*

powerless language, *p. 135*   you-language, *p. 138*   uncomplimentary comparison, *p. 139*

Comprehend It?

1. Define each of the key terms in Section 5.3. To further your understanding of these terms, create examples to support your definitions.

2. Explain each of the strategies from Section 5.3.

Apply It!

If you say to a friend, "You always take me for granted," you're making a blanket statement. A less provocative and perhaps more accurate statement might be, "There are times when I feel like you take me for

(continued)

granted," or "I feel like you expect me to be there for you at your recitals. I'd like you to show up to more of my family events." Come up with an example of a blanket statement. Rewrite it so that the message is expressed in a more positive and less provocative way, focusing on the behavior you'd like to see from your conversational partner.

5 chapter exercises

Assessing Your IPC: Powerless Language

Purpose: To monitor my use of powerless language.

Directions: Use the frequency scales below to assess how often you use powerless language in your conversations.

Hedges are words such as "kind of," "sort of," "perhaps," "I suppose," and "I guess." Using these words may make you come across as passive and less resolute. Compare statements A and B in each pair, below. Which are hedges?

> **A:** "I'm a little disappointed."
>
> **B:** "I am disappointed."

> **A:** "Maybe it would be better if we talked about something else."
>
> **B:** "I need us to talk about something else."

I hedge:

Rarely	Sometimes	Often	A lot
1	2	3	4

Hesitations can take the form of long pauses following words like "well" or "so." Hesitations also include verbal pauses, such as filler words like "um" and "uh." Hesitations may give others the impression you lack confidence or certainty. How might you make statements A and B sound less powerless?

> **A:** "I wish you would, um, uh, not do that."
>
> **B:** "Well . . . I can help you with that . . . uhh, let's see . . . hmm."

I hesitate:

Rarely	Sometimes	Often	A lot
1	2	3	4

Disclaimers, like hesitations, de-emphasize the important parts of a message. To sound less uncertain, simply omit disclaimers, like the ones in statements A and B, from your speech.

A: "This is probably a dumb question but . . ."

B: "It's not really my place to say this but . . ."

I use disclaimers:

Rarely	Sometimes	Often	A lot
1	2	3	4

A *tag question* at the end of a sentence may cause the statement to sound less certain or determined. How do statements A and B sound without tag questions?

A: We should send them a confirmation, don't you think?

B: Give it another try, what do you say?

I use tag questions:

Rarely	Sometimes	Often	A lot
1	2	3	4

Building Your IPC Skills: Reducing Defensiveness Using "I-Language"

Purpose: To practice using I-language effectively.

Directions: To communicate your needs without causing others to become defensive, use "I-language" focusing specifically on the behavior you'd like to see. Compare the two statements in column A with the corresponding statements in column B. Which would you rather hear from someone?

A	B
"You are late again."	"I really like it when you arrive on time."
"You always snap at me!"	"I appreciate when you're patient with me."

Replace the following statements with "I-language." You might begin your revised sentences with phrases like "I appreciate," "I enjoy," "I like," or "I value." Be sure to focus your statements on the behavior you would like to see.

1. "At dinner you dominated the conversation."

2. "You left this morning without saying goodbye."

3. "How many times do I need to remind you to charge your cell phone?"

4. "You hardly ever take me out with your friends anymore."

5. "You spend money faster than anyone I know."

Want to earn a better grade on your test? Go to INQUIZITIVE to practice actively with this chapter's content and get personalized feedback along the way.

6

Nonverbal Communication

learning objectives

Reading this chapter will help you:

- Appreciate the significance of nonverbal communication
- Understand the various types of nonverbal communication
- Practice techniques to improve nonverbal communication

Communication scholars Michael Kraus, Dacher Keltner, and Cassy Huang believe that NBA teammates who touch each other more win more. The researchers and their team watched every professional team play one game during the first two months of a regular season and recorded the number of times teammates touched each other, taking into account information such as fist bumps, high fives, and side hugs. In the end, teams with the highest levels of touch had the best win-loss records, and teams with the lowest levels of touch had the worst records.[1]

At the time of the study, the two top-performing teams had the most player-to-player touch: the Boston Celtics and Los Angeles Lakers. Interestingly, the two teams with the lowest rates of touch between teammates also had the worst records: the Sacramento Kings and Charlotte Bobcats. Team success is not the only thing correlated with touch frequency. Many of the best players in the NBA are the touchiest, including Kevin Garnett of the Boston Celtics, Chris Bosh of the Toronto Raptors, and Carlos Boozer of the Utah Jazz.[2]

How does touch play a role in a team's success? According to Kraus, Huang, and Keltner, players who share in the benefits of touch play better. Supportive, affectionate touch between teammates triggers the release of oxytocin, a brain chemical

Touch is a common form of nonverbal communication. During basketball games, players often convey messages to each other using touch. Research suggests that touch may even affect a team's success.

associated with bonding and trust.[3] Players also use touch in a motivational way. A high five expresses gratitude and shared excitement for individual and collective successes, while an arm around the shoulder or a quick head tousle conveys support when a game is not going well or a teammate makes a mistake.[4]

Along with touch, facial expressions, gestures, vocal tones, and posture help us convey and make sense of nonverbal messages. In this chapter, we'll (1) examine the importance of nonverbal communication, (2) explore the various types of nonverbal messages, and (3) identify ways to improve your nonverbal communication.

6.1 Significance of nonverbal communication

The next time you visit your local mall, find a comfortable spot to observe those around you. You may notice individuals speaking in dyads and small groups. What is happening in terms of touch? How much space do people maintain between one another? Where do their eyes go? Take note of their postures, gestures, and facial expressions. What do you see?

You may not be able to hear what's being said, but the nonverbal behavior of the people you're observing may allow you to make some fairly accurate assumptions. For example, if you're watching a group of teens talking near the entrance to a hot pretzel shop, you might be able to discern which one in the group is bored with the conversation. If you're observing a mother and her teenage son, you may notice that they're arguing about something without actually hearing any of their words.

Nonverbal communication is sending and receiving messages without the use of language. You communicate nonverbally whenever you smile, laugh, clap, point at something, or snap your fingers. Nonverbal communication is pervasive; it is happening all around you, all the time. In Section 6.1, we'll focus on how and why nonverbal communication plays an important role in your interpersonal communication.

Nonverbal communication is revealing

Suppose your roommate Liz asks if you have time to help her rearrange the living room furniture, and you reply, "Sure, I'm not too busy!" If you keep glancing at your watch, though, what will Liz think?

In Chapter 2 you learned that when your nonverbal communication contradicts your verbal communication, you're sending a *mixed message*. Research suggests that Liz will likely focus more on your nonverbal behavior—checking your watch—to determine what you really mean. Why? Social interactions have taught her (and you too) that we don't have as much conscious control over our nonverbal reactions.[5] Therefore, what we do in a given moment nonverbally is often more genuine and revealing than what we say.

One kind of nondeliberate nonverbal reaction occurs when you start to smirk or laugh when it's not appropriate. One of our students, Sima, shared another: When she gets upset or nervous, her lips start to quiver. She says, "I hate it because I can't seem to control it."

These examples illustrate leakage. **Leakage** refers to sudden or spontaneous—often uncontrollable—nonverbal reactions. Every time you blush, stammer,

nonverbal communication Sending and receiving messages without the use of language.

leakage Sudden or spontaneous—often unconscious—nonverbal reactions.

pace, fidget, glance away, bite your lip, get teary eyed, put your hand to your throat, or play with your hair, you may reveal what you're really thinking or feeling—whether you're aware of it or not.

In their work *Pragmatics of Human Communication*, scholars Paul Watzlawick, Janet Bavelas, and Donald Jackson state, "We cannot not communicate."[6] As long as someone can observe you, you are potentially sending messages that are nonverbal in nature. Others may interpret these messages accurately, but they may just as easily interpret them inaccurately. Nancy describes the latter situation in her narrative. Has something like this ever happened to you?

> "I was lying in bed the other night. I sighed loudly and turned over with my back to my husband, Mike. He translated that in a way I never intended: He thought I was mad at him, when in reality, I was just exhausted from a long day at the hospital and was uncomfortable lying on my back." –Nancy

Nonverbal communication is relational

The relationship between sender and receiver often influences the meaning and interpretation of nonverbal messages. Something as simple as silence, a form of nonverbal expression, may say a lot about a relationship. Mia Wallace (Uma Thurman) and Vincent Vega (John Travolta) allude to this in the film *Pulp Fiction*:

> **Mia:** Don't you hate that?
> **Vincent:** What?
> **Mia:** Uncomfortable silences. Why do we feel it's necessary to yak about [crap] in order to be comfortable?
> **Vincent:** That's a good question.
> **Mia:** That's when you know you've found somebody special. When you both can just . . . comfortably enjoy the silence.

The silence between friends may indicate that they feel at ease around each other. Your nonverbal communication may also reflect the relationship you *want* to have with someone. You may hug a close friend a little longer to express your desire to be closer to each other.

Cognitive valence theory suggests that a relationship may become closer or more distant depending on how relational partners perceive each other's nonverbal messages.[7] For example, what you do with your time is a form of nonverbal communication. Your relational partners may perceive how you prioritize your time positively or negatively, which may affect how they feel about you and their relationship with you.

Let's say you're hosting a party. You've invited Shay, a new coworker whom you're just getting to know. When she arrives, you take several minutes to talk to her and introduce her to some of your other friends. You also check on her throughout the night to see if she's having a good time. If Shay perceives your nonverbal communication positively—you took time to connect with her and make her feel welcome—cognitive valence theory suggests that this

cognitive valence theory
The idea that a relationship is influenced by how relational partners perceive each other's nonverbal behaviors.

immediacy The degree of closeness, liking, and connection in a relationship.

will likely reinforce the positive feelings she has toward you. Conversely, if you don't take the time to visit with Shay at your party or if you only give her a quick hello, she may feel slighted or even question why you invited her in the first place.

When you interact with someone, your nonverbal behaviors can foster immediacy. **Immediacy** is the degree of closeness, liking, and connection that relational partners feel toward each other. Behaviors correlated with higher levels of immediacy include smiling, touching others warmly and appropriately, speaking with animation, leaning in when someone is speaking, maintaining good eye contact, and listening attentively without interruption.[8]

When you communicate in ways that convey immediacy, your relational partners may respond in a similar manner. According to research, greater levels of immediacy are associated with positive outcomes:

- Waitresses who casually touch their customers on the hand, forearm, or shoulder, even just once or in a fleeting manner, receive bigger tips.[9]

- Speed dating participants who communicate with more nonverbal immediacy receive more date requests.[10]

- Students are more likely to evaluate their learning positively and score higher on cognitive learning measures when their teachers exhibit more nonverbal immediacy.[11]

- Managers who smile often, greet employees warmly, and express genuine emotions appear more approachable and personable to employees. These nonverbal behaviors foster a greater exchange of valuable feedback and ideas.[12]

Into the Wild tells the story of Christopher McCandless (Emile Hirsch), who abandons his possessions, gives all of his money to charity, and hitchhikes to Alaska to live in the wilderness. On his journey, he forms a special friendship with Ron Franz (Hal Holbrook). In this scene, how are their feelings for each other expressed nonverbally? On YouTube, search using the keywords: "Into the Wild (8/9) Movie CLIP - Let Me Adopt You?" (2:43)

Nonverbal communication is purposeful

Nonverbal communication may serve to complement, contradict, accent, regulate, or substitute for verbal communication. It may help to remember these functions using the acronym CCARS.

Complement

If you are teaching a friend how to use a new app on her cell phone, you may point to something on her screen, slow your rate of speech down to help her grasp what you're saying better, and move in closer so she can see what you're doing on your own phone. In this way, your nonverbal behaviors complement your words and their impact on the receiver.

In a job interview, it will work to your benefit to make sure that your nonverbal behaviors complement what you say. To convey confidence and professionalism, you'll use words that are powerful, direct, and descriptive. Your posture, eye contact, gestures, and style of dress can likewise make a positive impression—usually in a collectively subtle yet significant way. In fact, research suggests that job seekers who wear upper-class clothing,[13] offer firm handshakes,[14] gesture more, and look interviewers directly in the eye not only look and feel more confident but are more persuasive and improve their chances of being hired.[15]

Contradict

Your nonverbal communication may also contradict your words. To convey sarcasm, you may use your tone of voice to let your listener know that what you mean is just the opposite of what you're saying. For instance, you might say, "Isn't that *just great*," accompanied by an eye roll, to indicate that something is not great at all. Other examples of contradiction include yelling, "Angry? I'm not angry!" or giving a wink when you say you're telling the truth.

Accent

Just as you use exclamation marks, italics, bolded text, and emojis to emphasize parts of a typed verbal message, you may use various nonverbal devices to accent, or draw particular attention to, parts of a verbal message. For example, you might pound your fist on the table to underscore your anger. Or, while telling stories around a campfire, you may dramatize a scary moment by making a claw with your hand to mimic a creature poised to attack.

Regulate

Certain nonverbal behaviors can help you regulate the flow of a conversation. As we discussed in Chapter 4, we call this kind of behavior *conversational turn-taking*. For example, you may pause and slightly nod your head, a *turn-yielding signal*, to let someone know you are ready for them to respond. If you're not ready to let someone speak, your voice might get louder as you continue talking; this is a *turn-denying signal*. If you want your conversational partner to yield so you can speak, you can use a *turn-requesting signal* such as holding your hand out as if to say, "Stop, let me say something."[16]

Substitute

Sometimes a nonverbal message stands in as a substitute for a verbal message. For instance, a look of boredom says it all when you can't or don't want to verbalize, "I have no interest in what's happening here." Waving at a person signifies "hello," a shrug says "I don't know," and a finger to your mouth means "be quiet." One of our students, Fan, shared: "Whenever it was really loud and crowded in the hallway at school, my friends would point to me and gesture as if they were shooting a basketball. This meant, 'Are you free to play basketball after school?'"

A gift may also act as a substitute for a verbal message. For example, it may represent the wishful thinking of a gift giver who hopes the gift will influence you in some way.[17] When one of our students, Isaac, received a set of coasters from his mother on his birthday, he said, "I got the hint. I used to place my drinking glasses and beer bottles on her wood furniture, which could leave water marks. My mom takes great pride in how her living room looks. I think it was her way of saying that she wants me to use coasters from now on. Too bad she didn't get me a case of beer to go with the coasters."

section review

6.1 Significance of nonverbal communication

Nonverbal communication, the exchange of messages without the use of language, is both revealing and relational in nature. It may complement, contradict, accent, regulate, or substitute for verbal communication.

Key Terms

nonverbal communication, *p. 146*   cognitive valence theory, *p. 147*
leakage, *p. 146*   immediacy, *p. 148*

Comprehend It?

1. Define each of the key terms in Section 6.1. To further your understanding of these terms, create examples to support your definitions.

2. In your own words, describe how nonverbal communication is revealing and relational in nature.

3. Compare and contrast the functions of nonverbal communication: complement, contradict, accent, regulate, and substitute.

Apply It!

The Artist, a black-and-white silent film, tells the story of a film star who falls in love with an aspiring actress. Watch this scene between George (Jean Dujardin) and Peppy (Bérénice Bejo), and examine how their nonverbal messages complement, contradict, accent, regulate, and substitute for the use of words. On YouTube, search using the keywords: "The Artist Movie Clip: Something to Set You Apart." (3:16)

6.2 **Types of nonverbal communication**

American soldiers serving overseas in Afghanistan and Iraq rely on information provided by local civilians to root out terrorist cells and identify potential threats. When troops establish positive relationships with locals, they're far more successful. How do they accomplish this if they don't speak Dari, Pashto, or Arabic?

The Pentagon relies on a 3D video game called the *Rapid Tactical Language Training System* to teach soldiers to communicate interculturally. The game places soldiers in a variety of simulated social situations that they must navigate using basic gestures or hand signs when a language barrier exists. Soldiers also learn that certain nonverbal behaviors enhance or detract from their interactions. For example, they are taught to place a hand on their heart as they approach a resident to signal good intentions. They are also encouraged to get down on one knee and remove their sunglasses when talking to children so they appear less intimidating.

The program also demonstrates what not to do. Male soldiers learn that they should not walk up quickly to single Arab women, reach out to shake their hands, or touch them in any way; Islam, the majority religion in the region, prohibits nonessential physical contact between people of the opposite sex unless they are family members.

Apart from the video game, the Pentagon also engages soldiers in cultural sensitivity training to teach them about nonverbal culture differences. Iraqis, for example, tend to converse with louder voices and gaze into each other's eyes longer and more directly compared to Americans.[18] Why do you think this information is important for soldiers to know?

Competent nonverbal communication is an important goal of American soldiers: They are taught how to leverage various types of nonverbal communication in order to communicate effectively. You can also benefit by making this a goal in your own life. In Section 6.2, we'll learn more about the various types of nonverbal communication and how they can affect your interpersonal communication and relationships.

Acts of service and thoughtfulness

After enduring chemotherapy in her battle against breast cancer, 34-year-old Michelle Zettle of Idaho lost all of her hair. Knowing how much she loved her hair, her husband, father, sons, brother-in-law, mother-in-law's boyfriend, and several male colleagues all shaved their heads to help her feel less alone. Their nonverbal actions sent Michelle a tender message of love and support.[19]

In terms of acts of service and thoughtfulness, grander gestures tend to communicate stronger messages, but the little things we do can mean a lot to our relational partners, too. Dr. Barton Goldsmith, a marriage and family therapist and author of *Emotional Fitness for Couples*, states that it's the little nonverbal acts

FLOWERS THAT SAY TOO MUCH

YES, HERE I AM AGAIN. A GENERIC LITTLE ARRANGEMENT THAT SHOWS HE WAITED UNTIL THE LAST MINUTE, THEN DIALED SOME 800 NUMBER.

that increase love and devotion over the long run. He advises his readers to do thoughtful things out of the blue on a regular basis, like getting your partner's car washed or putting a picture of the two of you in a new frame and placing it on the coffee table.[20]

On the other hand, certain acts may disappoint or even offend your relational partners. Not following through on a promise you made or eating the last piece of pie without asking if anyone else wanted it are examples of harmful nonverbal messages. Someone may also interpret a last-minute gift, such as the one featured in this cartoon, quite negatively.

Appearance

Do physically attractive people have social advantages over less attractive people? For one, research suggests that good-looking men and women have an easier time getting dates.[21] In job interviews, attractive people are also at an advantage; in one study, conventionally attractive female and male candidates were 54% and 47% more likely to get a second interview compared to only 7% and 26% of unattractive candidates, respectively.[22] Another study found that attractive wait staff earned $1,261 more per year than their less attractive colleagues.[23]

Like it or not, attractiveness is an aspect of physical appearance that plays a role in our interpersonal communication—and altering our appearance can communicate nonverbal messages. While we cannot control all aspects of our appearance, we can use grooming, apparel, diet, and exercise to influence how we appear to others. For instance, we often strategically choose our clothing to establish status and power (suits and uniforms), enhance popularity (trendy clothes or new styles), or project a certain image, such as professionalism, casualness, or even a personal brand.[24] In addition, accessories such as watches, jewelry, purses, hats, and shoes may accentuate the look or style you wish to project to others.

Body language

One of our students, Beatrice, has been married to her husband, Jack, for 45 years. She can tell when he's thinking deeply about something because he pours himself a cup of coffee and paces with it back and forth in front of their bay window. When he is nervous, his right knee bounces. When Jack is particularly happy, his eyes light up and he smiles ear to ear.

Like Jack, your body language is potentially rich in meaning. Body language includes eye behavior, facial expressions, gestures, physical animation, and posture.

Eye behavior

What is usually the first thing you do when you want to communicate with someone? You look at the person, often directly and a little longer than normal.

If the other person is receptive, you'll receive eye contact in return. If you don't, it likely indicates that the person is not interested in conversation.

Gaze aversion is when you purposely limit or cut off eye contact with someone. Generally speaking, Americans perceive gaze aversion negatively; it may signal a lack of confidence, truthfulness, attentiveness, or politeness. On the flip side, some cultures in Africa and the Pacific Islands see eye contact between young people and their elders as highly disrespectful. One Peace Corps member serving as a teacher in Africa discovered this when community elders complained that the children in her class were coming home and looking them in the eye. The teacher had unknowingly violated social customs by requiring the children to look her in the eye when speaking.[25]

Eye behavior goes beyond eye contact. Perhaps your goal is to intimidate, establish your authority, communicate disapproval, or show defiance. You could use your eyes to stare someone down. You may also roll your eyes to convey disagreement or annoyance. Research suggests that the eye roll is one of the most hurtful and invalidating forms of nonverbal communication.[26]

Facial expressions

Humans can create over 10,000 different facial expressions.[27] Many communication scholars believe a person's face is the first thing we focus on when forming impressions.[28] We look to people's faces to size up their emotions, leadership potential, attractiveness, and trustworthiness.[29]

Facial management techniques are the expressions you make to either convey or mask your thoughts and feelings. You use these techniques intentionally to achieve a desired effect. For instance, you may furrow your brow to convey your seriousness when your partner makes light of a request you've made. Or, you might put on a fake smile to mask your envy when your friend brags about the dream vacation he has planned.

On the other hand, many of our facial expressions are unintentional; recall our discussion of *leakage* earlier in the chapter. As José describes, we may or may not be aware of the facial expressions that we make. Can you relate to José's narrative? What do you think José could do to improve?

> "My facial expressions get me into trouble. I've been accused of being aloof because I apparently have this 'blank look' when people talk to me. Just the other day my friend said to me, 'Never mind, you obviously don't care what I have to say.' It's not that I don't care, but my face communicates just the opposite. I am consciously trying to make my face more expressive." —José

gaze aversion The act of avoiding or limiting eye contact.

facial management techniques The expressions you make to either convey or mask your thoughts and feelings.

microexpression A form of nonverbal leakage specific to the face.

gesticulation The use of your arms and hands to communicate meaning.

Many of our unintentional facial messages are the result of **microexpressions**—a form of nonverbal leakage specific to the face. They are sudden, involuntary facial expressions, which flash an instant message. We typically have little control over microexpressions, yet they are very revealing to others.[30]

Gestures

Gesticulation is the use of your arms and hands to communicate meaning, including snapping, clapping, high-fiving, pointing, and beckoning with your hands. You may pinch your nose to let your roommate know his socks smell. To wish a friend good luck, you might cross your fingers or give a supportive fist bump.

The meanings we assign to gestural symbols are not culturally universal. For example, the "OK" sign we use in the United States is quite innocuous in its traditional meaning: "everything is good," "looking fine," or "you got it." However, depending on the communication context, it's now used by some as a symbol of white supremacy and hate—or it could be interpreted as such.[31] When people use this symbol in France, it stands for "you have zero worth." In parts of Greece and Turkey, its meaning is equivalent to the meaning of the middle finger in the United States, or "up yours."[32]

Physical animation

To *animate* is to bring to life. While gesticulation involves just your arms and hands, physical animation is the use of your arms, hands, face, chest, legs, shoulders or other parts of your body to create some sort of action sequence. For example, to get a laugh out of a friend, you might pretend to walk into a wall and fall down. If you wanted your 4-year-old nephew to think you are about to charge him like a raging bull, you may stick your chest out, lower your head, create horns on your head with your index fingers, and huff and puff as you paw on the ground with your foot.

Posture

Posture is the way you carry yourself; how you stand, sit, or lie down next to someone. Posture may include how you turn your body toward someone, whether you lean forward or backward, and if you sit or stand with your back straight or slouched. Other elements of posture include how you cross your legs in a seated position, where you plant your feet when you're standing, and whether your arms are crossed or hanging relaxed. Speaking with open arms, standing tall with your back straight and shoulders back, and holding your head up may add authority, poise, and confidence to your verbal messages.[33]

Voice

You convey meaning with your voice by laughing, groaning, yelling, whispering, sighing, whining, and using filler expressions such as "uh-uh" or "hmmmm." It's easy to get confused and assume that talking out loud is verbal communication alone. In fact, only the words themselves constitute verbal communication. *How* you say your words—or your *vocal* communication—is a form of nonverbal communication.

The ways in which your voice conveys meaning apart from language is called **paralanguage**. How you use your voice may influence the perceptions others have of your socioeconomic status, intelligence, persuasiveness, personality, attractiveness, and credibility.[34] There are many components of paralanguage, including *vocal pitch, rate, volume,* and *quality*.

Vocal pitch

Vocal pitch is the intonation or inflection in your voice ranging from high to low sounds. Can you think of the various ways you alter your pitch to convey meaning? Take the expression "oh." To convey excitement, you might say "Oh!" in a high tone. When you say "uh oh," the "oh" is pitched lower than the "uh," signifying, "I'm in trouble." How might you say "oh" to express mild surprise, indifference, or sudden understanding?

The meaning of a verbal message may change depending on your vocal emphasis—the specific words you choose to emphasize with your voice. For instance, you might say to a friend, "That's a great looking shirt. I love the tie dye," which sounds like a compliment. But, by raising your pitch just as you say "tie dye," and making it sound like you're posing it as a doubtful question, you can make your voice sound very sarcastic: "That's a great looking shirt . . . I love the *tie dye?*" Pitch helps you communicate not only sarcasm but also distrust, humor, and a host of other emotions.[35]

The results of a study conducted by communication researchers Miron Zuckerman and Kunitate Miyake suggest that speaking with a **monotone voice**— a tone of voice that is flat or unchanging—may make you sound less pleasant. A monotone voice is hard for most people to listen to for an extended period of time and is considered boring and tedious. People who speak with vocal variety are perceived as more dynamic and interesting.[36] For example, in one study, business managers who spoke with vocal variety were liked more by employees.[37]

Vocal rate

Vocal rate or *tempo* is the speed at which you speak. For instance, you might talk quickly to express excitement or slowly to convey something serious or important. Speaking at a faster rate is associated with higher levels of persuasiveness and listener interest. If it is important to give someone time to process and understand what you are saying, speaking at a slower rate is helpful. Speaking slowly also helps you emphasize key points, which can be especially helpful if you are discussing data or complex terms.

Pauses and moments of silence are also elements of vocal rate. You may pause when you're thinking of what to say next, or you may pause strategically to drive home a point. A pause or hesitation may communicate an unintentional

paralanguage The ways in which your voice conveys meaning apart from language.

vocal pitch The intonation or inflection in your voice ranging from high to low sounds.

monotone voice A tone of voice that is flat or unchanging.

vocal rate The speed at which you speak.

message. Consider this exchange between Lucy van Pelt and Charlie Brown in *A Charlie Brown Christmas*:

> **Lucy:** You do think I'm beautiful, don't you, Charlie Brown?
> **Charlie:** Well. . . (*pauses*)
> **Lucy:** You didn't answer right away. You had to think about it first, didn't you? If you really thought I was beautiful, you would've spoken right up. I know when I've been insulted.
> **Charlie:** Good grief!

Vocal volume

Vocal volume is how loudly or softly you speak. Speaking with a higher volume (but not too loudly) is socially desirable in American culture, while speaking too softly may give others the impression you're timid or lack confidence.[38] However, prolonged exposure to either high or low volume may annoy others or cause them to tune out. Varying the volume of your voice is an effective way to keep a listener engaged. For example, you might raise your voice in a meeting to bring up a new idea, or you might speak more softly to build suspense when sharing a story.

Vocal quality

Vocal quality relates to how well you enunciate and pronounce your words. **Enunciation** is vocalizing a word clearly. To enunciate effectively is to make your words sound sharp, crisp, and distinct; it may be hard for others to understand what you're saying if you mumble or slur your words. We offer some techniques to improve your enunciation in the *Building Your IPC Skills* exercise at the end of this chapter. **Pronunciation** is the act of saying a word correctly based on dictionary or phonetic rules. If you mispronounce a word, your conversational partner may experience confusion or feel compelled to correct you. Either way, this may affect how others perceive your intelligence.

vocal volume How loudly or softly you speak.

enunciation The act of vocalizing a word clearly so others can understand what you're saying.

pronunciation The act of saying a word correctly based on dictionary or phonetic rules.

In this scene from the TV show *Schitt's Creek*, Moira Rose (Catherine O'Hara) and her daughter Alexis (Annie Murphy) are working together to schedule a community event with apparently little success. Describe how they convey their mutual frustration with their body language and paralanguage. On YouTube search using the keywords: "Schitt's Creek - The Singles Have Arrived." (1:39)

Vocal utterances are the filler sounds you make between words or sentences, such as "um," "uh," and "you know." If you use too many vocal utterances, others may perceive you as less articulate, intelligent, confident, interesting to listen to, likeable, or persuasive.[39]

vocal utterances The filler sounds you make between words or sentences.

Physical environment

The physical environment in which communication takes place—including such factors as room temperature, lighting, seating arrangements, decor, and color selections—may influence IPC. In one study, for example, patients reported feeling five times more comfortable talking to their doctors in an open seating area than in a businesslike space in which the doctor sat behind a desk.[40] Researchers also discovered that professors with neat, attractive offices were perceived as more credible by their students compared to professors with unkempt or poorly decorated offices.[41]

Research suggests that wall, fabric, and artwork colors affect mood and energy level. Bright colors such as red and yellow are associated with energy and activity and may increase animation; blue and green, by contrast, are calmer colors. One study found that prison inmates displayed less violent behavior when the walls of their cell blocks were painted a particular shade of pink.[42]

Scent

Scent is another way to send nonverbal messages. Pleasing smells may enhance your interaction with someone.[43] If you want to send a message of calm and hospitality, you might put a tray of brownies in the oven. You might also use lemon-scented cleaning products in your home—a smell associated with health and cleanliness.[44]

It's important to note that people vary in their ability to perceive and willingness to tolerate certain smells, and some smells nearly always send a negative nonverbal message. A person who bathes infrequently may smell bad to you, sending a nonverbal message of carelessness, but individuals from other cultures who are very accustomed to the smell of natural body odors may think nothing of it. One of our students, Kara, shared that she couldn't understand why her friends were always too busy to come over to her house until one of her friends confided, "Your home smells too much like your dogs." She was so familiar with the smell that she didn't realize it was there.

To avoid sending your conversational partner a negative message, you might want to steer clear of foods with strong odors, like garlic and onions. Another source of bad breath is alcohol, which dries your mouth and allows odor-causing bacteria to proliferate. Coffee breath is also problematic. To mask any undesirable smells and keep close encounters pleasant, many people avoid wearing strong scents and use gum and breath mints at work and during social events.

proxemic theory The idea that people perceive space differently and use space to achieve their communication goals.

territoriality The tendency to claim user's rights to a space that you don't own.

Space

Proxemic theory is the idea that people perceive space differently and use space to achieve their communication goals. According to anthropologist Edward Hall, people prefer to operate within four spatial zones—intimate, personal, social, and public—depending on their goals and the relationships they have with their interactional partners (see **TABLE 6.1**). A major tenet of proxemic theory is that our sense of appropriate space is influenced by culture. For example, people in southern European, Latin American, and Middle Eastern cultures generally conduct face-to-face conversations in closer proximity than people do in England, Norway, or New Zealand.[45]

This is important to keep in mind if you are having a conversation with someone from another culture. If the person seems to stand or sit too close to you—or appears to step back or move over in one's seat to create more space, it may have a lot to do with that person's sense of normal interactive space.

You may enhance your IPC by how you manage space. You can create a more intimate, comfortable conversation between team members at work by seating them at a round table where everyone is at an equal distance from each other, somewhere between Hall's personal and social space zones. You may also encourage people to sit where they would feel most comfortable, or you may ask where it would be best for you to stand or sit depending on the situation to avoid breaking any explicit or implicit territoriality rules.

It's also important to consider how possessive people are about their space. When you arrive to class, where do you and your classmates sit? In the same seats class after class? As a guest at someone's home, were you ever told where not to sit at the dinner table? If you occupy another person's space, you may unintentionally communicate a message of disrespect or intrusion. **Territoriality** refers to the tendency to claim user's rights to a space that you don't own.

If you are in someone else's car, home, or office, you may find it advantageous to know and follow certain rules of etiquette. For example, if you're a passenger in someone's car, it's polite to ask permission to roll down your window or change

table 6.1	Edward Hall's Spatial Zones
Spatial Zone	**Who Can Enter?**
Intimate space (0–18 inches)	Romantic partners and in some cases extremely close friends and family
Personal space (18 inches–4 feet)	Friends and family
Social space (4–12 feet)	Acquaintances and strangers
Public space (12–25 feet)	Attendees of a large gathering, such as a lecture or meeting, where one person is the primary speaker[46]

the radio channel. If you're visiting a relative and the guest bedroom is too cold, you probably wouldn't change the room temperature yourself. You'd say, "It's a bit chilly in here. Would you mind turning up the heat a little?"

Time

How you manage time may communicate a message to someone whether you are aware of it or not. "Time is seen as a precious resource, a valuable and tangible commodity. We spend time, save it, make it, fill it, and waste it" write communication scholars Judee Burgoon, David Buller, and Gill Woodall in their book *Nonverbal Communication: The Unspoken Dialogue.*[47]

The time it takes you to return a phone call, how long you stay at a party, and the amount of time you spend with your children all suggest something about you: in turn, your promptness and professionalism, your sociability, and who and what is important to you. Allowing distractions to interfere with a conversation may communicate that you don't value your time with someone. Arriving too late and waiting too long to start a meeting may suggest that you don't care about other people's time and commitments.

Some cultures place a high priority on promptness and punctuality while others are more laid back. In the United States, for instance, if someone in New York invites you to a party that starts at 9:00 p.m., you aren't generally expected to arrive until 9:30 p.m. or later. In Salt Lake City, guests are generally expected to show up on time or a little early.[48]

Touch

Touch can convey many types of nonverbal messages—e.g., support, warmth, concern, and friendliness. Doctors who use appropriate touch with their patients get better reviews.[49] Students with autism participate more in class when they receive supportive touches from their teachers.[50] Pregnant women who are massaged by their partner or spouse report lower levels of anxiety, depression, and anger and higher levels of love and affection toward their partner.[51]

While not all forms of touch are well received, if it is considered appropriate and pleasant by the recipient, touch can enhance an interpersonal interaction and send a message of connectedness, acceptance, goodwill, camaraderie, warmth, love, or affection.[52]

Visual representations and sound

A couple, George and Thea, sometimes coordinate colors when they dress for social events. In their apartment, there are lots of photos of them taken on trips abroad, and when they have guests over, they sometimes play their wedding playlist on their sound system. Like George and Thea, you may use visual representations, sound effects, and music to communicate certain nonverbal messages—such as how you feel about your romantic partner and the relationship. You can use photos, drawings, avatars, colors, artwork, sound effects, music, and emojis to convey many different messages.

In this scene from the TV show *Big Little Lies*, Mary Louise (Meryl Streep) surprises her daughter-in-law Celeste (Nicole Kidman) when she shows up unexpectedly to a Halloween party. Celeste, along with her four friends present at the party, witnessed the death of Mary Louise's son, and Mary Louise is suspicious of their report to the police. As you watch the scene, focus on the nonverbal behaviors that the characters display. Which of their behaviors convey significant and subtle meaning? On YouTube, search using the keywords: "Big Little Lies: The Slap." (2:57)

Tattoos are very popular nonverbal visual representations. Approximately 33% of American adults sport at least one.[53] What motivates people to get tattoos? Many say that tattoos allow them to express their individuality. Others see them as a way to communicate their attachment to certain individuals, activities, and beliefs.

Are there any drawbacks to this form of nonverbal expression? People perceive tattoos differently based on their type and placement. One's overall amount of body art, age, and socioeconomic status play a factor, too. In one study, college students were asked to look at photographs of models with and without tattoos and to rate them based on their attractiveness and credibility. While the students didn't feel that the tattoos detracted much from the models' attractiveness, they did think that the tattoos lowered how professional or credible they appeared.[54]

section review

- -

6.2 Types of nonverbal communication

Nonverbal messages may be conveyed through acts of service and thoughtfulness, appearance, body language, voice, physical environment, scent, space, time, touch, visual representations, sound effects, and music. Specific nonverbal behaviors in each of these areas may hinder or enhance our IPC.

(continued)

Key Terms

gaze aversion, *p. 153*

facial management techniques, *p. 153*

microexpression, *p. 154*

gesticulation, *p. 154*

paralanguage, *p. 155*

vocal pitch, *p. 155*

monotone voice, *p. 155*

vocal rate, *p. 155*

vocal volume, *p. 156*

enunciation, *p. 156*

pronunciation, *p. 156*

vocal utterances, *p. 157*

proxemic theory, *p. 158*

territoriality, *p. 158*

Comprehend It?

1. Define each of the key terms in Section 6.2. To further your understanding of these terms, create examples to support your definitions.

2. Compare and contrast the following:
   - Body language: eye behavior, facial expressions, gestures, physical animation, and posture
   - Paralanguage: vocal pitch, rate, volume, and quality

   - Hall's spatial zones: intimate, personal, social, and public

3. Summarize the important communicative aspects of acts of service and thoughtfulness, appearance, physical environment, scent, time, touch, and visual or auditory representations.

Apply It!

A kindergarten teacher asks her students to indicate on a chart how they would like to be greeted at the start of every school day. To witness this on YouTube, search using the keywords "Warm & Lovely Morning Greeting from Mrs. Judy" (1:06). Which types of nonverbal communication do you see?

What makes this a positive interaction for the teacher and her students? How might this enhance the relationships she has with them? Be prepared to share your thoughts with a classmate or discussion group.

6.3 Ways to improve nonverbal communication

Some communication scholars estimate that 60–70% of the meaning we exchange in face-to-face communication is nonverbal.[55] Paying close attention to your nonverbal communication and how it affects others is an important aspect of skilled interpersonal communication. Making sure you're interpreting the nonverbal communication of others accurately is equally important.

Section 6.3 will explore six important methods for increasing your nonverbal communication competence.

Practice mindfulness

In Chapter 1 we first introduced the important concept of *mindfulness*. To be mindful is to clear your mind and patiently attend to what is happening within you and around you. Mindfulness is associated with openness, receptivity, and awareness. To practice mindfulness, create a quiet moment free of distractions to reflect on a previous conversation or envision a future conversation. This will help you connect more with your own thoughts, feelings, and communication behaviors.

Think about something that is happening in one of your relationships right now—whether positive or negative. What is happening? How does this make you feel and why? Reflect on your communication with your relational partner: not just what you said or didn't say but how you said it, and what you did or didn't do. Next, think about how you'd like to communicate with this person the next time you interact.

One thing you can do to practice mindfulness is to engage in self-monitoring. You may recall from Chapter 1 that *self-monitoring* is the process of thinking about and analyzing your communication with others. People who regularly self-monitor are more likely to express nonverbal behaviors that engender higher levels of liking, interest, and status—such as smiling frequently and speaking at an appropriate volume—compared to people who rarely self-monitor.[56] The dimensions of interest, liking, and status are explained in TABLE 6.2. How little or often do you engage in these behaviors?

Mindfulness can also help you detect the subtle nuances of meaning embedded in a person's message. Imagine that you ask your brother an important question while he's brushing his teeth. How does he react? Does he stop brushing suddenly? Does he seem calm or agitated? If he says, "Just a moment, I'm brushing my teeth," and then brushes his teeth much longer than normal, what does this

table 6.2	Nonverbal Indicators of Interest, Liking, and Status
Nonverbal Message	**Indicating Behaviors**
Interest	Leaning forward while listening; nodding frequently; making direct eye contact; smiling and laughing; keeping an open body orientation; taking more time to talk (less quick to end the conversation); using vocal and gestural expressiveness
Liking	Talking with a slightly louder voice and faster rate; casual touches and smiles; sitting or standing closer; initiating interaction; increasing opportunities to interact by attending the same social events or getting involved in the same activity
Status	Standing with an erect posture and downward head tilt; speaking first or standing when others are sitting; sitting at the head of a table; wearing the most formal attire; initiating touch such as handshakes and shoulder taps first and more often; entering a room first

suggest? Holding back one's verbal communication is itself a form of nonverbal communication!

To communicate mindfully, it helps to receive and process all messages—verbal and nonverbal—before you formulate a response. Paying close attention also helps you adjust your communication in a timely and effective manner. If you're out on a double date, for instance, and you sense tension between the couple you're with, you may quickly change the subject. At a committee meeting, you may notice that a colleague's remark was ignored and make sure the group revisits it.

The **interactive adaptation theory** originated by communication scholars Judee Burgoon, Lesa Stern, and Leesa Dillman describes how competent communicators adjust or alter their nonverbal communication to interact successfully with others.[57] For example, if your colleague, Nikki, is sitting down in the conference room, and you need to speak to her at length about something important, rather than walking up to her and standing in front of her while speaking, you may sit beside her so the two of you are speaking at eye level. This is an adaptive behavior. When you assume the posture, gestures, and facial expressions of others, they may feel more at ease or in sync with you.

Seek feedback

Nonverbal communication is also improved by seeking feedback. You learned in Chapter 2 that *metacommunication* is communicating about communication. When someone comments on your communication, either positively or negatively, you can ask questions that are specific to your nonverbal communication. For example, you might ask:

- "How can I express my thoughts better to you next time?"
- "How did I come across to you just now?"
- "What aspect of my nonverbal communication makes you say that?"
- "How often do I appear this way to you?"
- "Are my nonverbal behaviors inconsistent with my verbal behaviors?"

Asking questions about your nonverbal communication may help you become more aware of how you come across and what you can do better.

Another way to gain feedback is to recreate an earlier conversation in front of your mirror. Take note of your facial expressions, gestures, and posture. What do you see and hear? How does your voice sound to you? What kinds of looks are you giving with your face?

These methods of feedback may also alert you to your **adaptors**: nonverbal behaviors which satisfy a physical or emotional need or help you manage physical and emotional sensations better. These behaviors often occur without your conscious awareness. Examples include scratching an itch, licking your lips, clearing your throat, doodling on a piece of paper to escape boredom, and tapping a pencil impatiently on a desk. If you're feeling tense or anxious, you

interactive adaptation theory The idea that competent communicators alter their nonverbal communication to interact successfully with others.

adaptors Nonverbal behaviors which satisfy a physical or emotional need or help you manage physical and emotional sensations better.

might click a ballpoint pen, chew on a pencil, bite your lips, pace, or bounce your knees.

Adaptors may communicate unintentional or contradictory messages. Your conversation partners may also find them annoying or distracting. Once you are aware of the adaptors that show up the most in your IPC, you can begin to consciously modify them or replace them with less conspicuous behaviors if necessary.

Avoid jumping to conclusions

If you're having a conversation with your sister and she gets quiet all of a sudden, do you assume you've said something that has made her upset or uncomfortable? What else could explain her shift in behavior? Perhaps she was just deep in thought or she assumed you needed time to talk without being interrupted. Before you jump to negative conclusions about your conversational partners' nonverbal behaviors, think about other possible reasons for them. When you consider different explanations, you may respond more patiently, thoughtfully, and strategically.

For example, people with neurodevelopmental disorders such as Asperger's syndrome, a condition on the autism spectrum, may not pick up on the nonverbal reactions of others very well. They may show a lack of emotional expression or avoid eye contact when speaking. You may interpret their nonverbal behaviors the wrong way if you don't consider how their condition affects their communication.

What might make someone appear aloof, fidgety, or short-tempered? It could be something temporary, such as stress, drug use (prescription or nonprescription), fatigue, physical pain, or drinking too much coffee, all of which influence nonverbal behavior. On the other hand, some people are just naturally more guarded or reserved around people they don't know due to shyness. Rather than assume you understand the reason for these individuals' behaviors, entertain other possibilities. Factors other than what is readily apparent, as Alyssa notes in her narrative, are worth considering. How can you relate to her experience?

"My parents often received lots of compliments from people on how well my two siblings and I behaved in public. Little did they know that my family communicated back and forth constantly without speaking. My mother would remind us to say please, thank you, and other kind words by the way she looked at us. She would tell us to stand up and smile with a tap to the back of our necks or a scratch to her earlobe. We knew what these signals meant: *display good manners this instant, or else.*" –Alyssa

In this clip from the reality show *The Real Housewives of Atlanta*, Cynthia Bailey and Peter Thomas are trying to navigate their relationship now that they're no longer married and Cynthia is dating. They meet to discuss a recent social event that felt awkward for both of them. What was their nonverbal communication like at the event? How did they use this follow-up conversation to clarify their perceptions and future expectations? On YouTube, search using the keywords: "RHOA: Cynthia Bailey Confronts Peter Thomas About Avoiding Her." (1:29)

Clarify your perceptions

When you're uncertain about what's causing a person's nonverbal behavior, ask a question for clarification. You might ask, for example, "Did what I say make sense?" or "Are you upset with Grandpa?" In previous chapters and in the section immediately before this we've explored how people can make snap judgments based on their initial perceptions. In Chapter 3 you learned about *perception checking*. A perception check can help you clarify what lies behind a person's nonverbal behavior before you attach your own meaning to it.

A perception check starts with an observation statement using I-language that focuses on what you're picking up with your senses. You may start by saying, "I notice," "I sense," "I see," "I heard," or "I get the feeling," followed by a question or two for clarification. This kind of language, generally speaking, may come across as less intimidating and confrontational, especially when you express yourself in a matter-of-fact way and with a voice that doesn't sound sarcastic, condescending, or angry.[58] Here are three examples:

- "**I notice** you're looking away from me a lot as we are speaking." (Observation) "Is there a reason for this?" (Question)

- "**I see** that you're biting your lip." (Observation) "Are you holding back something you need to say? Is everything okay?" (Questions)

- "**I sense** some tension in your voice." (Observation) "Are you feeling a little stressed about your performance this evening?" (Question)

You'll notice that with each perception check, you're simply making a non-judgmental observation of a nonverbal behavior. This technique helps your conversational partners see how they are coming across to you. Ask questions

chapter exercises

Assessing Your IPC: Expressiveness

Purpose: To enhance my nonverbal expressiveness.

Directions: Have an imaginary conversation with someone while standing in front of a mirror. Pretend that you are telling a friend about something that happened to you the other day. Speak naturally—like you normally do. Observe how you gesture, your facial expressions, and what you do with your mouth and eyes. Do your facial expressions and gestures represent how you want others to perceive you?

Next, have the same imaginary conversation again, but alter the expressiveness of your delivery. Change the rate, pitch, and volume of your voice. Animate your face more or less. Raise your eyebrows. Make your eyes dance. Add gestures to punctuate what you're saying, or suppress fidgets. Practicing this privately may help you feel less inhibited and self-conscious around others in public.

Here are some other ways to incorporate imaginary interactions with your mirror:

1. After you watch a television show or movie, go to the mirror and see if you can imitate one of the charismatic or dynamic characters from the show.

2. Imagine you are confidently introducing someone to a group of your coworkers or friends.

3. Memorize and deliver a riddle, joke, or humorous story or share an interesting story about yourself. Add punch and animation to your verbal communication with your voice, face, hands, and body.

4. Explain an idea or opinion you have about something in the news today with added expressiveness.

Building Your IPC Skills: Voice Work

Purpose: To improve the quality of my vocal delivery.

Directions: For the next 21 days, take five minutes a day to exercise your voice in the following areas. Monitor your communication by asking yourself these questions: What do I see as the benefit of this exercise? Do I notice changes in how often I express vocal utterances? What is different about my vocal delivery?

To reduce vocal utterances:

1. Record a message for someone. Before sending the message, listen to it. If you hear a vocal utterance, delete the message and rerecord it until your message is free of filler words.

2. At the start of a conversation, ask your conversational partner to alert you to any vocal utterances you commit. This is a fun way to get rid of vocal utterances.

To improve enunciation:

Practice tongue twisters daily. Numerous online sites, such as www.tongue-twister. net, offer a number of them. As you say each word, really extend your mouth muscles and use your tongue to attack each syllable. Say the words clearly. Pick up your rate of speed each time. Here are a few to get you started:

- Six sick slick slim sycamore saplings.
- A box of biscuits, a batch of mixed biscuits.
- Red lorry, yellow lorry, red lorry, yellow lorry.

To avoid a flat, monotone voice:

Read out loud daily. Modulate your voice. Alter your vocal pitch, rate, and volume. Do this when you leave voicemail messages for other people. Listen to your outgoing message before sending it. If your voice is monotone, too slow, or flat, or if your enunciation is not clear, delete and rerecord the message. Read out loud and record your voice. Painful? Yes, sometimes. But it's a great way to gain more awareness of how you're using your voice.

Want to earn a better grade on your test? Go to INQUIZITIVE to practice actively with this chapter's content and get personalized feedback along the way.

7

Emotional Expression

On a Friday night date at their town's summer carnival, Kellen has her eye on an adorable oversize stuffed pug, and her boyfriend, Ryan, can win it for her by sinking a few shots at Basket Toss. After trying for quite some time—and spending $50 in the process—Ryan finally succeeds. As he hands the prize over to Kellen, he says, "I'll do anything for you, boo," and kisses her on the cheek.

Would Ryan have done this for just anyone? No—$50 is a lot of money for a guy who's taking classes full-time and working part-time. But for Kellen, his girlfriend of 3 months, he doesn't give it a second thought.

Ryan and Kellen are in the midst of what attraction researchers call the honeymoon phase. Couples who are newly in love experience lower levels of serotonin and higher concentrations of other chemical messengers, such as dopamine—a combination that mirrors the brain chemistry of people who have obsessive-compulsive disorder.[1] This may explain why Ryan and Kellen can't stop thinking about each other when they're not together, why they have fits of jealousy and possessiveness, and why they often forego sleep in favor of all-night talking marathons.

According to conventional wisdom, the honeymoon phase lasts anywhere from 6 months to 2 years. One study suggests it can exceed 30 months

The emotions we experience, like the romantic ones felt by this couple, play a powerful role in our interpersonal communication. When we express and manage them effectively, our emotions can lead to healthy and happy relationships.

depending on the couple.[2] But what happens when this early stage is over? As we'll discuss at the end of this chapter, interpersonal communication, not brain chemistry, may make staying in love possible.

Along with romantic enchantment, emotions such as distrust, joy, nostalgia, amusement, confusion, awe, excitement, and boredom color your perceptions and influence what you remember, what you think about, the choices you make, and how you relate to others. In this chapter, we'll (1) define emotions and examine their relationship to interpersonal communication, (2) identify common emotional challenges within relationships, and (3) explore ways to manage and express emotions with greater competence.

7.1 Emotion and IPC

Whenever Sharon visits her close friend Julia, she brings along her 3-year-old son Bradley. Like many toddlers, Bradley is prone to frequent meltdowns, and Julia feels stressed and anxious when he acts out. The last time Sharon and Bradley came over to Julia's apartment, Bradley dropped to the floor kicking and screaming, knocking over—and breaking—one of Julia's prized ceramic artworks. Sharon apologized for her son's behavior but didn't offer to pay for or replace the broken piece. Julia felt disrespected and stopped inviting her over.

After a few weeks apart from Sharon, Julia's frustrations began to dissipate, and she considered the situation again with a clear head. She was still upset about what happened, but she missed spending time with her friend even more. So, she came up with a solution: she would suggest visiting Sharon at her house next time. That way, Bradley might feel more comfortable, and he would be closer to his toys to keep himself entertained. If his behavior were to become too stressful for Julia, she could come up with an excuse to leave.

What do you think of Julia's idea? What would you say or do if you were in her position? The communication choices we make relative to our emotions are important because they can greatly affect our relationships. In Section 7.1, you'll learn about the many facets of emotion and its potential to influence your interpersonal communication and relationships.

Emotion is a process

An **emotion** (or feeling) is a psychological and physiological response to an activating event. The *psychological* reaction you have occurs in your mind—you become aware of something and have thoughts about it. The *physiological* reaction occurs within your body—your temperature or heart rate might change, and levels of certain hormones or brain chemicals may increase or decrease.[3]

To understand emotion as a process (see **FIGURE 7.1**), imagine you're at work and you overhear your coworker Warren talking about you with several other people in your department. This is the *activating event.* You are *perceptually aware* of and focusing your attention on what Warren is saying, and you arrive at a *cognitive interpretation*: he's talking about you in a very uncomplimentary way. At the same time, a physiological reaction occurs.[4] Your body temperature rises, your heart rate increases, and your muscles tense. Your nervous system triggers the release of certain hormones such as cortisol and norepinephrine.[5] How do you feel right now? You're angry! The combination of your cognitive interpretation and physiological reaction is what we call emotion.

emotion A psychological and physiological response to an activating event.

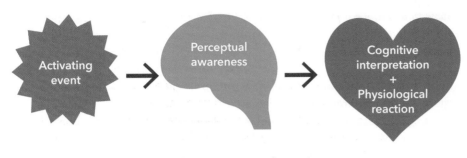

FIGURE 7.1 **Process of Emotion**

An activating event may cause you to experience a blend of emotions. **Blended emotions** are two or more emotions that you feel simultaneously. For instance, if Warren is someone you trust, hearing him talk badly about you may make you feel not only angry but also sad and betrayed. It's also possible to experience **conflicting emotions**—that is, two opposite emotions—at the same time. You may, for example, feel motivated to confront Warren but also dread doing so.

Sometimes you experience an emotion in response to an emotion. Have you ever felt guilty or ashamed after erupting at someone in a furious outburst? This is called a **meta-emotion**, an emotion about an emotion—or a feeling about a feeling.[6] You may feel embarrassed after you angrily confront Warren, for example.

Compared to an emotion, a **mood** is an emotional state that lacks a clear cause or contextual stimulus. A mood is tied to biochemical cycles associated with brain activity, sleep, and hormones. Have you ever felt like you were in a funk and didn't know why? Do you sometimes feel happy for no apparent reason? These are moods, not emotions. Moods generally last longer than emotions and are less intense, but they can affect your emotional reactions. For example, you may feel more irritated by a sibling's behavior if you're already in a bad mood.

Emotional experience and expression

Emotional experience is the internal sensation and identification of your own emotions. Many factors influence which emotions you experience; one in particular is how you choose to think about an activating event. Renowned psychologist Albert Ellis is considered the founder of **rational-emotive theory (RET)**. According to RET, your cognitive interpretation of an activating event has a lot more to do with your emotions than the event itself does. In other words, how you think about an event dictates how you will feel about it.[7]

For example, let's say your uncle shares a somewhat embarrassing story about you to family members who are gathered to celebrate a holiday. His story is an activating event. What you choose to think about your uncle's intentions and the story—whether negative (*He's trying to humiliate me again!*) or positive

blended emotions Two or more emotions that you feel simultaneously.

conflicting emotions Contradictory emotions that you feel at the same time.

meta-emotion An emotion about an emotion—or a feeling about a feeling.

mood An emotional state that lacks a clear cause or contextual stimulus.

emotional experience The internal sensation and identification of your own emotions.

rational-emotive theory (RET) The idea that your cognitive interpretation of an event has more to do with your emotion than the activating event does.

emotional contagion The transfer of feelings from one person to another.

emotional expression How you communicate your emotions to others.

(I have to admit, it's a pretty funny story)—may cause you to feel loved, honored, embarrassed, angry, indifferent, happy, sad, proud, or some combination of these emotions.

Another factor that plays a role in emotional experience is emotional contagion. **Emotional contagion** is the transfer of feelings from one person to another.[8] For instance, you may feel especially cheerful and lively when you're out to lunch with your bubbly, enthusiastic girlfriend. You may also find yourself feeling sad or happy at a funeral or wedding because the emotions commonly experienced at these events move through the area, traveling from person to person.

Emotional expression is how you communicate your emotions to others. You express your emotions verbally and nonverbally, directly and indirectly. For example, when Caleb arrives late to pick up Hakeem for their school's last home football game, Hakeem might verbalize his annoyance indirectly by asking, "Lose your watch?" Or, he could express his emotions directly: "You're late and I'm not happy about it. We've missed the first quarter."

Hakeem may also convey his displeasure nonverbally. He could do so directly, by giving Caleb a stern look or speaking with a sharp tone of voice, or indirectly, by sighing softly or casually glancing at his watch.

You may also try to conceal your emotions—that is, avoid emotional expression—for any number of reasons. For example, you may hesitate to express your love for someone if you fear rejection, or you may try to appear composed to help others stay calm in a crisis. You may remain silent or even smile at a joke you find distasteful to avoid an awkward moment.

Real Housewives of Atlanta reality star Phaedra Parks and her son Ayden are experiencing significant emotions on their way to Ayden's first day of school. Use the process of emotion—the activating event, perceptual awareness, cognitive interpretation, and physiological reaction—to describe their emotional experience. How do they express their emotions? On YouTube, search using the keywords: "RHOA: Ayden brings Phaedra to tears on his first day of school." (2:27)

Emotions are facilitative and debilitative

Is anger a positive or negative emotion? How about sadness or excitement? An emotion is *facilitative* or *debilitative* if it helps or hinders you in some way. From an interpersonal communication perspective, **facilitative emotions** help you improve the quality of your communication and enhance relational outcomes. **Debilitative emotions** have the opposite effect—they interfere with your ability to communicate and produce negative relational outcomes.[9]

Nervousness, for example, is potentially facilitative or debilitative. A little nervousness before a job interview may prompt you to prepare adequately ahead of time so that you perform at your best. Excessive nervousness, however, may cause you to stay up all night and feel fatigued during the interview.

In the following narrative, Lorana describes a situation she faced with her mother. How were her emotions both facilitative and debilitative?

> "At age 19 I was always angry and frustrated with my mom. We argued a lot, often in nasty ways, which hurt our relationship. These same emotions–anger and frustration–motivated me to venture out and become independent. After I moved out, we got along much better. It really helped improve our relationship!" –Lorana

The intensity, duration, and frequency of an emotion can make it more facilitative or debilitative. *Intensity* is the extent to which you feel something. *Duration* is how long you feel it, and *frequency* is how often you feel it. For example, if the stress of a looming deadline helps your work team stay focused and communicate quickly and efficiently, then it is facilitative; the emotion is high in intensity but short in duration. However, if your work team is constantly hit with multiple deadlines (frequency) over a short period of time (duration), it can be debilitative, especially if it causes infighting and burnout.

Emotional intelligence

Emotional intelligence (EI) is the ability to identify, manage, and express your emotions effectively. EI also includes the ability to perceive, understand the reasons for, and respond skillfully to the feelings of others.[10]

Exercising emotional intelligence can help you establish close, satisfying relationships.[11] A person with high EI makes conscientious decisions, uses appropriate humor, exhibits self-control in response to sudden provocations or outbursts, and is able to offer helpful emotional support without getting entangled in other people's problems.[12]

In the world of work, successful leaders often demonstrate communication characteristics associated with EI. For example, they may sense their employees' emotions and respond with empathy and care. **Empathy** is the ability to

facilitative emotion
An emotion that helps you improve the quality of your communication and enhance relational outcomes.

debilitative emotion An emotion that interferes with your ability to communicate and produces negative relational outcomes.

emotional intelligence (EI) The ability to identify, manage, and express your emotions effectively, including the ability to read and respond to the emotions of others.

empathy The ability to understand, appreciate, and value what someone else is feeling.

emotional display rules The social dos and don'ts of emotional expression.

understand, appreciate, and value what someone else is feeling. Empathy goes beyond acknowledging another person's emotions; it involves experiencing what that person feels. When you communicate with empathy, the other person can sense it.[13]

To some extent, your emotional intelligence is influenced by genetics and how you were raised, but it's also a form of intelligence that you can develop.[14]

The influence of culture and gender

Throughout your life you'll receive direct and indirect messages encouraging you to adhere to certain **emotional display rules**, or the social dos and don'ts of emotional expression.[15] For example, you may act very excited about a coworker's promotion even though you don't think she's the best person for the job. Why? You are following a social rule that was likely taught or modeled to you: A good friend shares in another's joy or sadness.

While some rules are instilled in us by others, we can also create our own emotional display rules. For example, you may make it a rule not to let your parents see you upset because you know they worry about you a lot.

It's difficult to talk about emotional display rules without mentioning culture and gender. Both play a role in how we perceive and express emotions.

Culture

You may belong to an organizational or societal culture that influences how you express your feelings. For example, one study found that 77% of soldiers returning from combat in Iraq and Afghanistan did not reveal their symptoms of depression and anxiety to their commanding officers largely out of fear that doing so may tarnish their evaluations in some way.[16] Conversely, soldiers returning from active military duty report feeling much more comfortable sharing their emotions within an encouraging, understanding environment, such as a private, confidential support group for veterans with post-traumatic stress disorder. Many anonymous online support groups are popular for this reason.[17]

Along with organizational cultures, broader societal cultures also influence how you perceive and express emotions. For example, people of different cultures vary in how they interpret emotions. Researchers have found that people in the United States tend to look more at a person's mouth to determine how they are feeling (that is, they look for a slight smile or frown), while in Japan, people are more likely to focus on a person's eyes.[18] In traditional Chinese culture, emotional expression is restrained. Comparatively, traditional Mexican culture encourages open displays of emotion.[19]

Gender

Men and women express emotions in ways that are more alike than different. However, some studies do suggest patterns in communication style that differ between gender lines. While the conclusions drawn from research are a bit mixed, generally speaking, women are more likely to express feelings such as joy and sadness outwardly and are better able to recognize emotions in others. Men are more likely to emote anger and aggression and are less likely to accurately recognize the emotions of others.[20]

Gender socialization plays a significant role in how we experience and express emotions.[21] In a provocative and thoughtful TED Talk, writer and activist Soraya Chemaly shares how men are often raised to suppress emotions that make them appear vulnerable, such as fear and grief. Women, in contrast, are socialized to mask feelings of anger or hostility. Women are told that it's not "ladylike" to lash out, but boys are not similarly shamed for aggressive behavior; it may be dismissed with the adage, "boys will be boys." To hear Chemaly speak, search on YouTube using the keywords: "The power of women's anger." (11:44)

Biology also plays a role in how we experience and express emotions. Males and females produce different levels of certain hormones,[22] which may influence the intensity of emotions such as aggression, love, sadness, euphoria, and excitability.[23] In addition, neuroimaging studies indicate that the functional connectivity of male and female brains is different, especially in the area of the amygdala, which is believed to regulate hormones, perceptions, and emotions.[24]

section review

7.1 Emotion and IPC

An emotion is a psychological and physiological reaction to an event. The emotional process begins with an activating event, followed by an awareness of the event, resulting in a cognitive interpretation and physiological response. Emotional experience is the internal sensation and identification of your own emotions. Emotional expression is how you communicate your emotions to others. Emotions may serve a facilitative (helpful) or debilitative (unhelpful) purpose in terms of your IPC and relationships. Emotional intelligence (EI) is the ability to identify, manage, and express emotions effectively, along with the ability to perceive, understand, and respond to the emotions of others. Culture and gender play a role in the establishment of emotional display rules.

Key Terms

emotion, *p. 172*	emotional experience, *p. 173*	debilitative emotion, *p. 175*
blended emotions, *p. 173*	rational-emotive theory (RET), *p. 173*	emotional intelligence (EI), *p. 175*
conflicting emotions, *p. 173*	emotional contagion, *p. 174*	empathy, *p. 175*
meta-emotion, *p. 173*	emotional expression, *p. 174*	emotional display rules, *p. 176*
mood, *p. 173*	facilitative emotion, *p. 175*	

(continued)

Comprehend It?

1. Define each of the key terms in Section 7.1. To further your understanding of these terms, create examples to support your definitions.

2. Compare and contrast:
   - emotions and moods
   - blended and conflicting emotions
   - facilitative versus debilitative emotions

3. Using a real-life scenario, explain how emotion is a process.

Apply It!

One aspect of emotional intelligence is the ability to accurately perceive and interpret the emotions of others. How well do you perceive emotions? You can take an illuminating online quiz by searching for:

"Emotional intelligence quiz-greater good" (greater-good.berkeley.edu/quizzes/ei_quiz). What does your score suggest? Share your results and impressions with a classmate.

7.2 Emotional challenges

One of our students, Jason, stumbled into an awkward situation while out to lunch one afternoon with his wife, Anna. Anna had gotten up from the table to refill her drink when Jason noticed a text message pop up on her phone that mentioned him by name. Curious, but against his better judgment, Jason tapped the message to read more. What did he find? A very long group text between Anna and four of her closest friends, all about how disgruntled they were with their husbands.

Jason's feelings were hurt. He felt shocked and betrayed, but he knew that Anna would feel the same if she found out that he'd read her text messages. What would you say or do if you were Jason?

Those of us in close, interdependent relationships are bound to experience emotional challenges from time to time. While there are many types of emotional challenges, in this section we'll highlight six in particular.

As you read Section 7.2, take some time to really think about each emotional challenge. Which ones are causing problems for you interpersonally? How often do they show up in your relationships, and why?

Emotional labor

One of our students, Sabrina, is a correctional officer. She strives to treat inmates with care, concern, and respect, but in order to do her job she also has to be suspicious, strong, and tough. She says, "It's taxing trying to juggle these different emotions."

emotional labor The effort it takes to generate, manage, and mask your emotions.

Sabrina describes the challenge of **emotional labor**, or the effort it takes to generate, manage, and mask your emotions. Some jobs require a lot of emotional labor.[25] For example, flight attendants are expected to be upbeat around passengers no matter how they might really feel. Emotional labor happens outside of work, too. In order to get along with a friend, family member, or romantic partner, for instance, you may feel like you have to suppress your frustrations to keep the peace.

One of our students, Carolyn, described how her grandmother is like a mom to her. She calls Carolyn at least once every day, sometimes more. She often drops off gifts to Carolyn's children or just stops by to ask how one of their doctor's appointments went. Each visit often turns into a lengthy chat. Carolyn says that her grandmother's efforts to be a part of their life mean a lot to her, but they also take an emotional toll on her at times. She often has to mask her negative feelings and fake the emotions her grandmother expects from her—such as gratitude and enthusiasm.

In close, long-term relationships, emotional labor imbalances are a common challenge. Within a family, the burdens of emotional labor may be distributed unequally if, for example, one parent is expected to do all of the discipline (not an easy thing to do from an emotional standpoint) or is the one the children always go to when they need help with a problem.

In situations where you're feeling burnt out from emotional labor, it's important to acknowledge it and find a healthy outlet or coping response. In the case of an emotional labor imbalance, talking openly to a relational partner about it and seeking solutions is essential.

Avoidance

Sometimes our emotions are made worse when we avoid interactions that are likely to trigger unpleasant emotions. **Avoidance** is the act of evading or skirting a person, interaction, or conversational topic. Avoidance behaviors include quickly changing the subject, not responding to a text, or acting like everything is fine when it's not.

You may rely on avoidance tactics to skip awkward or uncomfortable feelings in the short term, but the consequences may affect your relationships negatively in the long run. For example, not speaking up in meetings at work because you are shy or nervous may keep you in your comfort zone, but it's counterproductive if it keeps your good ideas from being heard. Not confronting a family member about a problem may allow you to sidestep an unpleasant interaction initially, but in the long term it may make you feel increasingly resentful.[26]

In addition, not talking openly about your feelings may result in passive-aggressiveness.[27] **Passive-aggressiveness** is a form of indirect hostility that allows the sender to appear outwardly noncombative. Let's say you're upset with your boss, Irene. You would be acting passive-aggressively if, rather than talking to her about it in a direct, honest, and productive way, you instead engaged in more indirect or covert behaviors that reflect your negative feelings toward her.

avoidance The act of evading a person, interaction, or conversational topic.

passive-aggressiveness A form of indirect hostility that allows the sender to appear outwardly noncombative.

Examples include "unknowingly" misinforming her about something, "forgetting" to do something she asks, or "accidentally" making a mistake that affects her adversely. In her absence, you may take longer than usual to return her calls. If Irene needs your assistance, you may make up a false excuse as to why you can't help her out.

If Irene senses that you're being passive-aggressive, she may get quite angry and confront you about it outright. She may also respond by being passive-aggressive in return, which would likely fuel the animosity between you.

Listed in **TABLE 7.1** are several types of avoidance.[28] How often do these avoidance behaviors occur in your interpersonal communication? What effect do they have on your emotions? What about your relationships? After reading about each one, see if you can identify the type of avoidance depicted in the cartoon.

It's important to point out that sometimes avoidance can benefit a relationship. Avoiding certain topics or interactions may help improve relationship satisfaction and draw attention away from irreconcilable differences.[29] For example, if you strongly dislike your best friend's new romantic partner, but he dismisses all of your concerns, it might be a good idea to avoid the topic in the future. If you know that nothing you say will change his mind, you may decide that preserving your relationship with him is more important than fighting over something you cannot control.

table 7.1	Types of Avoidance Behaviors
Types of Avoidance	**Description**
Clowning	Joking around to sidestep an uncomfortable topic or issue
Feigned apathy	Appearing not to care
Feigned ignorance	Acting as though you don't have certain knowledge when you do
Feigned helplessness	Pretending like you are not able to do something
Impervious admission	Refusing to acknowledge responsibility or admit wrongdoing
Impervious response	Shutting down or refusing to talk
Placating	Agreeing or going along to appease or pacify someone despite how you really feel
Sugarcoating	Being overly positive about things when problems surface; downplaying a conflict, making light of it, or acting as if everything is fine

Displacement

Imagine you've returned home after a rough day at work—your boss has been giving you a really hard time. As you try to start dinner, your kids run into the kitchen excitedly, laughing and screaming loudly as they try to peg each other with their toy guns. You suddenly lose your cool and yell, "I swear you two are driving me crazy! Stop playing and go finish your homework! And how many times do I have to tell you to clean up the mess in the living room? You only think of yourselves."

You see a look of surprise and sadness cross their faces at your sudden anger. They had nothing to do with your bad day, and now you're taking it out on them. **Displacement** occurs when you lash out at someone who is not the cause of your negative emotions. Anyone who does the littlest thing to annoy you may get the full brunt of your feelings.

If you are upset with how your boss treated you and you don't address the conflict constructively or work through your emotions (we'll discuss some emotional management techniques in Section 7.3), your feelings will likely linger, even if you try your best to mask them. In this situation, you could avoid displacing your negative emotions by taking a deep breath, counting to 10, and then letting your children know you're feeling grumpy and why: "Hey guys, I've had a very rough day at work and I'm feeling cranky. Would you give me 20 minutes to take some deep breaths and calm down? Some peace and quiet will help me. Let's have you play outside or in the basement."

To make sure your displaced emotions don't cycle through your communication partners, take some time to resolve your feelings when you catch them spilling over into your relationships with other people. If you take out your anger with your boss on your children, for instance, they will likely feel that they cannot express to you the hurt and anger you caused them. In turn, they might displace their feelings on each other or another sibling.

Trapping

Trapping is the act of asking someone to communicate in a certain way and then making that person regret doing what you've asked. A common example of trapping is asking someone for complete honesty. Let's consider Michelle, who finds herself in conflict with members of her soccer team and wants her girlfriend Morgan to tell her she's in the right. However, what she says is, "I want you to give me your honest opinion." When Morgan reluctantly answers, "I think your actions are only making things worse with your teammates," Michelle gets upset with her. She even gives her the cold shoulder for a while.

In another instance of trapping, Michelle asks Morgan, "Could you make plans for us this weekend? I know you don't like making plans, but I want you to show some initiative." Morgan comes up with some ideas and shares them,

displacement The act of lashing out at someone who is not the cause of your negative emotions.

trapping The act of asking someone to communicate in a certain way and then making that person regret doing what you've asked.

but Michelle acts unenthused and even suggests doing something else.

How would you feel if you were Morgan? In the first example, you might feel like Michelle set you up to make her mad. The next time Michelle asks you to be honest, you may simply tell her what you think she wants to hear to avoid a negative reaction. In the second example, you may feel reluctant to make plans for the two of you in the future. You may even say to Michelle, "Why should I bother making plans if you're just going to insist on doing what you want anyway?"

From a relational standpoint, it's important to guard against trapping. When our relational partners make an effort to meet our expectations, it's important that our communication choices support and encourage their efforts. If you were to go back to the situations you read involving Michelle and Morgan, what could Michelle say or do that is the opposite of trapping?

Withholding

When you feel slighted by someone or even deeply hurt, you may engage in the act of withholding. **Withholding** occurs when you purposely deprive someone of something they want or need in order to express your negative feelings. This is often used as a *compliance-gaining* strategy, which will be explored in Chapter 9. You may withhold attention, interaction, affection, intimacy, or access to opportunities or resources to express feelings of anger, hurt, or frustration. The silent treatment is an example of withholding. Not inviting someone to your party is another. Schoolchildren may exercise withholding by not allowing someone to sit with them at lunch or participate in an activity during recess.

Don McCabe, author of *To Teach a Dyslexic*, writes of how he withheld something as simple as eye contact as a way to vent his frustrations with teachers he considered unsympathetic to his learning disability. He writes:

> *I enjoyed baiting my teachers. My favorite stunt was to look out the window while the teacher was talking and act like I was not paying attention. Of course, I was listening intently. Inevitably, the teacher would try to make an example out of me. The teacher would call on me, fully expecting me to say "What?" And then she could tell me to pay attention. Only it never worked that way. I would answer the question without bothering to turn my head. More than once the teacher was so furious that I could look out the window and still answer the question that I was sent down to [the principal's] office.*[30]

withholding When you purposely deprive someone of something they want or need in order to express your negative feelings and exert control.

Withholding can also be used to manipulate and control a person's behavior. A blogger by the name of Ossiana Tepfenhart describes a previous relationship:

"When I did what he wanted me to do, he was attentive and caring. When I didn't? Well, he'd stonewall me, ghost me on dates, or just otherwise act icily toward me until I'd cave."

Ossiana goes on to write, "Over the months we dated, I felt more and more hurt. I began to question why he'd hurt me this way, or whether it was all really my fault. I began to wonder what was wrong with me. Any time I'd try to discuss this with him, he'd shut it down."[31]

Withholding often works as a compliance-gaining strategy because it is human nature to seek approval and belonging. When a relational partner withholds affection or acceptance, it hurts. No one likes rejection, especially when the person rejecting us is someone we want to be with. Withholding, however, puts a strain on a relationship. Many relationships become unhealthy or end because one or both partners revert to withholding as a means of emotional expression and control.

Irrational thinking

Many of our negative, debilitative emotions are supported by irrational beliefs, also referred to as **fallacies**. Fallacies may lead us to make communication choices that limit our ability to express and manage emotions effectively.[32] Common beliefs include the fallacies of *approval*, *causation*, *overgeneralization*, *perfection*, and *should*.

fallacy An irrational belief that feeds into negative, debilitative emotions.

fallacy of approval The belief that it's essential to seek and win everyone's acceptance and admiration.

The fallacy of approval

If you think it's essential to seek and win everyone's acceptance and admiration, you're operating from the **fallacy of approval**. While it's generally advantageous

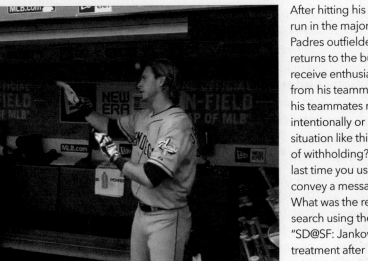

After hitting his first career home run in the major leagues, San Diego Padres outfielder Travis Jankowski returns to the bullpen expecting to receive enthusiastic congratulations from his teammates. Whether his teammates reacted this way intentionally or not, how might a situation like this fit the description of withholding? When was the last time you used withholding to convey a message to someone? What was the result? On YouTube, search using the keywords: "SD@SF: Jankowski gets silent treatment after home run." (0:45)

to get along with other people and help them when you can, this fallacy may cause you to go out of your way to make everyone happy to such an extent that you sacrifice your own principles and needs. You'll typically have a very hard time saying "no" to requests or speaking up when you disagree. You may sugar-coat everything and try too hard to be nice.

The fallacy of causation

When you're convinced that a communication choice will definitely result in a certain outcome, you're committing the **fallacy of causation**. For example, if you lost an expensive piece of jewelry that your mother lent you, you might think, *I can't possibly tell her I lost that ring, she'll be furious!* If you believe this, you might be right, but you may just as well be wrong. She may not get upset at all, or she may not get as upset as you predict.

In the same way, it's not accurate to blame someone for causing you to do something, especially when it comes to your emotions. For example, if you say to your friend Zane, "I wouldn't have gotten so mad at you if you'd simply texted me back," you're suggesting that you had nothing to do with your own anger, and instead Zane was the sole cause. Or, if you say, "I wouldn't have had so much to drink if we had left the party when I wanted," you're implying that Zane was the cause of your drinking behavior.

The fallacy of overgeneralization

The **fallacy of overgeneralization** entails taking a single instance (or an isolated occurrence) and believing that it's an enduring absolute. If you think, *I bombed that interview. I'm terrible at giving interviews*, you've interpreted one interview as proof that you don't interview well at all, or ever. This kind of overgeneralization can lead to feelings of hopelessness, frustration, and anxiety.

Overgeneralization can also affect your interpersonal communication with others. Let's say your friend Mikayla looks at her phone several times during a conversation with you and you say, "You're always glued to your phone." This would be an overgeneralization. An alternative would be to simply point out Mikayla's behavior using I-language: "I noticed you've looked at your phone a couple times. Is everything okay?" This communication choice doesn't overgeneralize Mikayla's behavior, and it's less likely to offend her.

The fallacy of perfection

You subscribe to the **fallacy of perfection** if you think it's essential to communicate exceptionally well all the time. While striving to communicate as effectively as you can, as often as you can is a good goal, to assume that one communication misstep makes you a complete failure is self-defeating. If you're influenced by this fallacy, you usually have a very hard time acknowledging your mistakes or admitting what you don't know. You may even mask your feelings of uncertainty or inadequacy because you believe that doing so is a sign of weakness.

fallacy of causation The belief that a communication choice will definitely result in a certain outcome.

fallacy of overgeneralization The belief that a single instance (or an isolated occurrence) signifies an enduring absolute.

fallacy of perfection The belief that it's essential to communicate exceptionally well all the time.

In this scene from the reality show *Teen Mom*, Cheyenne and her boyfriend Zach sit down to discuss what happened at a family barbecue. At what point in their conversation do you hear examples of the fallacy of should and the fallacy of overgeneralization? How is Cheyenne and Zach's conversation about this incident productive? On YouTube, search using the keywords: "Communication is Key | Teen Mom OG | MTV." (3:10)

The fallacy of should

If you expect others to think and behave like you do, and you get deeply disappointed when they don't, you're falling victim to the **fallacy of should**. The fallacy of should occurs when you think that someone hasn't done what is appropriate—what, in your view, *should* be done. Recognizing that your way is not the only way may help you avoid unnecessary arguments.

When you use the word *should*, you imply that one choice is right and any other choice is wrong. For example, if you say, "I should spend time with my parents this weekend," it implies that if you choose not to, you're guilty of something—perhaps not making your parents a priority. A better alternative would be to say, "I want to see my parents soon when it's a good time for both of us." You may find that it's better to spend time with them when it doesn't feel like an obligation. At certain times, it might increase your health and happiness to say something like, "I want to see my parents, just not this weekend. I'd rather go waterskiing with my friends instead."

fallacy of should The belief that others ought to think and behave just as you do.

section review

7.2 **Emotional challenges**

There are certain challenges associated with emotional experience and expression. These challenges, if not managed effectively, may damage a relationship. They include emotional labor imbalances, avoidance, displacement, trapping behavior, withholding, and fallacious thoughts. Common fallacies include the fallacies of approval, causation, overgeneralization, perfection, and should.

(continued)

Key Terms

emotional labor, *p. 178*

avoidance, *p. 179*

passive-aggressiveness, *p. 179*

displacement, *p. 181*

trapping, *p. 181*

withholding, *p. 182*

fallacy, *p. 183*

fallacy of approval, *p. 183*

fallacy of causation, *p. 184*

fallacy of overgeneralization, *p. 184*

fallacy of perfection, *p. 184*

fallacy of should, *p. 185*

Comprehend It?

1. Define each of the key terms in Section 7.2. To further your understanding of these terms, create examples to support your definitions.

2. Compare and contrast the fallacies of approval, causation, overgeneralization, perfection, and should.

Apply It!

Of the challenges you just read about—emotional labor, avoidance, displacement, trapping, withholding, and irrational thinking—which ones are the most difficult for you to deal with? Which ones affect your relationships the most? Why?

7.3 Improving emotional expression

Evelyn is on the phone with her daughter, Jackie, as she packs her luggage for a weeklong trip to visit her. Evelyn has just learned that Jackie won't be able to pick her up at the airport because she has a routine dentist appointment. Evelyn is upset and says:

> *I can't believe you're going to make me take a cab from the airport. I'm already flying a thousand miles to see you. I bought an expensive plane ticket, and now I have to pay a taxi driver to get dropped off at your house. You've known for almost two months that I was coming. It would have been nice to have you pick me up so we could grab some lunch. This is one heck of a way to greet your mother.*

Evelyn's feelings of frustration, anger, and hurt are coming across loud and clear. Her tone of voice punctuates her emotions. Did Evelyn express her feelings in the best manner? Jackie has feelings about her mom's message, too. What she says next will likely influence the direction of their conversation, and it may also influence the quality of their time together during Evelyn's visit. Their ability to effectively identify, manage, and express their emotions will affect their communication—which in turn will affect the relationship they have now and in the future.

In Section 7.3, we'll explore ways to expand your emotional intelligence. You will learn effective strategies for identifying, managing, and expressing your emotions—all skills that will help you achieve and maintain satisfying relationships.

Identify and manage your emotions

Has an argument with a family member ever ruined your day? If a social engagement is canceled, do you feel down about it for hours? How fast can you bounce back when something adversely affects you? How resilient are you emotionally?

Sometimes you may feel stuck in your negative emotions. Other people may say or do things that trigger these feelings, but no one can make you feel a certain way indefinitely. It's important to remember that you have the ability to alter your emotions: You can decide how important a communication event is to you and choose how you think about it.[33]

Any time you notice that your emotions are turning negative or becoming debilitative, find a quiet place—somewhere you can be alone for a few minutes—and talk yourself through the following seven questions. These questions are also a great way to recognize and avoid the fallacies we covered in Section 7.2. We're big proponents of doing this exercise out loud so you can hear yourself think.

Identify

What am I feeling? Use the words that best express the feeling you're having: "I feel tense," "I feel angry," or "I feel anxious." As you do this, pay attention to your body. Do you feel muscle tension in your neck or shoulders? Is your knee bouncing in a nervous fashion? Has your breathing or heart rate increased? Do you feel flushed or suddenly sweaty?

Why do I feel this way? Identify the activating event or trigger. There may be more than one: "I'm irritated because I don't have time to grocery shop, and there's no food in the house. I'm angry because the house is a mess, and I'm the only one who will clean it."

Manage

How can I look at my situation differently? Asking and answering this question can help you view a situation more positively. You might say, for example, "I can order takeout just for tonight. I'll have time to shop this weekend," and "If the house is a mess, it's not the end of the world."

You can also reorient your feelings by focusing on other priorities that warrant more of your time, thoughts, and energy: "I can shop (or clean) any time, but right now my focus is on my deadlines at work."

What can I do to make myself feel better? This question focuses your thoughts on solutions and constructive action. Think of various things that normally put you in a good mood and are healthy and productive—and start doing them. Identify and jot down small steps you can take to make things better, and then begin checking them off your list: "Today I'll use my lunch hour to go for a walk in the sun and get some exercise. I can also order groceries for pickup on my phone while walking."

What is outside of my control? Pinpoint what you don't have control over, and let it go. Focus on what is within your control: "I can't control how busy I am right now. I can't do anything about the house except to calmly explain my concerns to my roommates and ask them to do their chores by tomorrow night."

What is right about my life? Think about all of the good things in your life—from little things you may take for granted, like owning your own toothbrush or having access to a shower, to big things, like your health and the relationships that matter to you. You might say to yourself, "I am so glad I have the weekend off to catch up with a few chores and unwind."

What hasn't changed in my life? This is a great question to consider when life feels like it's spiraling out of your control. Rather than mull over what's changing, think instead about what is constant in your life: "I still enjoy my job despite the stress it causes me at times."

In his narrative, Devon explains one way that he and his family members would encourage each other to manage their negative emotions. How might you benefit from this approach?

"When I was a kid, I remember standing in the yard with my mom and sister. We had just given our dog Lucky a bath. She jumped out of the outdoor tub and started shaking her fur like crazy to dry off. She put her whole body into it. My mom said, 'See, you can do the same thing when you are angry or upset, just shake it off.' We stood there and shook our bodies just like Lucky. It was hilarious. Later, whenever one of us would get upset, someone would say, 'Just shake it off,' and imitate our beloved dog. It was hard not to laugh or smile." –Devon

Communicate your emotions competently

How often do you say something in the heat of the moment and later regret it? Have you ever sent a text impulsively? When handled carelessly, emotional expression can damage a friendship or the respect of your peers in a heartbeat; it can also contribute to long-term problems such as unsatisfying relationships or social isolation.

Sometimes a relational partner—whether a coworker, roommate, spouse, friend, or romantic partner—will say or do something that you didn't see coming. Perhaps it's a sudden display of emotion, a scathing remark, or a momentary lapse in judgment. You may be at a loss for words or so angry that you have to bite your tongue lest you say something mean—and pay for it later. How can you respond in these situations? Let's look at the following strategies for expressing your emotions effectively.

Postpone conversations strategically

Feelings such as anger, frustration, and grief may interfere with your capacity to think rationally and solve problems.[34] Even positive feelings such as excitement or pleasant surprise may make it difficult for you to communicate clearly, listen effectively, and respond patiently.[35]

If you're feeling distracted or overwhelmed by one of these emotions, consider postponing your conversation. In Chapter 4 you learned about *postponement*—deliberately delaying a conversation or response until you're ready to communicate effectively. Postponing gives you time to cool off and think about how best to respond. Taking several deep breaths or counting to ten are forms of postponement, as are longer breaks in conversation. You might give yourself ten minutes, an hour, or a day or two to pause and reflect before revisiting the subject.

When you suggest postponing a conversation, it may help to also propose some "homework." For example, Jayne senses that a conversation with her coworker Scott is getting tense. She could say, "How about we take a break from this discussion and come back to it tomorrow morning at 9:00 a.m.? Let's both think about how we want to divide up the responsibilities. Sound good?" Jayne might also say, "So that we're being mindful of each other, let's try to think about where we're both coming from and why, along with areas where we can compromise. What do you think?" This gives the cooling-off period a productive purpose.

Jayne and Scott are also using this time to gain perspective. **Perspective-taking** is the act of imagining that you are the other person in a given situation.[36] You can try to put yourself in the mind of your conversational partner(s). For example, Scott might contemplate one or more of the following questions:

- Why is this important to Jayne?
- Is there room for me to compromise or negotiate?
- How can I communicate that I understand where Jayne is coming from?
- Are there points that we both agree on? How might I acknowledge this?
- What questions can I ask to encourage Jayne to open up to me?
- Does Jayne deserve an apology? If so, how can I best express it to her?

Express your emotions asynchronously

In Chapter 2 you learned that *asynchronous communication* occurs when messages are sent back-and-forth with a delay in feedback. Sometimes it may help to convey your emotions in an asynchronous manner. If you're finding it really difficult to communicate with someone face-to-face, try writing a letter or an email. Relaying your thoughts and feelings to a friend, family member, coworker, or romantic partner in this way allows you to take as much time as you need to carefully and thoughtfully craft your message

perspective-taking The act of imagining that you are the other person in a given situation.

"It's my resignation in the form of a graphic novel."

before sending it. You might include something like this in your message:

> I don't intend for this letter to replace the conversation we'll have in person, but I need to start by putting my thoughts in writing. I appreciate you allowing me to do so in this manner. Let me know when it's a good time to talk.

When you write a letter or send an email, you eliminate the potential distractions of a face-to-face conversation: You can't get interrupted, sidetracked, or caught up in your own or the other person's emotions. This option may help you express what you need to say exactly how you want to say it, hopefully in a manner that is respectful and sensitive to the other person's feelings.

Research has also shown that writing out your thoughts and feelings is therapeutic, especially if it allows you to express your emotions honestly and openly.[37] You may never share what you've written, or if you do, it may be after letting a few days go by so you can gain more clarity regarding your feelings and how best to convey them.

Use I-language

"I feel ... because ... I need" statement A sentence structure that helps you focus on the behavior that affects you and what you'd like your relational partner to do.

As we discussed in Chapter 5, *I-language* is often an effective way to clearly state your message. If you need to confront a relational partner about a behavior that's troubled or upset you, you can do so in a way that focuses on how the behavior affects you emotionally and what you would like the person to do in the future. **"I feel ... because ... I need" statements** may help. Compared to you-statements, these statements come across as appropriately assertive but less harsh or abrasive, especially if they're expressed using a calm, polite, matter-of-fact voice.[38] Compare the negatively charged you-statements below with the more neutral "I feel" statements that follow. Which statements sound less confrontational to you?

- **A:** "You can't be counted on. You left me hanging again."
- **B:** "<u>I feel</u> frustrated <u>because</u> I had to wait 30 minutes and then call a cab. <u>I need</u> you to value my time by showing up when you say you're going to."

- **A:** "You put your uncle's feelings ahead of mine!"
- **B:** "<u>I feel</u> disrespected <u>because</u> your silence communicates that it's acceptable for your uncle to talk to me like that. <u>I need</u> you to speak up next time."

Validate

Ramón and Rick are star players for their high school basketball team. The game is intense and the outcome may affect their college basketball prospects.

Ramón: Rick, I've been open the last five times. You're not banking your shots so pass the ball.

Rick: You're right. I'm off tonight, and you've been open. Sorry, man. I'll look for you.

Ramón: I know there are some recruiters in the stands, and you must feel a lot of pressure. Relax. Show them how you can move the ball around.

The conversation begins with Ramón expressing his frustration with Rick. Rick validates Ramón, and Ramón reciprocates by validating Rick. **Validation** is the act of recognizing another person's stated or unstated thoughts, feelings, and needs. The purpose of validation is to acknowledge where a person is coming from, which leads to better communication and calmer emotions. There are many ways you can validate someone. Five of them are included in the acronym AAAAI:

- <u>Agree</u> with the facts or with the other person's perceptions.
- <u>Apologize</u> without making excuses—no "yeah, buts."
- <u>Acknowledge</u> the other person's thoughts and feelings.
- <u>Appreciate</u> the feedback you are receiving.
- <u>Identify</u> a solution.

validation The act of recognizing or acknowledging another person's stated or unstated thoughts, feelings, and needs.

When Rick says, "You're right. I'm off tonight," he's *agreeing* with the facts or at least with Ramón's perceptions. He *apologizes* and *identifies* a solution. Ramón *acknowledges* what he thinks Ramón is feeling—a lot of pressure to impress the recruiters.

Validating others can de-escalate or diffuse a tense situation. It's a confirming form of communication. If you were Ramón, how would you respond to Rick's communication? You'd likely find some of your negative feelings dissipate because you feel validated. You may even feel pretty good that you were able to identify a problem and have your teammate respond in such a mature and thoughtful manner.

Convey more gratitude

Taking time every day to think about what you have to be thankful for in life—perhaps as a part of a practice tied to deep relaxation exercises, meditation, or prayer—can do a lot to lift your spirits and well-being.[39] Expressing positive thoughts using words of praise, appreciation, and encouragement can do a world of good for your relationships too, whether at school, home, or work.

After hosting a dinner for their parents, Brooke (Jennifer Aniston) and her romantic partner Gary (Vince Vaughn) get into a major argument. After watching this scene pinpoint instances where Gary and Brooke could have validated each other using any of the A.A.A.A.I. validation approaches. How would validation help them to steer their conversation in a more positive, productive direction? On YouTube search using the keywords: "The BreakUp-fighting scene (2006)." (4:38)

For example, in the area of romantic relationships, a technique perfected by researchers John Gottman and Robert Levenson enables them to predict with 91% accuracy whether a couple is likely to stay together in the long run. How? By closely observing their interactions, Gottman and Levenson found they could separate the couples into two groups: those who were quick to compliment, praise, and assume the best in each other, and those who were not. The former group frequently used expressions of gratitude such as, "being here with you is really nice," or "I love having this time with you." These couples were far more likely to still be together, and happy, when the researchers checked in on them six years later.[40]

Make it a point every day to communicate the positive things you see in your relational partners. Let them know how they make your life better and what you appreciate about them. To help you turn this practice into a habit, try this technique. Put three pennies in your right pocket. Every time you express gratitude or offer a compliment, put one penny in your left pocket. Your goal is to get all three pennies in your left pocket by the end of the day. You can also do this with wristbands (switching three from your right wrist to your left wrist). You might even use your cell phone to track your daily effort.

Practice and seek forgiveness effectively

Saying you forgive a relational partner is one thing, but truly getting over a transgression and not allowing it to affect you is entirely different. Forgiveness is an emotional process that may require time and the ability to reconstruct your thoughts.

Holding on to resentment can be detrimental to your health, while practicing forgiveness can be beneficial.[41] In one study, when subjects were asked to think about and describe instances in which someone hurt them, their blood pressure and heart rate increased, as did their levels of muscle tension and perspiration. Holding grudges may induce a stress response that can affect heart health and immunity. Subjects also reported that ruminating about their grudges made them feel sad, angry, anxious, and less in control. When the subjects were asked to empathize with and project loving thoughts toward their transgressors, by contrast, their stress levels coasted downward.[42]

In order to forgive someone, it helps to stop dwelling on whatever that person did to wrong you. If you find yourself thinking about the offending behavior, tell yourself to stop, and then refocus your thoughts on something positive. You may even think to yourself, *I've let that go. I'm no longer going to allow this to affect me. I've moved past this.*

It's important to keep in mind that when you truly forgive someone, you also give up all rights to retaliate or to bring up the transgression again in future conversations. Research suggests that you can make the process of forgiveness easier if you don't say you've forgiven someone until you have done the emotional work necessary to move on. Also, if you express complete forgiveness to someone without attaching any conditions or stipulations, research suggests that you are less likely to harbor feelings of anger and hurt.[43]

When working through the negative feelings associated with someone's transgression, don't hold your feelings inside. Invite the person to sit down with you face-to-face and ask if you can explain your emotions and perspective without being interrupted. You can even share how you'd like to be listened to or what that person could do to make amends.

When you are attempting to forgive someone, it may help to recall the times in your life when you have wronged others and sought their forgiveness. Think about the past mistakes you've made and moments of poor judgment. Just as you are capable of transgressions, others are too. Perhaps someone gave you a second chance in the past. Here is an opportunity for you to do the same.

If you find yourself in a situation where you are the one seeking forgiveness, the following strategies can help. It may be easier to forgive someone— and for someone to forgive you—when forgiveness is sought in these ways:[44]

- Admit your wrongdoing. Do so without blaming anyone else or making excuses for your behavior.
- Apologize sincerely. Mean it with your words, voice, and body language.
- Make a firm commitment to not repeat the transgression.
- Try to make amends. Do something to make up for the hurt you've caused.
- Invite your relational partners to share how your actions affected them. Listen intently without interruption. Paraphrase what they say and validate their feelings.

Express your love to stay in love

At the start of this chapter, we introduced you to a couple, Kellen and Ryan, who are in the midst of what romance scholars call a honeymoon phase. What if we told you that expressing your emotions effectively can extend that period to 10, 20, or even 50 years? Studies have shown that the feelings associated with the honeymoon stage can exist in couples in both long-term and new romantic relationships.[45]

Romance researchers believe that certain practices may reinforce or kick-start a deeper romantic and emotional connection.[46] Try these behaviors to maintain or deepen your own romantic relationships:

- Stare into your romantic partner's eyes for at least two minutes on a regular basis while holding hands.
- Exercise together.
- Engage in more novel and spontaneous activities with each other and share your adventures with friends and family.
- Speak affectionately with your partner often. Make it a daily habit to praise, compliment, encourage, and show appreciation. Use endearing language with each other.

SOCIAL AWARENESS TOTAL _____	
0 1 2 3 4	I consider the impact of my decisions on other people.
0 1 2 3 4	I can easily tell if people around me are becoming annoyed.
0 1 2 3 4	I sense it when a person's mood changes.
0 1 2 3 4	I am able to be supportive when giving bad news to others.
0 1 2 3 4	I am generally able to understand the way other people feel.
0 1 2 3 4	My friends can tell me intimate things about themselves.
0 1 2 3 4	It genuinely bothers me to see other people suffer.
0 1 2 3 4	I usually know when to speak and when to be silent.
0 1 2 3 4	I care what happens to other people.
0 1 2 3 4	I understand when people's plans change.

SOCIAL SKILLS TOTAL _____	
0 1 2 3 4	I am able to show affection.
0 1 2 3 4	I am able to manage relationships well.
0 1 2 3 4	I find it easy to share my deep feelings with others.
0 1 2 3 4	I am good at motivating others.
0 1 2 3 4	I am a fairly cheerful person.
0 1 2 3 4	It is easy for me to make friends.
0 1 2 3 4	People tell me I am sociable and fun.
0 1 2 3 4	I like helping people.
0 1 2 3 4	Others can depend on me.
0 1 2 3 4	I am able to make someone else feel better if they are very upset.

Building Your IPC Skills: Validation

Purpose: To help myself practice using validation.

Directions: After reading the dialogue between Lara and her dad, think of your own scenario and characters. Create a dialogue where one character validates the other. Try to include at least three of the following approaches (AAAAI):

1. <u>Agree</u> with the facts or with the other person's perceptions.

2. <u>Apologize</u> without making excuses—no "yeah, buts."

3. <u>Acknowledge</u> the other person's thoughts and feelings.

4. <u>Appreciate</u> the feedback you are receiving.

5. <u>Identify</u> a solution.

Lara's dad keeps coming into her bedroom while she is watching a movie with her boyfriend, Felix—each time with some excuse. Finally, he comes in and sternly tells Lara that her boyfriend needs to leave. Lara confronts her dad later. Notice how his response includes each of the validation strategies numbered above.

Lara: Seriously, Dad. I'm 18. You came across as really mean and rude telling him to leave so abruptly like that. We weren't doing anything wrong. I don't recall ever being told Felix couldn't be in my room with the door open, and Mom lets him watch movies in my bedroom at her house.

Dad: (1) You're right, Lara. We haven't talked about this scenario yet. I let my feelings get the best of me. (2) I am sorry. (3) I'm sure that had to be uncomfortable and embarrassing for you both. I'll be sure to apologize to Felix next time I see him. (4) Thanks for telling me how you feel. (5) That said, I don't want the two of you in your bedroom together. Are there other options that seem fair to you and that I can feel more comfortable with?

Want to earn a better grade on your test? Go to INQUIZITIVE to practice actively with this chapter's content and get personalized feedback along the way.

8

Relationship Dynamics

learning objectives

Reading this chapter will help you:

- Understand the major principles of relationships

- Navigate the dynamics of relationship development

- Identify and manage dialectical tensions

Although wedding vows vary throughout the world, many are adapted from the *Book of Common Prayer*. Couples solemnly promise to stay together no matter what: "To have and to hold from this day forward, for better or worse, for richer or poorer, in sickness and in health, to love and to cherish, till death us do part."[1]

Interestingly, in Mexico City, lawmakers introduced legislation that would radically alter the meaning of this vow: Till death do us part–or until our next marriage renewal date, whichever comes first.

Under the proposed law, a marriage license would be good for two years. A couple could renew their marriage license and submit it to the appropriate court, or they could simply part ways.

If the couple decided not to renew the marriage license, their assets would automatically split 50-50 with equal child custody unless one or both of the spouses petitioned the court for a different arrangement. There would be no need for drawn-out divorce proceedings or hefty legal fees.[2]

Proponents of this legislation argue that short-term marriage renewals would force a couple to reevaluate their relationship more often A one-time, lifelong commitment lulls couples into complacency. There isn't a strong incentive to work on the marriage, and it becomes easy for partners to take each other and the relationship for granted.

Opponents say that the renewal concept is unromantic and reinforces a throwaway culture. It would make

Relationships start, stop, grow, endure, and end for many reasons. What do you see in this photo? Perhaps it's a wedding reception or company social hour. With so many people in attendance, there are sure to be many relational dynamics at play.

divorce too easy and plant doubts about the lasting potential of marriage. It also wouldn't make a breakup any less painful for the couple or their children.

What do you think about renewable marriage licenses? What are the pros and cons? If you were a lawmaker, would you vote in favor of this legislation or oppose it?

Marriage, like all relationships, can start, develop, thrive, teeter, and end for many reasons. In this chapter, we'll focus on relationship dynamics as they pertain to friendships, family, work, and romance, including (1) the principles of relationships, (2) the process of relationship development, and (3) how to manage common relational challenges effectively.

8.1 Principles of relationships

The late geriatric doctor Henry Lodge, renowned for his advice on aging, once stated, "Love, companionship, and community are woven deeply into [your] DNA. Emotional connection is a biological imperative, and [you'll] pay a high price for ignoring it."[3]

Psychologist Julianne Holt-Lunstad agrees. Her research team's exhaustive meta-analysis of 148 studies revealed that living without close relationships is just as detrimental to your overall health as smoking 15 cigarettes a day or suffering from an alcohol addiction, and it's even worse for you than obesity or a lack of exercise.[4] While not all relationships are good for you—those that are abusive, neglectful, or toxic—relationships that are positive, loving, and supportive are essential to your health. Many would say that they make life worth living.

One of our students, Lynn, shared, "My husband Ron died three years ago after a four-year battle with pancreatic cancer. In his last months, the hope of living long enough to see our daughter give birth to our first grandchild lifted his spirits and kept him going. On the day Alexis was born, my entire family was there to witness this miracle. When Ron held Alexis in his arms, he wept. We all did. We just held each other, overcome with joy and awe and sadness. This was the greatest moment of my life. Ron cherished his time with Alexis for the two remaining months he was with us."

Relationships greatly affect our health and well-being. In Section 8.1, we'll explore several additional principles that characterize relationships.

Relationships vary in significance

The demands of work, school, and day-to-day living take up most of your time. To unwind, you may prefer to work out, read, or watch TV alone. You have only a finite amount of time remaining to foster and maintain relationships.

A **strong tie** is a relationship that is significant to you. It has a strong influence on your thoughts, feelings, and behaviors. You may share a strong tie with someone you've known for a long time, such as a best friend, godparent, or cousin. You may also form a strong tie with someone you're just getting to know, such as a new roommate, stepsibling, or romantic interest.

A **weak tie** is a relationship that you do not take extra time or effort to develop. Weak ties exist more out of convenience or circumstance. You may, for example, have weak ties with cousins whom you only see at your family's annual holiday gathering. Interacting with them is nice and enjoyable, but you don't maintain your relationships with them outside of this context.[5]

strong tie A relationship that is significant to you.

weak tie A relationship that you do not take extra time or effort to develop.

Weak ties are not as substantial as strong ties, but they're nice to have. While most of us only maintain a handful of strong ties due to time constraints, weak ties can number in the hundreds—think of the friends you interact with on social media, the people you chat with at the gym, or the customers who frequent the coffee shop where you work. They often make work tasks and social occasions more enjoyable. They also provide companionship, networking opportunities, and a sense of community.[6]

You'll devote more time and energy to your strong ties than you will to your weak ties. For example, you likely interact with members of your family more than you interact with acquaintances. However, spending a lot of time with someone doesn't necessarily make your relationship with that person significant. For instance, you may work closely with certain coworkers but never really get to know them. Likewise, infrequent interaction doesn't make a relationship any less significant. Say, for instance, that you have a good friend who moved far away three years ago. You see each other about once a year while vacationing, and you always have a blast. You only call each other two or three times a year, but each time you do, it seems like only yesterday that you last spoke. You look forward to your conversations and think of each other often. Your interactions, while infrequent, are meaningful, and so your relationship is significant.

Relationships have upsides and downsides

Think back to some of the highlights of your life—your big wins, magic moments, and memorable firsts. They might stand out because you were able to share them with the people you care about. Relational partners make achievements worth celebrating. They're there for you when you need a hug, a pat on the back, or a shoulder to cry on. They can make you laugh, swoon, sing, and dance.

Relationships have numerous upsides, but they can also increase your obligations, stretch your patience, sap your energy, and deplete your financial resources. To meet the needs of your family or a romantic partner, you may have to sacrifice the development and maintenance of other relationships. Those you are the closest to are also the ones who may hurt and disappoint you the most. They may break your trust or your heart. Close relationships also have the potential to be abusive—emotionally, physically, or sexually.

> "After dealing with my previous boyfriend's possessiveness and paranoia, I'm letting every future dating partner know that I won't tolerate being drilled every day about my whereabouts. I refuse to drop my other male friends, and I will not completely write off an ex who I'm still friends with. I simply have zero tolerance for that kind of controlling behavior and would rather stay single than deal with that again." –Lilly

In her narrative, one of our students, Lilly, shares how she plans to ward off potential relationship downsides in the future. What do you think about her decision?

Relationships are often random and situational

Many relationships begin thanks to a fairly random set of circumstances. One of your authors, Leslie, has often heard the story of how her mom, Elvia, met her dad, Jeffrey. The first time that Elvia ever hailed a cab—she usually took the bus or hitched a ride with a family member—she flagged down the taxi that Jeffrey was driving. They talked at length over the course of the ride, and before Elvia stepped out of the cab, Jeffrey had asked her out to a movie. She agreed. They fell in love and were married two years later.

Relationships can start at any time, and they can end at any time. You may initiate a fast friendship with someone at a weekend retreat, while working a seasonal job, or during a stay at the hospital. These relationships may mean something to you in the short term, but when the situation changes—the retreat ends, you switch to another job, or you are discharged from the hospital—the relationship may end abruptly.

Relationships are voluntary and involuntary

Imagine you're folding towels in the laundry room of your apartment complex. A neighbor who lives down the hall walks in to put her wet clothes in the dryer, and the two of you strike up a lively conversation. If you choose to ask for her number or invite her over for coffee, you're initiating a voluntary relationship.

Other relationships are involuntary—that is, they exist whether we want them to or not. For example, your professors most likely didn't enroll you in their classes. When a company hires you, chances are, you won't get to choose your boss or work team. Some relationships exist because you choose them; others exist because life chooses them for you.

Relationships involve feelings

All relationships involve feelings that vary in intensity and duration.[7] Some of the most common are closeness, liking, love, passion, respect, and trust (see TABLE 8.1).

You may experience a blend of these emotions. For instance, you may both like and respect your boss. You may feel love, liking, and closeness toward a friend. Within certain relationships, you may experience some feelings but not others. You may respect a colleague, but not like her. You could also love someone you don't respect.

These feelings may change slowly or suddenly. You may gradually lose feelings of closeness toward a friend who seems too busy to spend time with you. If a family member offers to donate her bone marrow to help you overcome a life-threatening blood disease, this may quickly intensify the love and respect you have for her. A funeral, and the grieving process associated with it, may unify family members and deepen their level of closeness in the short and long term.

table 8.1	Relationship-Oriented Feelings
Closeness	A feeling of connection or immediacy with someone, such as a teammate or godmother.
Liking	A feeling of pleasant and positive affection for someone. If you like your neighbor, you probably enjoy interacting with her.
Love	A feeling associated with caring for and being cared for by someone. People who love each other feel committed to each other on some level.[8] There are various types of love; the love felt between a parent and child may feel different than the love shared by soldiers who serve together in combat.
Passion	A feeling of intense romantic affection or longing for someone, mixing joy, excitement, and sexual attraction. You may feel passion toward your fiancé or the person you're dating.
Respect	A feeling associated with looking up to or wanting to emulate a person who possesses certain qualities. You may respect a friend who bravely speaks out against social injustice. You may also respect someone who makes sacrifices on your behalf, such as a coach, teacher, or adult caregiver.
Trust	A feeling of certainty about the enduring nature of a relationship and what you can expect from someone. You may trust your boss because she communicates her expectations consistently and provides you with reliable support.

Researchers have identified various communication behaviors that engender closeness, liking, love, passion, respect, and trust. These behaviors include active listening, expressing yourself genuinely, and showing that you value another person's experiences and opinions.[9] Others are listed in the *Building Your IPC Skills* exercise at the end of this chapter. Take a few minutes now to complete the activity. Which behaviors would you like to incorporate in your own interpersonal communication?

Relationships are governed by rules

Rules theory suggests that relationships are held together and torn apart based on whether or not relational partners' adhere to certain rules.[10] As we established in Chapter 2, *rules* are guidelines for what we can or cannot do from a communication standpoint within an interpersonal system. A **relational rule**, therefore, governs what you can or cannot do within the context of a specific relationship. Some rules are established explicitly and others implicitly.

In Chapter 2, you learned that an *explicit rule* is established with communication that is very clear, obvious, and direct. For example, a mother may tell her son not to invite a friend over for dinner before asking her first, privately.

An *implicit rule* is established in a more indirect way, usually by observing someone's communication or picking up on subtle cues. During a meeting at work, for instance, you may refrain from asking a question while your supervisor is

rules theory The idea that relationships are held together and torn apart based on relational partners' adherence to certain rules.

relational rule A rule that governs what you can or cannot do within the context of a relationship.

Is it a relational rule violation if you date a close friend's ex? Some people may not have a problem with it. Others would have a serious problem with it—no matter what. Which factors would make it more or less acceptable to you if a friend wanted to date your ex? On the *Wendy Williams Show*, a member of the audience seeks advice. What advice would you give her? On YouTube, search using the keywords: "Ask Wendy: Dating Your Friend's Ex." (1:21)

speaking because you've noticed that no one else speaks up until your supervisor invites questions from the group.

Some relational rules, such as returning phone calls and texts in a timely manner, are established in all types of close relationships. Another common relational rule is that friends should stand up for each other if one is being treated unfairly; this rule is also regularly established between family members and romantic partners. Other widespread rules include keeping each other's secrets and offering help when needed.

Often, however, rules will differ from relationship to relationship.[11] For example, your supervisor at your old job may not have wanted you to raise concerns in a group setting unless you spoke to her about them first, but your new manager might foster more spontaneity during meetings. She may even tell you, "If there's a problem, just say something about it when we're all together so everyone can discuss it."

section review

8.1 Principles of relationships

Close, meaningful relationships are essential to your well-being. This is one of the many principles of relationships. In addition, relationships vary in terms of their significance and their upsides and downsides. They are often random and situational, and they may be voluntary or involuntary. While relationships involve various types of feelings, they are also regulated by rules.

(continued)

Key Terms

strong tie, *p. 200*   weak tie, *p. 200*   rules theory, *p. 203*   relational rule, *p. 203*

Comprehend It?

1. Define each of the key terms in Section 8.1. To further your understanding of these terms, create examples to support your definitions.

2. Summarize each of the following principles of relationships:

   - Relationships vary in significance.

- Relationships have upsides and downsides.
- Relationships are often random and situational.
- Relationships are voluntary and involuntary.
- Relationships involve feelings.
- Relationships are governed by rules.

Apply It!

Take a look at the first 10 posts made by your friends or people you follow on your favorite social media feed. If you don't use social media, pull up the contacts list in your cell phone and examine the first name under each letter. Which relationships are strong ties? Which ones do you consider weak ties? Why do you consider them strong or weak? Would you like to change the status of these relationships in any way? If so, how might you do so using your IPC?

8.2 Relationship development and maintenance

As we've established, relationships can begin anywhere. Let's say you enjoy exercising at the gym and you meet someone there with a similar routine. Working out together may encourage you to exercise harder and might make staying physically fit more enjoyable. You may even compete with each other using fitness trackers to see who burns the most calories or takes the most steps each week. Your shared interests and successes bring the two of you closer and motivate you to maintain the relationship. However, the relationship may devolve if your competition grows too intense or if you both can no longer make it to the gym at the same time.

In Section 8.2, we'll explore the factors that motivate people to initiate, cultivate, maintain, repair, and terminate relationships. We'll also explain the stages of forming and ending relationships.

Attraction

Attraction is the feeling of being drawn to someone; it happens when you find a person appealing in some way. **Short-term attraction** is the initial feeling that motivates you to begin and develop a relationship. For example, you may experience short-term attraction when you discover that a classmate has climbed Mount Kilimanjaro in Tanzania, something you'd love to do one day. **Long-term attraction** is the feeling that motivates you to maintain an existing relationship,

attraction The feeling of being drawn to someone you find appealing.

short-term attraction The initial feeling that motivates you to begin and develop a relationship.

long-term attraction The feeling that motivates you to maintain a relationship and, when necessary, repair or reconcile it.

and when necessary, repair or reconcile it. If you and a classmate frequently discuss your shared political views and start volunteering with a political party together, your shared views and political involvement will likely make you want to develop the relationship and sustain it in the long run.

What first attracts you to someone in the short term, however, may not always attract you in the long term. Say, for example, that you were initially attracted to the person you're seeing because of his good looks. After a couple of weeks, you may get tired of hearing friends say how lucky you are. Or, you may grow tired of watching others flirt with him—especially if he returns their flirtatious behavior!

Similarities and differences

What attracts you to a relationship: similarities or differences? Research suggests that you are more likely to cultivate relationships with people who are similar to you.[12] However, the things that make someone different can be appealing, too. For example, Ellen may want to pair up with her colleague Jedidiah on a quality improvement project because of his creativity. Ellen is more conventional and analytical, and she thinks that combining their ways of thinking will net the best results.[13]

There's a common misconception that opposites attract. This may be true in the short term, but similarities are more compelling than differences when it comes to long-term attraction. In other words, opposites attract, but close relationships between people who are dramatic opposites don't tend to last, especially if their differences do not complement each other.[14]

Do you agree with the research? Why or why not? To test your opinion and help you determine if similarities are more important than differences in your choice of a romantic partner, complete the *Assessing Your IPC* exercise at the end of this chapter.

Relational rewards versus costs

Think about a relationship you have with a close friend. What makes it appealing? What makes it worth maintaining? Your answer will probably include one or more of the types of attraction in **TABLE 8.2**. Each type of attraction is associated with certain relational rewards. A **relational reward** is something you receive from a relationship that you like and value.[15] A **relational cost** is something you don't like about or want in a relationship—for example, frequent arguing or putting up with a person's mood swings.

According to **social exchange theory**, your willingness to develop and maintain a relationship is based on an analysis of its rewards and costs. This calculation is like a mental scale that tips one way or the other—a relationship is either worth it or not worth it.[16] For example, a married couple may determine that the costs of their relationship outweigh its rewards, leading to a divorce.

Sometimes you compare the costs and rewards of an existing relationship with those of a potential relationship. Your perceptions may lead you to believe that

relational reward
Something you receive from a relationship that you like and value.

relational cost An aspect of a relationship that you don't like or want.

social exchange theory
The idea that your willingness to develop and maintain a relationship is based on a cost-benefit analysis.

table 8.2	Types of Attraction and Relational Rewards
Types of Attraction	**Relational Rewards**
Intellectual	• Engaging conversations • Witty banter • Lively storytelling • Meaningful philosophical discussions and debates
Belief-based	• Connections with people who share similar opinions, political stances, religious affiliations, and personal values • Opportunities to engage in activities related to shared beliefs
Social	• Being with someone who is fun to be around • Access to a person's friends and social network • Invitations to social events
Physical	• Increased social status or popularity • In a romantic or sexual relationship, increased physical desire
Emotional	• Feeling understood, listened to, and validated • Receiving sympathy and comfort from others • Opportunities to express feelings and concerns
Interest-based	• Opportunities to enjoy activities that are mutually satisfying • Fun, camaraderie, and friendly competition
Resource-based	• Access to desirable items, events, and opportunities that you couldn't obtain on your own

an alternative relationship has more to offer than your current relationship, a cognitive assessment referred to as the **comparison level of alternatives.**[17] You might compare your relationship with your parents, for instance, to the relationship you imagine you would have with your best friend's parents if you were their child. You may also do this with a romantic relationship. One study found that it's not uncommon for people to maintain online relationships with potential partners, called "back burners," in case their current romantic relationship goes sour.[18]

Another theory closely associated with social exchange theory, **equity theory,** suggests that your relationship satisfaction is higher when you sense that there is a fair exchange of costs and benefits between you and a relational partner. For example, let's say you co-own a business. If you believe that you're spending more time and money on the venture than your business partner is, but the two of you are splitting the profits 50-50, how might you feel about the partnership? Your relationship would likely suffer. However, if you contribute two-thirds of the money needed to cover startup costs, and your partner spends about two-thirds more time than you do working at the store, the two of you may consider it an even trade in terms of costs. As a result, you'll be happier running a business together.[19]

comparison level of alternatives The idea that you compare the costs and rewards of an existing relationship with those of a potential relationship.

equity theory The idea that your relationship satisfaction is higher when you and a relational partner share equally in the costs and benefits of your relationship.

Child genius Sheldon Cooper (Iain Armitage) meets fellow prodigy Paige (Mckenna Grace) in an advanced college physics class. Compare this scene from the TV show *Young Sheldon* to what you've read about how similarities and differences can influence attraction. How might Sheldon and Paige's similarities and differences make a friendship more or less likely? Compare your thoughts to the social exchange theory. On YouTube, search using the keywords: "Young Sheldon's new smart rival scenes." (3:48)

Adding up the relational rewards and subtracting the costs may seem a bit too simplistic when it comes to making decisions about your relationships. One reward may trump a dozen costs in terms of importance or significance. For example, your mother's love for you and the support that comes with it may overshadow the onslaught of chain emails she sends you each week, and her propensity to like and comment on every one of your posts on social media—including your friends' posts. You keep your relationship with your mom close and significant because the rewards that really matter to you far outweigh the costs.

Physical proximity

Another important factor in relational development and maintenance is proximity. **Physical proximity** is how near or accessible you are to someone. If you are in close physical proximity, the frequency and ease of communication makes a relationship more probable. This may explain why you are more likely to form a relationship with a classmate who sits next to you or a coworker whose cubicle is adjacent to yours.[20]

If you and a coworker have a mutual friend, there is a greater chance that all three of you will develop a friendship because you'll have more opportunities to see and interact with each other. You may also form relationships with people faster if you belong to the same clubs or organizations.[21]

physical proximity How near or accessible you are to someone.

That said, it's easier than ever to maintain relationships across physical distance thanks to electronic channels. If you move from California to Texas, for instance, you may maintain some of your relationships with friends, relatives, and colleagues from California over video chats, phone calls, email, and social media.

Self-disclosure

Self-disclosure is the act of revealing personal information about yourself—such as personal facts, opinions, feelings, and needs—to others. For example, if you reveal the fact that you have 12 points on your driver's license for speeding, you're also revealing that you tend to drive too fast; perhaps you're a bit impatient, an adrenaline junkie, or a reckless driver. What you disclose says a lot about what you value, how you think, and who you are. Others may form positive or negative thoughts or opinions about you based on what you disclose. Self-disclosure, therefore, may or may not benefit you interpersonally.

When you disclose information about yourself and others respond favorably, you tend to like them more. When you respond favorably to the self-disclosure of others, they will tend to like you more, too.[22] A favorable response to self-disclosure may include listening intently, smiling or laughing appropriately, asking engaging questions at the right times, and appearing pleased or interested. A favorable response typically does not include putdowns, criticism, unsolicited advice, or judgment.

Self-disclosure and reducing uncertainty

Self-disclosure is one way to reduce what you don't know about someone. When you disclose personal information, your relational partners tend to reciprocate and share things about themselves. This reduces uncertainty and satisfies your curiosity.[23]

Communication scholars Charles Berger and Richard Calabrese's **uncertainty reduction theory** holds that we tend to seek out information about relational partners or social situations to reduce any discomfort associated with uncertainties we have about them.[24]

A very common uncertainty reduction tactic is to ask a variety of questions to get someone to open up to you. When you first meet someone, you may try to find out what you have in common, what makes you different, and whether the person is someone you can like and trust. While these questions are more pronounced early in a relationship, they persist as long as a relationship exists because people and relationships change over time.

You might also share information about yourself to ease someone else's uncertainty. As Carl illustrates in his narrative, reducing uncertainty fosters familiarity and predictability—precursors to interpersonal trust. Have you experienced something similar as a result of self-disclosure?

Another theory that relates to self-disclosure and uncertainty reduction, the **social penetration theory**, suggests that the breadth and depth of self-disclosure

self-disclosure The act of revealing personal information about yourself to others.

uncertainty reduction theory The idea that we tend to seek out information about relational partners or social situations to reduce any discomfort associated with uncertainties we have about them.

social penetration theory The idea that the breadth and depth of self-disclosure influences a relationship's development.

"Amy, a member at the gym where I work, confided in me that she felt unfit, unhealthy, and unhappy. To let her know I understood her struggles, I told her about my lifelong battle with bad food choices. At first she didn't believe me. Then I showed her a picture of me before I started eating a healthy diet and exercising regularly. We really opened up to each other. She later told me that my self-disclosure added to my credibility and made her want to hire me as her personal trainer." –Carl

influences a relationship's development. Getting to know someone is a process that may occur quickly or slowly based on the willingness of relational partners to reveal a wide range of details about themselves (breadth) and varying degrees of private, personal information (depth).

With each act of self-disclosure, relational partners eliminate what is unknown about each other, bringing them closer to discovering each other's innermost thoughts, opinions, feelings, values, interests, and needs. Generally speaking, as breadth and depth increases, uncertainty is reduced, and feelings of liking and trust grow. This may not always happen, of course, especially if what you learn about your relational partner makes that person less appealing to you.[25]

The degree to which you disclose information may vary from relationship to relationship. With your doctor, for example, you may only talk about matters concerning your health. In this case, the breadth of your self-disclosure is limited. The depth of your disclosure, however, increases when you share intimate information about your health. With a coworker, on the other hand, you may talk casually about a range of topics such as your weekend plans or what you like to eat (high breadth), but you might share very little private information (low depth). Chances are, the breadth and depth of your self-disclosure is the greatest with your most trusted, intimate relational partners—a close family member, best friend, therapist, or romantic partner.

Communication scholar Michael Sunnafrank developed a theory that helps explain the relationship between self-disclosure, uncertainty reduction, and relational development. His **predicted outcome value theory** suggests that in your initial interactions with others, you'll use various communication strategies, like asking questions and self-disclosure, to assess whether it benefits you to have future interactions. If you expect that future interactions will yield the kind of relational rewards you value, you'll continue your efforts to connect.[26]

Self-disclosure and honesty

When you share personal facts, opinions, feelings, and/or needs, you may do so with varying degrees of honesty. You might embellish a story about yourself to impress a date. If you tell your mother about a fight you had with your coworker, you may leave out a few key details because you don't want to acknowledge your own bad behavior.

Research has revealed an interesting paradox: We tend to be both the most and least honest within the relationships that matter the most to us. While vulnerability and candid self-disclosure are key to experiencing the rewards associated with a close relationship,[27] you may find yourself lying more often, too, in order to maintain the relationship and its benefits.[28]

Benefits and risks of self-disclosure

There are many benefits to self-disclosure. Honest self-disclosure builds trust and increases feelings of passion, liking, love, closeness, and respect between relational partners.[29] Studies suggest that the quantity and quality of

predicted outcome value theory The idea that you'll use various communication strategies in your initial interactions with others to assess whether it benefits you to have future interactions.

self-disclosure between married couples is strongly correlated with relationship satisfaction.[30] In addition, revealing your experiences can help or inspire others, and sharing positive information about yourself may increase your own feelings of self-worth.[31]

However, self-disclosure has inherent risks and doesn't always lead to positive outcomes. You may make someone feel uncomfortable or a bit overwhelmed if you reveal too much information or very private information too early in your relationship. Someone could judge or reject you based on what you share. Others may feel that your self-disclosure puts pressure on them to reciprocate, and they might distance themselves from you as a result.

One of our students, Sebastian, shared, "One of my friends told a very personal secret to a mutual friend of ours. She made him promise not to say anything to anyone. He made someone else promise the same thing. Let's just say a lot of people made the exact same promise. Since then, I've been very careful to keep this proverb in mind: 'Confiding a secret to an unworthy person is like carrying sand in a bag with a small hole.'"

To avoid the negative outcomes of self-disclosure, consider the following questions before you share:

- Can I trust this person with this information?
- Did I clearly communicate that I want anything I share to be kept private?
- How could this disclosure affect me in the future?
- Is this the right time and place to disclose?
- Is my disclosure honest and accurate?
- What are my motives for disclosing? Do they reflect the ethics and morals I expect from others?
- Would it improve my relationship if I took more risks and disclosed more?

Relational stages

The **relational stages model** describes how relationships start, grow, endure, and end. There are 10 stages of relationship development and deterioration.[32] (see **FIGURE 8.1**).

While this model is most often used to describe the stages of a romantic relationship, many interpersonal communication scholars agree that it pertains to all types of relationships.[33] As you read through the stages, think about how they apply to your relationships with friends, family members, coworkers, and romantic partners. The first five stages are associated with a relationship that is coming together. The last five are associated with a relationship that is coming apart. Keep in mind that some of your relationships may involve all the stages, many of them, or just one or two. You and a relational partner may jump backward or forward from one stage to the next in the order presented, or you may

relational stages model A model that describes how relationships start, grow, endure, and end.

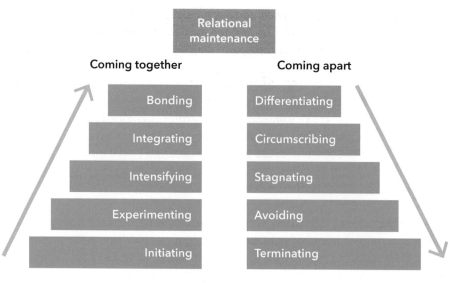

FIGURE 8.1 Relational Stages Model

skip one or more stages. Your current relationship may even be best described as a combination of two or more stages.

Initiating

The initiating stage starts with the first "hello," handshake, smile, or exchange of pleasantries. It's the interaction that sets a relationship in motion. Your first impressions—digital or in person—influence your desire to begin the initiating stage.

Experimenting

In the experimenting stage, you'll determine if a potential relationship warrants your continued interest. You may size a person up by engaging in small talk. **Small talk** is communication in which you disclose general information about yourself in order to get acquainted with someone. It may include basic facts about yourself, such as where you live, your hobbies, and what you do for a living. Your conversation may seem smooth and comfortable or strained and unpleasant. You may discover you have many—or very few—things in common.

What you learn may motivate you to pursue a closer relationship with a coworker or to seek a friendship with a teammate outside of your scheduled practices and games.

From a romantic standpoint, the experimenting stage may involve a first date or an unofficial meetup. Research suggests that most of our relationships don't advance any further than this stage.[34]

Intensifying

In the intensifying stage, you'll increase your interactions. Self-disclosure becomes more personal and substantive. You'll share more about your goals

small talk Communication in which you disclose general information about yourself in order to get acquainted with someone.

and future plans, tastes and preferences, opinions, and personal struggles. Little favors and tokens of friendship occur more frequently, such as offering a classmate a ride after school or sharing your extra water bottle with a teammate.

When romance is involved, relational partners may start going on formal dates or group outings together. Goosebumps, butterflies, and passionate feelings abound. However, as you learned in Chapter 7, it's difficult to stay in this honeymoon phase for long periods of time. This stage is usually short-lived or occurs in spurts.

Integrating

The integrating stage is marked by both parties' significant commitment to the relationship. A sense of shared identity develops; you and your relational partner may even start to give each other nicknames. You'll begin to form relationships with each other's friends and family and establish rituals for hanging out. For example, you may look forward to spending time with colleagues every Friday for happy hour or every Wednesday night for a dodgeball league.

In a romantic relationship, you may become "official" by deciding to see each other exclusively or posting your romantic status on social media. The two of you may do more things as a couple, and when talking about yourself, you increasingly replace "I" and "me" with "we" and "us." You may describe things as if you and your partner own them jointly: "our song," "our favorite restaurant," or "our plans." You may also refer to each other using terms of endearment such as "babe" or "boo."

In the intensifying and integrating stages, you work out the rules of your relationship. For example, is it okay to stop by your friend's house unannounced? Can you use a roommate's cologne without asking? Sometimes these rules are assumed but never discussed, which can turn into conflict when someone says "no" or gets upset.

Bonding

Long-term commitment and comfort are well established by the bonding stage. You are no longer out to impress; you and your relational partner accept each other, the good and the bad. The two of you have a longstanding history and a sense of certainty that you are in one another's lives for the long haul. You may refer to a friend as a lifelong friend or as your BF (best friend).

People usually formalize their relationships at this stage by moving in with each other, getting married, adopting a pet together, forming a business partnership, or jointly purchasing a major asset, like a boat, car, or vacation property.

Differentiating

In the intensifying, integrating, and bonding stages, you are likely to see similarities and differences as mostly positive. The differentiating stage occurs when relational partners begin to perceive one or more differences as highly undesirable or annoying. For example, while you initially found your friend's

Social psychologists Arthur Aron, Elaine Aron, and Edward Melinat believe that two complete strangers can fall in love in a single interaction. They ask subjects to sit across from each other and exchange answers to 36 predetermined questions.[35] Two college students were asked to participate in this experiment. Using their recorded conversation, describe how this relationship might take off using the terms associated with the "coming together" stages of a relationship. Did the subjects fall in love? On YouTube, search using the keywords: "Can 2 Strangers Fall in Love with 36 Questions Russell Kera." (9:05)

spontaneity fun and adventurous, you're beginning to resent her for some of the problems her free-spirited attitude has caused you.

In this stage, your needs and expectations change. You are more likely to experience conflict and feel frustration and resentment. In some cases, it may be best to allow the relationship to change or dissolve. However, if you are committed to growing the relationship, this stage requires greater understanding, accommodation, and a willingness to find new ways to connect.

You may experience differentiation when a good friend establishes a new friendship and starts spending less time with you. Or you might feel it when your younger brother begins to exert more independence and stops taking your advice. A close coworker could get a promotion and become your manager. Any of these changes may cause differentiation to occur. Your ability to communicate effectively and adjust to change will influence which stage you go to next—one that is associated with coming together (intensifying, integrating, or bonding) or coming apart (circumscribing, stagnating, or avoiding).

Circumscribing

A relationship is in the circumscribing stage when you and a relational partner face an issue with no apparent resolution. Confronted by this challenge, you may throw in the towel and go directly to the termination stage. Or, you may hang in there a little longer in the hope that things will get better.

In this stage, your issues become obvious to others. Certain topics are "off limits," or you may argue and complain more than you have in the past—complete with finger-pointing, expressions of hurt, and attempts to dredge up past grievances. Often, one or more unresolved issues have left you increasingly dissatisfied with the relationship, and your recent communication has not produced positive results.[36] If you feel that future attempts to communicate will fare no better, your motivation to resolve your difficulties may diminish.

Stagnating

At the stagnating stage, you and your relational partner reach a plateau. The quality of your communication has hit an all-time low. Rather than talk about the relationship or your feelings, you may stick with superficial and "safe" communication topics. One or both of you withdraw, and self-disclosure is reduced. There is little or no relational growth. You carry out activities without feeling or excitement; boredom and predictability is the new normal. It may even seem awkward—for instance, you might sit down together for a meal but have nothing to talk about. You may also feel stuck or trapped.

Avoiding

Because you and your relational partner continue to ignore key issues and topics you'll establish reasons to avoid interaction. Avoidant behavior may include such excuses as, "I won't be able to go on that trip we talked about because work has me busy this weekend." A spouse may spend extra hours at work to delay coming home. A roommate may keep to his room with his door closed when you are around. You may interact with a certain coworker only when it is absolutely necessary. People who live together and can't afford to move out may ignore each other, sleep in different rooms, or occupy separate living areas. On social media, people may unfollow each other.

Terminating

When a relationship ends, individuals disassociate and go their separate ways. Termination may occur in a simple, quick manner; you might say, "I can't be your friend any more" or "I need to end this." It may also occur when one or both individuals simply cut off all contact without warning or discussion. Online, you may block or unfriend someone on social media or change your relationship status.

Termination can be voluntary or involuntary. You might end a relationship on your own, or the decision to end a relationship might be made for you by your relational partner or someone else. For instance, a romantic partner or adult caregiver may insist that you stop all future interactions with someone for reasons that you may or may not consider justified. Some relationships end mutually—and others end because of life circumstances.

Moving from stage to stage

Now that you know about the different relational stages, let's explore how a relationship can move from one stage to another. Shifts may occur slowly, almost imperceptibly, but they can also happen suddenly. As we mentioned earlier, a relationship may skip several stages or move back and forth between stages as a result of one or more turning points.

"I started a new relationship. At the end of our first date, I was ready to slip into something more comfortable - my *old* relationship!

turning point An event that causes or signals a significant change in a relationship.

A **turning point** is an event that causes or signals a significant change in a relationship.[37] Kissing someone for the first time, a second date, moving away from home, doing someone a huge favor, saying something very hurtful during an argument, or winning the lottery are all potential turning points.

A turning point can shift the direction of a relationship. Let's say you ended a friendship several years ago because you felt betrayed by a friend in some way (a turning point). You unexpectedly run into this former friend at a mutual friend's baby shower. The two of you end up sitting at the same table, and something this person says or does causes you to soften and reconsider the relationship (another turning point). Your reunion may send the relationship from the termination stage right back to the intensifying stage.

Sometimes a turning point may move a relationship from a single stage to what seems like a combination of stages. For example, a student of ours, Connor, shared that his parents divorced when he was 17 years old. A year later, Connor's dad, Jared, started dating again. Connor didn't care for his father's new girlfriend, and he missed the good times when it was just him and his dad. He said their relationship was in the differentiating stage during this time period.

When Connor decided to talk to Jared about his feelings, the conversation didn't turn out well and things didn't get any better. His father's new romantic relationship and Connor's heartfelt conversation with his dad (and its outcome) were turning points that moved their relationship from the differentiating stage to a blend of the circumscribing and stagnating stages. If you were Connor, what would you say or do to effectively address your concerns with Jared?

section review

8.2 Relationship development and maintenance

Relationships are influenced by attraction, similarities and differences, comparisons of benefits and costs, proximity, and self-disclosure. Relationships evolve across 10 different stages.

Key Terms

attraction, *p. 205*

short-term attraction, *p. 205*

long-term attraction, *p. 205*

relational reward, *p. 206*

relational cost, *p. 206*

social exchange theory, *p. 206*

comparison level of alternatives, *p. 207*

equity theory, *p. 207*

physical proximity, *p. 208*

self-disclosure, *p. 209*

uncertainty reduction theory, *p. 209*

social penetration theory, *p. 209*

predicted outcome value theory, *p. 210*

relational stages model, *p. 211*

small talk, *p. 212*

turning point, *p. 216*

(continued)

Comprehend It?

1. Define each of the key terms in Section 8.2. To further your understanding of these terms, create examples to support your definitions.

2. Compare and contrast:
   - Long-term and short-term attraction
   - Social exchange theory and equity theory
   - Uncertainty reduction theory, social penetration theory, and predicted outcome value theory

3. Summarize how initial attraction, similarities and differences, comparisons of benefits and costs, proximity, and self-disclosure influence the formation of relationships.

4. Describe the various stages of relationships, from initiating to terminating. Think of five people in your life. Which relational stage are you in with each of these individuals?

Apply It!

Think about a relationship you have that is very satisfying to you. Now, think about one that is not. Write a list of rewards and costs for each. What is the ratio of costs to rewards in each relationship? (This may be qualitative, not quantitative.) How does the ratio of costs to rewards influence your relationship satisfaction? Relate your analysis to social exchange theory and equity theory.

8.3 **Managing dialectical tensions**

One of our students, Brice, wants to keep his work relationships strictly professional and uncomplicated. His coworker, Hadley, however, is trying to develop a friendship with him outside of work. In this case, Hadley wants a relationship that Brice isn't interested in.

The push and pull nature of relationships is of particular interest to interpersonal communication scholars who study dialectical tensions. A **dialectical tension** occurs when the needs or motivations of relational partners clash. In Section 8.3, we'll explore several types of dialectical tensions and identify strategies to manage them successfully.

Types of dialectical tensions

Dialectical tensions can pose serious relational challenges, but they aren't necessarily a bad thing. Dialectical tensions are a natural, normal occurrence in close, interdependent relationships; understanding them and talking freely about them using the right communication techniques can make adapting to them easier.

Though there are several types of dialectical tensions, we'll highlight four in particular: connection versus separateness, predictability versus novelty, openness versus privacy, and dependence versus autonomy.[38]

Connection versus separateness

One partner says, "I can't get enough time with you." The other says, "I can't get enough time away from you." These two sentiments capture the essence of the

---

dialectical tension The strain created between relational partners when their needs or motivations clash.

connection/separateness dialectical tension.[39] Sociobiologist Desmond Morris, author of the book *Intimate Behaviour*, refers to this as a "Hold me tight" and "Let me go" dialectic.[40]

Kaneshia describes the connection/separateness tension in her narrative. How can you relate to her experience?

"My friend Lindsey and I hung out a lot in high school. I had every class with her. We drove to school together. We were in the same clubs. She even joined my cheerleading squad. I was spending about 10 hours a day, 6 days a week with her. I started getting really annoyed with her and didn't know why. She wasn't doing anything purposely to bother me. To her, everything seemed fine between us, but I needed a break from her."–Kaneshia

The connection/separateness tension may also occur when one relational partner wants to connect by communicating on the phone or via text more or less often than the other. One of our students, Felipe, doesn't really like to talk on the phone, but his mother does. He says she often complains that he is too quick to get off the phone. She'll say to him, "What, you have more important things to do than talk to your own mother?"

Predictability versus novelty

Sometimes doing the same things in the same way is nice. Many people like routines and consistency. Other people, however, prefer change and spontaneity. When relational partners want just the opposite in this regard, it can create another kind of dialectical tension.

For example, Christine and Harish enjoy a Friday night ritual: Every week, they grab takeout from their favorite restaurant and play boardgames. Christine finds that her Friday nights with Harish are getting tedious. Harish, on the other hand, loves doing the same thing with her every Friday. To satisfy her desire for novelty, Christine may suggest going out to eat and inviting a couple or two to join them for dinner or taking off on a weekend excursion.

We may also see the predictability/novelty tension play out at work. Perhaps the department you oversee is in charge of planning your company's annual awards dinner. Several of your subordinates, bored by the way the event has been run in the past, enthusiastically propose sweeping changes. However, you like the traditions of the annual dinner. You know that upper management feels the same way and likely wouldn't support big changes. There is now a source of tension between you and your coworkers. How would you manage this dialectical tension effectively using your communication?

Openness versus privacy

At times, your relational partners may want you to divulge more personal information than you feel comfortable sharing, and vice versa.[41] For example, some family members may want unsavory or embarrassing family information kept secret—what goes on in the family, stays in the family—while others may feel it's a good thing to talk openly about it.

In a romantic relationship, partners may differ in their opinions about whether reading each other's email or text messages is acceptable. One of our students, Cora, shared how this tension put a tremendous strain on her relationship with her boyfriend, Karl. After about 8 months of serious dating, Karl asked her out of the blue, "Why do you keep picking up my phone to see who's calling me?" Cora was surprised by the question and responded that she was just curious—and that he should feel free to look at her phone.

Karl replied, "I don't look at your phone. I trust you. My last girlfriend insisted that I share my phone, email, and social media passwords with her. I did, but she made a big deal about my conversations with a few of my female friends. She assumed the worst and got upset over nothing. I don't want a repeat of that."

Cora said, "I'm not your ex, and I'm sure I'm not going to freak out like she did. I think sharing this kind of information, if mutual, is a sign of trust and reinforces it."

Cora equated trust with openness, while Karl likened it to respecting each other's privacy. Do you think it's a good idea to have unfettered access to a romantic partner's cell phone, email accounts, or social media profiles? Why or why not? Your answer may suggest that you have a greater or lesser need for openness (also referred to as transparency) or privacy. What do you think Cora and Karl could say and do to help them work out this dialectical difference?

Dependence versus autonomy

Questions such as "Why did you decide this for me?" and "Why can't I have a say?" may surface when one relational partner wants to make decisions independently and the other wants to do so mutually. One of our students, Eaden, found that he often argued with his wife at the supermarket about keeping their purchases within budget. Even though they came up with a grocery list together each week, both he and his wife would inevitably place extra items they individually wanted in the cart that the other hadn't agreed to—leading to a surprising total at the checkout counter. The two decided to budget for "no questions asked" purchases—that is, both can spend a certain amount of money on things they want to buy without the other's input or approval.

In relationships between parents and children, we often see the dependence and autonomy tension flare up when parents try to influence the choices their children make. Typically, the children want just the opposite—the freedom to make their own decisions. This tension can reverse itself when children grow up and want to make more decisions for aging parents who are unwilling to relinquish their independence.

In *Failure to Launch*, 35-year-old Tripp (Matthew McConaughey) enjoys the comforts of his parents' home. Unbeknownst to him, they are exhausted by his level of dependence. They hire Paula (Sarah Jessica Parker) to lure him into independent adulthood. Relate this scene to the dependence versus autonomy dialectical tension. On YouTube, search using the keywords: "Failure to Launch (1/10) Movie CLIP - Paula's Pitch (2006) HD." (2:21)

Managing dialectical tensions effectively

Now that you've learned about some of the common dialectical tensions, let's explore how you can address them effectively using interpersonal communication. Imagine that you're visiting your parents during a weeklong break from college. You want to spend time with them, but you also want to make time for your friends.

You'd like to have the freedom to spend part of your week off with your friends, but your parents are making plans with you that will make hanging out with other people quite difficult. This presents a dialectical tension. Your parents want a lot of connection, but you need some separateness.

The three-step method outlined below may help get you out of this tricky interpersonal situation: (1) Identify the tension or problem, (2) validate the other person's needs, and (3) focus on solutions. Let's take a look at a possible dialogue you might have with your dad:

- **Identify the tension:** "Hey Mom and Dad, I want to spend time with you both and I also would like to catch up with my friends who I haven't seen in a while."

- **Validate your relational partner's needs, thoughts, and feelings:** "I know we haven't seen each other much during the semester, and we're all looking forward to spending quality family time together."

- **Solution-based communication:** "Can we plan out the week so I can spend time with you and do a few things with my friends? When are you free? What would you like to do?"

In this scenario, you state your needs concisely using I-language. You validate your parents' need to spend time with you, and you propose an idea in a solution-based manner. What do you see as the benefits of this three-step approach? Are there any limits? How could you make this three-step approach work better?

In order to make decisions that are acceptable to both you and your parents, you may need to negotiate a bit. You can make this process easier by identifying what is most important to each of you. As you work out the details of how you spend your break, the outcome is better for everyone if you strive to satisfy each other's top priorities.

It often helps to work through dialectical tensions using language that facilitates constructive cooperation and compromise, perhaps beginning with a phrase such as, "how about." For example, you could say to your dad: "How about we plan on playing racquetball late Saturday morning at the gym? That way I can spend Friday night catching up with friends. Does that sound good to you?" This approach gives your dad a say and something to look forward to. If your suggestion doesn't work, you can negotiate a day and time that works better for him.

Are you experiencing one or more dialectical tensions with anyone right now? If so, why? Have you experienced a dialectical tension in the past? What type of impact did this have on your relationship?

section review

8.3 **Managing dialectical tensions**

Relationships will invariably encounter dialectical tensions. At times our needs or motivations are opposite to those of our relational partners. These tensions include connection versus separation, predictability versus novelty, openness versus privacy, and dependence versus autonomy. Clear, honest, and effective communication may help you work through these tensions. One approach involves three steps: identifying the tension, validating the person's needs, and initiating solution-based communication.

Key Term

dialectical tension, *p. 217*

Comprehend It?

1. Define *dialectical tension*. To further your understanding of this term, create an example to support your definition.

2. Compare and contrast each of the following dialectical tensions:
   - Connection versus separation
   - Predictability versus novelty
   - Openness versus privacy
   - Dependence versus autonomy

Apply It!

Think of a dialectical tension you've experienced before (or make one up). Draft a dialogue between you and another person in which a dialectical tension exists and use the three-step method to (1) identify the tension using I-language, (2) validate the person's needs, and (3) engage in solution-based communication.

chapter exercises

Assessing Your IPC: Interpersonal Attraction

Purpose: To determine if I am drawn more to potential romantic partners based on similarities or differences.

Directions: This assessment was suggested in Section 8.2, "Similarities and differences," on page 206. Research suggests that you are more likely to form a long-term romantic relationship with someone who is similar to you.[42] To help you determine if you agree or disagree with the research, look at the following characteristics. Indicate your preference for a potential romantic partner who meets these descriptions using the following scale:

Really dislike	Dislike	Neither like nor dislike	Like	Really like
1	2	3	4	5

_____ (A) Same or very similar religious beliefs

_____ (B) Different religious beliefs

_____ (A) Same or similar body structure (overall height, weight, body shape)

_____ (B) Different body structure (overall height, weight, body shape)

_____ (A) Similar level of physical attractiveness

_____ (B) Higher or lower level of physical attractiveness

_____ (A) Same race and/or nationality

_____ (B) Different race and/or nationality

_____ (A) Same or similar education level

_____ (B) Higher or lower education level

_____ (A) Similar socioeconomic background

_____ (B) Higher or lower socioeconomic background

_____ (A) Same level of ambition

_____ (B) Higher or lower level of ambition

_____ (A) Mostly similar values

_____ (B) Mostly dissimilar values

_____ (A) Mostly similar interests

_____ (B) Mostly different interests

_____ (A) Similar number of past sexual encounters and relationships

_____ (B) Considerably more or fewer past sexual encounters

_____ (A) Similar outlook on life

_____ (B) Very different outlook on life

_____ (A) Similar health habits (eating, smoking, exercise, grooming)

_____ (B) Dissimilar health habits (eating, smoking, exercise, grooming)

_____ (A) Similar family background (marital status of parents, number of siblings, closeness of family)

_____ (B) Dissimilar family background (marital status of parents, number of siblings, closeness of family)

_____ (A) Same or close in age

_____ (B) Significantly younger or older in age

_____ (A) Similar political views or party affiliation

_____ (B) Dissimilar political views or party affiliation

_____ (A) Similar tastes and preferences in terms of music, movies, clothing, and food

_____ (B) Dissimilar tastes and preferences in terms of music, movies, clothing, and food

_____ (A) Same sexual orientation

_____ (B) Different sexual orientation

_____ (A) Same interests in future family planning (number of children desired, plans to care for loved ones)

_____ (B) Different interests in future family planning (number of children desired, plans to care for loved ones)

Add up all of the scores for the items marked *A*. Next, add up the scores for the items marked *B*. A items represent how much you value similarities. B items represent how much you prefer differences. The higher of the two scores suggests that you most likely want a romantic partner that is more similar (A) or dissimilar (B).

In some cases, your answers to the B statements would depend on whether the difference was one you perceived as positive or negative. For example, you may see a potential partner's "higher or lower level of ambition" as a positive difference if your partner is more ambitious than you. Are there areas where you see differences as being more positive compared to others? Are there differences or similarities that would influence your level of attraction significantly?

Building Your IPC Skills: Improving Your "Like Factor"

Purpose: To identify aspects of my interpersonal communication that make me more relationally attractive.

Directions: This exercise is from Section 8.1, "Relationships involve feelings," on page 202. The IPC behaviors listed below are known to reinforce positive relational feelings such as closeness, liking, love, passion, respect, and trust. Label each statement with the number between one and four that best represents how often each behavior occurs in your interpersonal communication.

Rarely	Sometimes	Neutral	Often	A lot
1	2	3	4	5

_____ I offer to help others whenever possible.

_____ I create opportunities to interact with people.

_____ I give others a say in terms of activity choices.

_____ I arrange it so that activities I do with others are mutually enjoyable.

_____ I refer to people's positive qualities often. I compliment and praise others.

_____ I am reliable. I stick with plans and do what I say I'm going to do.

_____ I appear interested in what others have to say.

_____ I remember what people share with me and follow up with them to show I care.

_____ I return people's phone calls, texts, and social invitations promptly.

_____ I make people laugh and can laugh easily with them.

_____ I express myself in a positive and optimistic way.

_____ I try to look my best.

_____ I strive to be genuine and honest with the things I say.

_____ I share personal information about myself so others can get to know me.

_____ I listen to others without interrupting.

_____ I invite others to express their opinions and ideas.

_____ I show that I value people's opinions and ideas even if I disagree.

_____ I smile often and appear happy to see people.

_____ I engage in affectionate forms of touch when appropriate—hugs, handshakes, high fives.

_____ I express what others mean to me: "I value our friendship."

_____ I treat others to small tokens of affection and gifts—cards, notes, candy, food.

_____ I engage in acts of kindness—for instance, picking up friends who need a ride.

_____ I share my food or personal belongings with others.

_____ I offer words of encouragement and support to others in person and online.

_____ I remember people's names and use them during conversations.

Have a few people who know you rate your behavior by completing this assessment. How do their ratings compare to yours? What are the similarities and differences?

Your goal here is to increase your self-awareness. Try to be open and receptive to the information you receive. Express appreciation for it and avoid making excuses, blaming the other person for your behavior, or getting defensive. If you disagree, try simply saying, "Good to know. I appreciate what you are saying. Thank you." (With a smile!)

9

Interpersonal Conflict

Michael Wilder could whip out thousands of dollars from his wallet whenever he wanted. "Too Short," as his friends called him, often wore a bulletproof vest and carried a gun. He wasn't a rich executive, police officer, or secret service agent. He was simply a scared 17-year-old.

"Nobody paid attention to me. I wanted to feel loved and important, so I joined a gang. I made a lot of money selling drugs," Michael explains. Though the gang gave Michael a sense of belonging and plenty of cash, it was a dangerous life, and enemies were easy to come by.

One such enemy was 6-foot-6, 370-pound Yafinceio Harris, aka "Big B." Past interpersonal conflict fueled Michael and Yafinceio's hatred toward each other—and almost cost them their lives.

When Michael was out with a friend one night, he found himself in a fight with Yafinceio's cousin Terrance. A scuffle erupted and Terrance grabbed a baseball bat and struck Michael repeatedly. Michael's friend pulled out a gun and shot Terrance, killing him. Enraged by his cousin's death, Yafinceio put a contract out on Michael's life. One day, members of Yafinceio's gang caught up with Michael, and a high-speed car chase ensued. Knowing he could no longer outrun them, Michael jumped out of his car, made a wild dash on foot, and lost his pursuers in a large crowd of people.

Michael was later arrested and sent to prison for drug dealing. He hated being there, but at least felt relieved that he wouldn't have to worry about Yafinceio for a while—until he found out Yafinceio

Conflict and power struggles are inevitable in close, interdependent relationships. Our ability to communicate a conflict and work through it will affect our relationships. A coworker who lacks skills in conflict management may turn a simple meeting into a very tense situation.

was arrested months later and occupied a nearby cellblock at the same prison. Michael never saw him but was told that Yafinceio had recruited other prisoners to kill him. He lived in a constant state of fear.

Years later, Michael was released from prison. He decided to quit gang life altogether and enroll at the college where one of your authors, Bruce, teaches. On the first day of his English class, Michael arrived a few minutes late and hurriedly grabbed a front-row seat, completely unaware that Yafinceio was sitting in the back of the classroom!

When class ended, Michael got up to leave and was shocked when Yafinceio approached him. Michael didn't know what to do. Should he run? Should he call security? Michael alerted his professor. The professor led the men out of the classroom and asked what was going on. Despite their mutual suspicion, the two started talking about why they had disassociated from gang life.

Surprisingly, over the course of the semester, Michael and Yafinceio became friends. They later formed a community organization called Peace During War, which promotes peaceful conflict resolution.

Like Michael and Yafinceio, you've probably experienced a serious conflict with a relational partner before. Whether or not this conflict was serious to the point of being life-threatening, it likely had an impact on you and your relationship. What caused the conflict? Did your interpersonal communication affect the outcome in any way?

In this chapter, we'll (1) explore the dynamic nature of interpersonal conflict, (2) examine how power is managed within relationships, and (3) identify strategies to resolve conflict effectively.

9.1 The nature of interpersonal conflict

Six decades ago, brothers Adi and Rudolf Dassler formed a sports shoe company. Their shoes gained international appeal after American Jesse Owens sprinted to four gold medal victories in the 1936 Olympics while wearing a pair of them.

Later, an intense rift suddenly developed between the brothers, and they never spoke to each other again. Some townsfolk believed that Rudolf had an affair with Adi's wife. Others thought that a political debate resulted in an exchange of hurtful insults.

The two brothers disbanded the company and each struck out on his own: Adi formed Adidas and Rudolf launched Puma. They located their companies in the same town, Herzogenaurach, Germany, divided only by a river. If one company tried to hire a celebrity athlete to promote its brand, the other would offer a better deal to steal the endorsement.

When Adi and Rudolf's children took over, they shared the same animosities as their fathers and often vocalized them to each other and to their organizations. To this day in Herzogenaurach, those who wear Adidas often won't associate with those who wear Puma, and vice versa.

Recently, in an effort to de-escalate tensions between the townspeople, the CEOs of both companies agreed to play a friendly soccer game to symbolize sportsmanship and harmony. Rather than play against each other, the companies divided their employees and placed them on both teams. Organizers hope the game is a positive step toward mending the 60-year conflict.[1]

This story illustrates an important fact: Conflict is created and maintained by communication behaviors, and it has the potential to significantly affect relationships.

In Section 9.1, we'll explore the nature of conflict—what it is, why it occurs, and how to approach it.

What is conflict?

Interpersonal conflict is a perceived struggle or tension between two or more relational partners. The struggle or tension may involve strongly held differences of opinion, incompatible goals, or unmet needs. Conflict can occur in a split second or it can unfold over a period of time. Its course is determined by the communication choices of those involved.

Conflict can be expressed in both obvious and subtle ways. **Overt conflict** is communicated in a clear, straightforward manner. The strife between Adi and Rudolf Dassler is an example of overt conflict; both brothers directly acknowledged it with their words and actions. Overt conflict may occur dramatically with yelling, threats, and harsh words, or it may play out more calmly through pleasant and polite behavior.

On the other hand, **covert conflict** is expressed indirectly—one relational partner may hint at it in a snide comment while the other suddenly limits interaction or eye contact. Relational partners may also try to mask the conflict or act like nothing is wrong, but it's there.

Whether conflict is overt or covert, it starts with perception. In Chapter 3, you learned that *perception* is the mental process of receiving and interpreting sensory information—what you taste, touch, smell, see, and hear. Your *attributions* are the explanations you assign to your perceptions. Perception and attributions play a major role in interpersonal conflict.[2] Let's consider, for instance, a potential conflict between two sisters, Jasmin and Berina. Jasmin doesn't want anyone to use her printer because she has to pay for the expensive ink cartridges herself. Berina, however, keeps sending documents to the printer even though Jasmin has told her not to. If Jasmin sees Berina using her printer again (perception) and assumes Berina is ignoring her wishes (attribution), a conflict exists.

However, if Berina promises to use Jasmin's printer only for school projects and offers to pay Jasmin each time she prints something—and follows through on her promises—there may not be any conflict between them at all. Jasmin no longer perceives Berina's behavior as affecting her negatively, and Berina has access to a resource she needs.

To take another example, in her narrative, Dakotah describes a conflict she's having. As Dakotah points out, she perceives her future mother-in-law's behavior and attributes it to a lack of respect. This may cause Dakotah to feel angry, frustrated, resentful, sad, or anxious.[3] If Dakotah communicates her feelings to

> **interpersonal conflict**
> A perceived struggle or tension between two or more relational partners.
>
> **overt conflict** Conflict that relational partners express to each other in a direct and straightforward manner.
>
> **covert conflict** Conflict that relational partners mask or do not acknowledge openly.

> "Two weeks before my wedding, my fiancé's mother asked me for pictures so she could put a PowerPoint presentation together to show during our rehearsal dinner. I told her I wasn't a big fan of the idea. After our conversation, she went ahead and told my fiancé to send her the pictures. I felt like she went behind my back and didn't take my feelings into consideration."
> –Dakotah

conflict spiral A situation that occurs when relational partners address conflict in an increasingly hostile and mean-spirited manner.

past-digging The act of bringing up a negative memory you have of your relational partner to drive home a point.

beltlining The act of taking something a relational partner has disclosed to you in confidence and using it against this person in a future conversation.

gunny-sacking The act of bringing up a bunch of past, unexpressed grievances in the heat of an argument.

her fiancé's mother effectively, the conflict may end. But if Dakotah's communication isn't effective, or if her fiancé's mother reacts in a way that Dakotah perceives as discourteous, the conflict may escalate.

Conflict escalation

A **conflict spiral** occurs when relational partners address conflict in an increasingly hostile and mean-spirited manner. For example, in an angry outburst you may reveal a *dirty secret*, something that you've done but kept secret from your relational partner, such as "I did cheat on you with my ex!" or "I hate your cooking. I've been feeding it to the dog for years!" Revealing a dirty secret is a move designed to wound, and it can provoke an angry, impassioned reaction that escalates the conflict even further. Even if you later recant a secret that you weaponized in an argument—you might say, for instance, "I really didn't sleep with my ex. I just said that in the heat of the moment to get you upset"—the fact that you said anything at all may raise suspicion and plant seeds of doubt.

People caught up in a conflict spiral may also express *sudden-death statements* or breakup messages, such as, "I quit," "That's it, we're done," or "I'm moving out." These messages are hurtful and may cause the other person to fire back with, "Great! Let me pack your bags for you!"

There are several other communication behaviors associated with conflict escalation. One in particular is past-digging. **Past-digging** occurs when you bring up a negative memory you have about your relational partner to drive home a point. Past-digging often takes the form of accusatory questions or statements. You might say, for example: "You never show up for me! Where were you during my last tournament? The one you swore you'd go to?" Your relational partner may feel compelled to respond in a face-saving manner by bringing up a time when you didn't follow through on a promise you made, and the argument intensifies.

There are various forms of past-digging. Two of the most common and damaging ones are beltlining and gunny-sacking. **Beltlining**, or "hitting below the belt," occurs when someone discloses something very personal to you in confidence, or during a moment of vulnerability, and you use this information in a future conversation as a putdown or criticism.[4]

For example, imagine that Brianna opens up and reveals to her boyfriend, Jeremy, that she treated her ex badly during a rocky point in their relationship. Looking back, she feels terrible about it. Months later, when Jeremy and Brianna get into an argument, Jeremy, in a moment of anger, says, "I can't believe you're acting like this. I'm sorry, but I'm not your ex!" Ouch! Jeremy's comment hits below the belt. He doesn't have to refer to Brianna's past disclosure to make his point—he does so because it will hurt her.

Gunny-sacking is the act of bringing up a bunch of past, unexpressed grievances in the heat of an argument.[5] Gunny-sacking starts when a relational partner wrongs you in some way. Instead of addressing it openly, you keep your thoughts and feelings hidden. You carry them around with you in a metaphorical sack, and each time a bothersome behavior occurs, you stuff your thoughts and feelings away. Over time, the sack gets heavy. At some point, usually when you're upset, you'll dump out what you've stored in the sack and launch into a litany of complaints about the person's past behavior.

Along with the behaviors (beltlining and gunny-sacking) associated with past-digging, another problematic behavior associated with conflict escalation is *passive-aggressiveness*. In Chapter 7, you learned that passive-aggressiveness is a form of indirect hostility that allows the sender to appear outwardly non-combative. For example, a wife who doesn't like that her husband isn't helping enough around the house may deliberately start vacuuming nearby, making it more difficult for him to hear what he's trying to watch on TV. A first-string basketball player who is upset that the coach gave him less playing time than usual during the previous game might show up late to the next practice with a false excuse, keeping the coach from running important pre-game plays. The goal of passive-aggressive behavior is to convey your feelings, and often to punish someone, in a disguised manner or without direct confrontation. However, a relational partner may catch wind of your passive-aggressive behavior and respond in ways that add fuel to the fire.

Conflict rituals

A **conflict ritual** is a reoccurring pattern of communication that sparks and inflames conflict. For example, one of our students, Catherine, shared,

> For a while whenever I left my wet clothes in the washer, my mom would get snippy and say, "Your laundry is getting moldy again." I'd get defensive and we'd end up having an argument. I appreciate how she talks to me now. With a soft and pleasant voice she says, "Your wash is ready for the dryer. Do you need me to switch it over for you?" It's a kind reminder. I actually feel more motivated to stay on top of my laundry.

In this case, the conflict ritual was the argument that always followed the critique Catherine received when she did her laundry. By changing the way she conveyed her message, Catherine's mom helped the two of them stay clear of their conflict ritual.

Conflict and stress

Conflict is a source of stress, especially when it escalates (as in a conflict spiral) and when it reoccurs (as in a conflict ritual). In a study that focused on the effect conflict has on stress, couples were asked to submit saliva samples before and after an experimental conflict negotiation task. The samples collected after the task revealed increased levels of cortisol, a hormone associated with stress. Cortisol levels were even higher among couples who felt less secure about their relationship.[6] In another study, researchers found that elevated levels of cortisol lingered not only for parents who had argued, but also for their children, who had watched their parents argue. This was particularly true if the children blamed themselves for their parents' conflict.[7]

conflict ritual A reoccurring pattern of communication that sparks and inflames conflict.

de-escalation Using your communication to power down or decrease the intensity and scope of a conflict.

The stress caused by relational conflict may adversely affect your heart health, immune system, and sleep. In addition, when you're under stress, you're more likely to engage in unhealthy behaviors like smoking, drinking, and overeating.[8] Unresolved conflict is associated with reduced productivity at work, poor workplace morale, depression, argumentativeness, relationship demise, divorce, and domestic violence.[9]

Conflict de-escalation

While some conflicts are unavoidable, your communication choices may help you de-escalate or power down a conflict. To **de-escalate** a conflict is to decrease its intensity and scope. For example, if a client calls you to complain about a recurring billing error and you listen intently, apologize without making excuses, validate his feelings, and quickly identify a solution, your communication is likely to de-escalate the conflict.

You can also completely circumvent conflict with proactive communication. Imagine, for example, that you've promised your cousin Nadine that you'll arrive a little early to her baby shower to help set things up, but on the day of the party, you're running late. If you let Nadine know ahead of time, this reduces the potential problems your tardiness may cause—a better choice than just showing up late without warning and trying to explain after Nadine's already upset with you. We'll discuss more strategies for de-escalating conflict in Section 9.3.

Common causes of conflict

Some causes of conflict are more common than others.[10] Arguments between romantic partners, for instance, may stem more often from jealousy, perceived differences in commitment, and unmet emotional needs.[11] Friends are more

In this scene from the 2020 TV series *Party of Five*, Javier (Bruno Bichir) and his son Emilio (Brandon Larracuente) rely on technology to stay connected after Javier and his wife Gloria are deported to Mexico. An issue gets brought up. How would you use this scene to define interpersonal conflict? What do you think is the cause of their conflict? Does it appear to be expressed more in a covert or overt way? On YouTube, search using the keywords: "Party of Five Season 1, Episode 6 – Javier is worried Emilio is hiding something." (2:29)

likely to quarrel about the management of shared friendships and problems associated with planning social activities.[12] We can break the common sources of conflict into seven categories: change, incompatible values, scarce resources, interdependence, memory, meta-conflict, and undesirable behaviors.

Change

Change is a common source of conflict. Imagine, for example, that your employer's rapid growth or merger requires you and your coworkers to perform new, unfamiliar tasks. Conflict may arise if someone is slow or unwilling to learn or if there's ambiguity about who is responsible for doing which task.

Change can occur quickly. Take, for instance, a couple staring in disbelief at a positive pregnancy test. If a pregnancy is unplanned, and one partner is pleasantly surprised but the other partner is deeply disappointed or even scared, it could instigate a conflict. Other times, change occurs slowly—almost imperceptibly. Say your mother has always enjoyed gambling; it was never a real concern, but financial problems have started to surface as she spends more time at the casino. If she doesn't believe there is a problem or a reason to change, this could create conflict between the two of you because you feel it's important to look out for her.

Incompatible values

Your *values* are your priorities in life; what you consider important. What you value may include your commitments and relationships, along with your beliefs, goals, traditions, and affiliations. Incompatible values often lead to conflict. A dilemma may occur, for example, when one partner considers it important to celebrate certain dates on the calendar, and the other doesn't. Let's say Emma loves Valentine's Day; she makes dinner reservations at a fancy boutique hotel and buys her boyfriend, Shen, an expensive shirt to celebrate. When Shen arrives home from work, she hands him his gift, saying, "You'll love it! It's something you can wear tonight when we go out." Shen replies, "Go out? I'd rather just lay low tonight." Shen apparently hasn't made any plans for Valentine's Day, nor does he have a gift to give her. Emma is hurt and disappointed.

Shen knows Emma is upset, but he prefers to create romantic moments on a whim or when the moment is right, not when he feels obligated to do so because of a particular date on the calendar, especially one he feels is overly commercialized.

Emma doesn't see it Shen's way. She wants to do something special with Shen on Valentine's Day because it celebrates and kindles romantic love. What could Emma and Shen do from a communication standpoint to work through this conflict? Is there an outcome both could feel good about? What would you suggest?

Scarce resources

A scarce resource is something that is finite or available on a limited basis. Imagine you're sitting at the dinner table and can't wait to dig into the last piece of your dad's prized homemade lasagna. Your brother wants the exact same

"It's mine—and I'd apprecicate your not looking out of it."

thing. You both reach for it. Right now, the two of you are in conflict because of a limited resource. If you agree to share the last piece, this is a great way to resolve the conflict—just be sure to split it evenly!

Besides food, a scarce resource can be time, money, and space. For example, you usually only have a certain amount of time to sleep in a given day; if the quality of that time spent sleeping is affected by a sleep partner, conflict may arise. Take Sujin and her partner, Rachael. When Sujin sleeps, she needs a light on and runs a fan to create white noise. Rachael, on the other hand, can't sleep unless it's completely dark and quiet. Another couple, Zane and Amare, are at odds too. Zane sprawls out a lot and moves all over the bed while he sleeps. Amare is tired of getting kicked and elbowed at all hours of the night. For some couples, sleeping in separate beds is a solution that allows them to maximize the time they have to sleep soundly.

In fact, a survey of over 1,000 Americans found that approximately 62% of couples say they'd prefer to sleep alone, and 27% say they sleep in different beds because they are not sleep compatible.[13] Sleep researcher Neil Stanley, who does not sleep with his wife, thinks this is a good idea and advises that it's better for most couples not to share a bed for sleeping purposes.[14] Stanley points to various studies as evidence. One study in particular found that sleep-deprived couples were more likely to get into verbal fights.[15]

Interdependence

Interdependence is the degree to which you rely on a relational partner to help you achieve your goals and meet your needs. For example, in a college class, your grade may depend on a group project; you expect everyone in the group to take the assignment as seriously as you do. What if one of your groupmates is slacking? Because your grade depends on all members of the group doing their fair share and submitting quality work, you perceive that your classmate is interfering with your goals, which causes you to feel frustrated and angry. Doing well in school is important to you.

Managing finances is another major source of conflict that stems from interdependence. When you're casually dating someone, you make most money decisions independently; however, when you're cohabitating or married, interdependence is greater. The two of you will have to agree on such things as decorating and home improvement expenses, establishing a budget, debt reduction, savings, and investments—all of which can spark conflict if the two of you aren't on the same page.[16]

Memory disputes

"No, that's not what happened!" "I didn't say that!" "You mean to tell me you don't remember?" A memory dispute occurs when you and a relational partner remember past events or conversations differently. There are many reasons why memory disputes may occur. Some are perfectly innocent: Perhaps you can't remember something because you were distracted or tired at the time when it happened. You and a relational partner may also disagree on how a conversation went if you felt hurt by what the other person said or if there is a lack of trust between the two of you. You may then remember the conversation in a way that reinforces your feelings of hurt or suspicion.[17]

Memory is often used as a weapon in conflict. As you develop a relationship with someone over time, you'll share more personal information about yourself. While this self-disclosure fosters a strong bond, it also has the potential to provide your relational partner with ammunition to use against you in a future conflict (recall our discussion of *beltlining*). During the course of a relationship, you have the potential to do things—intentionally and unintentionally—that hurt your relational partner. Sometimes conflict is perpetuated by a past grievance lingering in the mind of the person affected by it.

Meta-conflict

Meta-conflict is conflict caused by the way you express conflict. For example, one of our students, Glenn, shared that in the past he'd sometimes flick his children on the head when they weren't listening to him. His wife, Traci, didn't like seeing him do that. What made the conflict between Glenn and Traci worse, according to Glenn, is that he'd made attempts to respect her wishes, but when he forgot and did it out of habit, Traci scolded him in front of the children, which made him feel belittled. He then responded by criticizing her reaction: "Stop yelling at me in front of the kids! Talk about bad parenting." Glenn and Traci's communication about their conflict made their conflict worse.

Undesirable behaviors

Someone's words or actions may really get under your skin, especially if you have to deal with that person's behavior frequently. For example, a colleague who works in the cubicle next to you may talk loudly when he's on the phone, which is very distracting. You may also feel frustrated that none of your coworkers refill the copy machine when it runs out of paper or fix their own paper jams.

Our students often talk about conflicts that stem from the undesirable behaviors of their roommates. Sarah shared that she's very annoyed by her new roommate's overzealous attempts to pursue friendships with her close friends. JaQuan dislikes it when his roommate uses his soap and shaving products without asking.

Approaches to conflict

Twelve years ago, our student Mary and her husband, Roger, agreed that it made sense for Roger to take on the role of stay-at-home dad to their young children. This arrangement worked out well: Mary's job offered adequate pay and benefits to cover the family, and Roger was great with the kids. Roger used his downtime to start a home-based business, and he enrolled in classes to advance his career. Today, the kids are 12 and 14 years old and attend middle school. Roger

In the TV series *Pose*, several teenagers who are rejected by their families form a family unit with Blanca (Mj Rodriguez), a transgender woman. Blanca is determined to see them realize their potential. Compare this scene between Blanca and Helena (Charlayne Woodard), the lead instructor at a prestigious dance school, to the seven sources of conflict highlighted in this section. Which source of conflict is evident in the clip? How might this source of conflict unfold from an IPC standpoint in both a positive way and a negative way? On YouTube, search using the keywords: "Pose Season 1 Real Mothers Scene." (1:38)

is still at home and not working. His business isn't flourishing as planned, and he's completed only five classes.

Mary is tired of being the sole breadwinner, but when she confronts Roger about it, he becomes quite defensive. Now, Mary completely avoids the topic. Roger has promised to do things to improve the situation, and she is begrudgingly giving him more time, even though Roger hasn't given her any specifics about his career plans.

What should Mary and Roger say and do to address their conflict effectively? Your answers may reflect how you view conflict and your preferred way of handling it. **TABLE 9.1** lists five styles of or approaches to conflict: competing, avoiding, accommodating, collaborating, and compromising.[18]

As you read over the table and the material that follows, see if you can pinpoint two of the approaches Mary is using to address her conflict with Roger. Also, identify which of the strategies you use most often with your relational partners. When and how often do you use them? What are the results?

Competing

If you view conflict in zero-sum terms—that is, either you win or you lose—you may favor a competing approach to conflict. **Competing** is a way of approaching conflict where you prioritize getting what you want above all else; you must "win" at the expense of others. You may refuse to take no for an answer, debate relentlessly, or walk away in the middle of a conversation that's not going your way. A competing approach may also lead to acts of direct aggression such as

competing A conflict approach that prioritizes getting what you want above all else; you must "win" at the expense of others.

table 9.1	Conflict Patterns and Outcomes	
Approach	**Characteristics**	**Outcome**
Competing	You're focused on winning at all costs.	I win. You lose.
Avoiding	You don't want to deal with the conflict.	I lose. You lose.
Accommodating	You're willing to sacrifice your needs for your relational partner(s).	I lose. You win.
Collaborating	You want the best possible outcome for you and your relational partner(s).	I win. You win.
Compromising	You will make some concessions in order to produce an acceptable outcome.	I win/lose. You win/lose.

ugly shouting, swearing, ridicule, or threats, and it may even escalate to physical intimidation or violence.

Avoiding

Avoiding is an approach that steers clear of all overt conflict. Research suggests that avoidance is the approach to conflict most often used by relational partners; individuals may pretend the conflict doesn't exist or stay quietly upset or simmer about an issue without addressing it.[19] This means that, even if a conflict appears nonexistent on the surface, it may emerge seemingly out of nowhere later.[20]

Two common forms of avoiding are skirting and sniping.[21] **Skirting** occurs when you avoid conflict by either joking about a problem or changing the topic of conversation. Take a couple, Raul and Elaina, for instance. Furious that Raul put off doing their taxes until the last minute, Elaina angrily brings it up while they're driving to their daughter's soccer game. Raul tries to make a joke about it, saying, "Don't get mad, you know you can't drive when you're in*tax*icated." He uses humor to disarm Elaina without seriously addressing her concerns.

Sniping occurs when you allude to a conflict but then back away from it. Imagine a friend calls you at the last minute to tell you he's made changes to the evening plans you'd agreed to. You're sniping if you tell him, "Don't bother to ask me what *I* want to do." When your friend tries to find out what you would rather do, you say, "Never mind," and refuse to talk about it further, avoiding immediate conflict.

Accommodating

Accommodating is a way of approaching conflict that prioritizes maintaining harmony at all costs. It's quite the opposite of competing. You accommodate

avoiding A conflict approach that steers clear of all overt conflict.

skirting The act of avoiding conflict by either joking about a problem or changing the topic of conversation.

sniping The act of alluding to a conflict but then backing away from it.

accommodating A conflict approach that prioritizes maintaining harmony at all costs.

collaborating A conflict approach that prioritizes finding an outcome that is ideal for everyone.

compromising A conflict approach in which you make some concessions that are less than ideal but acceptable to everyone.

by giving in to the needs or goals of others, sacrificing your own in the process—often to escape uncomfortable conversations or keep the peace.

For example, one of your authors, Leslie, once dated a guy named Jorge. Jorge was a tall, handsome, hardworking man with an infectious smile. Leslie really liked him, but she was caught off guard one night when Jorge told her that he wanted to start a family right away. He valued a very conventional type of marriage, and he asked her to quit her job as a professor to raise their children. Leslie loves her work and wouldn't think of leaving her profession for any reason. In response, she told Jorge that she could work full-time and raise children successfully. They discussed the issue rigorously but couldn't reach an agreement, and the relationship dissolved. Had Leslie given in to Jorge's wishes and ignored her own needs, she would have accommodated him as a conflict strategy.

Collaborating

Collaborating is a conflict approach that prioritizes finding an outcome that is ideal for everyone. Let's say that you and your two teenage children each want to do something different on vacation: You can't wait to relax by the pool; your son, Dillon, wants to book a whale-watching tour; and your daughter, Natalie, wants to go snorkeling. A collaborative way to resolve this conflict is for the three of you to find ways to fit all of the desired activities into your vacation in order to make everyone happy. Collaborating often takes more time and effort, and it requires listening, discussing, brainstorming, and other-centered thinking.

Compromising

There are times when finding a solution that satisfies everyone is extremely difficult, if not impossible. **Compromising** is a way of approaching conflict by making some concessions that are not ideal but acceptable to everyone. You may approach a conflict knowing that you want certain things, but you also care about your relational partner's needs. Recall the vacation example. If you only have time to do two of the three activities your family would like to do, you might flip a coin to determine who gets to decide, or you may agree to go snorkeling and whale watching, as long as Dillon and Natalie promise to give you extra pool time when the three of you vacation again later in the summer. When you compromise, you give up some things in return for gaining other things. The outcome is not completely ideal, but it's acceptable to everyone.

Research suggests that collaborating and compromising foster greater relational satisfaction, trust, and commitment. Competing approaches, on the other hand, tend to promote resistance, enmity, and ambivalence. Those who find safety and comfort in avoiding conflict may also find that avoidance stifles relational growth. And while there are times when accommodating may seem like a good choice, those who accommodate too often may find themselves feeling increasingly disappointed, disrespected, devalued, and dissatisfied with their relationships.[22]

Research also indicates that your preferred conflict management style (competing, avoiding, accommodating, collaborating, or compromising) may have a

In this scene from the TV series *Station 19*, firefighter Victoria (Barrett Doss) confronts her best friend Travis (Jay Hayden) about his decision to order a rookie to leave his side when his injuries and an intense fire threatened both of their lives. Which of the conflict approaches does Victoria use? On YouTube, search using the keywords: "Station 19 Victoria Tells Travis Why's She's Mad at Him." (1:55)

lot to do with personality traits like assertiveness and cooperativeness. *Assertiveness* is your willingness to advocate for your interests and needs. *Cooperativeness* is the extent to which you work with others and help them get what they want. If you lack assertiveness and you're not very cooperative, you're more likely to avoid conflict. If you are highly assertive, but not very cooperative, you're apt to handle conflict competitively. If you are highly cooperative and not very assertive, you'll tend to manage conflict using accommodation. If you are highly cooperative and assertive, you're more likely to use compromising and collaborating conflict approaches.[23]

Misconceptions about conflict

Conflict is a normal, inevitable occurrence, but misconceptions may affect how you approach conflict.[24] One misconception is that conflict is always bad for a relationship—that it is **deconstructive**. In reality, conflict can be good or bad depending on how relational partners perceive and handle it. If you work through conflict effectively, it is constructive. **Constructive conflict** results in positive relational outcomes, such as getting feelings out in the open and making decisions that are mutually satisfying. When you work out your differences with someone, it can strengthen the bond you share and improve your communication competence.[25]

Another common misconception is that conflict will go away with time if you just ignore it. A conflict may seem insignificant now, but it could intensify if it's not addressed early. If you believe that a conflict can't or won't get resolved, you might not even try to resolve it, or you may give up prematurely. Sometimes it's necessary to try various conflict management approaches to work out an issue with someone. Unless you get to the root cause of a conflict and resolve it successfully, it may pop up repeatedly over time.[26]

deconstructive conflict
Conflict that damages or hurts a relationship.

constructive conflict
Conflict that results in positive relational outcomes.

Finally, there's the belief that conflict means that a relationship is in trouble. If conflict goes unresolved and gets worse, that may be true. However, conflict itself doesn't necessarily mean that both parties are ready to end a relationship, even if the conflict is handled in ways that make you think the relationship is rocky. If you and a relational partner openly talk about a conflict, it shows that the relationship still matters to you. You care about it and want it to get better. When you don't bring up a conflict, the reverse is often true—you've checked out completely and no longer care.

section review

9.1 The nature of interpersonal conflict

Interpersonal conflict is a perceived struggle or tension between two or more relational partners. Conflict may influence your emotions and health. Effective communication can help you work through, minimize, or even prevent conflict. There are various sources of conflict, including change, incompatible values, scarce resources, interdependence, memory disputes, meta-conflict, and undesirable behaviors. There are also various ways to approach conflict: competing, avoiding, accommodating, collaborating, or compromising. Certain misconceptions may affect how you approach conflict.

Key Terms

interpersonal conflict, p. 229	beltlining, p. 230	competing, p. 236	collaborating, p.238
overt conflict, p. 229	gunny-sacking, p. 230	avoiding, p. 237	compromising, p.238
covert conflict, p. 229	conflict ritual, p. 231	skirting, p. 237	deconstructive conflict, p. 239
conflict spiral, p. 230	de-escalation, p. 232	sniping, p. 237	constructive conflict, p. 239
past-digging, p. 230	meta-conflict, p. 235	accommodating, p.237	

Comprehend It?

1. Define each of the key terms in Section 9.1. To further your understanding of these terms, create examples to support your definitions.

2. Explain how conflict starts with perception and attributions.

3. Describe how each of the following can be sources of interpersonal conflict: change, incompatible values, scarce resources, interdependence, memory, meta-conflict, and undesirable behaviors.

4. Compare and contrast the following approaches to conflict: competing, avoiding, accommodating, collaborating, and compromising.

Apply It!

Think of a significant interpersonal conflict you had with someone recently. Did change, incompatible values, scarce resources, interdependence, memory disputes, meta-conflict, and/or undesirable behaviors play a role in the conflict? What was your approach to the conflict? Was it competing, avoiding, accommodating, collaborating, or compromising? Was it the best approach? Why or why not?

9.2 **Power in relationships**

As tears stream down her face, Aliyah turns to her mother, Sandy, and says, "You are my mom, but you haven't been my mom for a long time. If I stopped doing everything for you, you would be dead in less than a month." Sandy chases her antianxiety, depression, and seizure pills with two pints of vodka a day. She drinks mouthwash when her vodka supply runs out.

Sandy's three daughters, son, and husband decide to confront Sandy together in her living room with the help of a professional therapist. The air is thick and what happens next is heart-wrenching. Sandy's loved ones spell out exactly what will happen if Sandy refuses to participate in a recovery program. The consequences include divorce and not being able to spend time with her grandchildren. The family's attempts to control and exert power over Sandy's addiction are shown on the reality TV series *Intervention*.

This example illustrates the challenges of managing power within relationships. Many interpersonal conflicts occur as a result of a power struggle—when two or more individuals are not willing to relinquish control or share power in a way that is mutually satisfying.

In Section 9.2 you'll gain a greater understanding of interpersonal power—and its relationship to conflict.

Power orientations

Interpersonal power is the ability to influence a relational partner's thoughts, feelings, and behaviors. The degree to which you prefer to exercise control and power in a relationship may fall along a continuum from abdicratic to autocratic. (See **FIGURE 9.1**.)

You are **abdicratic** if you prefer to relinquish control in most cases; you're more comfortable letting others take charge or make decisions. If this best describes you, you're a "happy follower." If you're a power seeker, you're more **autocratic**; you have a greater need to exercise control and have the final say more often. You're a "happy boss." In the middle of the two ends of the power spectrum is the **democratic** orientation. Someone described as democratic fluctuates between these two orientations quite comfortably depending on the situation or the relationship. You're as comfortable being in charge as you are letting others take over whenever you sense it's necessary.[27]

Let's compare all three power orientations. A father may allow his adolescent daughter to make her own decisions to encourage her to mature and develop

interpersonal power The ability to influence the thoughts, feelings, and behaviors of a relational partner.

abdicratic The power orientation characterized by a tendency to let others take charge or make decisions.

autocratic The power orientation characterized by a tendency to take charge and make decisions.

democratic The power orientation characterized by a fluctuating need for power; between abdicratic and autocratic.

Abdicratic	Democratic	Autocratic

FIGURE 9.1 Power Orientations

effective decision-making skills. This kind of parent is abdicratic. However, if he insists on making a lot of decisions for her without her involvement or say, he is more autocratic. Another father may share power with his daughter in certain situations, but when he thinks it's best to step in and have the final say, he does. If this is the case his power orientation is democratic. Which term describes your need for interpersonal power most of the time?

Interpersonal conflict may occur when relational partners are unwilling to be democratic or when both are either autocratic or abdicratic. The following dialogue between Pat and Kiri illustrates how conflict may arise between two abdicratic individuals. How would you rewrite the narrative to make their communication more productive?

> **Kiri:** Where do you want to go for dinner?
> **Pat:** I don't care. You?
> **Kiri:** I don't care either. We can go wherever. I'll let you decide this time.
> **Pat:** We could go to Logan's or TGI Fridays. Or, how about Olive Garden?
> **Kiri:** I don't care, just pick a place!
> **Pat:** But did you have a place in mind?
> **Kiri:** No. I was hoping you would just pick a place.
> (*Pat looks at Kiri blankly*.)
> **Kiri:** It's like this all the time. Sometimes it would be nice if you would just decide for us.

As this dialogue suggests, the way in which a relational partner perceives your use of power is important. (Kiri perceives Pat's use of power as unhelpful to the point of annoyance.) In order to satisfy everyone's power needs, effective communication and compromise may be necessary. Sometimes you need to relinquish power in order to accommodate a relational partner's autocratic needs, or you may need to take charge or make a decision when asked.[28] It may help to clarify who has a greater need for power in a given situation by asking questions such as, "Would you like me to handle this, or would you rather?" Other possible questions include, "How would you like us to proceed?" and "What would you like me to do?"

Sources of power

Is there someone you know who possesses a lot of interpersonal power? Chances are, this person controls a resource that you and others value, referred to as a **power currency**. A power currency can be money, sex appeal, or access to a desired social network.[29] For example, imagine you are a new student at a school, and you meet Miley, a leader of a peer group you'd like to associate with. Miley has interpersonal power because of her social currency. If Miley invites you to join her friends at lunch or attend a meeting for a club she's a member of, you may find yourself easily persuaded because she controls a resource you desire.

Someone who has less to lose if the relationship ends may also wield more interpersonal power. The **principle of least interest** suggests that a relational

power currency A desired resource that confers interpersonal power on the person who possesses it.

principle of least interest The idea that a relational partner who has the least interest in continuing the relationship may feel less inclined to yield or share power.

partner who doesn't value the relationship as much or has the least interest in continuing it holds more power in the relationship. This person may feel less inclined to accommodate, collaborate, or compromise because if the relationship deteriorates or ceases, it affects that person less than the other relational partner. For example, if your romantic partner says he's considering ending the relationship, but you are still very invested in it, he wields more interpersonal power than you. You may do more of what he wants in order to keep the relationship going. In business interactions, you may feel less inclined to negotiate a deal if you have other interested buyers; there is less to lose if the deal doesn't go through.[30]

Along with power currency and the principle of least interest, there are several other sources of power. In a 1959 study on interpersonal power, social psychologists John French and Bertram Raven identified and described five sources or bases of social power: reward, coercive, referent, legitimate, and expert power (see TABLE 9.2).[31] As you read about each power base, think about your most significant relationships. Are there bases of power you rely on more often with certain individuals? Are there bases of power others use to influence you? If so, which ones?

The ability to exercise interpersonal power from any of French and Raven's power bases depends a lot on the communication context.[32] For example, if you ran into your professor at a pub and she asked you to retake a test right then and there, you'd probably respond, "Are you kidding? I don't think so!" Your professor may have legitimate power in the classroom, but she certainly doesn't have it at a bar.

In addition, within a family context, parents typically wield the most interpersonal power, because they are the adults and can reward (*reward power*) and punish (*coercive power*) their children for good and bad behavior, respectively. Parents tend to relinquish their interpersonal power as their children reach

table 9.2	French and Raven's Five Power Bases
Reward power	You can reward someone with something desirable (with accolades, money, gifts, opportunities).
Coercive power	You can punish someone (cause harm, take something away, or withhold something of value).
Referent power	You can influence someone because you possess something that is highly desired or admired (physical beauty, a magnetic personality, popularity, success, or fame).
Legitimate power	You exercise power because of your title, credentials, or formal position. Power is given to you by an institution or governing body.
Expert power	You can persuade others because you have the knowledge, experience, or skills they lack.

adulthood, especially when their adult children move out and start living on their own, for the most part. However, as Fernando aptly describes in his narrative, power struggles may still occur between parents and their adult children. See if you can identify the power bases (reward, coercive, referent, legitimate, and expert) that Fernando's parents are trying to tap into.

"My parents rely a lot on me to take care of my younger siblings. This includes driving them to school and work. They bought me a nice car, and I spent a lot of money detailing it and adding expensive rims. When I told them I was ready to move out, they said the car would have to stay with them so my younger brother could drive it—even though I paid for all of the repairs and maintenance for four years! They also offered to pay more of my tuition if I stayed home. I feel like they want to control every part of my life." —Fernando

Compliance-gaining strategies

In an interview with Oprah Winfrey, actor Matthew McConaughey shared a story about his mom, Kay. Kay would often make Matthew and his two older brothers, Michael and Pat, a great breakfast to start the day. If Matthew and his siblings ever failed to show their appreciation for the food and her hard work, she would order them back to bed. According to Matthew, "She'd say, 'Don't come downstairs until you are ready to see the roses in the vase instead of the dust on the table.'"

Matthew's mom exercised coercive power when she withheld their breakfast until they changed their attitude. As you'll remember from Chapter 7, *withholding* occurs when you purposely deprive someone of something they want or need as a compliance-gaining strategy. **Compliance-gaining strategies** are the communication tactics you use to get others to do what you want them to do.[33]

To get a better sense of how these strategies work, consider the following example. Aiden, a construction manager, and Trey, a police detective, are dating exclusively. Aiden wants to move in with Trey. He first poses the idea nonchalantly one day, but Trey doesn't respond enthusiastically. A couple weeks later, while grilling out on Trey's back patio, Aiden points out that most of his belongings have made their way to Trey's house over the course of their 18-month relationship. Not only would the move be easy, Aiden says, but there would be clear benefits to pooling their assets and income under one roof. Aiden is using *logical appeals*—sound reasons, evidence, and facts—in an attempt to persuade Trey.

Although Trey sees the logic in what Aiden is saying, he balks at the suggestion. Aiden may then employ an *obligatory absolute*, a statement suggesting that a certain course of action would go against a well-established norm, standard, or expectation. An obligatory absolute is often expressed using words such as "should," "ought to," or "supposed to." Aiden may say to Trey, "People who love each other like we do *ought* to live together," or "We're the only couple I know who practically lives together but owns two homes."

compliance-gaining strategy A communication tactic that you use to get a relational partner to do what you want.

If this doesn't work, Aiden may employ a reciprocity appeal. You may recall from Chapter 5 that a *reciprocity appeal* occurs when you imply that it's time for your relational partner to return a favor with the intent of making that person feel guilty if they say no. Say that Aiden has helped Trey renovate his condo. He may use this as the basis of his next appeal: "Oh, I get it; it's great to have me here virtually living with you to help you renovate this place, but now that it's finished you want your space." Aiden might also say, "I've spent all this time helping you do what is important to you, but you can't do this for me?"

Aiden may use one or more of these tactics with varying degrees of success. If you use the same compliance-gaining tactic on someone repeatedly because it gets you what you want, clinical psychologist Claude Steiner calls this a **power play**.[34] For example, if your roommate feels guilty about having hurt you in some way, he may feel obligated to make up for it. You know he feels bad, and you capitalize on his guilt by asking him to do things for you. If you use this tactic on him repeatedly with success, it's a power play.

TABLE 9.3 lists additional verbal and nonverbal compliance-gaining strategies.[35] As you read through the table, label each strategy with the number between one and five that best reflects how often you use it (with 1 meaning "rarely" and 5 meaning "frequently"). Based on your scores, which tactics surface the most in your IPC? Do they work? If so, with whom and why? How might the tactic affect a relationship? Share your thoughts with a classmate or discussion group.

> **power play** When you use a compliance-gaining tactic on someone repeatedly because it gets you what you want.

table 9.3	Compliance-Gaining Strategies		
Type	**Description**	**Example**	**Score (1-5)**
Bargaining	You offer to do something for a relational partner if that person agrees to do something for you.	"If you cook dinner for my family, I'll buy you that high-end blender you keep talking about."	_____
Just this once	You promise that your relational partner will only have to do the disagreeable action once.	"I won't ask you to cook dinner for my family ever again."	_____
Pre-giving	You behave generously toward a relational partner because you want that person to do you a favor in the future.	"Did you enjoy the spa package I bought you? Glad to hear. Um . . . I hate to ask but could you make dinner for my family tonight?"	_____
Positive esteem appeal	You convince a relational partner that doing what you ask will make others think highly of that person.	"If you cook dinner, my family would love it—love *you*, I should say."	_____
Negative esteem avoidance	You convince a relational partner that refusing to do as you ask would make others think poorly of that person.	"My family will think you can't cook if you don't at least cook them something."	_____

(Continued)

table 9.3	Compliance-Gaining Strategies—cont'd		
Type	**Description**	**Example**	**Score (1-5)**
Only you	You appeal to a relational partner's ego, saying that no one else could do what you need done.	"No one can cook like you do."	_____
Personal expertise	You convince a relational partner to do something because you have experience in the matter, and that person can rely on your help.	"Don't worry. I know how to cook a perfect turkey—I'll be there to help if you need me."	_____
Relentless persuasion	You keep trying different persuasive approaches until you wear your relational partner down.	"I know you don't want to cook, but I can't help but think. . . ." "How about. . .?" "What if. . .?"	_____
Tradition	You insist that a relational partner do something because it has always been that way.	"My family always has a big dinner on Thanksgiving. The host has to cook!"	_____

In this scene from the TV series *Bridezilla*, a couple, Lessika and Jeremy, are having a conflict regarding an important aspect of their wedding. How do they use their communication to get what they want? Do you see an example of a compliance-gaining strategy in this clip? On YouTube, search using the keywords: "Altar Aftermath – Bridezillas." (3:35)

section review

9.2 Power in relationships

Interpersonal power is the ability to influence the thoughts, feelings, and behaviors of a relational partner. How you exercise interpersonal power can affect a relationship positively or negatively. Your need for power can range from abdicratic to autocratic. You can exert power from one or more of the following power bases: reward, coercive, referent, legitimate, and expert. You use compliance-gaining strategies to influence how others think and behave.

(continued)

Key Terms

interpersonal power, *p. 241*   autocratic, *p. 241*   power currency, *p. 242*   compliance-gaining strategy, *p. 244*

abdicratic, *p. 241*   democratic, *p. 241*   principle of least interest, *p. 242*   power play, *p. 245*

Comprehend It?

1. Define each of the key terms in Section 9.2. To further your understanding of these terms, create examples to support your definitions.

2. Compare and contrast the following power orientations: abdicratic, democratic, and autocratic.

3. Compare and contrast French and Raven's five bases of power: reward, coercive, referent, legitimate, and expert.

4. Describe five of the compliance-gaining strategies you read about in this section.

Apply It!

Think about one of your significant relationships. Which compliance-gaining tactics does your relational partner use to influence you? Do they work? Why or why not?

Now, think about French and Raven's five bases of power. Which bases of power is this person operating from?

9.3 Managing conflict effectively

One of our students, Courtney, once described a time when she was out with her boyfriend, Dustin, and two other couples at a restaurant. As a woman with a low-cut top walked by, Dustin appeared to stare very noticeably at her chest—with Courtney sitting right next to him. Embarrassed, she pinched his back to let him know she wasn't happy with his wandering eye.

Dustin responded by loudly exclaiming, "Ouch! Why did you pinch me just now?" in front of the other couples. Courtney felt even more humiliated. She laughed it off for the moment, but on their drive home, she confronted Dustin.

Courtney said, "How could you be so insensitive? I would never demean you like that. First, you obviously checked out another woman right in front of me and then you made a scene when I tried to discreetly let you know it wasn't okay." Dustin replied, "You're overreacting! I hardly looked at her, and you pinched me really hard. I just reacted in the moment!"

Where do you think this conversation is headed? In Section 9.3, we'll explore a variety of conflict resolution strategies that may help you defuse conflict successfully. As you're reading, consider how you might also use these techniques to prevent unnecessary conflict before it starts.

Approach conflict strategically

Let's return to Dustin and Courtney. What could they do to handle this conflict more effectively? Before Courtney says anything to Dustin about the incident, she could choose to wait a little longer to give her emotions a chance to simmer down, and she could pick a better time and place to broach the subject. Confronting Dustin when (1) it's been a long night and both of them are tired, (2) they've had a few cocktails, and (3) they're riding in the back seat of an Uber and their conversation is not private may not create an ideal communication context.

When Courtney decides to approach Dustin, she can let him know what she'd like to discuss and ask if it's a good time for him to talk:

> **Courtney:** Hey Dustin, I've been thinking about our date last night. I have something I'd like to share. Do you have a few minutes now to listen?

Courtney alludes to the topic and how much time she thinks is needed. She purposely asks Dustin if he has time to *listen*—not *talk*—because listening is the behavior she wants from him. Once Courtney and Dustin are in a good environment for their discussion, Courtney can address her conflict with Dustin using a benefit-of-the-doubt message, I-statements, and validation.

Benefit-of-the-doubt message

A constructive way for Courtney to start their discussion is with a benefit-of-the-doubt message:

> **Dustin:** What did you want to talk about?
>
> **Courtney:** It's about the woman I saw you staring at last night. I know that looking at her doesn't diminish how you feel about me.

In this scenario, Courtney expresses a **benefit-of-the-doubt message**—a statement that lets Dustin know she's not assuming the worst about his behavior or his intentions. He may feel less defensive if she starts the conversation in this way.

I-statements

When she addresses the conflict, Courtney should also steer clear of *you-statements*. You-statements suggest that Dustin definitely did something wrong and did so purposely to hurt Courtney. Notice how antagonistic a message like this sounds:

> **Courtney:** <u>**You made**</u> me very uncomfortable when <u>**you were**</u> staring at that woman last night. I pinched you to draw your attention to how I was feeling. <u>**You disrespected and embarrassed**</u> me when you asked "Why did you pinch me?" in front of everyone.

Contrast the you-statements in the message you just read to the I-statements in the following message.

> **Courtney:** <u>**I felt very**</u> uncomfortable when <u>**I saw**</u> you staring at that woman last night. I pinched you to draw your attention to how I was feeling. <u>**I felt**</u> disrespected and embarrassed when you asked, "Why did you pinch me?" in front of everyone."

Which message would you prefer to hear if you were Dustin?

Using the pronoun I helps Courtney communicate ownership of her thoughts and feelings. Courtney has the power to choose how she interprets Dustin's behavior, the importance she gives it, and ultimately how she feels about it. The pronoun I makes it clear that her perceptions, while accurate to her, are tentative and may not be what Dustin perceives or remembers.

Validation

Our communication may cause our relational partners to get defensive if they sense that we don't recognize or appreciate their thoughts, feelings, or needs.

Using Courtney and Dustin as an example, let's examine how validation reduces defensiveness and promotes understanding and cooperation. We learned in Chapter 7 that *validation* is the act of recognizing or acknowledging another person's stated or unstated thoughts, feelings, or needs.

After Courtney expresses her concerns, Dustin could validate Courtney by saying, "I can see why you were upset. My behavior made you feel uncomfortable and disrespected. That wasn't my intention at all. I certainly could have handled my reaction better though. I'm sorry."

Even if Dustin doesn't agree with Courtney's perception or her memory of the event completely, in order to help her get past this, he needs to acknowledge that his behavior affected her negatively. While he does state that it wasn't his intention to hurt her, he doesn't excuse his behavior ("I had too much to drink"), blame her ("You're just being insecure"), or minimize her feelings ("You're making this a big deal when it's not"). How might Courtney validate Dustin in return?

Encourage solution-based IPC

Solution-based communication focuses on potential solutions rather than the behaviors that started the conflict. Let's look again at how Courtney uses a benefit-of-the-doubt message and I-statements in her conflict with Dustin. Notice how these two techniques segue smoothly into solution-based communication.

> **Courtney:** I know that looking at another woman doesn't diminish how you feel about me. (*Benefit-of-the-doubt message*) But **I felt** very uncomfortable when I saw you staring, so I pinched you to draw your attention to how I was feeling. **I felt** disrespected and embarrassed when you asked, "Why did you pinch me?" in front of everyone. (*I-statements*) How would you like me to handle a situation like this in the future? Is there a better way to let you know how I'm feeling? (*Solution-based message*)

Courtney expresses a benefit-of-the-doubt message followed by I-statements that focus on Dustin's behavior without calling him any names or directing put-downs at him. She delivers a solution-based message focusing on productive, preventive *metacommunication*, a concept you read about in Chapter 2.

solution-based communication Communication that is focused on potential solutions rather than the behaviors that started a conflict.

"We could agree to disagree but then you'd still be wrong."

Research suggests that solution-based communication helps relational partners manage conflict productively.[36] It may also reduce an argument's duration and intensity, and it can promote more positive, facilitative emotions within a relationship.[37]

The goal of solution-based communication is to shift a conversation away from the behaviors that created a conflict to the behaviors that will prevent future conflict. When you communicate in a solution-based manner, you focus on what can make things better rather than the problem itself and who's at fault. You can use the following questions to initiate solution-based communication:

- "What would you like to see happen next time?"
- "What are some better ways to handle this?"
- "What are we both willing to commit to?"
- "How can we avoid this conflict in the future?"

Let's look at one more example to illustrate the use of validation and solution-based communication. Consider how Danielle's supervisor uses these two communication strategies. How would you feel if you were Danielle?

"I confronted my supervisor after she mentioned my slow sales numbers in front of other staff members during a meeting. She said, 'I'm sorry. You have every right to be upset. I made you look bad when I was trying to motivate the team by throwing challenges out. I shouldn't single anyone out. I will see that it doesn't happen again. I really appreciate that you came to me. Is there anything else I can do to rectify this?' She also appeared genuinely concerned. I felt much better after talking to her." –Danielle

Assume there is truth in every perspective

To resolve a conflict, it's helpful to develop a dual perspective. A **dual perspective** is the ability to understand your own and your relational partner's thoughts, feelings, and needs. Writer Paul Reps presents five positions by which you might analyze an existing conflict. Answering each of the questions listed in **TABLE 9.4** is also a great exercise to help you prepare for a challenging conversation. Positions 2 through 5 will likely promote a dual perspective.[38]

dual perspective The ability to understand your own and your relational partner's thoughts, feelings, and needs.

Focusing on positions 2 through 5 may not solve your conflict entirely, but you may change your mind regarding a plan of action. You'll likely gain some new insights—you may even feel better about the conflict. Research suggests that when you are able to analyze a conflict from more than one perspective, it triggers empathy, allows you to think in more complex and expansive ways, and enhances positive relational climates.[39]

table 9.4	Conflict Patterns and Outcomes	
Positions	**Description**	
Position 1 How am I right, and how are you wrong?	You cannot see the perspective that your relational partner is coming from. You only see the virtues of your own thoughts, feelings, and needs.	
Position 2 How are you right, and how am I wrong?	You acknowledge all the possible reasons why your relational partner's thoughts, feelings, and needs are justified, sound, or right. It requires you to acknowledge things about yourself that you find unpleasant.	
Position 3 How are we both right and wrong?	You identify how you are both right and wrong. You also identify the common ways that you and your relational partner think and feel about the situation.	
Position 4 How is the issue not as important as it seems?	You consider how important an issue really is. You may even try to see the situation as an opportunity to fix a problem or grow as relational partners, not as a calamity.	
Position 5 Where is there truth in all four perspectives?	You give all four positions a thorough review to see if you have acknowledged everything in a balanced manner.	

Follow conflict resolution steps

Imagine you're collaborating with a colleague, Stefan, on a sales presentation. The presentation may result in a lucrative business contract for your company, and it's an opportunity to showcase your skills. Upper management is looking to promote someone from within, so you want to put your best foot forward. When you review Stefan's PowerPoint presentation, though, it's not exactly what you'd like to see. The content is there, but it lacks visual appeal. You had pointed this out yesterday, but Stefan dismissed your concern. How should you approach this conflict with Stefan?

The following six steps (see **FIGURE 9.2**) are commonly associated with the conflict resolution and problem-solving process.[40]

Step 1: Identify your needs

Be sure you know exactly what you need and why. Can you articulate it to yourself out loud or in writing in a way that is very clear? In this case, in preparation for your conversation with Stefan, you might write: "I'd like to enhance some of the slides with graphics and animation. Why? I want to make all aspects of our presentation top-notch and possibly increase the odds of winning a contract."

FIGURE 9.2 **Conflict Resolution Steps**

Step 2: Share your needs

When you approach Stefan, keep your discussion to the present circumstance. For example, it might not go over well if you begin your conversation by saying, "Stefan, last time we did a sales presentation together, you ignored my ideas." You also want to avoid kicking things off with a criticism, such as, "Your work is too predictable and conventional."

Sometimes the best way to express your needs is to simply state what you'd like to see happen and why. Let's see how this conversation might unfold:

> **You:** Stefan, I like how you incorporated the company's logo in our PowerPoint presentation. Each slide is very easy to read.
>
> **Stefan:** Thanks.
>
> **You:** You're welcome. I'm eager to present our pitch tomorrow. It's a golden opportunity to showcase our talents to upper management. I know we both want to get that contract.
>
> **Stefan:** Yeah, we do. I think we will!
>
> **You:** I agree! That's why I'd like to make slides seven through twelve a little more sophisticated by adding a few graphics and some animation to jazz up the presentation.

You started the conversation by pointing out the positive aspects of Stefan's PowerPoint work before you stated the changes you'd like to see. Sometimes it's easier to digest a critique or suggestion after someone highlights the positive aspects of your work. You also mentioned something about the goals you share regarding the presentation, creating a sense of teamwork and solidarity. Finally, you stated clearly what you want to do to address your concern.

Step 3: Brainstorm

Let's assume that Stefan is willing to consider your ideas. It may help to come up with several possible options or ideas together. Promote unrestricted free thought and creative problem solving using a method called brainstorming. **Brainstorming** is the process of generating as many ideas as possible and jotting them down. The goal is to welcome all ideas without critique. To support this goal, you might say:

> **You:** Stefan, I have some ideas about how to enhance the presentation. Let's take a look at slides seven through twelve and brainstorm some options together.

Step 4: Evaluate your options

Analyze the strengths and weaknesses of the options you've brainstormed, considering each option's strengths, practicality, and anticipated results. You may do this by asking the following questions:

- ▪ "What are the pros and cons of each option?"
- ▪ "Can ideas be combined in any way?"
- ▪ "Which options seem fair and reasonable to both of us?"

brainstorming The process of generating as many ideas as possible without initial critiques.

You might need to integrate several ideas to create the best outcome. At this point, some compromising is usually necessary to reach a mutually satisfying decision. For example, if you want to add pie graphs to all of the slides, but Stefan doesn't, you may need to let your idea go and incorporate a few of his ideas. You might say:

> **You:** So Stefan, you don't think we need to do too much or go overboard with our graphics and animation. That is a good point. I agree. I'd like to add charts to slides four and six. Is that okay?

Your willingness to address Stefan's concerns and exercise flexibility will hopefully create a win-win outcome: one in which all parties feel good about a decision because everyone's thoughts and needs were taken into consideration.

When working through steps 2–4, it's important to keep the following suggestions in mind:

- If someone disagrees with you, try not to take it personally. You might even acknowledge the disagreement out loud and frame it positively by saying, "It appears we have different ideas. Great minds don't always think alike," or "We disagree and that's okay. I'm sure we can find common ground."

- Take an active-listening approach using the various positive verbal and nonverbal *back-channel cues* you read about in Chapter 4—for example, maintaining good eye contact, nodding your head responsively, and encouraging the speaker to elaborate—"Okay, good to know. What else?"

- Give your relational partner adequate time to speak without interruption. You can also paraphrase back what the person is saying in your own words. Be a good listener and encourage others to speak up.

Step 5: Implement a solution

Now that you've agreed on some changes, you implement your solution or idea. Decide who will do what and follow through with your decisions. It's always best to stay within the limits of what you've agreed to do, otherwise your relational partner may feel manipulated. For example, if you agree to enhance four slides and show them to Stefan later in the day, but you end up revamping the entire PowerPoint presentation, Stefan will likely get upset.

Step 6: Assess the solution

After you implement your solution, take some time to assess whether it has resolved your conflict successfully. You might look at the finished slides and ask Stefan what he thinks. Does the solution need some adjusting to produce better results? You can also decide to scrap a solution that isn't working and replace it with one that will. Examining the solution may require repeated conversations over time.

In *The Office*, the regional manager of the Scranton branch of the Dunder Mifflin Paper Company, Michael Scott (Steve Carell), attempts to use some of the conflict resolution steps you've just read about with his employees Pam (Jenna Fischer), Angela (Angela Kinsey), and Oscar (Oscar Nunez). Which steps did he use? What did he do well and what could he have done better? On YouTube, search using the keywords: "The Office – Conflict Resolution." (1:52)

section review

9.3 Managing conflict effectively

Approaching conflict effectively may involve the use of benefit-of-the-doubt messages, I-statements, and validation. As you work through a conflict, it may help to keep the conversation focused on solutions and consider the truth in every perspective. There are six steps you can take to address and handle conflict: identify your needs, share your needs, brainstorm, evaluate your options, implement a solution, and assess the solution.

Key Terms

benefit-of-the-doubt message, *p. 248*   dual perspective, *p. 250*

solution-based communication, *p. 249*   brainstorming, *p. 252*

Comprehend It?

1. Define each of the key terms in Section 9.3. To further your understanding of these terms, create examples to support your definitions.

2. Think of a time when you used some or all of the conflict resolution steps listed in this section (identify your needs, share your needs, brainstorm, evaluate your options, implement a solution, and assess the solution). Pair up with a classmate and describe what happened. What went well? What didn't?

Apply It!

Think of a recent conflict you've had with someone—or one you're having now. Read out loud the questions associated with Reps's conflict positions below. Try your best to consider the thoughts, feelings, and needs of

(continued)

your relational partner as you write out your answers to each question. Contemplate as many valid viewpoints as possible. How is an exercise like this beneficial?

- Position 1: How am I right, and how are you wrong?

- Position 2: How are you right, and how am I wrong?
- Position 3: How are we both right and wrong?
- Position 4: Is the issue as important as it seems?
- Position 5: Where is there truth in all four perspectives?

chapter exercises

9

Assessing Your IPC: Problematic Communication Behaviors

Purpose: To identify my preferred conflict management style.

Directions: Take the free online conflict styles assessment offered by the United States Institute of Peace. This instrument helps you evaluate how you prefer to manage conflict according to the five approaches discussed in Section 9.1 (with one exception: They refer to collaborating as "problem solving"). Based on your scores, which conflict style do you prefer the most? Which do you prefer the least?

To take the assessment and print the results, search using the keywords: "Conflict Styles Assessment United States Institute of Peace."

Building Your IPC Skills: Resolving Conflict

Purpose: To improve my use of several conflict management techniques.

Directions: With a classmate or discussion group, think of a situation that could potentially cause a conflict. Create a dialogue showing how you would use two or more of the following techniques in your approach.

Benefit-of-the-doubt message

I-statements

Validation

Solution-based communication

For example, you might say to a subordinate at work: "Despite getting overwhelmed at times with all of the reports I send you, you strive hard to catch my errors. (Benefit-of-the-doubt message) I noticed that a few miscalculations slipped by. (I-statement) Is there any way we can verify the data with the central office so we can get close to 100% accuracy?" Perhaps we can brainstorm some ideas. (Solution-based communication)

III

Contemporary Topics in Interpersonal Communication

10

Diversity and Inclusion

In a satirical CollegeHumor video titled, "I Don't See Race," four friends (Zac, Katie, Mike, and Grant) are sitting at a table with their laptops when Zac says, "There were so many incredible, super-diverse movies last year . . . movies that didn't just feature White people." Katie is seemingly unaware of this fact and replies, "Call me crazy, but I just don't see race. I guess I'm just the least racist person here."

Zac looks at her, bewildered, and says, "Race is often a pretty obvious thing to observe. It's not racist to notice." Katie laughs incredulously and says, "I only see one race: the human race." Grant chimes in and says to Katie, "You're only telling yourself that so you don't have to think about racism or confront your own prejudices."

Katie exclaims, "No, I'm not prejudiced, okay? I don't even judge [Mike] for being a woman!" Mike snaps back, "I'm a man, Katie. You know that." To that, Katie says, "No, honestly, I just guessed. . . . I don't see gender, and I don't see sex. I just see people." Zac replies, "Unless you're blind, you can tell that people have inherent differences." Katie replies, "Oh, I wouldn't know if I was blind or not because I don't see disabilities."

Katie even claims to not see baldness in people, including actor Bruce Willis, who Grant reminds her is "famously bald." To watch the full video, search YouTube using the keywords: "I Don't See Race." (3:33)

Human differences do exist, whether or not someone like Katie cares to notice them. Human

The group pictured works on team building. Their willingness to learn about and form relationships with people who are different from them will enrich their lives in many ways.

diversity comes in many forms. For instance, consider the diversity within your interpersonal communication class. What makes you unique compared to your professor and classmates? Consider your life experiences, age, race, educational background, physical attributes, abilities, gender, sexual orientation, ethnicity, and socioeconomic status.

The presence of diversity exists not only in your classroom but in your school, neighborhood, place of employment—even among your friends and family. As far as human diversity is concerned, there are so many things we can write about and discuss. In this chapter, we'll focus predominately on how (1) culture and (2) gender and sexual orientation play a role in your interpersonal communication. We'll also (3) explore how to communicate effectively with and among diverse groups of people.

10.1 Culture

In an article for a magazine focused on disability advocacy, undergraduate student Grace Tsao writes:

> I can remember distinct times when I was younger when my parents did not allow me to attend certain functions where a lot of first-generation Chinese, other than family, were in attendance. [. . .] They told me that these traditional Chinese would gawk at me and gossip about the fact that I use a wheelchair. They would look down on our family because only a family who has done wrong would deserve such a fate and shame. I didn't believe my parents at first. In fact, I accused them of being ashamed of [me]. They kept assuring me that they loved me no matter what, and that this sheltering was for my own good, because not all people would view my disability the way we did.[1]

As Grace grew older, she became increasingly aware of the negative effects sheltering had on her. Her parents didn't just isolate her from certain social events; they also never broached certain topics with her such as dating or marriage. Their reluctance to discuss these topics sent a clear message: that her disability made the possibility of romantic love highly unlikely.

Grace uses her writing to challenge cultural assumptions that promote practices like sheltering. She hopes that her work will change the way society views people with physical and mental disabilities. Many people have contacted Grace to thank her for her efforts.[2]

When Grace's parents emigrated from China to the United States, they brought their traditional Chinese culture with them. Culture played a role in their communication with Grace.

Culture is the shared language, beliefs, interests, values, and customs of an interpersonal system or society. In Chapter 2, we examined cultures within *interpersonal systems*—two or more interdependent individuals who rely on each other to accomplish personal and shared goals. Interpersonal systems include romantic relationships, families, work teams, and peer groups.

culture The shared language, beliefs, interests, values, and customs of an interpersonal system or society.

society A large grouping of individuals who share a common social identity.

A culture that is established within an interpersonal system, such as a family, sports organization, or business, may reflect and reinforce the culture of a society. A **society** is a large grouping of individuals who share a common social identity. You may form a common social identity with others based on where you live (for instance, in the United States we all identify as Americans). You may also share a common social identity with others based on your race (for example, Native American), ethnicity (such as Puerto Rican), religion (Catholic), common interests (members of an online gaming community), similar experiences (World War II veterans), or occupation (frontline medical workers).

In Section 10.1, we'll explore societal-based cultures and their influence on interpersonal communication and why it's important to communicate with greater cultural understanding.

Cultures exist within cultures

A **co-culture** (or *subculture*) is a smaller culture within a larger culture.[3] For example, a submarine crew of 130 sailors may spend as long as 3 months at sea together cramped in a submerged vessel 360 feet in length. To cope with the stresses of their job, Petty Officer First Class Kevin Watson and his off-duty crew race down passageways on makeshift Go-Karts, host zany fashion show competitions, and carry out some interesting initiation rituals for shipmates crossing the equator for the first time.[4]

Kevin's submarine crew is an interpersonal system with its own unique culture. It's a co-culture that incorporates aspects of the larger culture of the U.S. Navy. The U.S. Navy is a co-culture within a larger military culture: the U.S. Armed Forces (Air Force, Army, Navy, Marine Corps, and Coast Guard). The U.S. Armed Forces are a co-culture within an even larger U.S. culture. Just as there are smaller interpersonal systems within larger interpersonal systems, there are smaller societal cultures within larger societal cultures.

Enculturation and acculturation

Enculturation (ihn-CUHLT-uhr-A-shuhn) is the process of learning about and adopting the norms and values of your own culture. *Values* are commonly held standards of what is important or unimportant, appropriate or inappropriate, and right or wrong in a given culture. For example, if you grew up in the United States, it's likely you were taught (enculturated) that burping out loud during or after a meal is something to avoid if possible. It's considered rude, gross, or embarrassing. However, in parts of Asia or the Middle East, burping is encouraged! It means you enjoyed your meal, and it's a compliment to the chef.[5]

Acculturation (uh-CUHLT-uhr-A-shuhn) is the process of learning about and adopting the norms and values of a different culture. For example, Petty Officer Kevin Watson, whom you just read about, had to acculturate to life aboard a submarine when he enlisted in the navy. To fit in and thrive in an unfamiliar culture, he paid attention to what he was told and observed what was going on around him, adjusting his behavior accordingly.

Acculturation may involve **code-switching**—an effort to assimilate into a different culture while maintaining roots in your own culture. Code-switching involves changing your language or speech patterns, dress, posture, and

co-culture A smaller culture within a larger culture.

enculturation The process of learning about and adopting the norms and values of your own culture.

acculturation The process of learning about and adopting the norms and values of a new culture.

code-switching The effort to assimilate into a different culture while maintaining roots in your own culture.

mannerisms among people who don't share your cultural affiliation. The purpose of code-switching is usually to fit in and get along. For example, Black Americans may speak "Black English" (also referred to as African American Vernacular English or Ebonics) with each other, and then switch to General American English when talking to someone of another race, particularly someone they don't know well. Other minority groups in the United States, such as the Latino community, may speak Spanish with members of their own culture but switch to English when speaking to individuals outside of their culture.

In the film *Dear White People*, a group of Black students decides to buck the social pressure to be more "White" at a fictitious Ivy League college. The film satirizes how Black people often juggle different social identities depending on the situations they find themselves in.

The main character, Samantha, is voted to lead an all-Black house on a predominately White campus. She is aware of the racial divide and wants to meet the cultural expectations of her **in-group**, or the group she identifies with. In this case, Samantha's in-group is composed of her Black housemates. However, she's also a campus-wide leader who is forming friendships with several White students. These students are part of an **out-group**, or a social group she doesn't identify with. Each group has a different set of expectations for Samantha.

Samantha tries to balance her affiliation with both cultures without coming across as "too White" or getting accused of "trying to be White" by members of her in-group—a social dilemma called the race-acting hypothesis.[6] You'll get a good sense of this by watching the video referenced in the caption featuring Samantha and her friend Gabe.

Gabe (Justin Dobies) tries to convince his romantic interest, Samantha (Tessa Thompson), to just be herself in this scene from *Dear White People*. Use this clip to describe the concepts of acculturation and code-switching. On YouTube, search using the keywords: "Dear White People (8/10) Movie CLIP - Who Am I? (2014) HD." (3:19)

Samantha is juggling the expectations of more than one culture. She is Black, but she's also a woman, a student, an American, etc. According to law professor Kimberlé Crenshaw's **theory of intersectionality**, social identity markers (for example, being a woman and being Black) do not exist independently of each other. Together, they make up who you are and influence how others (including societal institutions) treat you. For example, if Samantha is the only Black female member of an all-White male campus organization, she may feel different because of her race and her gender. Members of the out-group may even make her feel more or less included or relate to her differently because of her intersectionality.[7]

Like Samantha, you may discover that your intersectionality (the social identity markers that make you unique compared to others) places limits on you or puts you at a disadvantage in some way. One of your authors, Bruce, has a friend named Leelan. Leelan was born in the United States to two foreign-born parents. His mother is of British, Indian, and Spanish descent, and his father is of African and Caribbean descent. When Leelan visits his extended family in Trinidad and Tobago, he catches flack for not speaking fluent Spanish and for "looking and sounding too Americanized." He says, "Because I look like them, they expect me to be like them." A family friend once told him, "Leelan, you're so handsome—wouldn't it be nice if you didn't have that accent?"

Leelan is treated differently because of his ethnicity and nationality in the United States as well. As a young, attractive, multiracial man, many of the men he dates seem to be primarily interested in his looks. He says, "I have to play the game—answer all of their questions about my racial/ethnic heritage and go on a date to figure out their true intentions. It's very annoying." Because of the layers of his intersectionality—his age, nationality, attractiveness, and ethnicity—Leelan realizes that, in certain social contexts, others perceive and treat him differently.

Social norms vary from culture to culture

In Chapter 2 you learned that *norms* are the customary ways of communicating and doing things in certain social settings—and they often differ across cultures. For example, norms for dating are not universal. In Spanish culture, the marriage potential of a couple is often acknowledged openly by the second date. In New Zealand, romantic interest is expressed in peer group settings, and it's rare to date someone exclusively if you haven't socialized with that person's friends first. In India, you'd typically schedule a first date weeks in advance—with your romantic interest's parents.[8]

Dating rituals are not the only social norms that vary from culture to culture. During a class discussion, one of our students, Boyd, told us about his time studying abroad in Egypt and the United Arab Emirates. He wasn't accustomed to several of the social norms there, and he shared an interesting observation:

> *Arab men often hold hands and put their arms around each other while standing and walking. It isn't uncommon to see them sitting next to each other in deep*

theory of intersectionality
The idea that social identity markers do not exist independently of each other. Together, they may make you feel similar to or different from others—and affect how others treat you.

conversation and one man's hand is on the other man's thigh. Arab men often greet each other with a kiss. Warmth, friendship, and kinship are expressed this way. Males in the Middle East are—generally speaking—very affectionate with each other.

Another student of ours, Meera, did a double take when a classmate used a professor's first name to get his attention. An international student from India, Meera uses "Sir" and "Madam" to address professors in her home country—"to not do so," she says, "is highly disrespectful." When she speaks to an American professor in this way, she's encouraged to drop the formalities. Meera says, "It's something I'm still getting used to."

In addition to Boyd and Meera's personal accounts, the results of studies published by intercultural communication researchers offer further evidence of differences in social norms across cultures.[9] Here are a few examples:

- In traditional Japanese culture, not making eye contact with someone conveys respect. In Finnish culture, people tend to expect eye contact and perceive a lack of eye contact as a sign of disrespect: "Look at me when I'm talking to you!"[10]

- Most North Americans who are White are uncomfortable with long pauses during a conversation; however, in Native American cultures, extended silences are often preferred, especially when social situations are ambiguous.[11]

- Romantic partners in the United States are much more open to public displays of affection than are romantic partners in Korea.[12]

- Italians gesture more often and more elaborately than do people in the United States.[13]

- Compared to Germans, people in India tend to disclose less personal information in their online communication.[14]

- In North American culture, social events and meetings generally start on time, but in Latin American cultures like those in Argentina and Colombia, it is not uncommon for social guests to arrive approximately one to two hours after a gathering's starting time. To show up on time is perceived as rude. People may arrive to scheduled business meetings 20 minutes to an hour late.[15]

These research findings may apply to most people within a culture, but not everyone. Are there Americans who gesture more than Italians? Yes. Are all Korean couples less affectionate in public compared to American couples? No. Individual exceptions exist. Not every person who belongs to a particular culture practices all of its norms.

As far as norms are concerned, it's important to remember that you interpret the communication behaviors of others from your own cultural perspective. Just as you may find yourself surprised or confused by how people from other cultures communicate, they may find your communication just as surprising or confusing. They'll observe you through their cultural lens, too.

Cultural value dimensions between cultures

How you speak, dress, behave, and think is influenced by the interactions you've had with relational partners throughout your life, including the messages you've received from various institutions and print or electronic media. Your interpersonal communication may—and often does—mirror and reinforce the cultural values and practices of your society.[16]

Societal cultures fall somewhere within a range in terms of their social values and practices. Intercultural researchers have identified five cultural value dimensions or orientations: individualistic to collectivistic, low to high context, low to high power distance, masculine to feminine, and polychronic to monochronic.[17]

Individualistic to collectivistic

An **individualistic culture** places more of an emphasis on individual self-determination and success. Personal freedom and autonomy are highly valued. Groups look to individuals to lead and move initiatives forward. Corporate and educational co-cultures tend to measure and reward performance on an individual basis. Families steer children toward independence early in life. The elderly strive to maintain their independence late into life to avoid burdening their children. Western cultures (British, Australian, Canadian, and French, for example) are predominantly individualistic. The United States ranked first compared to 52 other countries in terms of its individualistic tendencies.[18]

A **collectivistic culture** emphasizes interdependence and doing what's best for the group or country, including one's team, employer, or family. These cultures de-emphasize individual success and competition and communicate with a strong "we" and "us" focus. Collectivistic cultures tend to promote a family culture in which elders live with their adult children and young adults live with their parents. Extended family is also more likely to live together, and for long periods of time, especially in times of need. Countries with collectivistic cultures include: Guatemala, Indonesia, the Philippines, Russia, Pakistan, North Africa, and China.[19]

Low to high context

A **low-context culture** values direct, assertive communication and getting things done. Relationships start and end more quickly, conflict is addressed openly and directly, and communication is more formal.[20] For example, a company may have a detailed employee handbook that spells out all the rules employees are expected to follow. German, Norwegian, Swedish, and North American cultures are considered low-context cultures.

A **high-context culture** emphasizes indirect and informal communication and in-group harmony. It discourages

individualistic culture
A cultural orientation characterized by a heavy emphasis on individual success and self-determination.

collectivistic culture
A cultural orientation characterized by an emphasis on interdependence and teamwork.

low-context culture
A cultural orientation characterized by communication that is formal, direct, and focused on getting things done.

high-context culture
A cultural orientation characterized by the high value placed on indirect and informal communication as well as in-group harmony.

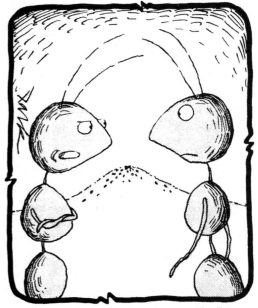

"I hear you've been spreading individualism around the hill again."

overt conflict and disagreements. For example, if you were a business owner, rather than addressing a conflict openly during a meeting, you would observe your employees' subtle facial expressions, eye contact, or silence to sense when they are unhappy about something. You would then allude to it indirectly or talk about it privately in order to come up with a solution.

In business transactions, individuals from low-context cultures skip the small talk and get right to business, but in high-context cultures, potential business partners spend a lot of time getting to know each other before they reach any agreements. Deals are often sealed with a handshake or an unwritten verbal agreement. High-context cultures emphasize compromise, cooperation, and relaxed negotiations, even when the end results are less than ideal. Japanese, Native American, Korean, Mexican, and Arab cultures are considered high-context cultures.[21]

Low to high power distance

The average person in a **low power distance (LPD) culture** has a relatively high chance of advancing from one socioeconomic level to another by means of education and ambition. Rags-to-riches stories are more common and celebrated in LPD cultures. You'll also hear friends, family members, and coworkers speak their minds about organizational and community leaders openly and directly. LPD cultures value equality and are more open to social change and diverse lifestyles. Countries with LPD cultures include New Zealand, Denmark, Israel, Canada, Sweden, and the United States.

In a **high power distance (HPD) culture**, political power is delegated to a few. It is uncommon to challenge or question authority. If you are born into a certain social class, you are expected to stay there—to know your place and form relationships only with individuals of the same socioeconomic status. HPD cultures place a high value on tradition, strict laws, and adherence to certain beliefs. Children are socialized to respect the authority and wisdom of parents, teachers, and leaders. Countries noted for having HPD cultures include North Korea, Russia, India, the Philippines, China, and Nigeria.[22]

Masculine to feminine

In a **masculine culture**, gender roles are very distinct. Men are expected to be strong, emotionally stoic, and assertive. They have greater status and power, and they're encouraged to strive for monetary and career success. Women are socialized to be modest, tender, and focused on improving quality of life via traditionally feminine roles. In all aspects of life, ambition and competition are viewed as masculine traits. Japanese, Austrian, Venezuelan, Italian, Mexican, and Jamaican cultures are considered more masculine, and the United States is also thought to have a masculine culture.[23]

In a **feminine culture**, gender roles are less distinct. Men and women are raised to practice modesty, cooperation, and compromise for the sake of maintaining harmony and close relationships. The characteristics associated with ambition and success are less gender specific. The political, social, and economic rights

low power distance (LPD) culture A cultural orientation that values equality and allows for greater socioeconomic mobility.

high power distance (HPD) culture A cultural orientation characterized by rigid social hierarchy and deference to power and authority.

masculine culture A cultural orientation characterized by distinct gender roles and a generally high social status for men.

feminine culture A cultural orientation characterized by less distinct gender roles and a relatively egalitarian status for men and women.

and opportunities for both sexes are more egalitarian. In feminine cultures, men are often granted paid paternity leave to help with raising their children.[24] Boys and girls are taught that it's okay to express uncertainty, to nurture, and to show emotion. The Swedish, Norwegian, Portuguese, Dutch, and Chilean cultures are considered feminine.[25]

Polychronic to monochronic

In a **polychronic culture** (PAH-lee-KRAH-nihk) the pace of life is generally slower and people have a more laid-back approach to time. Appointments are not as common. Plans often change and interruptions are easily tolerated, especially when a social opportunity presents itself. People are less preoccupied with the exact time of day. For example, if your family is getting together for dinner, family members may not even ask what time the meal will start; they'll just arrive sometime around the usual dinner hour. Polychronic cultures place a greater emphasis on the present (what's happening in the here and now) and are less concerned about schedules and deadlines. Indian, Caribbean, Kenyan, and Latin American cultures are considered polychronic cultures.

A **monochronic culture** (MAH-noh-KRAH-nihk) promotes a fast-track life. Time is seen as a precious commodity, something that you gain or lose. "Time is money" is a popular mindset. People prefer to follow a schedule, stick to it, and make things happen sooner rather than later. Delays are less tolerated. Monochronic cultures emphasize punctuality—showing up on time. Countries like Germany, Canada, the United States, and Switzerland, along with the Scandinavian countries of Norway, Belgium, Denmark, and Sweden, are considered monochronic.[26]

Cultural value dimensions within cultures

It is important to note that there is just as much variation along these five spectrums within cultures as there is between cultures. For example, urban areas within the United States, such as New York City and Washington, D.C., are typically low power distance, low context, and monochronic compared to Hawaii and rural parts of the southern United States.

In addition, plenty of cultural differences exist between the cultures within interpersonal systems and societal cultures. For example, while your country may be considered a monochronic culture, your family may live life and treat time in a very polychronic way.

Rather than making assumptions about people because of their culture, you can use this information responsibly by considering how culture may play a role in how someone is communicating with you. For example, if you are speaking to someone from another culture, say someone who is from the Mediterranean or South America, you may notice that they'll stand closer to you than you're used to. You may step back to give yourself more room, but your conversational partner may take a step toward you to close the awkward gap. People's sense of personal space varies from culture to culture.[27]

polychronic culture
A cultural orientation characterized by a flexible approach to time.

monochronic culture
A cultural orientation characterized by a strict, scheduled approach to time.

Importance of cultural awareness

Let's say you have a classmate, Sevvy, from the Democratic Republic of the Congo. Sevvy often arrives a few minutes late to your study group and gets unusually quiet at lunch if the friends at your table start a spirited debate. What would you think about this behavior? Would you assume that he doesn't respect other people's time, or that he doesn't have many strong opinions?

As you get to know Sevvy, you learn that the pace is much slower in Congo than it is in the United States. Sevvy's culture is more relaxed about time (polychronic) and values group harmony (high context) over public disagreement. With a better understanding of Sevvy's culture, you can interpret his behavior in a more accurate and accepting way. Your cultural knowledge will also help you enlighten others who might otherwise misinterpret his communication.

Cultural awareness is important because it can influence how we send and interpret messages—and what happens as a result. This is highlighted in Glover's narrative. Can you imagine the following scenario happening to you?

"I took a trip to Thailand to visit my girlfriend Boonsri. Several of her close friends joined us at a bar. At the end of the night, Boonsri gave me the bill to pay for everyone's drinks. I thought, 'What! This is a big tab!' Later she told me she gave me an opportunity to demonstrate 'Nam Jai,' which means generosity. Nam Jai is very important in Thai culture. I'm glad I responded positively to her gesture. I made a very good impression. She chuckled when I later asked, 'Would you mind giving me a little more of a heads-up next time?'" –Glover

section review

10.1 Culture

Culture is the shared language, beliefs, interests, values, and customs within an interpersonal system or a society. A society is a large grouping of individuals who share a common social identity. Cultures within cultures are called co-cultures. You learn about your own culture and the cultures of others through the processes of enculturation and acculturation, respectively. Norms–common ways of communicating and behaving in social settings–vary from culture to culture and tend to fall within five cultural value dimensions: individualistic to collectivistic, low to high context, low power distance to high power distance, masculine to feminine, and polychronic to monochronic. It benefits you interpersonally when you increase your awareness of cultural differences.

(continued)

Key Terms

culture, *p. 260*

society, *p. 260*

co-culture, *p. 261*

enculturation, *p. 261*

acculturation, *p. 261*

code-switching, *p. 261*

in-group, *p. 262*

out-group, *p. 262*

theory of intersectionality, *p. 263*

individualistic culture, *p. 265*

collectivistic culture, *p. 265*

low-context culture, *p. 265*

high-context culture, *p. 265*

low power distance (LPD) culture, *p. 266*

high power distance (HPD) culture, *p. 266*

masculine culture, *p. 266*

feminine culture, *p. 266*

polychronic culture, *p. 267*

monochronic culture, *p. 267*

Comprehend It?

1. Define each of the key terms in Section 10.1. To further your understanding of these terms, create examples to support your definitions.
2. Compare and contrast the following:
   - Culture and society
   - Enculturation and acculturation
   - In-group and out-group
3. If you were to move to another part of the world, which cultural orientations would you prefer and why? How might they influence your interpersonal communication and relationships?
   - Individualistic or collectivistic
   - Low or high context
   - Low or high power distance
   - Masculine or feminine
   - Polychronic or monochronic

Apply It!

Imagine you'd like to fit in with members of an out-group. You might try to incorporate some of their language and expressions as you interact with them. This form of code-switching may enhance your communication and assist you in the acculturation process. But what if your efforts make you look like the lead character in this video? On YouTube, search using the keywords: "The Guy Who Over-Pronounces Foreign Words." (2:31) With a classmate, discuss some of the problems you see. What other issues can arise when you try to fit in with an out-group? What behaviors should you avoid? Which are acceptable?

10.2 Gender and sexual orientation

Who talks more: men or women? When we ask students this question, most of them agree: "Women, hands down." One of our students, Blake, chimed in, "Yeah, my girlfriend is constantly prodding me to 'say how I feel' or 'open up more.' When I get up in the morning, Kia is wide-awake talking a mile a minute. When I come home from a ten-hour shift, dog-tired, she's ready to analyze every little thing going on between us."

Some of our students aren't so convinced. Malania sees the opposite in her boyfriend, Amar, who is "the antithesis of the silent man" and "won't stop talking." Is it fair to say that women are chattier, or is this an inaccurate assumption? Interpersonal communication research can shed some light on this question.

One study measured how often adult men and women talk. Subjects wore digital devices called sociometers, which measure the frequency of speech. In the project scenario, women spoke more often than men; however, when the subjects formed work groups of seven or more members, the men spoke more. In the unstructured social scenario, they found no significant difference in how often men and women spoke. Women did speak more than men when the social gathering got larger.

So, in other words, men talked more in larger groups that had been assigned a work task, while women spoke more in smaller work groups and in larger social groups. In social situations involving small groups, men and women talked just as much.[28] This study dispels the popular notion that women talk a lot more than men. The differences between how much men and women talk may not be that great. If differences exist at all, the social setting is a possible factor.

In Section 10.2, we'll examine insights gleaned from research on gender's relationship to interpersonal communication. We'll also explore the growing body of research that is helping us learn more about the relationship between IPC and sexual orientation.

Gender, sexual orientation, and IPC

How does gender affect your interpersonal communication? How does it shape your frame of reference and the way you perceive the communication of others? While men's and women's communication styles are more similar than they are different, sometimes we overlook gender differences and expect others to communicate just like we do. Gender communication research helps us understand one another better, making our communication more productive and satisfying. It is also helpful to understand the role a person's sexual orientation plays in interpersonal communication.

Biological sex

biological sex A biological distinction determined at birth and characterized by genetics and physical attributes.

intersex Possessing a combination of male and female biological traits and/or chromosomes.

gender identity Your sense of being a man, woman, neither, or both.

cisgender A gender identity whereby a person's gender and biological sex match.

nonbinary A gender identity whereby a person identifies as both genders or neither.

Before we can consider how different genders communicate, we should first explain the differences between biological sex, gender identity, and gender expression. **Biological sex** is determined at birth and categorized by genetics and physical attributes. If you are born with female biological traits and two X chromosomes you are considered female, and if you are born with male biological traits and XY chromosomes you are considered male. You are **intersex** if you were born with a combination of male and female biological traits and/or a different chromosome configuration, such as XXY.[29] Being intersex is a naturally occurring variation in humans. According to the Intersex Society of North America, approximately 1 out of every 100 babies born is considered intersex.[30]

Gender identity

Gender identity is your sense of being a man, a woman, neither, or both. Gender identity can correlate with your biological sex or it can differ from it. You may consider yourself **cisgender** (SIHS-jehn-dehr) if your gender identity matches your biological sex. If you identify with or express yourself as both genders, or do not identify strongly with either, you may say that you are **nonbinary** (some

Aspiring country music singer Jaimie Wilson describes the conversations he's had with friends and family regarding his gender identity. Which conversations did he find helpful—and hurtful? As you consider these questions, relate what Jaimie says in this video to the concept of social norms. On YouTube, search using the keywords: "How did I know I was transgender? Jaimie Wilson." (12:49)

people prefer the terms *gender nonconforming* or *genderqueer*). If your gender identity is the opposite of your biological sex, you may identify as **transgender**. For example, a person assigned male at birth may identify as a woman, in which case she is a transgender woman.

Nonbinary and transgender individuals may embrace their gender identity with the support of family and friends, along with the help of medical and mental health professionals. Some will initiate a process called transitioning, which may involve altering their appearance, the use of hormones, cosmetic surgery, and/or gender confirmation surgery.[31]

Gender expression

Gender expression is the way in which you express your gender, typically through your interests, behaviors, and communication style. Gender expression is often described in one of three ways: feminine, masculine, or androgynous. These terms are culturally determined social constructs that vary depending on one's societal culture. Generally speaking, the following descriptions of each form of gender expression are common in most cultures.

Feminine expression is consistent with the interests, behaviors, and communication style traditionally associated with femininity. In the United States, traditionally feminine interests include child-rearing, fashion, and decorating. Behaviors include attending to one's appearance, building and nurturing relationships, and offering emotional support.

A traditionally feminine communication style is indirect, emotionally expressive, and intimate in terms of self-disclosure.[32] Feminine expression is more animated, with a wider range of facial expressions, vocal variety, smiling, and

transgender A gender identity whereby a person's gender and biological sex do not match.

gender expression The way in which a person prefers to express their gender, typically through interests, behaviors, and communication style.

feminine expression A gender presentation consistent with the interests, behaviors, and communication style traditionally associated with femininity.

masculine expression A gender presentation consistent with the interests, behaviors, and communication style traditionally associated with masculinity.

androgynous expression A gender presentation that mixes masculine and feminine interests, behaviors, and communication styles.

sexual orientation The enduring romantic and sexual attraction you have to individuals of a certain sex or gender identity.

gay A sexual orientation characterized by attraction to individuals of the same sex.

straight A sexual orientation characterized by attraction to individuals of the opposite sex.

bisexual A sexual orientation characterized by attraction to individuals of both sexes.

pansexual A sexual orientation characterized by attraction to individuals of both sexes and all gender identities.

gesturing. Vocal tones are softer and higher. The language of feminine expression is more descriptive, emphasizing humility, using more questions, and incorporating more words related to emotions.[33]

Masculine expression is consistent with the interests, behaviors, and communication style traditionally associated with masculinity. Traditionally masculine interests may include sports, building and repairing things, and hunting/fishing, while behaviors include risk-taking, competition, and leadership.

A traditionally masculine communication style is associated with shorter sentences, logical thought processes, assertiveness, and directness.[34] Masculine nonverbal expression emphasizes firm handshakes, few facial expressions, wide postures, and using up more space with one's body. Vocal tones are lower and louder. The language of masculine expression focuses more on task completion, declarative statements, giving advice, and promoting one's social status.[35]

Androgynous expression is a mix of masculine and feminine expression.[36] For example, a woman may enjoy doing crafts (traditionally a feminine activity) and love fishing (traditionally a masculine interest). She may speak directly (a masculine characteristic) and feel very comfortable disclosing her feelings (a feminine characteristic). She may speak with a lot of animation (a feminine characteristic) and initiate firm handshakes (a masculine characteristic).

While there is certainly no right or wrong way to express your gender, certain types of gender expression may confer advantages and disadvantages. Interestingly, research suggests that androgynous expression may free you to pursue and excel at a greater variety of interests and careers. A communication style that combines the positive traits of masculine and feminine expression is associated with higher levels of relationship satisfaction,[37] self-esteem,[38] creativity,[39] and workplace success.[40] In addition, if you're comfortable communicating in ways that are more androgynous, you may have an easier time adapting to the communication style of others.

Sexual orientation

Your **sexual orientation** is the enduring romantic or sexual feelings you have toward individuals of a certain sex or gender identity. If you are primarily attracted to individuals of the same or opposite sex, you are considered **gay** (homosexual) or **straight** (heterosexual), respectively. The word homosexual is considered an outdated and pejorative term by many within the LGBTQ (lesbian, gay, bisexual, transgender, and queer) community.[41] The word gay is preferred in casual conversations. Also keep in mind that the word gay may describe a man or woman, while the word lesbian is only used to describe women.

There are several terms beyond gay and straight you can use to describe your sexual orientation. You may identify as **bisexual** if you are sexually or romantically attracted to individuals of either sex, or **pansexual** if you are attracted to individuals regardless of their biological sex or gender identity. Some may find these terms and others constricting and/or inexact and instead prefer the term

queer to describe their non-straight identity. The term is also used to refer to the LGBTQ community as a whole.

It is also possible to have an enduring lack of sexual interest in others, in which case you may identify as **asexual**. One of our students, Harminder, describes his asexuality in the following narrative. Can you relate to what he says in any way? How might Harminder's sexual orientation influence his interpersonal communication in dating situations?

> " I can find someone attractive, but I just don't have a desire to be intimate. I did have sex with a girl once to see if it would spark any interest. It was like when I played golf for the first time—it was a fairly pleasant experience, but I'm totally okay with never doing it again. To me romantic connection is more of an emotional experience." –Harminder

Now that we've explained different identities related to gender and sexual orientation, go back and choose the descriptors that best align with how you perceive your biological sex, gender identity, gender expression, and sexual orientation. How might your responses differ from those of your classmates, coworkers, friends, and family? Now, think about why it's important to factor your own and someone else's gender and sexual orientation into your daily interactions. How might the knowledge you've gained in this section benefit you interpersonally? In the sections that follow, we'll discuss what researchers have to say about this question.

Gender differences in IPC

According to a number of popular relationship advice authors, men and women are from different worlds in terms of communication—"Men are from Mars and Women are from Venus." In reality, communication scholars are more likely to use this metaphor: "Men are from North Dakota, and women are from South Dakota."[42] Research that focuses on cisgender subjects suggests that men and women communicate in ways more alike than different.[43] For example, one study found that men and women use emojis very similarly online and in text messages.[44]

Research does suggest, however, that there are verbal and nonverbal differences in the way men and women communicate—generally speaking.[45] As you continue reading, consider why it's important to have an awareness of these differences.

Verbal differences

■ Men tend to speak using short, fragmented sentences (for example, "Looking good!" versus "That dress looks stunning on you."). Women use more intensive adverbs and words related to feelings ("I *really* love what you've done to the place.").[46]

■ Women disclose more personal information to each other, and men disclose more personal information to women than they do to other men.[47]

- Men are more prone than women to employ competitive verbal behaviors, such as demands, boasts, and threats, especially with other men. They are more likely to use topic avoidance with opposite-gender peers.[48] Women are more likely than men to use compromising strategies with both sexes.[49]

- Men interrupt women more often than women interrupt men.[50]

- Men apologize less often during or after confrontations, and one reason may have to do with their perceptions of whether they think an apology is warranted.[51]

- Women are more reluctant than men to negotiate higher starting salaries.[52]

Nonverbal differences

- Women engage in more eye contact than men during conversations.[53]

- Men like more space around them when standing. Women stand closer to each other while speaking. Men spread their legs further apart when sitting, while women tend to keep their legs together and their arms close to their body.[54]

- Men are more likely than women to use their nonverbal communication to physically intimidate someone.[55]

- Women are more expressive than men when they listen. They engage in more head nodding, smile more, and use more vocal encouragers, such as "hmmm" and "uh-huh."[56]

- Women tend to cry or tear up more than men.[57]

- Men are less likely to touch other men, whereas women tend to touch each other more.[58]

Like intercultural differences, gender differences are generalizations. Look at the results of every study cited in this section, and you'll likely think of people you know who are exceptions. One of your authors, Bruce, witnesses this on a daily basis in his work as a relational therapist. After years of marital strife, one couple, Ursula and Samad, determined that the best way to get along was to divorce. They started seeing Bruce to help them plan "the best divorce possible." This meant that they wanted to part ways in a loving, respectful way and co-parent effectively during the transition. Samad was far more expressive with his back-channel cues. Ursula interrupted Samad quite a bit more—both communication behaviors that, according to research, occur more often with the opposite gender.

What causes gender-specific differences in how people communicate? Many studies point to biology and socialization. First there's biology, in which the hormones estrogen and testosterone play an important role.[59] Research that focused on cisgender males and females found that at the average onset of puberty, females may have as much as 9 times more estrogen (a hormone linked to emotion) in their body than males do, and males may have up to 16 times more testosterone (a hormone linked to aggression) than females.[60] Hormonal differences may partially explain why males tend to act out more aggressively,[61] while females experience greater emotional arousal.[62]

Another biological difference affecting communication can be found in the brain. A study that compared over a thousand MRI scans showed that an average adult female brain has more neurological connectivity in the areas known to aid language.[63] This may explain why women tend to speak in longer sentences than men do.[64]

Finally, studies on socialization point to differences in how male and female children are taught to express themselves. For example, mothers talk more about emotions with their young daughters than with their sons, and they engage their daughters in more nurturing, care-taking activities.[65]

As far as socialization is concerned, it's important to note that societal cultures often promote certain **gender schemas**—beliefs about what it means to be male or female. **Gender socialization** is the process of teaching children how to act in ways that align with the cultural expectations of their biological sex. For example, parents may give their children certain toys to play with or steer them into activities or careers that they consider more appropriate for their gender.

It's important to note that what parents find gender appropriate varies from culture to culture. For example, in China, some elementary schools require boys to take an oath "to be real men" and participate in a program on how to be masculine. These efforts started after teachers became concerned that too many boys were participating in elastic band skipping, a recess activity popular with girls.[66] The Chinese government also released a textbook targeted to fourth and fifth graders on the differences between boys and girls, called *Little Men*.[67]

gender schemas Pervasive cultural beliefs about what it means to be male or female.

gender socialization The process of teaching children how to act in ways that align with the cultural expectations of their biological sex.

When a real-life firefighter, surgeon, and fighter pilot visit this elementary classroom, the students' assumptions about gender are met with a surprise. Why is a lesson like this so important? Relate your answer to what you've read about gender differences, socialization, and gender schemas. On YouTube, search using the keywords: "A Class That Turned Around Kids' Assumptions of Gender Roles!" (2:07)

Research on IPC and sexual orientation

Research on interpersonal communication specific to queer persons is limited, but interesting findings do exist. For example, gay men and lesbians look for the same qualities in a romantic partner as straight people do. Same-sex couples argue just as much as opposite-sex couples, but gay couples are less likely to argue about money. Gay people are also more likely than straight people to maintain closer ties with former romantic partners.[68] Compared to straight people, gay, lesbian, and bisexual individuals are more likely to place greater importance on friendships and assign a more familial meaning to them, especially if their immediate families do not accept their sexual orientation.[69]

The results of other studies suggest the following:

- Gay couples are more expressive with their private affection and positive emotions compared to heterosexual couples with children and no less than heterosexual couples without children.[70]

- Compared to straight couples, gay and lesbian couples tend to use more humor and stay calmer during conflict, and they are less likely to rely on dominance tactics to exert power.[71] Lesbian couples report more effective conflict resolution styles and higher relationship satisfaction when compared to gay men and straight couples.[72]

- In a review of 79 studies by researchers at Cornell University, it was found that 75 out of the 79 studies determined that children of same-sex parents are just as likely to grow up socially well-adjusted as children raised by opposite-sex parents.[73] Another study found that children raised by lesbian parents were more socially well-adjusted (academically competent with fewer social problems) than children raised by same-sex male and opposite-sex couples.[74]

- Same-sex married couples are more likely to report greater coordination and satisfaction with caring for aging parents and parents-in-law compared to opposite-sex couples. Straight women felt less support from their husbands and were more likely to report that their husbands undermined their efforts to care for their parents.[75]

What insights can you gain by reading about these findings? If you were asked to provide some possible explanations, what would you say? As with the gender-related findings we discussed earlier, keep in mind that the results of these studies don't pertain to all individuals, couples, or families.

section review

10.2 Gender and sexual orientation

Our study of gender incorporates information about biological sex, gender identity, and gender expression. Generally speaking, research shows that some gender differences in communication

(continued)

do exist and are likely influenced by biology and socialization. However, men and women communicate in ways that are more alike than different. Research also suggests that differences exist in the way relational partners communicate and relate to each other based on their sexual orientation.

Key Terms

biological sex, *p. 270*

intersex, *p. 270*

gender identity, *p. 270*

cisgender, *p. 270*

nonbinary, *p. 270*

transgender, *p. 271*

gender expression, *p. 271*

feminine expression, *p. 271*

masculine expression, *p. 272*

androgynous expression, *p. 272*

sexual orientation, *p. 272*

gay, *p. 272*

straight, *p. 272*

bisexual, *p. 272*

pansexual, *p. 272*

queer, *p. 273*

asexual, *p. 273*

gender schemas, *p. 275*

gender socialization, *p. 275*

Comprehend It?

1. Define each of the key terms in Section 10.2. To further your understanding of these terms, create examples to support your definitions.

2. Compare and contrast:

- Nonbinary, cisgender, and transgender
- Masculine, feminine, and androgynous expression
- Gay, straight, bisexual, pansexual, queer, and asexual

Apply It!

In an interview with *Sports Illustrated*, former University of Massachusetts basketball player Derrick Gordon shares what happened after he acknowledged his sexuality to his teammates and family. What was the coming out process like for him, and why is coming out a significant, ongoing event in the lives of lesbian, gay, and bisexual individuals? How did Gordon's sexuality affect his interpersonal communication before and after his coming out? On YouTube, search using the keywords: "Derrick Gordon: Being True." (3:57)

10.3 Diversity and IPC competence

One of our students, Chandah, shared this in class:

Two years ago, I met the sweetest, nicest guy in the world—who just so happens to be an atheist. My family is super religious, but I fell for Chad big-time. I was torn. We had many long talks about why he chose not to believe in God or associate with organized religion. I started reading several books, such as The God Delusion by Richard Dawkins and Letter to a Christian Nation by Sam Harris, to understand Chad better. Even though it was unsettling for me to read these works, they opened my mind. I felt challenged to think more critically about my religious views. I also began to read the Bible analytically and not from a blind-faith perspective. I now consider myself an atheist. 'Atheist' is a taboo word in my family. I have encountered hostility and aggressive conversion attempts from concerned friends. Someone I work with runs a local freethinkers meeting and invited me to go. It's so nice to spend time with others who are so open to various philosophies and points of view. I can be myself and not feel like the biggest outcast.

dichotomous thinking A way of thinking in which you see things as strictly one way or another.

ethnocentrism The tendency to view the beliefs and practices of one's own culture or co-culture as superior to others.

Chandah is now hesitant to bring her boyfriend around her parents. She worries that her parents will not accept Chad and will react negatively once she tells them that her beliefs have changed. What do you think Chandah should do? How can she and Chad constructively address an issue like this with her parents, friends, and family?

Viewing differences negatively is a common source of interpersonal conflict. In Section 10.3, we'll underscore the importance of understanding and valuing diverse viewpoints, beliefs, and people and highlight helpful ways to do so in your interpersonal communication.

Monitor dichotomous thinking

It's difficult to consider and appreciate the complexities of people, issues, and situations if you approach them with an all-or-nothing mindset. **Dichotomous thinking** (di-KAH-tah-mahs) occurs when you view situations as strictly one way or another; something is either good or bad, right or wrong. For example, Chandah's parents may think that it is good or right to believe in their faith and that it is bad or wrong to not believe in it. Their strict adherence to this belief may cause them to get quite upset once they learn that Chandah no longer shares their faith. They may even try to persuade Chandah to disavow her nonreligious beliefs in a way that damages the relationship they have with her.

To avoid dichotomous thinking, Chandah's parents could gather more information—perhaps read some of the works Chandah has read—before expressing their opinions. They could try to examine the situation from as many angles as possible, and they could make an effort to be curious: *Why is Chandah no longer religious?*

Today, there is so much information online about the freethought movement and secular humanism that a quick search would give Chandah's parents answers. Of course, asking their daughter to share her new beliefs with an open mind is also helpful.

Challenge stereotypes and prejudices

Dichotomous thinking may feed into **ethnocentrism**—the tendency to evaluate other cultures and co-cultures through the lens of your own. Often, ethnocentric thinking means that you view the beliefs and practices of your own culture or co-culture as superior to others or assume that your group is better than another group. Ethnocentric beliefs are often grounded in *stereotypes*. As discussed in Chapter 3, *stereotypes* are overly simplistic, preconceived impressions or assumptions you have about a group of individuals. Some stereotypes may lead you to say things that offend others, such as "You can dance pretty good for a White guy," or to an Asian person, "You don't know how to use chopsticks, *really?*"

"I try not to be judgemental but I see everything in black and white."

If you have little or no experience interacting with people who are different from you, you may form initial impressions that support a stereotype. For example, if you allow negative stereotypes to influence how you perceive people with disabilities, you may focus on their limitations and overlook their strengths.

Ethnocentrism and stereotypes are also correlated with prejudice. **Prejudice** is a negative belief or feeling you have toward a group of people or someone you perceive as belonging to a certain group. For example, a relational partner may express a prejudicial attitude by saying, "She's trying to do a man's job," or "He's not acting his age, he's too old for that kind of behavior."

Specific types of prejudice have their own labels. TABLE 10.1 lists several other types of prejudice. For example, if you harbor prejudicial views toward a person of a certain race or ethnicity, this is called **racism**. While the words *race* and *ethnicity* are complex in meaning and often expressed interchangeably, *race* generally refers to the biological differences between groups of people based on skin color and physical characteristics. *Ethnicity* relates to differences on the basis of nationality, language, and culture.

Like all of the "isms" you see in Table 10.1, racism exists on an individual and institutional level.[76] The prejudicial views one has of a particular race or ethnic group is individual racism. You may, for example, know of a family member who owns a store and makes disparaging comments about patrons of his who are of a different race or ethnicity. These prejudices were likely handed down by his family or community when he was young and will be difficult to remove.

Institutional racism is the collective prejudice that members of an organization share, especially those in positions of power. In the United States, and much of the world, institutionalized racism favors White people, causing BIPOC (Black, Indigenous, and People of Color) to experience many inequities. For example, White police officers have been shown to have more violent encounters, and to shoot and kill, Blacks and Hispanics at much higher rates than they do White people.[77] Institutional racism can also be found in the health care, educational, and financial systems of the United States.

prejudice A negative belief or feeling toward a group of people or people perceived as belonging to a certain group.

racism Negative beliefs and feelings toward other races.

sexism Negative beliefs and feelings toward the opposite sex.

ageism Negative beliefs and feelings toward other age groups.

classism Negative beliefs and feelings toward people of a different socioeconomic background.

ableism Negative beliefs and feelings toward people with disabilities.

heterosexism Negative beliefs and feelings toward non-heterosexual individuals. This term is often used interchangeably with the word *homophobia,* the fear of non-heterosexual individuals.

cisgenderism Negative beliefs and feelings toward people who do not identify with the biological sex they were given at birth.

table 10.1	Types of Prejudice
Type	**Prejudice Based On:**
Sexism	A person's biological sex
Ageism	A person's age
Classism	A person's socioeconomic status
Ableism	A person's disability
Heterosexism	A person's non-heterosexuality
Cisgenderism	A person's gender identity

discrimination The act of treating a person in a hurtful or unfair manner due to prejudice.

unconscious bias A prejudicial belief you hold that you are not aware of.

similarity assumption An automatic and uninformed belief that others are like you in some way.

Treating a person in a negative or unfair manner because of prejudice is called **discrimination**. For example, a male supervisor might refuse to consider qualified female staffers for promotion. In another case, an interviewer could ask you specific questions about your marital, family, or pregnancy status—which is illegal—and decline to hire you based on your answer. A parent who tries to discourage a child from dating someone of a different race or ethnicity is communicating in a discriminatory manner.

If we communicate and behave in ways that are prejudicial and discriminatory, not only does it hurt others but it can seriously damage reputations, relationships, and careers. For example, Tim Hunt, a renowned biochemist, won the Nobel Prize for unlocking the secrets of the cell cycle. While he received international praise for his work, a comment he made garnered even more attention: colleagues and thousands of Internet users sharply rebuked him after others heard him say that women were a problem in the lab because "You fall in love with them, they also fall in love with you, and then when you criticize them, they cry." Under mounting pressure, Hunt resigned as honorary professor at University College London.[78]

While many people claim not to have any prejudices, most fall prey to some form of unconscious bias. An **unconscious bias** is a prejudicial belief you hold that you are not aware of. Unconscious bias may cause you to overlook and undervalue those who have a lot to offer. For example, a supervisor at work may unknowingly seek the input of her female employees over her male employees to help her plan a large company party. The underlying bias may stem from the assumption that planning a party is something women have more experience with or enjoy doing. The male partners at a law firm may schedule squash games and overlook inviting their female partners because they assume the women in the firm wouldn't be interested or competitive in the sport.

When people act according to their unconscious biases, they often don't realize they are doing so. Nevertheless, their actions place others at a disadvantage. For example, if the male partners of the law firm form bonds outside the formalities of work, they're more apt to trade insider information, offer candid advice or leads, and develop loyalties; those who are left out miss out on these opportunities.

Unconscious bias may also cause you to make a similarity assumption. A **similarity assumption** is an automatic, uninformed belief that others are like you in some way. If you are cisgender and straight, for example, do you assume that everyone around you is too? To avoid expressing such a similarity assumption, you can use gender-neutral words when talking to others. If you're chatting about romance or dating, rather than asking a guy, "Do you have a girlfriend?" you might instead ask, "Are you dating anyone?"

While it's important to acknowledge our conscious and unconscious prejudices—and strive to challenge and hopefully change them—it's also essential to

In this scene from the TV show *Silicon Valley*, Jared (Zach Woods) and Richard (Thomas Middleditch) blunder through an interview with Carla (Alice Wetterlund). Use this scene to describe unconscious bias and how members of an in-group may focus too much attention on differences in a way that may make members of an out-group feel more different than they'd prefer. On YouTube, search using the keywords: "Silicon Valley 'woman engineer.'" (2:39).

recognize that we may unintentionally make others feel uncomfortable when we try too hard to counter prejudice. For example, a professor may repeatedly ask the only Black student in a predominantly White classroom to share his thoughts on race issues. The professor's intentions are perhaps good; she wants to acknowledge his presence and she values his perspective as a Black person. What he says could enlighten the other students, but it may make him feel singled out.

Embrace diversity

One of our students, Deandre, was at an inclusive, eclectic club one evening when a guy complimented him on his looks and offered to buy him a beer. Deandre recounted, "I told him simply, 'Sure, if you don't mind that I'm straight.' He laughed and said, 'No not at all.' We just drank a beer at the bar and talked for a while. We hang out all the time now, and he's my boy. He's gay, and I'm straight, but we have a lot in common and enjoy each other's company."

Getting to know people from diverse backgrounds may expand your frame of reference, enrich your life, and help you foster a greater number of meaningful relationships. Research also suggests that our prejudicial beliefs about others often change once we get to know them.[79]

The process of promoting diversity and making all people feel welcomed, valued, and accepted is called **inclusion**. A desire to interact with everyone can foster an inclusive perspective. Evelia describes in her narrative how she feels when she meets someone who approaches interactions this way. Are you someone she would feel comfortable talking to? If so, why?

inclusion The process of promoting diversity and making all people feel welcomed, valued, and accepted.

"Being bilingual is a good thing, but to speak two very different languages fluently isn't easy. I sometimes stay quiet because I doubt I'll get my point across as desired. It really helps when I sense a native English speaker is friendly and seems genuinely interested in me and what I have to say. Someone who is patient and gives me time to answer a question really helps as well." —Evelia

Expand your cultural knowledge

Gaining more competence in your communication also involves expanding your knowledge of people from diverse cultures. If you ever find yourself surfing YouTube, click on videos that feature the lives of people who belong to other cultures or co-cultures. Many radio shows and podcasts feature themes of diversity and inclusion and aim to introduce listeners to new perspectives. NPR hosts several such podcasts on its website, including: *We Are Not a Monolith*, *The She Said Project*, and *Same Same Different*. Check them out!

Your college campus may also sponsor lectures and workshops that focus on issues of diversity and inclusion. Your authors, Bruce and Leslie, learned a lot by taking time to attend a panel discussion featuring members of the LGBTQ community who shared their personal experiences, including how their straight and cisgender relational partners help them feel included and respected. Here are a few ideas we gleaned from the workshop that you might like to consider:

- If someone makes a derogatory comment about someone who is LGBTQ, speak up. Silence communicates that you may condone it. A simple statement like: "I'm uncomfortable with your comments," or "Please don't say that around me," is effective.

- If someone says, "I think (s)he's gay," a nonchalant response like "okay" is neutral. A response like "good for her" or a simple "cool" works too if you wish to be affirming.

- Refrain from calling something "gay" in a pejorative manner. Also avoid saying "the gay lifestyle," which suggests that all LGBTQ individuals are the same or live a certain way. There is a lot of diversity within the community.

- Use the name and pronouns that match a transgender individual's gender identity. When you're not sure about someone's gender, ask a simple question such as: "What pronouns do you prefer to go by?"

- Support your relational partners, regardless of their gender identity or sexuality, when they act, dress, pursue activities, or communicate in ways that fall outside traditional gender norms. For example, teasing a male friend for wearing pink may put pressure on him to conform to a norm that limits his self-expression. It's especially helpful if parents acknowledge the existence of other sexual orientations and gender identities without judgment when discussing related topics with their children.[80]

You can also expand your awareness of and appreciation for human diversity in a number of other ways.

- Go out of your way to work with, recruit, train, and promote someone from outside your organization.

- Attend political rallies sponsored by parties you're not aligned with and participate with an open mind.

- Strive to sit next to or get to know the international students in your class.

- Read a religious book other than the one your faith is based on.

- Visit museums and art galleries featuring exhibits from other countries.

- Learn about the dos and don'ts of intercultural communication by reading popular books like *Multicultural Manners: Essential Rules of Etiquette for the 21st Century*, by Norine Dresser, or *Do's and Taboos around the World*, by Roger Axtell.

- Take classes on race, gender, sexuality, and world studies.

- Watch movies that not only enlighten you about various cultures and co-cultures but also challenge stereotypes and prejudices. Examples include *The Hate U Give*, *Boy Erased*, *Moonlight*, *Arranged*, *The Lunchbox*, *Spanglish*, *Sweet Destiny*, *Mammoth*, and *The Joy Luck Club*.

Another thing you can do is invite people who are different from you to teach you about their practices, beliefs, and life experiences. Keep in mind that no one is obligated to answer your questions, and some may find it distressing or

The reality show *Push Girls* chronicles the lives of five women who were paralyzed by accident or illness. In this clip, Angela Rockwood, Auti Angel, Mia Schaikewitz, and Tiphany Adams each share what their disability means to them. How did watching this video make you feel? How would a close relationship with any of these individuals enrich your life? On YouTube, search using the keywords: "Push Girls, If You Can't Stand Up, Stand Out." (2:48)

draining to be asked. But if you find yourself in the right circumstances, here are some respectful ways you can approach the topic:

- "This is new to me. What is the customary way to handle this?"
- "I would love to learn more about this aspect of your culture. Can you tell me about . . . ?"
- "I am curious about your faith. Would you mind sharing with me the significance of . . . ?"
- "Some of your artwork (or jewelry, clothes, music) is unfamiliar to me. I like it. May I ask about its origins?"

section review

10.3 Diversity and IPC competence

A willingness to learn about and appreciate human diversity can enhance your IPC and relationships. It helps if you challenge dichotomous thinking with open-mindedness and curiosity. Identifying and challenging your own prejudices is also essential. Making an effort to get to know others who are different from you will also help you communicate more effectively with all kinds of people.

Key Terms

dichotomous thinking, *p. 278*	sexism, *p. 279*	heterosexism, *p. 279*	similarity assumption, *p.280*
ethnocentrism, *p. 278*	ageism, *p. 279*	cisgenderism, *p. 279*	inclusion, *p. 281*
prejudice, *p. 279*	classism, *p. 279*	discrimination, *p. 280*	
racism, *p. 279*	ableism, *p. 279*	unconscious bias, *p. 280*	

Comprehend It?

1. Define each of the key terms in Section 10.3. To further your understanding of these terms, create examples to support your definitions.

2. Compare and contrast the following key terms:
   - Prejudice and discrimination
   - Racism, sexism, ageism, classism, ableism, heterosexism, and cisgenderism

Apply It!

American actor and director Justin Baldoni explains how gender socialization limits our ability to create meaningful and rewarding relationships. What do you think about his message? How would taking the time to watch TED Talks like this expand your frame of reference and improve your understanding of human diversity? Relate what Justin says to the concept of dichotomous thinking and the section on challenging prejudices. To watch Justin's talk, search YouTube using the keywords: "Why I'm done trying to be 'man enough.'" (18:32)

chapter exercises

Assessing Your IPC: What Is Your Level of Cultural Sensitivity?

Purpose: To determine how open I am to learning about and pursuing relationships with individuals who are from different cultures and co-cultures.

Directions: Take a free, online assessment to determine if your interest in other cultures is low, average, or high. Intercultural communication scholars Guo-Ming Chen and William Starosta created this scale, and you can find it by searching online for "Cultural Competence/Intercultural Sensitivity Scale."[81]

Building Your IPC Skills: Diversity and IPC Competence

Purpose: To learn about and appreciate human diversity.

Directions: In the next couple of weeks, make a point to accomplish one of the bulleted diversity immersion suggestions we highlighted in Section 10.3 (p. 283). Describe to a classmate or discussion group what you did and the insights you gained as a result!

11

Communication and Technology

learning objectives

Reading this chapter will help you:

- Assess your use of communication technology
- Understand the bright and dark sides of the disinhibition effect
- Identify ways to use communication technology effectively

Sara, a 31-year-old marketing manager from San Francisco, originally didn't think that Tinder was for her. "I heard about it in a funny, joking, laugh-about-it way," she admitted. "But I started hearing that friends of mine had met significant others on this app, and I thought, maybe it's not just this hookup thing. It's for finding relationships." Now she has a serious boyfriend whom she met on the app, and after a year of dating, they're poised to move in together.[1]

Romain, on the other hand, is not a fan of Tinder. He lamented, "I'm not getting any matches! What's wrong with my profile? Is it my bio? My photos? What algorithm is Tinder using?"

Like Sara and Romain, you may enthusiastically—or begrudgingly—use technology to find a potential romantic partner. You almost certainly use it daily to communicate with other people in your life.

Technology channels and their various applications, such as cell phones and dating apps, respectively, significantly expand our capacity to develop and maintain relationships. In this photo, a woman uses her cell phone to communicate, perhaps with a potential date, while her friends look on in delight.

How do you use communication technology? What effect does it have on your relationships? In this chapter, we'll explore (1) the nature of technology-mediated communication, (2) the disinhibition effect, and (3) ways to use communication technology effectively.

11.1 The nature of technology-mediated communication

Technology-mediated communication (TMC) is the process of exchanging and assigning meaning to messages that are facilitated by technology channels and applications. *Technology channels* are pathways through which technological messages flow. They include the Internet, telephone landlines, cellular networks, and devices such as personal computers, tablets, and cell phones. *Technology applications* are the ways in which technology can be used. Examples include online dating and social networking, email, video-conferencing, and multiplayer gaming.

According to the **media ecology perspective (MEP)**, technology isn't just something you use; it becomes a part of you. It reshapes and reorganizes your IPC values, perceptions, and behaviors.[2] In other words, technology isn't neutral. It's always changing, and you're changing right along with it. According to the MEP, communication technology will, by its very nature, affect you in ways that are both good and bad.

Not everyone agrees with this perspective, however. Some critics of the MEP say that technology is a tool subject only to the whims of its users. They argue that technology doesn't inherently make your interpersonal communication better or worse and that you determine the effect it has on you.

What do you think? How easy—or difficult—is it to control your use of technology and its influence on your interpersonal communication and relationships?

One of the liveliest discussions we have with our students is whether TMC is good or bad for relationships. Students who are fans of TMC are quick to point out the positives. For example, one of our students, Teresa, is legally deaf; she relies on I-Caption technology, which converts voice communication to text in real time. Thanks to technology, Teresa is able to participate in meaningful phone conversations with family and friends.

Her classmate, Shakyia, shared, "I grew up not knowing one of my cousins. We found each other on Facebook! We were able to meet each other for the first time face-to-face using a video-conference app."

Dominic, another student of ours, recently moved to the area. He attended a movie screening—something he found out about by joining an online meetup group for film enthusiasts—and made four new friends that evening.

For all of its positives, however, our students are quick to point out that TMC has its drawbacks. As you are about to learn, TMC has the potential to negatively affect our interpersonal communication and damage our relationships.

technology-mediated communication (TMC) The process of exchanging and assigning meaning to messages that are facilitated by technology channels and applications.

media ecology perspective (MEP) The idea that technology reshapes and reorganizes your interpersonal communication values, perceptions, and behaviors.

Keep the media ecology theory in mind as you read Section 11.1. Our goal in this section is to encourage you to reflect on your use of TMC as we explore some of the interpersonal challenges associated with it. See if you can identify any areas for self-improvement!

Less richness

Thanks to cell phones and the Internet, you can see that your out-of-state cousin is throwing a graduation party just by looking at his social media, and you can send him a congratulatory note instantly. You can text a friend to wish her luck before her military deployment—and do it anytime, from pretty much anywhere. You can even respond to emails, as 59% of American adults do, while sitting on . . . yep . . . a toilet.[3]

Technology makes communication quick, easy, and efficient. For these reasons, texting and online messaging are popular communication methods. In Chapter 2, you learned that texts and online messages are *asynchronous*—there's a delay in the feedback you receive, which means you and your conversational partner can't influence each other's communication in real time.

Compared to face-to-face (F2F) and voice-to-voice (V2V) interactions (which are *synchronous*), asynchronous communication is generally considered a less rich form of communication. *Richness* refers to the amount of information you're able to transmit and how fast you can send and receive feedback. For example, when you tell a joke to a friend in person, you can see his physical expressions and hear his laughter right then and there. If you send the joke via text, you'll receive far fewer cues —perhaps only an "LOL" message—and his response may come much later in the day.

An overreliance on asynchronous communication channels may cause us to skip the complex thought processes and richer exchange of information we experience with spontaneous real-time talk. Psychologist Sherry Turkle, author of *Alone Together*, believes that the popularity of text and online messaging makes it easier for relational partners to sidestep complex or difficult conversations. As an example, Turkle cites an "I'm sorry" text, which she believes does not have the same richness as an F2F apology. She states, "A full-scale apology means I know I've hurt you, I get to see that in your eyes. . .You get to see that I'm uncomfortable, and with that, the compassion response kicks in. There are many steps and they're all bypassed when we text."[4]

In addition, as we increasingly rely on asynchronous communication channels, we run the risk of becoming ill at ease with F2F and V2V interactions.[5] Turkle describes a conversation she had with a woman whose son is only comfortable communicating via text; the woman's 16-year-old son will only talk on the phone with relatives, and only after she's urged him to.[6] Turkle also reports that a teen, who relies on texting for nearly everything, told her that "someday, but certainly not now, I'd like to learn how to have a conversation."[7]

Do you agree with the concerns raised by Turkle and other researchers about what we may lose or even avoid in our communication because of technology?

To what extent has technology replaced your F2F and V2V communication? What effect has TMC had on the richness and quality of your communication?

Jealousy and insecurity

In a groundbreaking study testing the effects of cell phones on interpersonal communication, researchers set up conversations between pairs of strangers and had them sit down to chat—with half of the pairs a few feet away from a cell phone, and the other half in a cell phone–free environment. Those who spoke within sight of the cell phone felt less connected with their conversation partner. They were also more likely to say that their conversation partner lacked authenticity and empathy.[8]

Because cell phones connect us to a wide network of people, their mere presence can introduce an element of competition into a conversation or relationship. If your friend sets her cell phone on the table while you're having lunch, she sends the message that you have her attention so long as someone else doesn't vie for it. Seeing your relational partner's cell phone may provoke jealousy and insecurity—consciously or subconsciously.

Social media is another source of jealousy within relationships. According to psychologist Amy Muise, social media gives "people access to information about their romantic partner that would otherwise be [unavailable to them]. This may include details about their partner's friendships and social exchanges, especially interactions with previous romantic or sexual partners."[9]

The accessibility of this information may make it tempting to check whether your romantic partner has any new followers or to monitor how often your partner likes or comments on another person's posts. You may even attempt to provoke a jealous response in your partner by posting something online. According to Muise, increased use of social media to monitor your partner can foster a vicious cycle of insecurity and jealousy.[10]

As you learned in Chapter 8, the *comparison level of alternatives* may lead people to believe that an alternative relationship has more to offer them than their current relationship does. If you are dissatisfied with your current relationship, social media may offer an array of enticing potential new partners. The simple fact that social media allows people to connect with anyone at any time—a connection that may lead to romantic interest—can also make partners anxious about the stability of their relationships.

Research suggests that people's insecurities about their romantic partners' digital lives are warranted, to some extent. According to one study, 42% of users of a popular dating app were currently married or in a committed romantic relationship.[11] Another study found that 70% of subjects said they had frequently maintained digital connections with at least one ex or a friend who they secretly would like to pursue romantically.[12] Researchers refer to these potential romantic relationships as *back burners*. Another study suggests that men have twice the number of back burners compared to women. This same study found that, on average, men and women in romantic relationships exchanged sexual, romantic, or flirtatious messages online with two or more individuals other than their current romantic partner.[13] This behavior is now referred to in the research literature as **digital infidelity**.

Does having a backup relationship mean that someone is any less committed to their relationship? Not necessarily, but technology may make it easier and more tempting to start and maintain emotional affairs and sexual liaisons. A correlation does exist between heavy Facebook use and higher incidences of emotional cheating, physical cheating, breakups, and divorce.[14]

On the other hand, some couples rely on technology to cultivate transparency and prevent infidelity. According to a Pew Research Center study, roughly 67% of married or committed couples share their online passwords with each other, 27% use the same email account, 11% can access each other's online calendars, and 11% share a social networking profile.[15]

Many couples find technological transparency helpful, but it can also be a point of conflict. One partner may value openness and accountability while the other prefers greater privacy. What do you think is the best way to balance these different preferences?

Those who support the media ecology perspective would argue that if today's technology didn't exist, the jealousy and insecurity it causes wouldn't exist either. Others propose that jealousy and insecurity are common experiences in romantic relationships regardless of communication technology.[16] Some of us simply have jealous tendencies and insecurities, while others do not.[17] Do your own online behaviors play a bigger role in stoking or mitigating jealousy and insecurity than the technology itself?

Phone snubbing

One of our students, Emma, shared how her husband, Corbin, would often arrive home from work while talking on his cell phone, ignoring Emma until he finished his conversation. She missed the days when they would come home and eagerly greet each other with a hug and a kiss.

After Emma expressed her concerns, Corbin made it a point to finish his phone calls in the garage before walking in the door. Though Emma appreciates his gesture, she still questions whether he values their time together: "I hear him pull into the driveway and wait twenty or thirty minutes for him to finish talking, and I wonder, 'who is so important that he has to carve away time we'd otherwise have together?'"

Emma is feeling "phubbed" or phone snubbed. **Phone snubbing** is the act of making it seem like your time on your cell phone is more important than your time with a relational partner. Common phone snubbing behaviors include:

- Checking your cell phone during a lull in a conversation
- Propping your phone on a table so the screen is visible "just in case"

---

digital infidelity The act of secretly exchanging sexual, romantic, or flirtatious messages online with someone who is not your current romantic partner.

phone snubbing The act of making it seem like your time on your cell phone is more important than your time with a relational partner.

- Disrupting a conversation to check a message
- Keeping your cell phone within arm's reach at all times
- Showing more interest in your phone than your romantic partner while in bed at night

Emma is not a fan of phone snubbing—and she's not alone. In one study, 22.6% of couples said that it caused ongoing conflict in their relationship.[18] If we were to ask your relational partners whether you phone snub them, what would they say? How is your use of technology in this regard affecting your relationships? In Zain's narrative, he tries to avoid phone snubbing but runs into another communication problem. Can you relate?

"I often shut my cell phone off when I'm with my sons. Friends and family get mad at me because I don't pick up their calls or respond to their texts fast enough. I believe we're never truly present when we are always on alert, with our phones vibrating in our pockets to update us about every possible thing. When I shut off my phone, I'm one hundred percent present with the person I'm with. I am doing more for that relationship than I'm doing by giving fragments of myself to a bunch of others." –Zain

Zain's effort to limit distractions during his F2F interactions is a good thing, but some of his friends and family members want his immediate attention when they reach out to him electronically. Zain says, "If I try to meet their expectations, the friends and family I'm with will get phubbed."

Do you carry your cell phone with you everywhere you go? Do you check it just about every time it alerts you to a call, email, or text? Do you assume your relational partners do the same—or that they should? If someone is slow to return your cell phone call or text, do you ever feel irritated, disappointed, anxious, or even suspicious?

If you answered "yes" to any of these questions, a proponent of the media ecology perspective would say that cellular technology has altered your IPC expectations and behaviors. However, you could also argue that cellular technology itself isn't completely to blame: It only influences your behavior and expectations to the extent that you allow it to do so.

Technology's addictive potential

One of the reasons we've integrated technology (or technology has integrated itself) so deeply into our lives is because of its addictive potential. One study asked 1,000 students attending 12 colleges in 10 different countries to voluntarily abstain from using mobile phones, laptops, TVs, and social networking sites for one day. A majority couldn't do it. Going without technology for just 24 hours caused one out of five students to experience noticeable withdrawal symptoms, including heart palpitations, confusion, anxiety, irritability, jealousy, and depression.[19]

Claire Dunphy (Julie Bowen) is ignored by members of her family once too often and declares a weeklong ban on all personal devices. Her husband Phil (Ty Burrell) turns the ban into a contest. Watch what happens in this episode of *Modern Family*. What appears to influence the Dunphys' communication more: the technology itself or the users of the technology? On YouTube, search using the keywords: "Modern Family - No Internet Contest." (4:40) (3:16)

What makes communication technology so addictive? With a quick swipe of your thumb or click of your mouse, you have instant access to a plethora of stimulating games, apps, photos, videos, and posts. You can also interact electronically with people you like. These enticements may trigger your brain to produce dopamine, a chemical messenger believed to fuel pleasure-seeking behaviors.[20]

You use technology, technology gratifies you, and dopamine causes you to seek more gratification. Psychologists refer to this as the **dopamine loop**. Have you ever searched for something online and kept clicking from one article or post to another? You suddenly realize that a significant amount of time has passed and you're reading something totally unrelated to your original search. If this has happened to you, you've experienced the dopamine loop at work.

When your phone vibrates, rings, or glows to let you know that you have a new message—signaling that someone is paying attention to you—your brain secretes dopamine, initiating another dopamine loop. This may explain why most people unlock their cell phones more than 150 times a day.[21]

One of our students, Kristen, shared an experience about the addictive potential of communication technology. Kristen recently moved from one side of the state to the other, and she missed her old friends. After her move, she initially used social media to stay in touch with them. She said, "I thought technology would make it easier for me, but I think it only made things worse. I could see my friends posting about all the things they were doing, and I couldn't participate. After school, I was on social media for hours every day. I got pretty lonely. Eventually I realized I needed to start reaching out to my new classmates."

dopamine loop The cycle of pleasure-seeking behavior caused by the brain chemical dopamine.

Two doctoral students at MIT, Robert Morris and Dan McDuff, were at one point spending a combined 50 hours a week on social media. They were inspired to invent a "shocking" device to help them overcome their online compulsion. Is there a real market for something like this? Would you benefit from their device? Why or why not? On YouTube, search using the keywords: "Pavlov Poke." (1:45)

Another student, Christopher, broke his wrist and was required to wear a cast for three weeks. He was temporarily out of work and spent much of his time playing an online multiplayer role-playing game, World of Warcraft (WoW). He shared, "Being out of work, not in school, and with nothing better to do, I got caught up in the fantasy role-playing and the competitive challenge of going to the next level. Lured by other players who invite you on quests based on your skill level, I soon became a WoW junkie. I started hanging out less and less with family and friends—and stayed holed up in my apartment with the shades closed in front of my game console."

Are Kristen and Christopher's experiences unusual? In the United States, people ages 16–24 report spending an average of 2 hours and 8 minutes on social media per day, a 76% increase since 2012.[22] Among all U.S. adult gamers (those who say they play at least once a week), 11.6% say that they spend on average more than 20 hours a week playing video games on their mobile devices, personal computers, and consoles.[23]

As you increase the time you spend on social media and gaming, you're more likely to feel lonely and depressed—and jeopardize your well-being and interpersonal relationships.[24] One woman posted on an online support group for people who are separated or considering divorce because of their partner's obsession with online gaming: "Your husband's behavior stops making sense. He trades sharing good times and memories with you for time with strangers he has met online."[25]

Recent research, however, suggests that gaming in short spurts or sporadically may actually reduce depression and anxiety for some people.[26] It may serve as a distraction from thoughts that exacerbate depression and anxiety.[27] In addition, multiplayer video gaming may lead to meaningful online friendships, which would enhance a person's well-being.[28]

To determine if your use of communication technology meets the criteria of an addiction, complete the *Assessing Your IPC* exercise at the end of this chapter. We'll explore some ways to use technology responsibly in Section 11.3 of this chapter.

section review

11.1 **The nature of technology-mediated communication**

Technology-mediated communication is the exchange of messages as facilitated by technological devices and their various platforms. According to the media technology perspective, technology reshapes and reorganizes your interpersonal communication values, perceptions, and behaviors. Four IPC challenges associated with TMC include less richness in communication, jealousy and insecurity in relationships, phone snubbing, and technological addiction.

Key Terms

technology-mediated communication (TMC), *p. 288*

media ecology perspective (MEP), *p. 288*

digital infidelity, *p. 291*

phone snubbing, *p. 291*

dopamine loop, *p. 293*

Comprehend It?

1. Define each of the key terms in Section 11.1. To further your understanding of these terms, create examples to support your definitions.

2. In your own words, explain the IPC challenges associated with TMC (less richness, jealousy and insecurity, phone snubbing, and technological addiction). Based on what you've read, how would you like to improve your own use of TMC?

Apply It!

To help you assess the amount of time you devote to internet browsing, online gaming, and social media use compared to other activities, complete the *Building Your IPC Skills* activity at the end of this chapter. You may find the results very illuminating!

11.2 **The disinhibition effect**

Thanks to technology, the line between private and public has blurred. Before the advent of TMC, you may have kept certain thoughts to yourself or only shared them with a trusted confidante. Whereas now, you might feel comfortable expressing them on Twitter, Instagram, WhatsApp, or any number of other electronic platforms—where a lot of people might see them. Typing your thoughts into a device creates a certain level of psychological distance, which may lower your inhibitions and enable you to say things that you ordinarily wouldn't say to someone's face. A receiver's reaction to your message isn't immediately apparent, and there's a delay in terms of any consequences.

From behind the safety of a computer screen, someone may, in a knee-jerk fashion, weigh in on a political subject they don't know much about on Facebook. Another person may fire off a tweet about "friends who are not real friends" in a hasty, harsh, and unwise manner. When someone is standing or sitting a few feet from you, on the other hand, you might think twice before saying what you really think or feel.

Research suggests that the asynchronous nature of online and text messaging has a **disinhibition effect**: it may cause you to express yourself more candidly and less guardedly than you otherwise would in person.[29]

In Section 11.2, we'll take a look at both the bright side and the dark side of the disinhibition effect.

The bright side of disinhibition

A friend of one of your authors, Emmanuel, posted this message when he needed help moving: "Hey guys, if anyone in the area is free Saturday to help me move into my new apartment, you'd be a life saver. I'll have beer in the fridge and pizza in the oven!" Within 15 minutes, one friend had offered his truck, and several others said they could help move boxes. Emmanuel doesn't find asking for help easy, but using social media to send a request without putting his friends on the spot made it much more comfortable for him.

Like Emmanuel, you may feel less reluctant to ask for or offer help and support when you can do so with TMC. The disinhibition effect may explain the popularity of online support groups and the rise in online opportunities to offer or seek helpful advice, emotional encouragement, coaching, counseling, and mentoring.[30] If someone you know is being unfairly or harshly criticized online, the disinhibition effect may also empower you to express your support virtually.[31]

The disinhibition effect is perhaps even more pronounced when people have the ability to remain anonymous. In many online settings, you can keep your identity a secret and your presence invisible. Apps and sites such as Whisper and PostSecret allow you to anonymously confess things you are not proud of—to acknowledge things about yourself, your relationships, and your decisions that you wouldn't feel comfortable sharing otherwise. This can result in **catharsis**, the release of negative emotions such as stress, fear, or guilt when you divulge personal struggles and secrets. Many participants in online chats, for example, report feeling quite relieved after sharing their secrets.[32]

The disinhibition effect may also accelerate the development of close relationships. You tend to grow closer to others as you get to know them. In Chapter 8, you learned about *self-disclosure*—the act of revealing personal information about yourself. Self-disclosure is generally a gradual process when it happens in person, but it may occur at a faster pace electronically; it may also become more intimate and revealing—in which case it becomes **hyperpersonal communication**.[33]

In *Love, Simon*, Simon Spier (Nick Robinson) meets "Blue," a male student who goes to the same high school, online. Their anonymity creates a safe space to get to know each other. Simon starts to fall in love with Blue and tries to figure out who he is, leading to many humorous and dramatic moments at school. How do your online and in-person relationships differ? Identify the various technology channels and applications shown in this clip and relate their use to the disinhibition effect. On YouTube, search using the keywords: "Love, Simon Official Trailer #2 2018." (2:45)

The asynchronous, disinhibited nature of TMC creates a unique hyperpersonal context that tends to accelerate the discussion of personal topics and the development of relationships. Reciprocity reinforces hyperpersonal communication. For example, with the greater ease and freedom to express yourself that comes along with the disinhibition effect, you may not hold back as much when sharing your thoughts, feelings, needs, and experiences. The person you're communicating with will likely do the same.[34] This hyperpersonal context can thus enhance many of our F2F relationships as well. When we are not with our relational partners physically, we can still engage with them in very meaningful and enjoyable online and cellular communication.

The disinhibition effect may also help shy individuals initiate conversations and ease into social interactions more comfortably and confidently. In online communication, you can assume whatever you want about the reaction you're getting from someone—which may reduce your inhibitions—and you can hide your own reactions to the messages you receive. For example, the person who asks you out on a date through a dating app can't see you break out in a celebratory dance in your living room.

In fact, those of us who are more introverted in F2F interactions may become quite extroverted online. Furthermore, research suggests that shy individuals can meet many of their social needs and establish close relationships using online channels.[35] Initiating relationships online may make it easier for introverts to establish F2F relationships later. One of our students, Boyd, alludes to this in his narrative. How can you relate to his experience?

"I find it way easier to start relationships online. I can tell if the other person isn't interested based on how long it takes to get a response, the length of the response, and content of the message. Approaching someone in person is riskier and more nerve-racking. What if they don't like me? Getting publicly rejected is much more embarrassing than being rejected online." —Boyd

There is concern, however, that shy people may rely too much on technology and use it to replace F2F interactions, as we discussed in Section 11.1. The big research question is whether technology does more to alleviate, perpetuate, or worsen F2F and V2V shyness.[36] What do you think? How can those of us who are shy use communication technology to overcome our shyness in person?

The dark side of disinhibition

Research also suggests that the disinhibition effect can compel us to communicate in inappropriate, hurtful, or dishonest ways.[37] Such behaviors include sexting, flaming, cyber harassment, ghosting, and catfishing. They have the potential to severely damage our relationships, and they may have negative legal consequences as well.

Sexting

Sexting is the exchange of nude or seminude photos, videos, and sexually suggestive language via text messaging. According to one study, 82% of adults surveyed admitted to sexting within the previous year.[38] While sexting can be beneficial to some relationships, especially established long-distance romantic relationships, sending a sext to another person who finds it inappropriate, embarrassing, or insulting may hurt a relationship, and can be considered sexual harassment.[39] In addition, because sexts are easily savable and shareable, they can take on a life beyond what the sender originally intended. If a sext lands in the wrong hands, that person may choose to weaponize it and damage the sender in some way.

Research shows that sexting can become an inadequate crutch for real intimacy. One study found that men who are more fearful of attachment or less comfortable with emotional intimacy engage in sexting behaviors more often. They may resort to sexting as their primary way to show emotional interest, something that, if done too early, too often, or with the wrong person, may sink a romantic relationship before it gets off the ground.[40]

Flaming

The disinhibition effect can lead people to exchange extremely harsh words with each other when they never would have been so antagonistic in person. This hostile exchange of online messages is known as **flaming**. Flaming often takes the form of a disagreement that turns into a volley of sharp retorts or hurtful insults. It is often laced with profanity and antagonistic abbreviations. A series

sexting The exchange of nude or seminude photos, videos, and sexually suggestive language via text messaging.

flaming The hostile exchange of online messages, often in the form of insults.

of comments on Facebook between Melissa and Rachel is an example of flaming. How might an exchange like this escalate a conflict or damage a relationship?

> **Melissa:** LMAO that is so not the answer I would give. Goes to show a stupid question begets a stupid answer.
>
> **Rachel:** Really, Mel? I'm sure YOU haven't ever asked a STUPID question before. Is there such a thing as a stupid question? We all don't know everything Mel. But of course, you know everything, right? SMH!

You can find another, more humorous example of flaming by searching YouTube using the keywords: "Caroline stole my broccoli casserole recipe Tiktok." (0:49)

Flaming can begin in many ways: openly hostile from the start, or more indirect. A person may complain about someone or air their "dirty laundry" without initially using the other person's name or referencing their specific actions. However, the subject of such a rant is often thinly veiled and their identity apparent to at least a few readers.

We also see flaming occur in any forum in which individuals can converse and reply to each other, such as multiplayer online gaming, when some players, in the heat of the moment, swear at each other, call each other names, and use derogatory language, including language that is racist, sexist, and/or homophobic.

Cyber harassment

The disinhibiting effect of TMC can bring out our worst selves in other ways. **Cyberbullying** occurs when someone repeatedly posts disparaging remarks or photos about another person online. Cyberbullying may take the form of taunts, negative comparisons, put-downs, gossip, and threats. The Cyberbullying Research Center estimates that nearly 25% of all teens will be a victim of cyberbullying, and more than 15% admit to cyberbullying others.[41]

While cyberbullying is usually associated with the actions of young people online, in fact, this type of behavior extends to all ages. **Cyberstalking** is the act of ongoing surveillance paired with the malicious use of technology. It can include identity theft, threats, coercion, and slander. ABC News featured a television story about a man's fiancée who went on a cyberstalking rampage after their breakup. She not only got hold of and changed his passwords but also used his email address to send embarrassing photos of him to his coworkers. She even used phone-masking technology to make it appear that he was calling her phone in violation of a protective order.

Another aspect of cyber harassment has many child psychologists and advocates concerned: parents who post humiliating videos of their children on social media in an attempt to inflict emotional punishment. At one point there were at least 30,000 such child-shaming videos posted on YouTube.[42]

Clinical psychologist Deborah Donison states, "In situations where I've worked with families or children who've experienced this kind of humiliation or shame,

cyberbullying The act of repeatedly posting disparaging remarks or photos about another person online. It may include taunts, negative comparisons, put-downs, gossip, and threats.

cyberstalking The act of ongoing surveillance paired with the malicious use of technology.

there's increased resentment toward the parents. [. . .] Unfortunately it also teaches these kids in a sense that publicly humiliating another person is an okay thing to do."[43]

If you or someone you know is harassed online, the social networking sites you're using will likely allow you to block individuals or report abusive comments. They may lock the offender's profile or ban the person's IP address—the unique numerical label assigned to each device that connects to the Internet. For information regarding your rights and helpful resources, visit the U.S. Department of Health and Human Services' anti-bullying website: www.stopbullying.gov or call the Victim of Crime Resource Center hotline: 1-800-842-8467.

Ghosting

The ability to communicate with others at a physical distance without having to look them in the eye or see their reaction may encourage impolite and selfish behavior. Have you ever gone on a couple of dates or spent weeks in online communication with a potential dating partner, only for the person to suddenly break off all communication without explanation? Perhaps you've communicated with someone on social media, it seems like a friendship is forming, and then without warning the person starts to ignore you.

This behavior is referred to as **ghosting**, and it is considered disrespectful, unkind, and hurtful. Instead of ghosting someone whom you no longer wish to communicate with, experts recommend that you simply tell the other person that you've enjoyed spending time together, but you're not feeling a strong enough connection to move forward. Or, in the case of cutting off platonic online communication, provide a legitimate reason—that perhaps you're quite busy or that the demands of life make it difficult for you to pursue new friendships. It's better than leaving someone hanging.

Catfishing

The ability to remain anonymous when communicating virtually, coupled with the disinhibition effect, may make it tempting to engage in dishonest behavior online. If no one can touch you or possibly recognize you, who's to stop you from acting as you wish and taking advantage of others? Nev Schulman, a New York photographer, can attest to this. When he was in his twenties, he found himself in a deep romantic online relationship with a woman named Megan. His brother, Ariel, saw a few red flags and convinced Nev to allow him to investigate Megan. They discovered she was someone completely different. Nev and Ariel turned their story into a documentary film called *Catfish*, which later sparked a television series called *Catfish: The TV Show* on MTV. The film and show gave rise to the word **catfishing** to describe the practice of pretending to be someone you're not online.[44]

ghosting The act of cutting off all communication with no explanation.

catfishing The act of pretending to be someone you're not online.

Manti Te'o, a 21-year-old University of Notre Dame linebacker, was catfished as well. During Manti's senior year of college, he was led to believe that his girlfriend, Lennay Kekua, had died of leukemia within hours of his grandmother's passing. After receiving this tragic news, Manti still managed to lead his team to a 20–3 upset against Michigan State, racking up 12 tackles, a fumble recovery, and key quarterback sack to dominate the game.[45]

A media firestorm erupted. Sports media and the Notre Dame community showered Manti with support. This was until *Deadspin*, a sports blog, broke the story that evidence of Manti's girlfriend—whom Manti had communicated with exclusively online—could not be found anywhere. She didn't exist. Manti soon learned that "Lennay" was really Ronaiah Tuiasosopo, a former high school star quarterback and a casual friend of Manti's. Ronaiah used Facebook photos of a friend to convince Manti that he was "Lennay."[46] To learn more about Manti's story, search YouTube using the keywords: "Manti Te'o full interview on Katie Show."

Post-cyber-disclosure panic

Have you ever felt distressed or anxious after sending a message electronically? If so, you've experienced what psychologists call **post-cyber-disclosure panic**. This reaction is also associated with feelings of dread or regret, which usually arise the moment you realize your message could be misunderstood or could affect you or someone you care about in a negative way. You might feel this panic after engaging in any of the TMC behaviors described in this section.

Prior to cell phones or the Internet, workers sometimes gathered in the break room or around the water cooler to complain about their boss. Today, thanks to the disinhibition effect, you might feel compelled to take your grievances online. Let's say that, after a particularly rough day at work, you tweet: "I don't know what part of the day I hate my boss the most . . . 5:30 a.m. when I'm at work and he isn't, or 3 p.m. when I have to see his stupid face."[47]

It may feel cathartic to post something like this, and others may like your tweet or respond with laughing emojis, but the moment it dawns on you that this tweet could get to your boss, you'll likely experience post-cyber-disclosure panic.

It's important to remember that relational partners can access, record, save, and share your cellular and online communication and activities in ways that you don't intend. Employers have a legal right to monitor your computer and cell phone if they are company-issued devices. The data they gather may serve as hard-to-refute proof in a legal proceeding, employment investigation, or hiring decision.

In several high-profile divorce and custody cases, electronic messages have been used as evidence. One case involved a woman who took a screenshot of the profile her husband maintained on a dating site while they were married— on which he had described himself as single and childless. She used this as evidence during a primary custody hearing. In another case, a woman claimed her husband was lying to the court when he said that she was rarely around for their children's activities. She was speechless when subpoenaed evidence proved she was playing interactive online games instead of attending her children's school functions.[48]

post-cyber-disclosure panic The dread, regret, or anxiety you feel after sending an online message.

section review

11.2 The disinhibition effect

Communicating using technology may cause us to divulge more personal information sooner and react more intensely and less guardedly than we otherwise would in person. This phenomenon is referred to as the disinhibition effect. There is a bright side to the disinhibition effect: When communicating online, you might feel freer to ask for and seek help, and online communication may help you speed up the process of initiating and developing relationships. There is also a dark side to the disinhibition effect. It is believed to play a role in online behaviors such as sexting, flaming, cyber harassment, ghosting, and catfishing. You may experience post-cyber-disclosure panic—anxiety or dread—after posting or sending something electronically that might come back to haunt you later.

Key Terms

disinhibition effect, *p. 296*

catharsis, *p. 296*

hyperpersonal communication, *p. 296*

sexting, *p. 298*

flaming, *p. 298*

cyberbullying, *p. 299*

cyberstalking, *p. 299*

ghosting, *p. 300*

catfishing, *p. 300*

post-cyber-disclosure panic, *p. 301*

Comprehend It?

1. Define each of the key terms in Section 11.2. To further your understanding of these terms, create examples to support your definitions.

2. In your own words, describe the bright side and dark side to the disinhibition effect.

3. Brainstorm additional examples not mentioned in the chapter that illustrate how the disinhibition effect has both a bright side and a dark side.

Apply It!

Review the electronic messages you've sent or posted within the last 72 hours. Did the disinhibition effect help you express something important or make a real connection, or did it somehow play a negative role in your communication? Write down your thoughts regarding this question and share them with a conversation partner or discussion group.

11.3 Using communication technology effectively

One of our students, Patricia, shared that she received several intimidating emails from her new boss, Dawn, before she met her in person. Patricia states, "Dawn's emails came across as very stern. I had the impression she was not a nice individual. I was actually a little terrified to talk to her at first. When I met her in the office, I thought, *this can't be the same person.* Dawn walks around with a bright smile on her face, stopping to say hello to all her employees. In one-on-one meetings, she tells me everything I need to know in a way that makes me feel competent and trusted."

Dawn, despite her excellent F2F communication skills, creates a negative impression and causes potential interpersonal problems with her employees because of the tone of her email messages. Do you know people who come off very differently online than they do in person? Can you think of other TMC behaviors that have negatively affected your relationships?

In Section 11.3, we'll explore several strategies to help you improve your TMC with the goal of improving your relationships.

Office etiquette and email use

If you are in a managerial position, keep in mind that most employees see online communication as an efficient way to send brief updates, reminders, agendas, and minutes from meetings; however, they also value the meaningful dialogue associated with F2F interaction with managers. Meetings are a better venue for communication when the goal is to work out problems, build rapport, celebrate accomplishments, and make decisions that affect the entire group.[49]

Experts offer the following guidelines for how to interact in the workplace. These recommendations may also improve your TMC outside of work with friends, family members, and romantic partners:[50]

- When an issue involves a performance critique or rule violation, conduct communication F2F, privately, and only with those who need to be present.

- When you really need to know if an employee, colleague, or supervisor understands your message, it's usually best to communicate F2F. This makes it easier to demonstrate something, clarify information, and read important nonverbal cues.

- Be sure to get permission before sending out an email about someone's hospitalization, illness, miscarriage, accident, or death in the family. Your colleague may want these events kept private or may have plans to share this information in a different way or at a later time. This guideline also applies to happier occasions, such as birthdays, pregnancies, weddings, engagements, and retirements.

- Format your emails with the appropriate etiquette and level of formality. If you are unsure of how to address a person, who to copy or blind copy on an email, or how to best format your emails, search online using the keywords "Business email etiquette basics." Judith Kallos offers tips and strategies on her website.

Cell phone etiquette

When we ask our students to name one thing they would change about how their relational partners use their cell phones, the most popular answer seems to be: Make my time with you important. Don't phone snub me!

You can avoid phone snubbing your conversational partners in a number of ways. For instance, you can silence your ringtone and vibration alerts, which may decrease how often you check your phone. If you are expecting an important call, tell the person you're with ahead of time and ask if it is okay to take the call (a very polite thing to do)! If you receive the call, excuse yourself, walk away, and return promptly.

You can also establish communication rules regarding times and occasions when technology is off-limits. One of our students, Jackson, a basketball player, shared that during team dinners, his teammates put their cell phones in the center of the table. Anyone who reaches for his cell phone has to buy everyone a round of appetizers.

Apps such as ShutApp and StayFocusd can bolster your self-discipline. They'll temporarily disable your phone or block certain apps for a specified period of time. Newer smartphones have built-in tools to help you monitor your cell phone use and restrict the use of apps at certain times. To learn about an array of options, visit the blog *TechWiser* by searching online using the keywords: "12 best apps to keep you off your phone."

Navigating social media

Knowing when and how to use social media can be difficult. When posting on social platforms, it helps to remember the *golden rule*: Treat others the way you wish to be treated. For example, it's considerate to ask people if it's okay to take their picture, tag them in your posts, or upload photos of them. Be sure to give those who are in any photos you post an opportunity to see how their image is captured. How would you feel if someone posted an embarrassing or unflattering photo of you?

Another clear way to avoid a social media blunder is to avoid calling people out online. As mentioned in Section 11.1, naming names and airing dirty laundry can often lead to flaming. Take a moment and think: *Would I like my personal business spread all over the web? If I post inflammatory content without much context, will it help or hurt the situation?* Remember, you cannot take back online comments. The Internet is forever.

It also helps to consider whether using social media is the best way to initiate a conversation, and if you choose this option, what is the best approach. In addition, it may help if you encourage others to communicate with you F2F or V2V if those approaches work better for you, as Monica describes in her narrative.

"Recently a guy messaged me on social media to tell me he's seen me around campus. He was wondering if he could get my number so he could ask me out. I couldn't help but think: *Where and when did he see me, how did he get my name, and why hadn't he approached me to say hello or even introduce himself?* I had never seen him before, so it kind of creeped me out. Instead of going back and forth with online messages, I simply told him to introduce himself to me the next time he saw me, and we could go from there." –Monica

In many instances, the best way to introduce yourself to someone is in person. Using social media to follow up on good old-fashioned F2F interaction is generally well received by most people. The obvious exception occurs when individuals establish profiles on dating apps—platforms that are specifically designed to help people initiate contacts and relationships online.

A social etiquette blogger named Grace Bonney offers an extensive guide of things to do and not to do across all types of popular social media platforms. Take a moment to read her article by searching online using the keywords: "Modern Etiquette: Social Media Do's & Don'ts."

Responding to provocative electronic messages

If an electronic message you receive rubs you the wrong way, consider the following questions: Am I misinterpreting some of the words? Am I keeping in mind that I can't make out this person's facial expressions, body language, or voice?

If a message you receive causes you to feel angry or upset, don't respond right away. Wait a day or two: A cooling-off period will help you gain your composure and think rationally. Before you respond, try to answer these questions: How can I respond in a manner that is polite, mature, and professional? How would I want others to judge my communication if they had the opportunity to do so?

Here are some additional suggestions:

- Ask yourself if it would be best to invite the person who sent the offending message to call V2V or talk F2F (both rich-channel environments).

- Respond to a message that is abrasive or lacks clarity with a friendly greeting and a question. You might write, for example: "Hi Erica. Thank you for the email. I'm not sure how to interpret your message. Would you please clarify what you mean? Can I call you?"

- Use a nonthreatening *I-statement* focusing on the message you received, including a follow-up question for clarification.

> **You: I received** your email stating that you don't think we're a good fit for you. (Observation) Is there anything you can share with me to help us improve our hiring and recruitment processes? (Question for clarification)

Digital detoxes

One way you can use communication technology more effectively is to use it less. One of our students, Maranda, laments:

> *With so many conversations to be had, responses to return, portals to check, it's no wonder why we feel so stretched thin all of the time. We post birthday messages every day to people we hardly know and respond to social media posts just to stay relevant. Relationships have shifted from quality to quantity.*

Do you agree with Maranda? Why or why not? If you agree, you're not alone, as evidenced by several prominent movements to unplug from technology. For example, acoustic rock and blues musician John Mayer urged his Twitter followers to join him in a weeklong "digital detox." The Vatican got on the "digital fasting" kick, with Catholic bishops urging the faithful to abstain from virtual communication during the religious season of Lent.[51]

Several resorts and vacation outlets are offering "back-to-basics" vacations free of digital distractions. For example, at Earthshine Lodge in Lake Toxaway, North Carolina, guests are encouraged to relinquish their electronic devices and spend time hiking, stargazing, zip-lining, and talking with loved ones in rocking chairs overlooking the mountains. One guest, Jeanna Freeman, stated, "It was exhilarating being away from my cell phone and free of it. I hadn't felt that good and connected with those I really care about in a long time."[52]

Psychologist Sherry Turkle is a fan of these back-to-basics initiatives. She says digital detoxes are helping us reconnect with others and ourselves. In a thought-provoking TED Talk, Turkle warns that, due to our reliance on technology, being disconnected from it, even for short periods of time, can prove difficult. If the peace and quiet of solitude becomes foreign to us, we replace it with distractions and busyness.[53] To see her complete talk, search YouTube using the keywords: "Connected, but Alone?" (19:49)

Making ourselves technologically unavailable to others frees us to daydream, soak up nature, meditate, make plans for the future, reminisce, and think about

Adults at Camp Grounded in Mendocino, California, surrender their electronic devices in exchange for solar carving, stilt walking, dodgeball, superfood truffle making, and acro-yoga. As you watch this video, imagine you're there as a camper. How might you benefit from an experience like this? On YouTube, search using the keywords: "Camp Grounded - Mendocino, California Session 2016." (6:43)

our relationships and what really matters to us. Intentionally disconnecting can deliver a host of benefits, including improvements in memory consolidation and goal-driven thoughts, and increased creative expression, moral reasoning, and compassion.[54]

chronic sleep deprivation (CSD) A cumulative reduction in the length and quality of sleep.

Technology and bedtime use

People who use electronic devices right before going to bed are less likely to report getting a good night's sleep or waking up refreshed.[55] Changes in sleep patterns occur as you stay awake with technology (thanks to the dopamine loop) and push back your normal sleep time later and later over time—as much as 1 to 3 hours per night. In addition, the bright light (referred to as blue light) from digital screens may disrupt your brain's production of melatonin, a hormone that helps you fall asleep sooner and attain the deep, restful sleep you need.[56]

Chronic sleep deprivation (CSD) is the cumulative reduction in the length and quality of sleep. CSD affects memory, concentration, and alertness, and it increases your risk of depression, anxiety, hypertension, heart disease, diabetes, memory disorders, impaired driving, and weight gain.[57]

How does your quality of sleep affect your ability to listen and speak during the day? Do you become less patient, agreeable, and pleasant to be around? Research suggests that sleep deprivation may affect our communication skills in various ways. In one study, participants who were deprived of sleep for just one night performed less skillfully on a collaborative work task that required them to listen and follow instructions than did participants who got a full night's sleep.[58]

Another study noted differences in the communication behaviors of doctors after they worked a night shift. For example, they were less likely to ask questions for clarification during interpersonal interactions.[59]

Sleep experts recommend that you establish a sleep time for the weeknights and weekends—and try to stick to it. Turn off all of your electronic devices (TVs, cell phones, tablets, e-readers, laptops, and computers) at least an hour before your regular sleep time. Replace the stimulating effects of technology with a routine that gets you ready for the next day. You might lay out your clothes, pack your lunch, or make a to-do list. To help you clear your mind and relax, dim the lights, light a candle, play soothing (meditative or instrumental) music, take a hot bath or shower, and/or read a book that's not too captivating or engrossing.[60]

"I've diligently spent the last eight hours saving an entire colony of elves from a pack of vicious dragons and your only concern is that it is 2 am?"

section review

11.3 Using communication technology effectively

This section provides a number of recommendations to help you improve your technology-mediated communication, including tips on the proper use of email, cell phones, and social media. In addition, giving yourself more digital detoxes or breaks and regulating your use of technology at night may help you improve your well-being and interpersonal communication.

Key Term

chronic sleep deprivation (CSD), *p. 307*

Comprehend It?

1. Define chronic sleep deprivation. To further your understanding of this term, create an example to support your definition.

2. Which suggestions for improving your use of communication technology were the most helpful to you and why? How do you plan to make improvements in these areas?

Apply It!

Scroll through your social media posts and consider your activity over the last 30 days. Ask yourself the following questions:

- Are any of my posts or activities not aligned with my relationship goals and commitments?
- Which of my posts might offend someone? Who? Would any of these posts hurt my reputation, friendships, or career—now or later?
- What do I focus on with my online comments and posts? Do I focus on anything too much? For example, do I criticize certain things or poke fun at a particular person too often?
- How often do I post about my own successes or about such things as money, alcohol, materialistic goals, or looks? What do I need to take a second look at before posting?
- If a potential employer were to look at my social media activity, is there anything I've posted that could hurt my chances of being hired?

(11) chapter exercises

Assessing Your IPC: Smartphone Compulsion Test

Purpose: To assess my level of smartphone reliance.

Directions: Complete the Smartphone Compulsion Test, a free, 15-item online assessment developed by psychiatrist David Greenfield, director of the Center for Internet and Technology Addiction. To find this assessment, search using the keywords: "Smartphone Compulsion Test." Based on your answers, does your attachment to your device fall in the normal, mild, moderate, or severe range? Based on the results, are there changes you'd like to make regarding your smartphone use? If so, what would you like to do and why?

Building Your IPC Skills: Time Assessment

Purpose: To assess the time I devote to the Internet (for nonacademic and non-work purposes), online gaming, and social media compared to other activities.

Directions: For the next 24 hours, set an alarm on your cell phone to go off every 4 hours during the day. Each time the alarm rings, record the activities you engaged in during this 4-hour period and the amount of time spent doing them. Activities may include browsing social media, exercising, socializing with others in person, studying, watching TV, working, cleaning, napping, eating, and volunteering. Once the 24-hour period is up, add up the time you spent doing each activity. What do your calculations suggest about your use of time?

Do this again for another 24 hours, but this time purposely decrease the time you spend using technology and watching TV by at least 50%. Was this difficult to achieve? Did you notice any changes in your productivity, energy level, moods, or the quality of time you spent with significant relational partners? If so, what were these changes? If you were to continue this activity for the next few days, how might it help you better manage your time and priorities?

12

Ethics and Civility

After Michigan State University's softball team suffered a disappointing 16–1 loss to Notre Dame, a reporter asked MSU star outfielder Alyssa McBride how it felt to see her team lose despite her exceptional talent. Alyssa confirmed that she could speak off-the-record, and then she said, "Honestly, I wish I would've gone to a different school." Soon after the interview, Alyssa's coaches scolded her in their office for making disparaging remarks about MSU's softball program, and asked her if she still wanted to play out the rest of the season.

In the days following Alyssa's "off-the-record" comment, the team's assistant coach pitched fast-balls straight at her during two separate batting practices. One pitch bruised her left arm as she tried to shield her face, and another hit her wrist.

Afterward, a teammate told Alyssa about a conversation she'd overheard between the head coach and the assistant coach just before the first batting-practice incident. Presumably in reference to Alyssa, the assistant coach had asked, "So I can hit her?" The head coach replied, "Yes, you can hit her because I can't." The teammate hadn't said anything to Alyssa right away because she couldn't imagine that the coaches would actually do anything to hurt her.

The university opened an investigation into Alyssa's claims. Meanwhile, the coaches denied any wrongdoing. Several players were asked to corroborate Alyssa's story, but they declined to comment. Ultimately, investigators and local prosecutors lacked sufficient evidence to discipline or

Trust is established when we communicate ethically. When trust is lacking, we may find ourselves in situations like the one featured in the photo. The couple is on date, but they appear not to trust each other—see how they're sneaking glances at each other's devices?

press charges against the coaches.[1] However, private text messages retrieved by police investigators from the cell phones belonging to Alyssa and the coaches suggest a mutual animosity did exist between them.[2]

This story raises several ethical questions. Should Alyssa have bad-mouthed her team to the reporter? Did the reporter leak Alyssa's comments to the coaches? Did Alyssa's coaches conspire to injure her with fast pitches and lie to investigators about

it? Did any of Alyssa's teammates withhold information from the investigators? Were the coaches falsely accused? Were any of the players intimidated by the coaches to stay silent?

It's possible that a number of unethical behaviors are at play here. What would you do if you were in a situation like this—either as a reporter, coach, school administrator, or player? Your answers to these questions may vary depending on the values that guide how you communicate—that is, your sense of interpersonal ethics. In this chapter, we'll (1) explain the significance of interpersonal ethics, (2) explore the role that deception plays in our relationships, and (3) identify ways to improve ethical decision-making.

12.1 Significance of ethical IPC

One of our students, Sharon, shared, "My close friend of forty years, Grant, owns two homes. One is five minutes away from where I work, and the other is two blocks from where I live in Douglas, Michigan. A month ago, I was in a car accident and totaled my Jeep. I was pretty shaken up about it, and I needed someone to drive me home from work while I waited for my car to be repaired. One Friday my regular ride had to cancel, so I asked Grant if he could help me out. He said, 'Sure, I can give you a ride. I'm nearby right now and plan on heading to Douglas this weekend anyway.'"

When Sharon called Grant later in the day to confirm the time that he'd be able to pick her up, Grant said that a contractor was working at his home in Douglas and needed to show him an unexpected repair requiring his immediate approval. Grant told her to be ready in 15 minutes. Sharon went on to say,

There was no way I could wrap up work that quickly, so I asked if he could give me thirty minutes. He told me, rather callously, that he couldn't wait and I would need to find a ride from someone else. I was so hurt by Grant's unwillingness to wait. I have helped him out on many occasions when it was very inconvenient for me. I seriously don't know if I can ever get past this.

Sharon felt that Grant's dismissiveness and unwillingness to help her violated several ethical principles—repaying obligations, flexibility, double standards—and their relationship suffered for it. Like Sharon, have you ever seriously questioned a relationship because a relational partner's behavior fell short of your ethical expectations? If so, that person did not live up to your interpersonal communication ethics.

Interpersonal communication ethics are the set of beliefs, values, and principles that guide communication behaviors within a relationship. Your IPC ethics help you determine whether a communication choice is right or wrong, moral or immoral.

You judge the communication of others based on your own interpersonal ethics. Similarly, others judge your communication according to their interpersonal ethics. Your judgments—and their judgments—affect your relationships in positive and negative ways.

interpersonal communication ethics
The beliefs, values, and principles that guide communication behaviors within a relationship.

In Section 12.1, we'll describe the characteristics of ethical communication and explain why they are important in maintaining healthy relationships.

Ethical standards of IPC

What makes a communication behavior ethical or unethical? There are multiple ways of measuring and defining ethical behavior. The National Communication Association, a professional organization made up of communication scholars, teachers, and professionals, has established a Credo for Ethical Communication. The credo focuses on five ideals that characterize ethical communication: respect, responsibility, integrity, fairness, and truthfulness.[3] To help you remember these ideals, use the acronym RRIFT. You may be more familiar with other standards for ethical behavior, including the golden and platinum rules: Treat others the way *you* wish to be treated, and treat others the way *they* wish to be treated, respectively.

Five ethical ideals

The first ideal of RRIFT is respect. You communicate with **respect** when you value someone's time, safety, health, possessions, feelings, and needs. Imagine that your roommate has a big test in the morning and is studying in your room. You can respect her time and needs by keeping the room quiet or by going someplace else if you'd like to talk or play loud music.

You communicate with **responsibility** when you own your actions, respond reliably, and act proactively to solve interpersonal problems. Suppose you make a mistake at work. Instead of hiding your mistake or blaming it on someone else, the ethical way to communicate about it is to take responsibility for it: You would tell your manager about your mistake and apologize.

You communicate with **integrity** when your behaviors mirror your convictions. If you disapprove of gossiping, for example, you communicate with integrity if you refrain from engaging in it. Imagine that your cousin starts to share some uncomplimentary gossip about your Aunt Nancy. If you stop your cousin and say, "Hey, let's not spread this kind of information around. I know Aunt Nancy would feel hurt if she knew we were talking about her like this," you're communicating with integrity.

You communicate with **fairness** when you play by the same rules as everyone else and ensure that others have equal access to resources, information, and opportunities. For example, let's say a professor has a surprise quiz planned for his class on Wednesday. During his office hours the day before, he has a conversation with one of his students and hints that there may be a pop quiz the next day. He's not communicating this information in the spirit of fairness if he hasn't shared this with every student. It would be more fair to announce the quiz to all of his students at the same time.

respect When you value someone's time, safety, health, possessions, feelings, and needs.

responsibility When you own your actions, respond reliably, and act proactively to solve interpersonal problems.

integrity When your behaviors mirror your convictions.

fairness When you play by the same rules and ensure that everyone has equal access to resources, information, and opportunities.

"We need to draw the line on unethical behavior. But let's draw it with an Etch-a-Sketch and don't be afraid to shake it a little."

You communicate with **truthfulness** when your communication is accurate and sincere. Communicating truthfully includes not withholding the truth. For example, if you buy something expensive for yourself when you know it's not in your family's budget, hiding the purchase from your spouse is not truthful communication. Truthfulness is admitting your purchase—and doing so before you're asked.

Applying the principles of respect, responsibility, integrity, fairness, and truthfulness to your communication choices can help you ensure that you are communicating ethically. To help you determine whether your interpersonal communication behaviors conflict with the RRIFT standards, complete the *Assessing Your IPC* exercise at the end of this chapter. Which behaviors occur most often and least often in your communication?

The golden and platinum rules

Another approach to ethical communication incorporates the golden rule. The **golden rule** encourages you to treat others the way you wish to be treated. It reminds you to think empathetically when you communicate with others.

However, your relational partners may not appreciate or agree with your ethical reasoning based solely on how *you* wish to be treated. Therefore, another perspective to consider is the **platinum rule**: Treat others the way *they* wish to be treated. This approach recognizes that other people's priorities, values, needs, and feelings may differ from yours.

For example, let's say you want to financially help your nephew, Scott, who is struggling to make ends meet while going to college full-time. If you were Scott, you'd welcome the offer of financial support (golden rule). But Scott feels uncomfortable taking the money—he values his independence. If you respect his wishes when he turns you down, you are applying the platinum rule.

Moral absolutism and relativism

While the RRIFT standards and the golden and platinum rules offer fairly straightforward guidelines for communicating ethically, there is some debate about what makes particular communication choices ethical or not. **Moral absolutism**, or the *objective* view of ethics, suggests that certain behaviors are always right and others are always wrong, no matter the circumstances. In other words, according to moral absolutism, an action is unethical if it is not okay for anyone to do it, anywhere, at any time.

Moral relativism, or the *subjective* view of ethics, considers the particular circumstances surrounding an action to determine whether it is ethical. According to this perspective, not all ethical questions have black or white answers, nor are all ethical choices intrinsically right or wrong.

Let's use an example to illustrate the difference between the two perspectives. Say you're at a party with a friend who is in a committed romantic relationship, and he starts talking to someone flirtatiously. He notices the look you're giving

truthfulness When your communication that is accurate, sincere, and doesn't omit information.

golden rule A moral decision-making approach in which you strive to treat others the way you wish to be treated.

platinum rule A moral decision-making approach in which you strive to treat others the way they wish to be treated.

moral absolutism The belief that certain actions are right or wrong no matter the circumstances.

moral relativism The belief that a given action is more or less ethical depending on the circumstances.

him and says, "What? I'm just being extra nice to someone who's extra attractive. Nothing wrong with that."

If you take a moral absolutist view of the situation you would say that it's always unethical to flirt with other people when you're in a committed romantic relationship. Therefore, there's no wiggle room here: Your friend behaved unethically. Alternatively, you may look at your friend's communication behavior from a moral relativist perspective. Perhaps you would think: *He was just having a bit of fun—he didn't do anything wrong. He didn't try to go beyond flirting, and no one's feelings were hurt.*

Are your ethical views on flirtation more absolute or relative? If you're in a romantic relationship, do you know if your partner feels the same way? According to one study, although couples believed they shared similar expectations about ethical behaviors such as online flirtation and emotional fidelity, partners' responses to hypothetical scenarios revealed that their beliefs were less aligned than they thought.[4]

To make sure you and your romantic partner are on the same page, it may help to have a candid conversation that centers around questions such as: What specific behaviors count as flirting? Are we allowed to engage in any flirtatious behaviors with others when we're with each other? What about when we're not together? What is unacceptable at all times?

Ethical choices are challenging at times

Choosing to communicate ethically is not always easy. For example, imagine that you and a friend are nurses who work on the same floor, and you notice that she fumbles a routine procedure. When you confront her about it, she admits to misusing Vicodin again. She asks you to overlook her mistake and promises that she'll get some private help.

Do you keep your friend's confession a secret, even though she's responsible for the health and safety of patients on your floor? If you report it, will this jeopardize her job? How might this affect your friendship? You may feel torn between your loyalty to her and your allegiance to the professional ethical standards you're sworn to uphold. What is the most ethical way to handle this situation? What would you say and do?

Other ethical choices have lower stakes but are no less challenging. Journalist Amy Sohn writes about her colleague Todd, who faces one such ethical dilemma. He is vehemently opposed to having children—so much so that he had a vasectomy at the age of 26. Todd laments, "If I bring it up on the first date, it can be off-putting. If I bring it up a few months into the relationship, there are hurt feelings. Even waiting a week or so can result in the person feeling angry and betrayed."

Todd's goal is to find (and keep) a dating partner, but he's not sure when and how to disclose the information about his vasectomy without sabotaging his

In this clip from the movie *Something's Gotta Give*, Erica (Diane Keaton) steps into a restaurant and sees her love interest, Harry (Jack Nicholson), having dinner with another woman. Erica feels betrayed and storms out. What information would you need to have, beyond what the scene provides, to determine if Harry's behavior is ethical or unethical? Incorporate the concepts of moral absolutism and relativism in your analysis. On YouTube, search using the keywords: "Something's Gotta Give" posted by GuilleG3. (3:40)

dating prospects. The ethic of **duty to disclose** calls on us to be transparent with our intentions and share information in a timely manner when it may involve or affect another person.[5] Amy writes that after careful consideration, Todd decided the most ethical thing to do going forward was to tell women about his decision before their first date.[6]

Another challenging aspect of ethical communication is the obligation to give our relational partners **significant choice**. When we ask our relational partners to make decisions, our communication is ethical to the extent that we give them the ability to make free and fully informed choices. A choice is free if it is made voluntarily with no manipulation or coercion involved, and it's fully informed if the person making the choice has all of the necessary and available information in a timely manner, with all of the time needed to make a sound decision.[7] Todd's decision to communicate about his vasectomy before the first date meets the ethical standards of duty to disclose and significant choice.

Unethical communication damages relationships

A student of ours, Erin, describes a time when a friend's communication behavior affected their relationship negatively. As you read Erin's narrative, imagine yourself in her situation. If one of your close friends were to do to you what Erin's friend did to her, how might it affect your relationship?

Erin's relationship with Veronica ended because of a significant relational transgression. A **relational transgression** is an unethical action taken by someone you know that hurts you or makes you feel betrayed. Common relational transgressions include not honoring promises, embarrassing or disrespecting a relational partner in front of others, and manipulating a relational partner into doing what you want without any concern for how it will affect this person.

duty to disclose The ethical obligation to share information in a timely manner when it may involve or affect another person in some way.

significant choice The ethical obligation to give a relational partner the ability to make free and fully informed decisions.

relational transgression An unethical action taken by a relational partner that hurts you or makes you feel betrayed.

> "I was really interested in a guy named Mitchell. My friend Veronica said to me, 'Watch out with that one, he's a player, trust me.' Because of her warning, I kept him at a distance when he showed a lot of interest in me. Afterward, Mitchell started liking Veronica, and she immediately started dating him. I learned later that she manipulated me into thinking he was not someone I should date because she wanted to date him. I had no interest in being her friend after that." –Erin

The lingering negative feelings you have as a result of a relational transgression are referred to as **ongoing negative affect**. In her narrative, Erin writes that the ongoing negative affect she feels as a result of Veronica's unethical behavior is so great that she no longer wants to be Veronica's friend. Veronica not only loses a friend because of her actions but may also find her reputation and credibility tarnished if Erin tells their other friends what happened. Veronica could lose the respect and trust of her peers, a difficult—sometimes impossible—thing to earn back.

When a relational transgression causes ongoing negative affect, you have several options: You might choose to work through your ongoing negative affect, you may decide that you can't or don't want to, or you might continue the relationship but distance yourself emotionally from the person who hurt you.

Many factors will influence which path you choose. For example, the type of relationship you have with the person who wronged you may make a difference. Is this person your best friend or a casual acquaintance? Was the transgression deliberate or accidental? Did it occur once or multiple times? You may also find it harder to hold a grudge if you've done something very similar and were forgiven for it. Other factors include:

- How satisfied you are with the relationship
- How emotionally committed you are to the relationship
- How fearful you are about losing the relationship
- How empathetic you choose to be
- How much you rely on the person
- How much pressure you feel to "get over it"[8]

Unethical actions hurt both the people that are affected by them and the people who commit them. If you behave unethically toward someone, you may feel guilty about it. Guilt is not a pleasant emotion to live with. When you're living with guilt, your own thoughts, feelings, and behaviors are repugnant to you. This guilty conscience can cause you to fall victim to a perceptual mind trap known as projection.[9]

Projection is the mental process of assuming that a relational partner is guilty of doing something—or is capable of doing something—that you've done yourself. Projection may cause you to unfairly accuse or distrust your relational partners.

ongoing negative affect
The lingering negative feelings you have toward someone as a result of a relational transgression.

projection The mental process of assuming that another person is thinking, feeling, or behaving as you would in a given situation.

In this scene from the television show *Gilmore Girls*, Rory (Alexis Bledel) stays out all night after a school dance. She comes home to find her mother, Lorelai (Lauren Graham), and grandmother, Emily (Kelly Bishop), arguing about her. Rory tries to thank Lorelai for speaking up for her, but is surprised by her mother's mixed message. How does this scene depict the concept of projection? On YouTube, search using the keywords: "Rory and Dean (23) Gilmore Girls." (4:57)

The saying "it takes one to know one" may ring true in some instances, but sometimes our perceptions of others are simply skewed by the guilt we feel for having done something that goes against our conscience. For example, Madeline often borrows clothing from her sister, Ann, without her permission—something she has been asked repeatedly not to do. She feels guilty about it, but this doesn't stop her. When one of Madeline's shirts goes missing, she immediately assumes Ann is the one who took it. Madeline's guilty conscience causes her to project her own behavior onto Ann.

Ethical communication strengthens relationships

When relational partners witness your ethical behavior, it builds interpersonal trust. **Interpersonal trust** is a person's firm belief in the ability, reliability, and honesty of another person. Research suggests it is an essential interpersonal need. Relational partners can avoid feelings of uncertainty, insecurity, worry, cynicism, disappointment, resentment, anger, and sadness if they establish and maintain trust in each other.[10]

Though Skyler, one of our students, was disheartened when she found out that a coworker, Lizzy, had complained behind Skyler's back to other coworkers about a mistake she made, she was happy to hear that her coworkers Leah and Mackenzie stuck up for her by countering the criticism with a kinder, fairer response to her mistake. Skyler said, "I was angry at Lizzy, who was bad-mouthing me, but I felt good—appreciative of and closer to Leah and Mackenzie—knowing they had my back like that."

interpersonal trust A firm belief in the ability, reliability, and honesty of another person.

Another of our students, Lauren, said:

When I ask my boyfriend, Tye, what he thinks, I know he tells me the truth. I count on that because I value his thoughts. Experience has shown me that when it might be tempting for him to sugarcoat his response, deny something, or tell me what he thinks I want to hear, he says it like it is. I'd rather hear the truth even when it's not packaged beautifully. He has inspired me to do the same. I know that I love him more because of it.

Knowing that others trust and admire you for your character is not just good for your relationships; it can also boost your self-esteem and well-being. Research suggests that making a conscious effort to communicate ethically increases your ability to manage impulses and exercise self-control.[11] Communicating ethically also helps you avoid unnecessary stress and mental anguish, deteriorating relationships, and social isolation.[12]

Institutional and legal consequences of unethical IPC

Organizations and institutions—such as schools, banks, and workplaces—form their own standards of ethical IPC behavior. Following these standards helps us avoid unwanted academic, financial, and employment consequences, such as demotions, school expulsion, fines, license suspensions, and loss of employment (including loss of business contracts and endorsements).

In addition, many IPC ethics are codified in law. Certain IPC behaviors may result in court-issued fines, civil lawsuits leading to financial payouts and other forms of financial restitution, probationary travel restrictions, restraining orders, and prison time. Examples of IPC behaviors that may be subject to these consequences include bribery, defamation of character, domestic abuse, extortion, blackmail, fraud, and invasion of privacy (see **TABLE 12.1**).

One of the most prevalent unethical IPC behaviors within organizations is harassment. **Harassment** is any behavior that makes a person feel uncomfortable, threatened, or unsafe. Such behaviors include intimidation, unwanted sexual attention or pressure, harsh criticism, unwelcome humor, false accusations, name calling, teasing, and threatening a person's job security or safety. This last behavior includes purposely interfering with a person's ability to perform a job effectively.[13]

Harassment can occur anywhere—including in places where you might not expect it. When NFL player Jonathan Martin quit the Miami Dolphins after just one year in the league, he cited harassment from his teammates as the cause. One day, as he sat at a table to eat lunch with several players, all of them got up and left. This was the last insult Martin could tolerate, and the next day, he left the team. Martin's high-profile accusations sparked a national debate and an exhaustive investigation by the NFL.

The NFL discovered that Martin had encountered relentless bullying and ridicule from three players, particularly offensive guard Richie Incognito. Incognito, who was suspended by the NFL, blamed locker-room culture for his behavior;

harassment Any behavior that makes a person feel uncomfortable, threatened, or unsafe.

table 12.1	Unethical IPC Behaviors	
Unethical Behavior	**Definition**	**Example**
Bribery	Enticing someone to do something unethical by offering money, property, or special favors	A classmate says he'll give you money to do his share of a group project, even though he's earning a grade for his work.
Defamation of character	Damaging someone's reputation by saying (*slander*) or writing (*libel*) false or misleading things about that person	An angry ex spreads lies about her former boyfriend on social media in an attempt to get even.
Domestic abuse	Hurting or threatening to hurt a family member, roommate, or romantic partner physically, emotionally, or sexually	Your romantic partner uses verbal or nonverbal behaviors to intimidate you, such as raising a fist or a hand as if to strike you or block your escape route.
Extortion	Threatening to do something bad to a person in order to acquire money, property, or desirable opportunities	A coworker tells you he'll inform your supervisor that you called in sick—when you actually went on a fun, two-day excursion—if you don't give him your prized weekend shifts.
Blackmail	Threatening to do something bad to someone to ensure that the person keeps something a secret, or threatening to reveal compromising or injurious information in order to acquire something in return	Your boss threatens to fire you if you speak to the press about the health code violations at the restaurant where you work.
Fraud	Pretending to be someone else or manipulating someone through trickery or misrepresentation for personal gain	Someone you've met online pretends to be romantically interested in you or creates a false identity in order to extract money or favors from you.
Invasion of privacy	Intruding into someone's personal life without permission in a purposeful and unwelcome manner	Your dormmate turns on your webcam without you knowing and records a private interaction you're having with someone. He then shows the recording to others.

others faulted Martin for not speaking up for himself or reporting the behavior to the coaching staff or team owners sooner.

Some sports commentators questioned how a 6-foot-5, 312-pound professional football player could even feel threatened by a teammate, let alone bothered by put-downs and hazing. Others jumped to Martin's defense, saying the size of a person's body doesn't offer any defense against the emotional distress of unremitting mean-spiritedness.[14]

If an individual is told to stop a behavior that fits the definition of harassment but persists, the person being harassed can seek institutional and legal recourse. And if a company or organization, like the Miami Dolphins, fails to take action to stop harassment in the workplace, the Equal Employment Opportunity Commission can fine it for perpetuating a **hostile work environment**. Such an environment exists when employees engage in harassment without facing corrective or disciplinary action.

> **hostile work environment**
> A workplace in which employees engage in harassment without facing corrective or disciplinary action.

section review

12.1 Significance of ethical IPC

Interpersonal ethics are the beliefs, values, and principles that guide communication behaviors within a relationship. The ethical ideals of respect, responsibility, integrity, fairness, and truthfulness (RRIFT) are standards for assessing IPC behavior. Moral absolutism is the view that certain communication behaviors are never justified and always wrong. Moral relativism, on the other hand, leaves room to consider the circumstances when determining whether a behavior is ethical. Ethical communication choices can be challenging and may damage or strengthen your relationships. There are institutional and legal consequences associated with certain unethical IPC behaviors.

Key Terms

interpersonal communication ethics, p. 312	golden rule, p. 314	relational transgression, p. 316
respect, p. 313	platinum rule, p. 314	ongoing negative affect, p. 317
responsibility, p. 313	moral absolutism, p. 314	projection, p. 317
integrity, p. 313	moral relativism, p. 314	interpersonal trust, p. 318
fairness, p. 313	duty to disclose, p. 316	harassment, p. 319
truthfulness, p. 314	significant choice, p. 316	hostile work environment, p. 321

Comprehend It?

1. Define each of the key terms in Section 12.1. To further your understanding of these terms, create examples to support your definitions.

2. Compare and contrast the following:
   - IPC ethical ideals: respect, responsibility, integrity, fairness, and truthfulness
   - Moral absolutism and moral relativism

3. Why is ethical communication challenging at times?

4. Explain how your ethical communication choices can hurt or enhance your relationships.

Apply It!

Describe how the following communication behaviors are potentially unethical using the ethical standards of RRIFT:

- Your professor habitually arrives late to class.
- You come to a party with a friend and she leaves without telling you.

- Your best friend gets upset every time you go out with your other friends.
- A coworker withholds information that you need to do your job effectively.
- A relative comes across as very religious but engages in behaviors that are not aligned with her beliefs.

12.2 Deception within relationships

David Hempleman-Adams has piloted a hot-air balloon across the geographic North Pole. He's ascended the highest peak on every continent. He even completed a 300-mile solo hike to the geomagnetic north pole pulling a 150-pound sled in minus-50-degree weather. When he left to go to the North Pole, he told his family he was going on a ski trip with some friends. In fact, he doesn't tell them about many of his adventures. David thinks, "What's the point in worrying them?"

Often, David's feats come as a surprise to his wife, Claire. Once, she picked up a copy of Britain's *Daily Telegraph* and came across a story featuring an adventurer who had plunged 20 feet down a frozen waterfall. Despite severely torn ligaments in his left ankle, he managed to limp 60 miles before seeking medical attention. The adventurer was her husband! Now, Claire, an attorney who manages the home full-time, says, "Nothing surprises me anymore."[15] If you were Claire, would you tolerate deception like this from your spouse?

In Section 12.2, we'll explore the role deception plays in relationships and consider how and when it can be used ethically and unethically.

Types of deception

Deception is communication behavior that deliberately misleads another person, including any communication that is not completely honest or forthcoming.[16] **TABLE 12.2** lists various types of deception. As you read about each one, see if you can pinpoint the types of deception evident in the story you just read about David. How does he keep Claire in the dark about his adventures?

In addition, as a form of self-monitoring, choose a number that most accurately reflects how often you participate in these deceptive practices. Use the following scale: 1 = *Never*, 2 = *Rarely*, 3 = *Sometimes*, 4 = *Often*, or 5 = *A lot*. What do your responses suggest? To what extent are you deceptive in your face-to-face, phone, and online communication?

Reasons for deception

Interpersonal deception is quite common. Three decades of research by University of Massachusetts scholar Robert Feldman have led him to conclude that two or three deceptive acts occur in just about every 10-minute conversation. In one of his studies, participants didn't even know they lied until they watched themselves on video.[17] Why is deception such a widespread behavior?

We commit deceptive acts to maximize desirable outcomes and minimize what we find unpleasant. For example, if you fake an interest in your boss's weekend plans because having a positive rapport with him may benefit you at work, you are acting deceptively to maximize a positive outcome. If you call in sick so that you don't have to present at a meeting you're not prepared for, you're acting deceptively to avoid an unpleasant experience.

---

deception Communication behavior that is meant to deliberately mislead another person.

table 12.2	Types of Deception		
Type of Deception	**Definition**	**Example**	**Score (1-5)**
Concealment	Covering up your unethical behaviors	You open a family member's mail and reseal it to make it look unopened.	_____
False Excuses	Making up an untrue reason for your behavior	You say you're late because the traffic was terrible even though you're actually late because you slept in and left your house at the last minute.	_____
False Association	Making it appear as if you have a relationship with someone when you don't	You take a selfie with a local celebrity you just met and post: "Always nice to hang out with this guy!"	_____
Feigned Ignorance	Pretending you don't know something that you actually know	Your dad texts you to remind you to take out the trash, but when he gets home, you pretend you never saw the text.	_____
Insincerity	Saying something that is not authentic	After a play, you compliment a cast member on her performance when you don't really mean it.	_____
Minimizing	Downplaying certain aspects of the truth	You're angry with your roommate for not paying his share of the rent on time. When he finally pays up and apologizes, you shrug and say, "It's no big deal," even though that's not how you feel.	_____
Omission	Intentionally withholding information	Your boss asks how you handled a phone call from a difficult customer. You leave out certain details, such as "I put her on hold an extra two minutes because I didn't like her attitude."	_____
Outright Lying	Saying something that is false	Your friend compliments you on your designer handbag and asks where you bought it. You say, "New online, of course," even though it's secondhand.	_____

If your deception is successful, you may experience **duping delight**: a feeling of gratification the moment you realize you just fooled someone and got away with it.[18] A feeling of duping delight often follows a successful bluff. In a game of cards, you bluff when you bet heavily on a weak hand to get your opponents

duping delight The feeling of gratification you get the moment you realize your deception succeeded.

Watch this scene from the television show *Stranger Things*, featuring Mike (Finn Wolfhard); his love interest, El (Millie Bobby Brown); Mike's mother, Karen (Cara Buono); and El's adoptive father, Jim (David Harbour). What types of deception do you see? If you had to venture a guess, is there a possible indication of duping delight in this clip? On YouTube, search using the keywords: "Stranger Things 3 - Mike Lies To Eleven On The Phone." (2:35)

to fold. You also bluff when you threaten someone but do not have the intention or means of following through with the threat.

Once you've experienced duping delight, it may motivate you to try to deceive people again. What are some of the reasons that you use deception? How frequently does duping delight influence your interpersonal interactions? Do you find that you deceive others even when it makes you feel guilty or causes relational problems? Do you find that you deceive others even when it makes you feel guilty or causes relational problems?

Is deception always unethical?

In some cases, deception isn't necessarily unethical. It may serve as a "social lubricant" to ease conversations and make interactions more pleasant or interesting. For example, you might exaggerate a story or brag about your ability to do something to spark some laughs at a party. You may also refrain from saying how much you like someone until you feel the moment is right.

Research suggests that downplaying your feelings, avoiding harsh comments, and holding back on things you really want to say may help preserve a close relationship. Deception may serve to protect a person's feelings, help relational partners avoid unnecessary conflict, or promote a positive work climate.[19]

Some acts of deception are even considered benevolent. Misleading or dishonest communication meant to help the receiver is called **benevolent deception**. Your parents may not tell you about your father's most recent medical scare because there is nothing you can do about it and they don't want to stress you out or worry you during exam week. They are being considerate of your feelings and want you to do well academically.

benevolent deception
Misleading or dishonest communication behavior meant to help the receiver.

As Javonti states in his narrative, medical assistants who care for Alzheimer's patients may deceive them at times to spare them unnecessary heartache or stress.[20] How is his use of deception with his elderly patient Donald benevolent?

"One of my elderly patients, Donald, has advanced Alzheimer's disease. He often asks me if he is going to see his wife, Vesta, later in the day. Because of his memory loss, he doesn't remember that she passed away three years ago. If I said, 'Sorry, no, she's dead,' it would be like he was hearing it for the first time. He'd become distraught. So I first try to distract him. If that doesn't work, I think it's in his best interests if I say, 'Yes you will,' or 'Not today but tomorrow.' He soon forgets he even asked the question or what my answer was." –Javonti

Another form of deception that may not raise any ethical concerns is deceptive affection. **Deceptive affection (DA)** occurs when we don't express our true feelings.[21] In other words, how you express your affection is not aligned with how you actually feel. DA may occur because it's necessary or expected within a relationship. In some cases, not engaging in DA may create an awkward moment or raise unnecessary concerns. For example, if your romantic partner sends you a text saying "I miss you," you may respond, "I miss you, too," even though you're actually enjoying your alone time. DA doesn't just occur between romantic partners: It may also include consoling a friend with a hug, even though it feels awkward to do so, or greeting your grandma with a kiss just because she expects one.

Along with DA, other forms of deception can enhance a relationship. For instance, you might put on a smiling face for your friend's birthday party even though you're in a terrible mood, or you might keep the news about your promotion to yourself when your friend calls to tell you he was fired.

Would you consider the examples in this section ethical or unethical communication behaviors? What circumstances would influence your decision? Or, is your answer unequivocal? Keep these questions in mind as you read about high- and low-stakes deception.

Low-stakes versus high-stakes deception

Imagine a coworker asks you how you are doing, and you reply, "Great!" If you don't actually feel great, is this completely honest? No, it isn't, but you may not have the time or energy to go into the details of your life with every person who asks how you're doing (and the people who ask may not have the time or energy to listen to those details). This is known as **low-stakes deception**, or dishonest communication, where the consequences, if any, are minor or unsubstantial. This type of deception is generally harmless and often makes life easier.

deceptive affection (DA)
Communication that does not express your true feelings.

low-stakes deception
Misleading or dishonest communication behavior perceived as harmless.

The repercussions of high-stakes deception, however, are potentially severe. **High-stakes deception** is dishonest communication that is likely to be harmful to a relationship. For example, how would you feel if you found out that your romantic partner repeatedly lied about staying late at work when she was really out at a bar with her ex? Maybe she even crafted a story about a project she had to stay late for to keep the lie going. This makes the deception even more grievous—and high-stakes. If you are the victim of high-stakes deception, you might think: *I'm not just upset that you lied to me. I'm more upset that I can't ever believe what you say anymore.*

High-stakes deception often requires a lot of effort to pull off. If you're maintaining a consequential lie, you have to guard against saying or doing something that contradicts an earlier lie, or you have to remember details you've shared in previous conversations in order to keep your lie consistent. To hide your lie, you might also have to go to great lengths to cover up your behavior.[22]

Compared to how you might feel after making a low-stakes lie, you may experience more anxiety, worry, guilt, depression, and self-loathing as a result of your high-stakes deception. You might have to work hard to suppress these emotions to avoid suspicion. It also takes more emotional energy to simulate false feelings.[23]

Detecting deception

Are there reliable signs or signals, that indicate deception? What does communication research have to say? The results of numerous studies are mixed.[24] Under certain conditions, however, a person who is trying to deceive you may:[25]

- Speak with a higher-pitched voice
- Appear nervous or anxious
- Pause when a question is very easy to answer
- Add unnecessary details to an answer
- Give a very short answer when more elaboration would be expected
- Alter their rate of speech
- Stumble over words
- Avoid eye contact or look at you more directly for a longer period of time

Keep in mind, however, that these behaviors are useful indicators of deception only to the extent that they're different from a person's everyday behavior. There are often other reasons behind suspicious behavior, and people may exhibit many of the behaviors you just read about even when they are being completely honest. For example, a person may give you a short answer to a question if the person has uncomfortable feelings or is defensive about the topic. Just being accused of something may cause a completely innocent person to fidget, stutter, or become restless.

Numerous studies have tested how well participants can detect lies. A team of researchers examined over 206 studies that focused on the ability of subjects to detect deception. They found that on average, subjects could discriminate between a lie and a truthful statement with about 54% accuracy.[26] With online interactions, the accuracy of deception detection plummets. When asked to identify specific instances when they felt a conversational partner was being dishonest, participants in one study performed better when conversations took place face-to-face (they correctly identified 67% of all lies) than they did when conversations took place via video conferencing (they correctly identified only 45% of all lies).[27]

Confronting deception

If you suspect that a relational partner is deceiving you, you can confirm it directly, indirectly, or covertly. It's even possible you'll get closer to the truth depending on the approach you use.[28]

Keep in mind, though, that no matter which approach you take, there is no guarantee that you'll get "the whole truth and nothing but the truth." Although some people respond better to certain approaches than to others, in general, it's best to express yourself using an even, calm voice when confronting people about possible deception. Avoid confrontational nonverbal behaviors such as eye-rolling and finger-pointing, and stay away from facial expressions associated with disbelief, disgust, or anger.

Direct approach

If you decide to take the direct approach, you ask a question or make a statement point-blank: for instance, "Did you just lie to me?" or "I don't think you're telling me the whole truth." Although the direct approach may get you the answer you're looking for, it may be perceived as confrontational or accusatory. In Section 12.3, we explain two ways to approach a person directly and constructively using I-statements and a two-step perception check.

Indirect approach

You can also use an indirect approach to get to the truth. You may ask a question like, "Did anything happen while I was gone?" or "Is there something you want to tell me?" Instead of a direct question like, "Did you take money out of the till?" you may say to an employee, "Hm. . . we came up short again last night. I wonder what's going on." You would then pause and observe the employee's reaction.

When you sense that someone is reticent to share their honest thoughts and feelings, you can make it easier for them using another indirect approach. Relational partners may feel more comfortable telling you what they've heard from others if you don't ask them to identify who said what. They may also reveal their own thoughts or opinions when it is under the guise of what they've heard others say. Questions like this may work well: "Have you heard any complaints?"; "What do your teammates think about our new offensive plays?"; or "Are there any ideas being bounced around the office?"

Covert methods

Sometimes we rely on deception to prove deception. One technique is to bluff or pretend you already know the truth. Here's one example:

> **Josh:** Jeremiah, we need to talk about your taking my car out for secret joyrides. I know you did it, so don't even pretend you didn't.

If Jeremiah hesitates or doesn't jump to his own defense, Josh now has a pretty good indication that Jeremiah took his car for a ride without asking. Do you think this approach is ethical? What are some potential drawbacks with this approach?

section review

12.2 Deception within relationships

Interpersonal deception is any communication behavior that is not completely honest or forthcoming. We commit deceptive acts to maximize desirable outcomes and minimize what we find unpleasant. Deception can be ethical, unethical, or somewhere in between. Some acts of deception are benevolent. Others are low-stakes—that is, harmless—or high-stakes, if the repercussions are more severe. Verbal and nonverbal behaviors may signal deception; however, they may indicate other things too. We may confront suspected deception directly, indirectly, or covertly.

Key Terms

deception, *p. 322*

duping delight, *p. 323*

benevolent deception, *p. 324*

deceptive affection (DA), *p. 325*

low-stakes deception, *p. 325*

high-stakes deception, *p. 326*

Comprehend It?

1. Define each of the key terms in Section 12.2. To further your understanding of these terms, create examples to support your definitions.

2. What are some of the reasons why we deceive others?

3. Compare and contrast low-stakes, benevolent, and high-stakes deception.

4. Identify and describe some of the verbal and nonverbal cues associated with deception. Why are they not always reliable?

5. Explain the three approaches you can use to confront deception: direct, indirect, and covert.

Apply It!

Withholding or omitting information is a form of deception. Are you keeping information from someone you know? Is this secrecy unethical? Answer the following questions and compare your responses to the ideals of RRIFT (respect, responsibility, integrity, fairness, and truthfulness) from Section 12.1.

- Is my secrecy affecting or will it affect my relationship partner negatively?
- Is it reinforcing an unethical behavior?

- Is it making me want to do something unethical?
- Is it not allowing someone to make a fully informed decision?
- Is it giving someone a false perception or expectation?
- Would I want to know this information if the roles were reversed? If so, why?

12.3 Ways to improve ethical decision-making

Metacommunication, as we've learned in Chapter 2, is communication about communication. This may include communication with our relational partners about standards for ethical communication. For example, you might sit down with a roommate and talk about the communication behaviors you associate with ethical roommate communication. With a work team, you may brainstorm the ethical behaviors everyone wishes to see from one another. You may facilitate a discussion with members of your family to identify shared goals for ethical family communication.

In Section 12.3, we'll examine additional approaches to help you clarify your ethics, commit to them, and promote ethical IPC.

Confront unethical communication constructively

Sometimes it's not easy to talk to your relational partners about their unethical behavior. However, as much as you may want to avoid confrontation, failing to address such a behavior may communicate that you condone it or that you're willing to tolerate it.

Imagine that one of your relational partners is behaving or wants to behave in a way that falls short of the ideals of respect, responsibility, integrity, fairness, and truthfulness. In earlier chapters, we explain the effective use of *I-statements*. An I-statement is a constructive way to address an ethical dilemma.

First, state a feeling you have about the behavior in question and say why you have this feeling. Then, follow this statement with another statement that clearly expresses the behavior you want to see instead. Use I-language, beginning your sentences with phrases such as "I need," "I value," or "I appreciate." Here are two examples:

- "**I'm concerned** we often commit to social engagements but cancel out at the last minute. **I don't want** our family and friends to think we're unreliable or that we don't value their invites. **I'd like** us to follow through on our commitments."

- "**I'm disappointed** you've made up your mind and won't consider my ideas. **I'd like** to have more of a say when it comes to planning this trip."

Rather than jumping to any conclusions or accusing a person of unethical communication, it may also be prudent to first determine if your perceptions are accurate. With a *two-step perception check* (see Chapter 3), you state the behavior that makes you suspicious or uncomfortable using the pronoun I followed by a word like *noticed, saw, heard,* or *sense.* You follow your I-statement with a question or two for clarification. A two-step perception check comes across as less antagonistic or snappish compared to an accusatory you-statement, especially if your voice and body language are calm, even-keeled, and matter-of-fact.

In the two examples below, you sense that a family member is not telling you the truth.

> **You:** <u>I noticed</u> you shifted nervously in your seat just now. (Observation) Does my question make you feel uncomfortable for some reason? (Question for clarification)

> **You:** <u>I heard</u> you include a lot of unnecessary details in your answer. (Observation) Is there a reason why? (Question for clarification)

Recognize and encourage ethical behaviors

You can encourage ethical communication by recognizing it and voicing your appreciation when you see it. When you make a choice to do what's right, acknowledge it to yourself using *intrapersonal communication* or self-talk (which we discussed in Chapter 3). Here are some examples:

- I was tempted to lie to her, but I didn't. I chose to be honest. I like that about myself.

- I feel good that I said I felt uncomfortable with the gossip my cousin was sharing with me today.

- I didn't yell or resort to name calling when I got angry with Mom last night. That's how I like to handle my anger.

You can also applaud others when they communicate ethically. For example, you can encourage your relational partners to communicate honestly by saying how much you appreciate honest behavior when it happens. Here are a few examples:

- "I really like that you told me this even though you were worried about my reaction."

- "I thought it was very considerate of you to acknowledge how others played a role in your success."

- "I appreciate you telling me when you talk to or spend time with Jake. It makes me feel more secure."

Own your communication choices

If you behave unethically and commit a relationship transgression, there are a number of ways you can reduce the intensity and duration of your relational partner's ongoing negative affect. No matter which way you choose, admitting that you are at fault is an important first step in the healing process. Acknowledge your mistakes without rationalizations or excuses. Use the language of responsibility, for example: "I was wrong," "I should have . . . ," "Next time I will . . . ," or "I need to work on . . ."

TABLE 12.3 identifies four communication methods that may start a healing dialogue.

Two of the most effective, though often overlooked, methods described in Table 12.3 are making amends and promising to work on our behavior. Both

table 12.3	Four Ways to Promote a Healing Dialogue
Communication Method	**Example**
Express remorse.	"I feel bad that I said you were a lousy friend. I'm sorry."
Take responsibility.	"I let my feelings get the best of me. I was wrong."
Make amends.	"I want to make it up to you somehow. "
Promise to work on the behavior.	"I will do my best to make sure I don't do this again."

methods involve forethought and follow-through, and they make it clear to our relational partners that we mean what we say.

To make amends, you may ask a relational partner if there's anything you can do to make things right, or you can suggest something specific. For example, if you canceled dinner with a friend at the last minute, you could say, "Since I left you hanging, I'd like to treat you to dinner at that restaurant you were raving about last week. When are you free?"

You can also ask your relational partner if there is a behavior you could work on that would help heal your relationship. You show particular good faith if you can name something you'll be working on without prompting. For example, if you said something culturally insensitive to a friend you may say, "I know it's not your job to educate me about your culture. I'll read about it on my own time so I don't offend you like this again."

It's important to remember that even if you take responsibility for your unethical behavior and work toward repairing the relationship, you cannot always expect your relationship to return to normal. The person you've wronged may perceive any offer to make amends as insufficient or even an attempt at manipulation. The same goes for promising to work on your behavior.

If you find yourself in this scenario, and you have tried the other methods of repairing a relationship listed in Table 12.3, sometimes the best thing to do is validate the person's feelings. Doing so shows that you understand your actions have caused severe harm and that you respect the person's decision not to forgive you. You may say, "I understand I've really hurt you and that our relationship can't go back to what it was. I hope one day I can earn your forgiveness."

By the same logic, you do not have to accept another person's attempt to reestablish a relationship. If you doubt an apology is sincere, or if the harm caused by the other person's unethical behavior is severe enough, you may say, "Thank you for your apology and offer to make amends, but I cannot forgive you for your actions."

Be honest, sensitive, and tactful

Many interpersonal communication scholars and moralists believe that we should strive to be as honest as possible because honesty is the building block of trust. Others say that honesty in general is ideal but point out that there are times when complete honesty is not the best policy. When is it more ethical not to be completely honest? We covered some examples of this in Section 12.2. Your authors endorse this perspective: Strive to be completely honest, *but* be honest with sensitivity and tact. This approach will create room for vulnerability, deeper intimacy, and opportunities for growth in your relationships.

One of our students, Aarush, shared that he was once placed in a tricky situation when his girlfriend, Jessica, surprised him with a homemade dinner that took her 2 hours to prepare. Aarush did not like the meal. What could he have said that's honest yet sensitive and tactful? How would you have approached the situation?

"I didn't want to hurt her feelings, but I also didn't want to lie to her—or eat the dish again! I told her, 'Babe, I can see you put your heart into this casserole. It took a long time to make. I like how you're trying out some new meal ideas. Thank you. It was too spicy for me, and I'm not a fan of pork. But because you went way out of your way to make this, let me treat you to some frozen yogurt.'" –Aarush

Aarush gives Jessica a warm hug and a kiss on the cheek. He offers to clean up the kitchen. Jessica may feel disappointed that Aarush didn't like what she prepared. However, she'll most likely appreciate the fact that it wasn't easy for him to tell her the truth, and she won't hold his honesty against him. In fact, Aarush's sensitive and tactful candor may deepen Jessica's trust in him.

Think of an effective way to communicate a message honestly—with sensitivity and tact—in the following situations with a romantic partner:

- Telling your partner your whereabouts, even if it may raise suspicions
- Mentioning that a friend of yours was someone you once dated
- Being open about your intimacy needs
- Divulging that you're having doubts about your future as a couple
- Admitting that you did something your partner asked you not to do
- Responding to the question, "Do I look good in this?"

Disagree with civility

civility The level of politeness and courtesy you extend to a conversational partner.

Conversations can get testy and confrontational when speakers disagree with each other's points of view. How you communicate disagreement can lead to a meaningful, enlightening, and productive conversation, or it can lead to hostilities and hurt feelings. If you disagree with someone, there is a way to convey it respectfully and with civility. **Civility** is the level of politeness and courtesy you extend to a conversational partner.

This commercial features relational partners admitting, quite candidly, their mistakes and transgressions with each other. How do the characters in this scenario own up to their communication choices? What kind of responses do they get? What do you think is the ad's central message? On YouTube, search using the keywords: "This AD on truthfulness is going viral around Social Media." (2:45)

An example of a civil behavior is *active listening* (see Chapter 4). If you want to influence a person's thinking and keep a conversation from becoming hostile, you have a greater chance of doing so if you practice active listening. Show that you are willing to listen without interrupting. Convey that you understand your conversational partner's point of view by *paraphrasing*—a technique that we explained in Chapter 4. Validate or agree with the speaker if and where you can before you explain why you disagree. Next, ask if the speaker is willing to hear you explain your point of view. Imagine you're speaking to a coworker, Dominic:

> **You:** (*After listening to Dominic without interrupting*) So, you think the United States spends a disproportionate amount of taxpayer money hosting the United Nations with little to nothing to show for it.
> **Dominic:** I don't just think so. I know so.
> **You:** While I can see where you're coming from, countries do need to pay their fair share to keep the U.N. running. I don't agree that it's a complete waste of our money. Can I share with you why?
> **Dominic:** Sure.
> **You:** Okay. Thanks. Without the U.N., we might not have an institution that brings all countries together in one place to solve global issues. Plus, I'm sure it helps our local, state, and national economies in terms of all the visitors it brings to the U.S.

This approach models that you are willing to listen to and acknowledge Dominic's point of view. You say you disagree without sounding like you're completely dismissing or discrediting his thoughts. You ask if you can share your point of view and then continue once he indicates that he's receptive. Since you have modeled active listening and validation, hopefully, Dominic will reciprocate and do the same for you.

In **TABLE 12.4**, the statements on the left come across as disrespectful and are not very productive. If you tend to use these statements when you disagree

table 12.4	Civil Disagreement
Disrespectful Language	**Respectful Language**
You're wrong.	I see it differently.
That's not true.	What I understand is . . .
You don't know what you're talking about.	I have information I'd like you to consider.
I have a better idea.	I have an alternative idea.
Nonsense . . . Democrats do it all the time.	Is this behavior limited to just one party?
That's unrealistic.	Can we sustain this in the long term with the resources we have?
You'd have to be an idiot to vote for . . .	I'm not a fan of that candidate, but I'm glad to hear you plan to vote. Can I share my view on the candidate?
You've got to be kidding, right? You *really* believe that?	Sounds like our beliefs differ in this regard.

with others, you can replace them with the neutral statements or questions on the right.

Communicate strategically when things get intense

Disrespectful, hurtful, manipulative, and controlling behaviors often occur during heated conversations. To avoid communication behavior that others may view as unethical, there are several strategies you can apply:

- When a relational partner needs a "cooling off" period, allow this person time to calm down. Postpone or delay the conversation. Agree on a mutually convenient time to talk later.

- When a relational partner wrongs you in some way, talk about it directly and privately. Don't involve others. Respect everyone's right to privacy. Safeguard this person's positive reputation at work and within your social and family circles.

- Honor the need to cry. Crying is a natural, normal response for men and women. Avoid labeling this behavior as "weak," "foolish," or "emotional." When crying is discouraged, you or your relational partner may shut down, avoid conversations, or bottle up emotions.

- Don't force a potentially heated conversation when a relational partner is sick, fatigued, highly anxious, intoxicated, depressed, or has a lot going on at work.

- Avoid labels or words that are demeaning or degrading, such as "You're acting crazy," or "You're being overly sensitive." This includes condescending expressions such as "Here you go again," "You're entitled to your wrong opinion," and "That's ridiculous."

- Don't hit below the belt by taking advantage of what you know about the other person's psychological vulnerabilities. If a person has opened up to you in the past in a trusting way about an earlier mistake or a personal struggle, don't bring it up during an argument to prove a point in a hurtful way.

- Avoid bottling up or stockpiling unexpressed grievances to the point that your conversation partner is overwhelmed by all of them once you unleash them.

section review

12.3 **Ways to improve ethical decision-making**

There are several ways to improve our ethical communication. We can confront unethical communication constructively, recognize and encourage ethical communication, and own our communication choices. We can also practice honesty with sensitivity and tact; communicate disagreement in a civil, respectful way; and practice strategies to avoid unethical behaviors when a conversation gets heated.

Key Terms

civility, *p. 332*

Comprehend It?

1. Define civility. To further your understanding of this term, create an example to support your definition.

2. Explain how to use I-statements effectively when you need to confront someone about a perceived unethical behavior and create your own example.

3. How can we encourage ethical communication within our relationships?

4. How can we effectively own our communication choices?

5. How can you disagree with someone in a civil, respectful way?

6. Describe the strategies you think you need to work on to help you avoid unethical communication behaviors when a conversation gets heated.

Apply It!

Complete the *Building Your IPC Skills* exercise at the end of this chapter.

chapter exercises

Assessing Your IPC: Measuring Your Ethical Behavior

Purpose: To help me assess my ethical communication.

Directions: Certain interpersonal communication behaviors fail to live up to the ideals of respect, responsibility, integrity, fairness, and truthfulness (RRIFT). As a form of self-monitoring, read each behavior listed below. How often does each behavior occur in your communication? Try to be as accurate as possible. Use the following scale:

1	**2**	**3**	**4**	**5**
Never	**Rarely**	**Sometimes**	**Often**	**A Lot**

_____ I behave secretly or withhold information even though I know it could adversely affect a relational partner in some way.

_____ I listen to conversations that are not meant for me.

_____ I read the private journals, text messages, or emails of others without their knowledge or consent.

_____ I persuade others to do things that are destructive, illegal, or unsafe.

_____ I threaten to physically, emotionally, and/or financially harm people for personal gain.

_____ I share private information with others when I'm asked not to.

_____ I spread rumors or engage in the act of gossiping—sharing uncomplimentary, socially damaging information about a person to others.

_____ I say or do things to promote negative stereotypes.

_____ I ridicule or mistreat others because of their race, ethnicity, culture, beliefs, sexual orientation, gender, size, or disabilities.

_____ I pretend I'm listening intently to others when I'm not.

_____ I refuse to consider other people's feelings, opinions, or needs.

_____ I embarrass others in public when I'm angry or upset.

_____ I use violence or physical intimidation to exercise power or control.

Take a look at your scores. Which behaviors occur more or less often? In what ways would you like to improve your ethical communication? Compare your self-analysis with the perceptions of others. Select a few significant individuals to evaluate you. Do they perceive your ethical communication differently? Find out why—in an appreciative and mindful way, of course—and ask what would it take to change their perceptions.

Building Your IPC Skills: Your Ethical Playbook

Purpose: To clarify, develop, and monitor my ethical communication.

Directions: Using the five ideals of ethical communication—respect, responsibility, integrity, fairness, and truthfulness—identify the specific behaviors from the exercise above that you wish to commit yourself to improving. These are your goals or intentions.

Refer to this activity often to assess your progress. You'll make your plan of action very clear and measurable if you are specific about what you intend to say and do consistently. You can use this exercise as a form of daily or weekly self-monitoring. Ask yourself the question: Were my behaviors aligned with my goals?

Think about the ethical behaviors you're pursuing in terms of the meaningful relationships in your life, whether in the contexts of family, work, friendship, or romance.

Goal: To communicate responsibly	Behaviors: (How will I be responsible?) 1. I will return calls and texts in a timely manner. 2. I will follow through on the commitments I make. 3. I will make myself available when people need me whenever I can. 4. I will readily admit when I make a mistake and apologize.
Goal: To communicate respectfully	Behaviors:
Goal: To communicate with integrity	Behaviors:
Goal: To communicate fairly	Behaviors:
Goal: To communicate in a trustworthy manner	Behaviors:

endnotes

Chapter One

1 McCafferty, M. (2007, Jan). I tracked down the man who broke my heart. *Glamour*, 153–154.

2 Chapman, G. (2015). *The 5 love languages: The secret to love that lasts*. Northfield Publishing.

3 Clark, R. A., & Delia, J. G. (1979). *TOPOI* and rhetorical competence. *Quarterly Journal of Speech*, 65(2), 187–206. https://doi .org/10.1080/00335637909383470

4 Chou, C., & Cooley, L. (2018). *Communication Rx: Transforming healthcare through relationship-centered communication*. McGraw-Hill; Ogolsky, B. G., & Bowers, J. R. (2013). A meta-analytic review of relationship maintenance and its correlates. *Journal of Social and Personal Relationships*, 30(3), 343–367. https://doi .org/10.1177/0265407512463338

5 Mikkelson, A. C., York, J. A., & Arritola, J. (2015). Communication competence, leadership behaviors and employee outcomes in supervisor-employee relationships. *Business and Professional Communication Quarterly*, 78(3), 336–354. https://doi.org/10 .1177/2329490615588542

6 McLaren, R. M., & Pederson, J. R. (2014). Relational communication and understanding in conversations about hurtful events between parents and adolescents. *Journal of Communication*, 64(1), 145–166. https://doi.org/10.1111/jcom.12072

7 Kemp, A. H., Arias, J. A., & Fisher, Z. (2017). Social ties, health and wellbeing: A literature review and model. In A. Ibáñez, L. Sedeño, & A. M. García (Eds.), *Neuroscience and social science: The missing link* (pp. 397–427). Springer. https://doi.org/10.1007 /978-3-319-68421-5_17

8 Yoshimura, S. M., & Berzins, K. (2017). Grateful experiences and expressions: The role of gratitude expressions in the link between gratitude experiences and well-being. *Review of Communication*, 17(2), 106–118. https://doi.org/10.1080/1535859 3.2017.1293836; see also: Horstman, H. K., Maliski, R., Hays, A., Cox, J., Enderle, A., & Nelson, L. R. (2016). Unfolding narrative meaning over time: The contributions of mother–daughter conversations of difficulty on daughter narrative sense-making and well-being. *Communication Monographs*, 83(3), 326–348. https://doi.org/10.1080/03637751.2015.1068945

9 Brown, S. L., Fredrickson, B. L., Wirth, M. M., Poulin, M. J., Meier, E. A., Heaphy, E. D., Cohen, M. D., & Schultheiss, O. C. (2009). Social closeness increases salivary progesterone in humans. *Hormones and Behavior*, 56(1), 108–111. https://doi.org/10.1016 /j.yhbeh.2009.03.022

10 Chen, Y., & Feeley, T. H. (2014). Social support, social strain, loneliness, and well-being among older adults: An analysis of the Health and Retirement Study. *Journal of Social and Personal Relationships*, 31(2), 141–161. https://doi.org/10.1177/0265407513488728

11 Savage, B. M., Lujan, H. L., Thipparthi, R. R., & DiCarlo, S. E. (2017). Humor, laughter, learning, and health! A brief review. *Advances in Physiology Education*, 41(3), 341–347 https://doi .org/10.1152/advan.00030.2017; see also: Louie, D., Brook, K., & Frates, E. (2016). The laughter prescription: A tool for lifestyle medicine. *American Journal of Lifestyle Medicine*, 10(4), 262–267. https://doi.org/10.1177/1559827614550279

12 Musick, K., & Meier, A. (2012). Assessing causality and persistence in associations between family dinners and adolescent well-being. *Journal of Marriage and Family*, 74(3), 476–493. https://doi.org/10.1111/j.1741-3737.2012.00973.x

13 Evans, R., Pistrang, N., & Billings, J. (2013). Police officers' experiences of supportive and unsupportive social interactions following traumatic incidents. *European Journal of Psychotraumatology*, 4(1), https://doi.org/10.3402/ejpt.v4i0.19696; see also: Stephens, C., & Long, N. (2000). Communication with police supervisors and peers as a buffer of work-related traumatic stress. *Journal of Organizational Behavior*, 21(4), 407–424. https:// doi.org/10.1002/(SICI)1099-1379(200006)21:4%3C407::AID -JOB17%3E3.0.CO;2-N

14 Elsenbruch, S., Benson, S., Rücke, M., Rose, M., Dudenhausen, J., Pincus-Knackstedt, M. K., Klapp, B. F., & Arck, P. C. (2007). Social support during pregnancy: Effects on maternal depressive symptoms, smoking, and pregnancy outcome. *Human Reproduction*, 22(3), 869–877. https://doi.org/10.1093/humrep /del432

15 Morikawa, M., Okada, T., Ando, M., Aleksic, B., Kunimoto, S., Nakamura, Y., Kubota, C., Uno, Y., Tamaji, N., Furumura, K., Shiino, T., Morita, T., Ishikawa, N., Ohoka, H., Usui, H., Banno, N., Murase, S., Setsuko, G., Goto, S., . . . Ozaki, N. (2015). Relationship between social support during pregnancy and postpartum depressive state: A prospective cohort study. *Scientific Reports*, 5, Article 10520. https://doi.org/10.1038/srep10520

16 American Heart Association. (2016, December 20). *Avoiding deadly holiday heart attacks*. https://news.heart.org/avoiding -deadly-holiday-heart-attacks

17 Fleshner, M., & Laudenslager, M. L. (2004). Psychoneuroimmunology: Then and now. *Behavioral and Cognitive Neuroscience Reviews*, 3(2), 114–130. https://doi.org/10.1177/1534582304269027; see also: Segerstrom, S. C., & Miller, G. E. (2004). Psychological stress and the human immune system: A meta-analytic study of 30 years of inquiry. *Psychological Bulletin*, 130(4), 601–630. https://doi.org/10.1037/0033-2909.130.4.601

18 Sillars, A. L. (2010). Interpersonal conflict. In C. R. Berger, M. E. Roloff, & D. R. Roskos-Ewoldsen (Eds.), *The handbook of communication science* (2nd ed., pp. 273–290). Sage.

19 Harburg, E., Kaciroti, N., Gleiberman, L., Julius, M., & Schork, M. A. (2008). Marital pair anger-coping types may act as an entity to affect mortality: Preliminary findings from a prospective study (Tecumseh, Michigan, 1971–1988). *Journal of Family Communication*, 8(1), 44–61. https://doi .org/10.1080/15267430701779485; see also: Newsom, J. T.,

Mahan, T. L., Rook, K. S., & Krause, N. (2008). Stable negative social exchanges and health. *Health Psychology, 27*(1), 78–86. https://doi.org/10.1037/0278-6133.27.1.78

20 Welch, M. R., Sikkink, D., & Loveland, M. T. (2007). The radius of trust: Religion, social embeddedness and trust in strangers. *Social Forces, 86*(1), 23–46. https://doi.org/10.1353/sof.2007.0116

21 Parks, M. R. (2015). Weak and strong tie relationships. In C. R. Berger & M. E. Roloff (Eds.), *The international encyclopedia of interpersonal communication.* Wiley Blackwell. https://doi.org/10.1002/9781118540190.wbeic041; see also: Sandstrom, G. M., & Dunn, E. W. (2014). Social interactions and well-being: The surprising power of weak ties. *Personality and Social Psychology Bulletin, 40*(7), 910–922. https://doi.org/10.1177/0146167214529799

22 Koerner, F. A., & Fitzpatrick, M. A. (2002). Understanding family communication patterns and family functioning: The roles of conversation orientation and conformity orientation. *Annals of the International Communication Association, 26*(1), 36–65. https://doi.org/10.1080/23808985.2002.11679010; see also: Barbato, C. A., Graham, E. E., & Perse, E. M. (2003). Communicating in the family: An examination of the relationship of family communication climate and interpersonal communication motives. *Journal of Family Communication, 3*(3), 123–148. https://doi.org/10.1207/S15327698JFC0303_01

23 Koesten, J. (2004). Family communication patterns, sex of subject, and communication competence. *Communication Monographs, 71*(2), 226–244. https://doi.org/10.1080/0363775052000343417; see also: Avtgis, T. A. (1999). The relationship between unwillingness to communicate and family communication patterns. *Communication Research Reports, 16*(4), 333–338. https://doi.org/10.1080/08824099909388734

24 Koesten, J. (2004). Family communication patterns, sex of subject, and communication competence. *Communication Monographs, 71*(2), 226–244. https://doi.org/10.1080/0363775052000343417; see also: Avtgis, T. A. (1999). The relationship between unwillingness to communicate and family communication patterns. *Communication Research Reports, 16*(4), 333–338. https://doi.org/10.1080/08824099909388734

25 Saad, L. (2015, June 8). *Fewer young people say I do—To any relationship.* Gallup. https://www.gallup.com/poll/183515/fewer-young-people-say-relationship.aspx

26 Traister, R. (2016). *All the single ladies: Unmarried women and the rise of an independent nation.* Simon and Schuster.

27 Shea, C. T., Davisson, E. K., & Fitzsimons, G. M. (2013). Riding other people's coattails: Individuals with low self-control value self-control in other people. *Psychological Science, 24*(6), 1031–1036. https://doi.org/10.1177/0956797612464890

28 Rath, T. (2006). *Vital friends: The people you can't afford to live without.* Gallup Press.

29 Indiana University. (2014, November 19). *When it comes to teen alcohol use, close friends have more influence than peers.* ScienceDaily. https://www.sciencedaily.com/releases/2014/11/141119084953.htm

30 Gallup. (2013). *State of the American workplace.* https://news.gallup.com/reports/199961/state-american-workplace-report-2017.aspx

31 Rath, T. (2006). *Vital friends: The people you can't afford to live without.* Gallup Press.

32 West, K. (2007, November 19). The top five reasons employees hate their jobs. *National Business Research Institute Blog.* https://www.nbrii.com/employee-survey-white-papers/the-top-5-reasons-employees-hate-their-jobs

33 Hanson, G. C., Hammer, L. B., & Colton, C. L. (2006). Development and validation of a multidimensional scale of perceived work-family positive spillover. *Journal of Occupational Health Psychology, 11*(3), 249–265. https://doi.org/10.1037/1076-8998.11.3.249; see also: Grzywacz, J. G., Almeida, D. M., & McDonald, D. A. (2002). Work-family spillover and daily reports of work and family stress in the adult labor force. *Family Relations, 51*(1), 28–36. https://doi.org/10.1111/j.1741-3729.2002.00028.x

34 Spott, J., Pyle, C., & Punyanunt-Carter, N. M. (2010). Positive and negative nonverbal behaviors in relationships: A study of relationship satisfaction and longevity. *Human Communication, 13*(1), 29–41.

35 Kirchier, E. (1988). Marital happiness and interaction in everyday surroundings: A time-sample diary approach for couples. *Journal of Social and Personal Relationships, 5*(3), 375–382. https://doi.org/10.1177%2F0265407588053007

36 Dafoe Whitehead, B., & Popenoe, D. (2001, June 27). *Singles seek soul mates for marriage.* Gallup. https://www.gallup.com/poll/4552/singles-seek-soul-mates-marriage.aspx

37 National Communication Association. (1999). *How Americans communicate.* https://teachingfsem08.umwblogs.org/files/2008/05/roper-poll-on-communication.pdf

38 Espiner, T. (2007, December 14). *Survey: People skills valued over those for IT.* CNET News. https://www.cnet.com/news/survey-people-skills-valued-over-those-for-it

39 National Association of Colleges and Employers. (2016). *Job outlook 2016: The attributes employers want to see on new college graduates' resumes.* https://www.naceweb.org/career-development/trends-and-predictions/job-outlook-2016-attributes-employers-want-to-see-on-new-college-graduates-resumes

40 Sageev, P., & Romanowski, C. J. (2001). A message from recent engineering graduates in the workplace: Results of a survey on technical communication skills. *Journal of Engineering Education, 90*(4), 685–693. https://doi.org/10.1002/j.2168-9830.2001.tb00660.x

41 McKinley, C. J., & Perino, C. (2013). Examining communication competence as a contributing factor in health care workers' job satisfaction and tendency to report errors. *Journal of Communication in Healthcare, 6*(3), 158–165. https://doi.org/10.1179/1753807613Y.0000000039

42 Burton, S. K. (2006). Without trust, you have nobody: Effective employee communications for today and tomorrow. *Public Relations Strategist, 12*(2), 32–36.

43 Seitel, F. P. (2004). *The practice of public relations* (9th ed.). Pearson/Prentice Hall.

44 Spitzberg, B. H., & Cupach, W. R. (1989). *Handbook of interpersonal competence research.* Springer-Verlag.

45 Barry, R. A., Bunde, M., Brock, R. L., & Lawrence, E. (2009). Validy and utility of a multidimensional model of received support in intimate relationships. *Journal of Family Psychology, 23*(1), 48–57. https://doi.org/10.1037/a0014174

46 Giles, H., Coupland, N., & Coupland, J. (1991). Accommodation theory: Communication, context, and consequence. In H. Giles,

J. Coupland, & N. Coupland (Eds.), *Contexts of accommodation* (pp. 1–68). Cambridge University Press.

47 Johannesen, R. L. (2001). Communication ethics: Centrality, trends, and controversies. *Annals of the International Communication Association, 25*(1), 201–235. https://doi.org/10.1080/23808985.2001.11679004

48 Tongue, J. R., Epps, H. R., & Forese, L. L. (2005). Communication skills for patient-centered care: Research-based, easily learned techniques for medical interviews that benefit orthopaedic surgeons and their patients. *Journal of Bone and Joint Surgery, 87-A*(3), 652–658.

49 Lundquist, L. M., Shogbon, A. O., Momary, K. M., & Rogers, H. K. (2013). A comparison of students' self-assessments with faculty evaluations of their communication skills. *American Journal of Pharmaceutical Education, 77*(4), Article 72. https://doi.org/10.5688/ajpe77472

50 Boren, J. P., & Veksler, A. E. (2011). A decade of research exploring biology and communication: The brain, nervous, endocrine, cardiovascular, and immune systems. *Communication Research Trends, 30*(4), 4–31.

51 Corsten, S., Konradi, J., Schimpf, E. J., Hardering, F., & Keilmann, A. (2014). Improving quality of life in aphasia—Evidence for the effectiveness of the biographic-narrative approach. *Aphasiology, 28*(4), 440–452. https://doi.org/10.1080/02687038.2013.843154; see also: Rodríguez Muñoz, F. J. (2013). Pilot assessment of nonverbal pragmatic ability in people with Asperger syndrome. *Psychology of Language and Communication, 17*(3), 279–294. https://doi.org/10.2478/plc-2013-0018; Simpson, R. L. (2011). Meta-analysis supports Picture Exchange Communication System (PECS) as a promising method for improving communication skills of children with autism spectrum disorders. *Evidence-Based Communication Assessment and Intervention, 5*(1), 3–6. https://doi.org/10.1080/17489539.2011.570011

52 Wackman, D. B., Miller, S., & Nunnally, E. W. (1976). *Student workbook: Increasing awareness and communication skills.* Interpersonal Communication Programs.

53 Goleman, D. (2006). *Social intelligence: The new science of human relationships.* Bantam Books; see also: Schraw, G. (1998). Promoting general metacognitive awareness. *Instructional Science, 26,* 113–125. https://doi.org/10.1023/A:1003044231033; Sypher, B. D., & Sypher, H. E. (1983). Perceptions of communication ability: Self-monitoring in an organizational setting. *Personality and Social Psychology Bulletin, 9*(2), 297–304. https://doi.org/10.1177%2F0146167283092015

54 Langer, E. J. (2009). *Counterclockwise: Mindful health and the power of possibility.* Ballantine Books; see also: Carson, S. H., & Langer, E. J. (2006). Mindfulness and self-acceptance. *Journal of Rational-Emotive and Cognitive-Behavior Therapy, 24*(1), 29–43. https://doi.org/10.1007/s10942-006-0022-5

Chapter Two

1 Rademacher, T. (2006, March 4). Retiring Zeeland teacher takes the (cup) cake. *Grand Rapids Press,* A24.

2 Lovering, D. (2011, July 15). *Love letter delivered 53 years late.* Reuters. https://www.reuters.com/article/us-loveletter-lost/love-letter-delivered-53-years-late-idUSTRE76E35D20110715

3 Fried, S. (2006, April). Confessions of a naked man. *Ladies' Home Journal,* 78–80.

4 Connors, J. V. (2011). Systems theory and interpersonal relationships. In J. V. Connors, *Interpersonal Peacemaking Reader* (pp. 309–324). University Readers.

5 Compton, C. A., & Dougherty, D. S. (2017). Organizing sexuality: Silencing and the push–pull process of co-sexuality in the workplace. *Journal of Communication, 67*(6), 874–896. https://doi.org/10.1111/jcom.12336

6 Burgoon, J. K. (2016). Expectancy violations theory. In C. R. Berger & M. E. Roloff (Eds.), *International encyclopedia of interpersonal communication* (1st ed., pp. 1–9). Wiley.

7 Jiang, L. C., & Hancock, J. T. (2013). Absence makes the communication grow fonder: Geographic separation, interpersonal media, and intimacy in dating relationships. *Journal of Communication, 63*(3), 556–557. https://doi.org/10.1111/jcom.12029

8 Kohl, P. (1991). *Hole in the garden wall.* Simon & Schuster.

9 Edwards, R. (2011). Listening and message interpretation. *International Journal of Listening, 25*(1–2), 47–65. https://doi.org/10.1080/10904018.2011.536471

10 Cloven, D. H., & Roloff, M. E. (1991). Sense-making activities and interpersonal conflict: Communicative cures for the mulling blues. *Western Journal of Speech Communication, 55*(2), 134–158. https://doi.org/10.1080/10570319109374376

11 Prochazka, J., Ovcari, M., & Durinik, M. (2020). Sandwich feedback: The empirical evidence of its effectiveness. *Learning and Motivation, 71,* Article 101649. https://doi.org/10.1016/j.lmot.2020.101649; see also: Reddy, S. T., Zegarek, M. H., Fromme, H. B., Ryan, M. S., Schumann, S.-A., & Harris, I. B. (2015). Barriers and facilitators to effective feedback: A qualitative analysis of data from multispecialty resident focus groups. *Journal of Graduate Medical Education, 7*(2), 214–219. https://doi.org/10.4300/JGME-D-14-00461.1; Davies, D., & Jacobs, A. (1985). "Sandwiching" complex interpersonal feedback. *Small Group Behavior, 16*(3), 387–396. https://doi.org/10.1177/0090552685163008

12 Burgoon, J. K., & Hoobler, G. D. (2002). Nonverbal signals. In M. L. Knapp & J. A. Daly (Eds.), *Handbook of interpersonal communication* (3rd ed., pp. 240–299). Sage; see also: Burgoon, J. K., Birk, T., and Pfau, M. (1990). Nonverbal behaviors, persuasion, and credibility. *Human Communication Research, 17*(1), 140–169. https://doi.org/10.1111/j.1468-2958.1990.tb00229.x

13 Proctor II, R. F., & Wilcox, J. R. (1993). An exploratory analysis of responses to owned messages in interpersonal communication. *ETC: A Review of General Semantics, 50*(2), 201–220; see also: Argyle, M., Alkema, F., & Gilmour, R. (1971). The communication of friendly and hostile attitudes by verbal and non-verbal signals. *European Journal of Social Psychology, 1*(3), 385–402. https://doi.org/10.1002/ejsp.2420010307

14 Kruger, J., Epley, N., Parker, J., & Ng, Z.-W. (2005). Egocentrism over e-mail: Can we communicate as well as we think? *Journal of Personality and Social Psychology, 89*(6), 925–936. https://doi.org/10.1037/0022-3514.89.6.925

15 Walther, J. B., & Tidwell, L. C. (1995). Nonverbal cues in computer-mediated communication, and the effect of chronemics on relational communication. *Journal of Organizational Computing, 5*(4), 355–378. https://doi.org/10.1080/10919399509540258

16 Morris, M., Nadler, J., Kurtzberg, T., & Thompson, L. (2002). Schmooze or lose: Social friction and lubrication in e-mail negotiations. *Group Dynamics: Theory, Research, and Practice, 6*(1), 89–100. https://psycnet.apa.org/doi/10.1037/1089-2699.6.1.89

17 Bevan, J. L. (2014). Dyadic perceptions of goals, conflict strate-gies, and perceived resolvability in serial arguments. *Journal of Social and Personal Relationships, 31*(6), 773–795. https://doi.org/10.1177/0265407513504653; see also: Baltzersen, R. K. (2013). The importance of metacommunication in supervision processes in higher education. *International Journal of Higher Education, 2*(2), 128–140. https://doi.org/10.5430/ijhe.v2n2p128

18 Wannarka, R., & Ruhl, K. (2008). Seating arrangements that promote positive academic and behavioural outcomes: A review of empirical research. *Support for Learning, 23*(2), 89–93. https://doi.org/10.1111/j.1467-9604.2008.00375.x

Chapter Three

1 Donaldson-James, S. (2012, August 16). *Conjoined twins Abby and Brittany Hensel: 'Normal - whatever that is.'* ABC News. https://abcnews.go.com/Health/conjoined-twins-abby-brittany-hensel-astound-doctors-normalcy/story?id=17021596

2 Sülflow, M., Schäfer, S., & Winter, S. (2019). Selective attention in the news feed: An eye-tracking study on the perception and selection of political news posts on Facebook. *New Media & Society, 21*(1), 168–190. https://doi.org/10.1177/1461444818791520

3 Honeycutt, J. M., & Bryan, S. P. (2011). *Scripts and communication for relationships.* Peter Lang Publishing.

4 Todd, R. M., Talmi, D., Schmitz, T. W., Susskind, J., & Anderson, A. K. (2012, August 15). Psychophysical and neural evidence for emotion-enhanced perceptual vividness. *Journal of Neuroscience, 32*(33): 11201–11212. https://doi.org/10.1523/JNEUROSCI.0155-12.2012

5 MacKinnon, S. L., & Boon, S. D. (2012). Protect the individual or protect the relationship? A dual-focus model of indirect risk exposure, trust, and caution. *Journal of Social and Personal Relationships, 29*(2), 262–283. https://doi.org/10.1177/0265407511431178

6 Hampton, A. J., Fisher Boyd, A. N., & Sprecher, S. (2019). You're like me and I like you: Mediators of the similarity–liking link assessed before and after a getting-acquainted social interac-tion. *Journal of Social and Personal Relationships, 36*(7), 2221–2244. https://doi.org/10.1177/0265407518790411; see also: Sunnafrank, M., & Ramirez, A., Jr. (2004). At first sight: Persistent relational effects of get-acquainted conversations. *Journal of Social and Personal Relationships, 21*(3), 361–379. https://doi.org/10.1177/0265407504042837

7 Nakane, I. (2007). *Silence in intercultural communication: Percep-tions and performance.* John Benjamins Publishing.

8 Samovar, L. A., Porter, R. E., & McDaniel, E. R. (2010). *Communi-cation between cultures* (8th ed.). Wadsworth, Cengage Learning.

9 Remland, M. S., Jones, T. S., Foeman, A., & Rafter Arévalo, D. (2015). *Intercultural communication: A peacebuilding perspective.* Waveland Press.

10 Horan, S. M., & Houser, M. L. (2012). Understanding the com-municative implications of initial impressions: A longitudinal test of predicted outcome value theory. *Communication Education, 61*(3), 234–252. https://doi.org/10.1080/03634523.2012.671950

11 Hargie, O. (2011). *Skilled interpersonal communication: Research, theory, and practice* (5th ed.). Routledge.

12 Sprecher, S., Treger, S., & Wondra, J. D. (2013). Effects of self-disclosure role on liking, closeness, and other impressions in get-acquainted interactions. *Journal of Social and Personal Relationships, 30*(4), 497–514. https://doi.org/10.1177/0265407512459033

13 Knobloch-Westerwick, S., & Meng, J. (2009). Looking the other way: Selective exposure to attitude-consistent and counterat-titudinal political information. *Communication Research, 36*(3), 426–448. https://doi.org/10.1177/0093650209333030

14 Oliveira-Pinto, A.V., Santos, R. M., Coutinho, R. A., Oliveira, L. M., Santos, G. B., . . . Lent, R. (2014). Sexual dimorphism in the human olfactory bulb: Females have more neurons and glial cells than males. *PLoS ONE, 9*(11), Article e111733. https://doi.org/10.1371/journal.pone.0111733

15 Cleveland, J. N., Stockdale, M., & Murphy, K. R. (2000). *Women and men in organizations: Sex and gender issues at work.* Lawrence Erlbaum Associates.

16 Lillington, D. (2014, March 30). Do gays influence property values? *Urban Economics.* https://sites.duke.edu/urbaneconomics/?p=1054

17 Dalton, P., & Fraenkel, N. (2012). Gorillas we have missed: Sus-tained inattentional deafness for dynamic events. *Cognition, 124*(3), 367–372. https://doi.org/10.1016/j.cognition.2012.05.012

18 Simons, D. J., & Chabris, C. F. (1999). Gorillas in our midst: Sustained inattentional blindness for dynamic events. *Perception, 28*(9), 1059–1074. https://doi.org/10.1068/p281059

19 DePauw University. (2007, February 26). *Former Delta Zeta members tell their story to CNN and NBC affiliate* [Press release]. https://www.depauw.edu/news-media/latest-news/details/18984/

20 Stacey, M. (2015, November 20). My sorority dumped me. *Cosmopolitan.* https://www.cosmopolitan.com/college/news/a49556/my-sorority-dumped-me; Dillon, S. (2007, February 25). Sorority evictions raise issue of looks and bias. *The New York Times.* http://www.nytimes.com/2007/02/25/education/25sorority.html?_r=0

21 Rader, D. (2007, February 4). You can find a way to heal. *Parade,* 4-6.

22 Weigel, D. J., Lalasz, C. B., & Weiser, D. A. (2016). Maintaining relationships: The role of implicit relationship theories and partner fit. *Communication Reports, 29*(1), 23–34. https://doi.org/10.1080/08934215.2015.1017653

23 Bodie, G. D., Honeycutt, J. M., & Vickery, A. J. (2013). An analysis of the correspondence between imagined interaction attri-butes and functions. *Human Communication Research, 39*(2), 157–183. https://doi.org/10.1111/hcre.12003

24 Honeycutt, J. M., Vickery, A. J., & Hatcher, L. C. (2015). The daily use of imagined interaction features. *Communication Monographs, 82*(2), 201–223. https://doi.org/10.1080/03637751.2014.953965; see also: Hatzigeorgiadis, A., Zourbanos, N., Galanis, E., & Theodorakis, Y. (2011). Self-talk and sports performance: A meta-analysis. *Perspectives on Psychological Science, 6*(4), 348–356. https://doi.org/10.1177/1745691611413136

25 Veale, D., Kinderman, P., Riley, S., & Lambrou, C. (2003). Self-discrepancy in body dysmorphic disorder. *British Journal of Clinical Psychology, 42*(2), 157–169. https://doi.org/10.1348/014466503321903571

26 O'Neil, J. M. (2008). Summarizing 25 years of research on men's gender role conflict using the gender role conflict

scale: New research paradigms and clinical implications. *The Counseling Psychologist, 36*(3), 358–445. https://doi.org/10.1177/0011000008317057; see also: Kubic, K. N., & Chory, R. M. (2007). Exposure to television makeover programs and perceptions of self. *Communication Research Reports, 24*(4), 283–291. https://doi.org/10.1080/08824090701624155

27 Crawford, W. S., Kacmar, K. M., & Harris, K. J. (2019). Do you see me as I see me? The effects of impression management incongruence of actors and audiences. *Journal of Business and Psychology, 34*(4), 453–469. https://doi.org/10.1007/s10869-018-9549-6

28 Mruk, C. J. (2006). *Self-esteem research, theory, and practice: Toward a positive psychology of self-esteem* (3rd ed.). Springer; see also: Pyszczynski, T., Greenberg, J., Solomon, S. Arndt, J., & Schimel, J. (2004). Why do people need self-esteem? A theoretical and empirical review. *Psychological Bulletin, 130*(3), 435–468. https://doi.org/10.1037/0033-2909.130.3.435

29 Campbell, J. D., & Lavallee, L. F. (1993). Who am I? The role of self-concept confusion in understanding the behavior of people with low self-esteem. In R. F. Baumeister (Ed.), *Self-esteem: The puzzle of low self-regard* (pp. 3–20). Plenum Press. https://doi.org/10.1007/978-1-4684-8956-9_1

30 Buhrmester, D., Furman, W., Wittenberg, M. T., & Reis, H. T. (1988). Five domains of interpersonal competence in peer relationships. *Journal of Personality and Social Psychology, 55*(6), 991–1008. https://doi.org/10.1037/0022-3514.55.6.991

31 Baumeister, R. F., Campbell, J. D., Krueger, J. I., & Vohs, K. D. (2003). Does high self-esteem cause better performance, interpersonal success, happiness, or healthier lifestyles? *Psychological Science in the Public Interest, 4*(1), 1–44. https://doi.org/10.1111/1529-1006.01431

32 Murray, S. L., Rose, P., Bellavia, G., Holmes, J. G., & Kusche, A. G. (2002). When rejection stings: How self-esteem constrains relationship-enhancement processes. *Journal of Personality and Social Psychology, 83*(3), 556–573. https://doi.org/10.1037/0022-3514.83.3.556

33 Bishop, J., & Inderbitzen-Nolan, H.M. (1995). Peer acceptance and friendship: An investigation of their relation to self-esteem. *The Journal of Early Adolescence, 15*(4), 476–489. https://doi.org/10.1177/0272431695015004005

34 Mesmer-Magnus, J., Viswesvaran, C., Deshpande, S., & Joseph, J. (2006). Social desirability: The role of over-claiming, self-esteem, and emotional intelligence. *Psychology Science, 48*(3), 336–356.

35 Baumgardner, A. H., Kaufman, C. M., & Levy, P. E. (1989). Regulating affect interpersonally: When low esteem leads to greater enhancement. *Journal of Personality and Social Psychology, 56*(6), 907–921.

36 Ybarra, O. (1999). Misanthropic person memory when the need to self-enhance is absent. *Personality and Social Psychology Bulletin, 25*(2), 261–269. https://doi.org/10.1177/0146167299025002011

37 Judge, T. A., Erez, A., Bono, J. E., & Thoresen, C. J. (2002). Are measures of self-esteem, neuroticism, locus of control, and generalized self-efficacy indicators of a common core construct? *Journal of Personality and Social Psychology, 83*(3), 693–710. https://doi.org/10.1037/0022-3514.83.3.693

38 Floyd, K. (2002). Human affection exchange: V. Attributes of the highly affectionate. *Communication Quarterly, 50*(2), 135–152. https://doi.org/10.1080/01463370209385653

39 Baumeister, R. F. (2001). Violent pride: Do people turn violent because of self-hate or self-love? *Scientific American, 284*(4), 96–101.

40 Baumeister, R. F., Campbell, J. D., Krueger, J. I., & Vohs, K. D. (2003). Does high self-esteem cause better performance, interpersonal success, happiness, or healthier lifestyles? *Psychological Science in the Public Interest, 4*(1), 1–44. https://doi.org/10.1111/1529-1006.01431

41 Vohs, K. D., & Heatherton, T. F. (2001). Self-esteem and threats to self: Implications for self-construals and interpersonal perceptions. *Journal of Personality and Social Psychology, 81*(6), 1103–1118. https://doi.org/10.1037/0022-3514.81.6.1103

42 DiPaola, B. M., Roloff, M. E., & Peters, K. M. (2010). College students' expectations of conflict intensity: A self-fulfilling prophecy. *Communication Quarterly, 58*(1), 59–76. https://doi.org/10.1080/01463370903532245; see also: Alberts, J. K., Nakayama, T. K., & Martin, J. N. (2007). *Human communication in society*. Pearson.

43 Rosenthal, R., & Jacobson, L. (1992). *Pygmalion in the classroom: Teacher expectation and pupils' intellectual development* (Newly expanded ed.). Crown House.

44 McCroskey, J. C., Booth-Butterfield, S., & Payne, S. K. (1989). The impact of communication apprehension on college student retention and success. *Communication Quarterly, 37*(2), 100–107. https://doi.org/10.1080/01463378909385531

45 McCroskey, J. C. (2009). Communication apprehension: What have we learned in the last four decades. *Human Communication, 12*(2), 157–171.

46 McCroskey, J. C. (1982). *An introduction to rhetorical communication: A Western rhetorical perspective* (4th Ed). Prentice-Hall.

47 Holmstrom, A. J., & Kim, S. Y. (2015). The mediating role of cognitive reattribution and reappraisal in the esteem support process. *Communication Research, 42*(1), 60–86.

48 Goffman, E. (1971). *Relations in public: Microstudies of the public order*. Basic Books.

49 Crawford, W. S., Kacmar, K. M., & Harris, K. J. (2019). Do you see me as I see me? The effects of impression management incongruence of actors and audiences. *Journal of Business and Psychology, 34*(4), 453–469. https://doi.org/10.1007/s10869-018-9549-6

50 Batsch, N. L., & Mittelman, M. S. (2012, September). *World Alzheimer Report 2012: Overcoming the stigma of dementia*. Alzheimer's Disease International. https://www.alz.co.uk/research/WorldAlzheimerReport2012.pdf

51 Hopwood, C. J., Donnellan, M. B., Blonigen, D. M., Krueger, R. F., McGue, M., Iacono, W. G., & Burt, S. A. (2011). Genetic and environmental influences on personality trait stability and growth during the transition to adulthood: A three-wave longitudinal study. *Journal of Personality and Social Psychology, 100*(3), 545–556. https://doi.org/10.1037/a0022409

52 McCrae, R. R., & Terracciano, A. (2005). Universal features of personality traits from the observer's perspective: Data from 50 cultures. *Journal of Personality and Social Psychology, 88*(3), 547–561. https://doi.org/10.1037/0022-3514.88.3.547; see also: McCrae, R. R., & Costa, P. T. (1987). Validation of the five-factor model of personality across instruments and observers. *Journal of Personality and Social Psychology, 52*(1), 81–90. https://doi.org/10.1037/0022-3514.52.1.81

Chapter Four

1 Vangelisti, A. L. (2015). Communication in personal relationships. In M. Mikulincer & P. R. Shaver (Eds.), *APA handbook of personality and social psychology: Vol. 2. Interpersonal relations and group processes* (pp. 371–392). American Psychological Association.

2 Weger, H., Bell, G. C., Minei, E. M., & Robinson, M. C. (2014). The relative effectiveness of active listening in initial interactions. *International Journal of Listening, 28*(1), 13–31. https://doi.org /10.1080/10904018.2013.813234

3 Janusik, L. A. (2010). Listening pedagogy: Where do we go from here? In A. D. Wolvin (Ed.), *Listening and human communication in the 21st century* (pp. 193–224). Blackwell.

4 Burleson, B. R. (2011). A constructivist approach to listening. *International Journal of Listening, 25*(1–2), 27–46. https://doi.org /10.1080/10904018.2011.536470

5 Li, H. Z., Cui, Y., Wang, Z., Leske, I. P., & Aguilera, L. (2010). Backchannel responses and enjoyment of the conversation: The more does not necessarily the better. *International Journal of Psychological Studies, 2*(1), 25–37. https://doi.org /10.5539/ijps.v2n1p25

6 Chłopicki, W. (2017). Communication styles — An overview. *Styles of Communication, 9*(2), 9–25; see also: Brownell, J. (2010). The skills of listening-centered communication. In A. D. Wolvin (Ed.), *Listening and human communication in the 21st century* (pp. 141–157). Blackwell.

7 Weger, H., Bell, G. C., Minei, E. M., & Robinson, M. C. (2014). The relative effectiveness of active listening in initial interactions. *International Journal of Listening, 28*(1), 13–31. https://doi.org /10.1080/10904018.2013.813234

8 Corps, R. E., Gambi, C., & Pickering, M. J. (2018). Coordinating utterances during turn-taking: The role of prediction, response preparation, and articulation. *Discourse Processes, 55*(2), 230–240. https://doi.org/10.1080/0163853X.2017.1330031

9 Villaume, W. A., & Bodie, G. D. (2007). Discovering the listener within us: The impact of trait-like personality variables and communicator styles on preferences for listening style. *International Journal of Listening, 21*(2), 102–123. https://doi.org /10.1080/10904010701302006; see also: Sargent, S. L., & Weaver, J. B. (2003). Listening styles: Sex differences in perceptions of self and others. *International Journal of Listening, 17*(1), 5–18. https://doi.org/10.1080/10904018.2003.10499052

10 Stewart, M. C., & Arnold, C. L. (2018). Defining social listening: Recognizing an emerging dimension of listening. *International Journal of Listening, 32*(2), pp. 85–100. https://doi.org/10.1080 /10904018.2017.1330656; see also: Itzchakov, G., Kluger, A. N., Emanuel-Tor, M., & Gizbar, H. K. (2014). How do you like me to listen to you? *International Journal of Listening, 28*(3), pp. 177–185. https://doi.org/10.1080/10904018.2014.917929; Johnston, M. K., Weaver, J. B., Watson, K. W., & Barker, L. B. (2000). Listening styles: Biological or psychological differences?, *International Journal of Listening, 14*(1), 32–46. https://doi.org/10.1080/10904018 .2000.10499034

11 Stewart, M. C., & Arnold, C. L. (2018). Defining social listening: Recognizing an emerging dimension of listening. *International Journal of Listening, 32*(2), pp. 85–100. https://doi.org/10.1080 /10904018.2017.1330656; see also: Itzchakov, G., Kluger, A. N., Emanuel-Tor, M., & Gizbar, H. K. (2014). How do you like me to listen to you? *International Journal of Listening, 28*(3), pp. 177–185. https://doi.org/10.1080/10904018.2014.917929; Johnston, M. K., Weaver, J. B., Watson, K. W., & Barker, L. B. (2000). Listening styles: Biological or psychological differences?, *International Journal of Listening, 14*(1), 32–46. https://doi.org/10.1080/1090401 8.2000.10499034

12 Myron, W. & Kester, L. (2006). *Intercultural competence: Interpersonal communication across cultures.* (5th ed.). Pearson, Allyn, & Bacon.

13 Dindia, K., & Kennedy, B. L. (2004, November). Communication in everyday life: A descriptive study using mobile electronic data collection. Paper presented at the annual conference of the National Communication Association, Chicago, IL.

14 Brownell, J. (1990). Perceptions of effective listeners: A management study. *Journal of Business Communication, 27*(4), 401–415. https://doi.org/10.1177/002194369002700405

15 Versfeld, N. J., & Dreschler, W. A. (2002). The relationship between the intelligibility of time-compressed speech and speech in noise in young and elderly listeners. *Journal of the Acoustical Society of America, 111*, 401–408. https://doi.org/10.1121 /1.1426376

16 Fadiman, C. (Ed.). (1985). *The Little, Brown book of anecdotes.* Little, Brown.

17 Beebe, S. A., Beebe, S. J., & Ivy, D. K. (2016). *Communication: Principles for a lifetime* (6th ed.). Pearson.

18 Cusen, G. (2018). Interruptions in medical consultations: Issues of power and gender. *Journal of Linguistic and Intercultural Education, 11*(1), 49–66. https://doi.org/10.29302/jolie.2018.11.1.4; see also: Palmer, M. T. (1989). Controlling conversations: Turns, topics, and interpersonal control. *Communication Monographs, 56*(1), 1–18. https://doi.org/10.1080/03637758909390246

19 Spitzberg, B. H. (2000). What is good communication? *Journal of the Association for Communication Administration, 29*(1), 103–119.

20 McComb, K. B., & Jablin, F. M. (1984). Verbal correlates of interviewer empathic listening and employment interview outcomes. *Communication Monographs, 51*(4), 353–371. https:// doi.org/10.1080/03637758409390207

21 King, E., & Sumner, M. (2015). Voice-specific effects in semantic association. *Cognitive Neuroscience, 20*(4), 580; see also: Dubner, S. J. (2016, July 20). What are gender barriers made of? (Episode 254) [Audio podcast episode]. In *Freakonomics.* https://freakonomics. com/podcast/gender-barriers/

22 Delia, J. G. (1972). Dialects and the effect of stereotypes on interpersonal attraction and cognitive processes in impression formation. *Quarterly Journal of Speech, 58*(3), 285–297. https:// doi.org/10.1080/00335637209383125

23 Heaton, H., & Nygaard, L. C. (2011). Charm or harm: Effect of passage content on listener attitudes toward American English accents. *Journal of Language and Social Psychology, 30*(2), 202–211. https://doi.org/10.1177/0261927X10397288

24 Aarts, H., Custers, R., & Veltkamp, M. (2008). Goal priming and the affective-motivational route to nonconscious goal pursuit. *Social Cognition, 26*, 555–577. https://doi.org/10.1521/ soco.2008.26.5.555

25 Shargorodsky, J., Curhan, S. G., Curhan, G. C., & Eavey, R. (2010). Change in prevalence of hearing loss in US adolescents. *Journal of the American Medical Association, 304*(7), 772–778. https://doi.org/10.1001/jama.2010.1124

26 World Health Organization. (2015). *Hearing loss due to recreational exposure to loud sounds: A review.* https://apps.who.int/iris/bitstream/10665/154589/1/9789241508513_eng.pdf

27 Levey, S., Levey, T., & Fligor, B. J. (2011). Noise exposure estimates of urban MP3 player users. *Journal of Speech Language and Hearing Research,* 54(1): 263–277. https://doi.org/10.1044/1092-4388(2010/09-0283)

28 National Health Service. (2018, January 17). *5 ways to prevent hearing loss.* https://www.nhs.uk/live-well/healthy-body/top-10-tips-to-help-protect-your-hearing/

29 Lin, F. R., Ferrucci, L., Metter, E. J., An, Y., Zonderman, A. B., & Resnick, S. M. (2011) Hearing loss and cognition in the Baltimore Longitudinal Study of Aging. *Neuropsychology,* 25(6), 763–770. https://doi.org/10.1037/a0024238; Lin, F. R., Metter, E. J., O'Brien, R. J., Resnick, S. M., Zonderman, A. B., & Ferrucci, L. (2011). Hearing loss and incident dementia. *Archives of Neurology,* 68(2), 214–220. https://doi.org/10.1001/archneurol.2010.362

30 Covey, S. R. (1989). *The 7 habits of highly effective people: Powerful lessons in personal change.* Simon & Schuster.

31 Weger, H., Castle, G. R., & Emmett, M. C. (2010). Active listening in peer interviews: The influence of message paraphrasing on perceptions of listening skill. *International Journal of Listening,* 24(1), 34–49. https://doi.org/10.1080/10904010903466311

32 Warren, J. E., Sauter, D. A., Eisner, F., Wiland, J., Dresner, M. A., Wise, R. J. S., Rosen, S., & Scott, S. K. (2006). Positive emotions preferentially engage an auditory-motor "mirror" system. *Journal of Neuroscience,* 26(50), 13067–13075. https://doi.org/10.1523/JNEUROSCI.3907-06.2006

33 Spunt, R. P. (2013). Mirroring, mentalizing, and the social neuroscience of listening. *International Journal of Listening,* 27(2), 61–72. https://doi.org/10.1080/10904018.2012.756331

34 Janusik, L. (2005). Conversational listening span: A proposed measure of conversational listening. *International Journal of Listening,* 19(1), 12–28. https://doi.org/10.1080/10904018.2005.10499070

35 Hayes, J. (2002). *Interpersonal skills at work* (2nd ed.). Routledge.

36 Geiman, K. L., & Greene, J. O. (2019). Listening and experiences of interpersonal transcendence. *Communication Studies,* 70(1), 114–128. https://doi.org/10.1080/10510974.2018.1492946

37 Guntzviller, L. M., MacGeorge, E. L., & Brinker, D. L. (2017). Dyadic perspectives on advice between friends: Relational influence, advice quality, and conversation satisfaction. *Communication Monographs,* 84(4), 488–509. https://doi.org/10.1080/03637751.2017.1352099; see also: Burleson, B. R. (2003). Emotional support skills. In J. O. Green & B. R. Burleson (Eds.). *Handbook of communication and social interaction skills* (pp. 551–594). Erlbaum.

38 Keaton, S. A., Bodie, G. D., & Keteyian, R. V. (2015). Relational listening goals influence how people report talking about problems. *Communication Quarterly,* 63(4), 480–494. https://doi.org/10.1080/01463373.2015.1062407

39 Jones, S. M. (2011). Supportive listening. *International Journal of Listening,* 25(1–2), 85–103. https://doi.org/10.1080/10904018.2011.536475; see also: Doohan, E. (2007). Listening behaviors of married couples: An exploration of nonverbal presentation to a relational outsider. *International Journal of Listening,* 21(1), 24–41; Burleson, B. R., & Goldsmith, D. J. (1998). How the comforting process works: Alleviating emotional distress through conversationally induced reappraisals. In P. A. Anderson & L. K. Guerrero

(Eds.), *Handbook of communication and emotion: Research, theory, applications, and contexts* (pp. 248–280). Academic Press.

40 Wortman, C. B., & Boerner, K. (2007). Beyond the myths of coping with loss: Prevailing assumptions versus scientific evidence. In H. S. Friedman & R. C. Silver (Eds.), *Foundations of health psychology* (pp. 285–324). Oxford University Press.

Chapter Five

1 Mapes, M. J. (2011). *You can teach a pig to sing.* The Aligned Leader Institute.

2 Kitzinger, C. (2000). How to resist an idiom. *Research on Language and Social Interaction,* 33(2), 121–154. https://doi.org/10.1207/S15327973RLSI3302_1; see also: Burger, J. M. (1986). Increasing compliance by improving the deal: The that's-not-all technique. *Journal of Personal and Social Psychology,* 51(2), 277–283. https://doi.org/10.1037/0022-3514.51.2.277

3 Hosman, L. A., & Siltanen, S. A. (2006). Powerful and powerless language forms: Their consequences for impression formation, attributions of control of self and control of others, cognitive responses, and message memory. *Journal of Language and Social Psychology,* 25(1), 33–46. https://doi.org/10.1177/0261927X05284477

4 Floyd, K., & Morman, M. T. (2006). *Widening the family circle: New research on family communication* (1st ed.). Sage; see also: Floyd, K. (2002). Human affection exchange: V. Attributes of the highly affectionate. *Communication Quarterly,* 50(2), 135–152. https://doi.org/10.1080/01463370209385653

5 Myers, S. A., Byrnes, K. A., Frisby, B. N., & Mansson, D. H. (2011). Adult siblings' use of affectionate communication as a strategic and routine relational maintenance behavior. *Communication Research Reports,* 28(2), 151–158. https://doi.org/10.1080/08824096.2011.565276

6 Huston, T. L., Caughlin, J. P., Houts, R. M., Smith, S. E., & George, L. J. (2001). The connubial crucible: Newlywed years as predictors of marital delight, distress, and divorce. *Journal of Personality and Social Psychology,* 80(2), 237–252. https://doi.org/10.1037/0022-3514.80.2.237

7 Gumperz, J. J., & Levinson, S. C. (1996). *Rethinking linguistic relativity.* New York: Cambridge University Press.

8 Tohidian, I. (2009). Examining linguistic relativity hypothesis as one of the main views on the relationship between language and thought. *Journal of Psycholinguistic Research,* 38, 65–74. https://doi.org/10.1007/s10936-008-9083-1; see also: Whorf, B. L. (1956). The relation of habitual thought and behavior to language (1939). In J. B. Carroll (Ed.), *Language, thought, and reality: Selected writings of Benjamin Lee Whorf* (pp. 134–159). MIT Press.

9 Fong, M. (2000). The crossroads of language and culture. In L. A. Samovar & R. E. Porter (Eds.), *Intercultural communication: A reader* (9th ed., pp. 211–216). Wadsworth.

10 Chen, K. M. (2013, April). The effect of language on economic behavior: Evidence from savings rates, health behaviors, and retirement assets. *American Economic Review,* 103(2), 690–731. https://dx.doi.org/10.1257/aer.103.2.690

11 Koppelman, K. L., & Goodhart, R. L. (2005). *Understanding human differences: Multicultural education for a diverse America.* Allyn & Bacon.

12 Fine, G. A., & Beim, A. (2007). Introduction: Interactionist approaches to collective memory. *Symbolic Interaction,* 30(1), 1–5. https://doi.org/10.1525/si.2007.30.1.1

13 Graham, E. E., Papa, M. J., & Brooks, G. P. (1992). Functions of humor in conversation: Conceptualization and measurement. *Western Journal of Communication, 56*(2), 161–183. https://doi.org/10.1080/10570319209374409

14 Ramírez-Esparza, N., Gosling, S. D., Benet-Martínez, V., Potter, J. P., & Pennebaker, J. W. (2006). Do bilinguals have two personalities? A special case of cultural frame switching. *Journal of Research in Personality, 40*(2), 99–120. https://doi.org/10.1016/j.jrp.2004.09.001

15 Collins, R. (2007, August 14). Braintree fire mishap report released. *The Patriot Ledger.* https://www.patriotledger.com/article/20070814/NEWS/308149746

16 Hayakawa, S. I., & Hayakawa, A. R. (1991). *Language in thought and action.* Harcourt.

17 Steinmetz, K. (2017, May 17). This is what 'bae' means. *Time.* https://time.com/3026192/this-is-what-bae-means/

18 Mazer, J. P., & Hunt, S. K. (2008). "Cool" communication in the classroom: A preliminary examination of student perceptions of instructor use of positive slang. *Qualitative Research Reports in Communication, 9*(1), 20–28. https://doi.org/10.1080/17459430802400316; see also: Mazer, J. P., & Hunt, S. K. (2008). The effects of instructor use of positive and negative slang on student motivation, affective learning, and classroom climate. *Communication Research Reports, 25*(1), 44–55. https://doi.org/10.1080/08824090701831792

19 Kline, S. L., Simunich, B., & Weber, H. (2009). The use of equivocal messages in responding to corporate challenges. *Journal of Applied Communication Research, 37*(1), 40–58. https://doi.org/10.1080/00909880802592623

20 Makin, V. S. (2004). Face management and the role of interpersonal politeness variables in euphemism production and comprehension. *Dissertation Abstracts International, 64*, 4077; see also: McGlone, M. S., & Batchelor, J. A. (2003). Looking out for number one: Euphemism and face. *Journal of Communication, 53*(2), 251–264. https://doi.org/10.1111/j.1460-2466.2003.tb02589.x

21 Crisp, Q. (1985). *Manners from heaven: A divine guide to good behavior.* Harper & Row.

22 Keillor, G. (2005). *A Prairie Home Companion pretty good joke book* (4th ed.). HighBridge Company.

23 Pidd, H. (2009, March 29). New all-white England kit could highlight stains of defeat. *The Guardian.* https://www.theguardian.com/football/2009/mar/29/new-england-kit-white

24 Smith, B. L., Smith, T. D., Taylor, L., & Hobby, M. (2005). Relationship between intelligence and vocabulary. *Perceptual and Motor Skills, 100*(1), 101–108. https://doi.org/10.2466/pms.100.1.101-108

25 Oetzel, J. G., & Ting-Toomey, S. (2003). Face concerns in interpersonal conflict: A cross-cultural empirical test of the face negotiation theory. *Communication Research, 30*(6), 599–624. https://doi.org/10.1177/0093650203257841

26 Vinson, L. R., Johnson, C., & Hackman, M. Z. (1993). Explaining the effects of powerless language use on the evaluative listening process: A theory of implicit prototypes. *International Listening Association Journal, 7*(1), 35–53. https://doi.org/10.1080/10904018.1993.10499113; see also: Jensen, J. D. (2008). Scientific uncertainty in news coverage of cancer research: Effects of hedging on scientists' and journalists' credibility. *Human Communication Research, 34*(3), 347–369. https://doi.org/10.1111/j.1468-2958.2008.00324.x

27 Bradac, J. J., & Mulac, A. (2009). A molecular view of powerful and powerless speech styles: Attributional consequences of specific language features and communicator intentions. *Communication Monographs, 51*(4), 307–319. https://doi.org/10.1080/03637758409390204; see also: Hosman, L. A., Huebner, T. M., & Siltanen, S. A. (2002). The impact of power-of-speech style, argument strength, and need for cognition on impression formation, cognitive responses, and persuasion. *Journal of Language and Social Psychology, 21*(4), 361–379. https://doi.org/10.1177/026192702237954

28 Cassell, J., & Tversky, D. (2005). The language of online intercultural community formation. *Journal of Computer-Mediated Communication, 10*(2), Article JCMC1027. https://doi.org/10.1111/j.1083-6101.2005.tb00239.x

29 Rentscher, K. E., Rohrbaugh, M. J., Shoham, V., & Mehl, M. R. (2013). Asymmetric partner pronoun use and demand–withdraw interaction in couples coping with health problems. *Journal of Family Psychology, 27*(5), 691–701. https://doi.org/10.1037/a0034184

30 Rittenour, C. E., & Kellas, J. K. (2015). Making sense of hurtful mother-in-law messages: Applying attribution theory to the in-law triad. *Communication Quarterly, 63*(1), 62–80. https://doi.org/10.1080/01463373.2014.965837

31 Kubany, E. S., Richard, D. C., Bauer, G. B., & Muraoka, M. Y. (1992). Impact of assertive and accusatory communication of distress and anger: A verbal component analysis. *Aggressive Behavior, 18*(5), 337–347. https://doi.org/10.1002/1098-2337(1992)18:5<337::AID-AB2480180503>3.0.CO;2-K

32 Prochazka, J., Ovcari, M., & Durinik, M. (2020). Sandwich feedback: The empirical evidence of its effectiveness. *Learning and Motivation, 71*, Article 101649. https://doi.org/10.1016/j.lmot.2020.101649; see also: Reddy, S. T., Zegarek, M. H., Fromme, H. B., Ryan, M. S., Schumann, S.-A., & Harris, I. B. (2015). Barriers and facilitators to effective feedback: A qualitative analysis of data from multispecialty resident focus groups. *Journal of Graduate Medical Education, 7*(2), 214–219. https://doi.org/10.4300/JGME-D-14-00461.1; Davies, D., & Jacobs, A. (1985). "Sandwiching" complex interpersonal feedback. *Small Group Behavior, 16*(3), 387–396. https://doi.org/10.1177/0090552685163008

Chapter Six

1 Kraus, M. W., Huang, C., & Keltner, D. (2010). Tactile communication, cooperation, and performance: An ethological study of the NBA. *Emotion, 10*(5): 745–749. https://doi.org/10.1037/a0019382

2 Slam Staff. (2010, February 23). Study: Touching leads to success, or something. *Slam Magazine.* https://www.slamonline.com/archives/study-touching-leads-to-success-or-something/; see also: Abbott, H. (2010, Feb 23). Study: Good players aren't afraid to touch teammates. *ESPN.* https://www.espn.com/blog/truehoop/post/_/id/13761/study-good-players-arent-afraid-to-touch-teammates

3 Kraus, M. W., Huang, C., & Keltner, D. (2010). Tactile communication, cooperation, and performance: An ethological study of the NBA. *Emotion, 10*(5): 745–749. https://doi.org/10.1037/a0019382

4 Hertenstein, M. J., Holmes, R., McCullough, M., & Keltner, D. (2009). The communication of emotion via touch. *Emotion, 9*(4), 566–573. https://doi.org/10.1037/a0016108

5 Burgoon, J. K., & Hoobler, G. D. (2002). Nonverbal signals. In M. L. Knapp & J. A. Daly (Eds.), *Handbook of interpersonal communication* (3rd ed., pp. 240–299). Sage.

6 Watzlawick, P., Bavelas, J. B., & Jackson, D. D. (1967). *Pragmatics of human communication: A study of interactional patterns, pathologies, and paradoxes.* Norton.

7 Andersen, P. A., Guerrero, L. K., & Jones, S. M. (2006). Nonverbal behavior in intimate interactions and intimate relationships. In V. Manusov & M. L. Patterson (Eds.), *The SAGE handbook of nonverbal communication* (pp. 259–278). Sage.

8 Burgoon, J. K., Guerrero, L. K., & Floyd, K. (2016). Nonverbal communication. Routledge; see also: Ray, G. B., & Floyd, K. (2006). Nonverbal expressions of liking and disliking in initial interaction: Encoding and decoding perspectives. *Southern Communication Journal, 71*(1), 45–65. https://doi.org/10.1080/10417940500503506

9 Guéguen, N., & Jacob, C. (2005). The effect of touch on tipping: An evaluation in a French bar. *International Journal of Hospitality Management, 24*(2), 295–299. https://doi.org/10.1016/j.ijhm.2004.06.004

10 Houser, M. L., Horan, S. M., & Furler, L. A. (2008). Dating in the fast lane: How communication predicts speed-dating success. *Journal of Social and Personal Relationships, 25*(5), 749–768. https://doi.org/10.1177/0265407508093787

11 Mazer, J. P. (2013) Associations among teacher communication behaviors, student interest, and engagement: A validity test. *Communication Education, 62*(1), 86–96. https://doi.org/10.1080/03634523.2012.731513

12 Richmond, V. P., & McCroskey, J. C. (2000). The impact on supervisor and subordinate immediacy on relational and organizational outcomes. *Communication Monographs, 67*(1), 85–95. https://doi.org/10.1080/03637750009376496

13 Kraus, M. W., & Mendes, W. B. (2014). Sartorial symbols of social class elicit class-consistent behavioral and physiological responses: A dyadic approach. *Journal of Experimental Psychology: General, 143*(6), 2330–2340. https://doi.org/10.1037/xge0000023

14 Stewart, G. L., Dustin, S. L., Barrick, M. R., & Darnold, T. C. (2008). Exploring the handshake in employment interviews. *Journal of Applied Psychology, 93*(5), 1139–1146. https://doi.org/10.1037/0021-9010.93.5.1139

15 Slepian, M. L., Ferber, S. N., Gold, J. M., & Rutchick, A. M. (2015). The cognitive consequences of formal clothing. *Social Psychological and Personality Science, 6*(6), 661–668. https://doi.org/10.1177%2F1948550615579462; see also: Segrin, C. (1993). The effects of nonverbal behavior on outcomes of compliance gaining attempts. *Communication Studies, 44*(3–4), 169–187. https://doi.org/10.1080/10510979309368393

16 Cappella, J. N. (2014). Controlling the floor in conversation. In A. W. Siegman & S. Feldstein (Eds.), *Multichannel integrations of nonverbal behavior* (pp. 69–98). Psychology Press.

17 Devito, J. (2013). *The interpersonal communication book* (13th ed.). Pearson.

18 Zielke, M. A., Evans, M. J., Dufour, F., Christopher, T. V., Donahue, J. K., Johnson, P., Jennings, E. B., Friedman, B. S.,

Ounekeo, P. L., & Flores, R. (2009, March/April). Serious games for immersive cultural training: Creating a living world. *IEEE Computer Graphics and Applications.* https://personal.utdallas.edu/~maz031000/res/IEEE_Article.pdf

19 Self Magazine Staff. (2004, October). Expressions of love. *Self Magazine,* 106.

20 Goldsmith, B. (2005). *Emotional fitness for couples: 10 minutes a day to a better relationship.* New Harbinger Publications.

21 Poulsen, F. O., Holman, T. B., Busby, D. M., & Carroll, J. S. (2013). Physical attraction, attachment styles, and dating development. *Journal of Social & Personal Relationships, 30*(3), 301–319. https://doi.org/10.1177/0265407512456673

22 Busetta, G., Fiorillo, F., & Visalli, E. (2013). Searching for a job is a beauty contest. MPRA (Munich Personal RePEc Archive) Paper No. 49382, Munich University Library. https://dx.doi.org/10.2139/ssrn.2331921

23 Parrett, M. (2015). Beauty and the feast: Examining the effect of beauty on earnings using restaurant tipping data. *Journal of Economic Psychology, 49,* 34–46. https://doi.org/10.1016/j.joep.2015.04.002

24 Richmond, V. P., McCroskey, J. C., & Hickson, M. L. (2012). *Nonverbal behavior in interpersonal relations* (7th Ed). Allyn & Bacon.

25 Matsumoto, D. (2006). Culture and nonverbal behavior. In V. Manusov & M. L. Patterson (Eds.), *The SAGE handbook of nonverbal communication* (pp. 219–236). Sage.

26 Rancer, A. S., Lin, Y., Durbin, J. M., & Faulkner, E. C. (2010). Nonverbal "verbal" aggression: Its forms and its relation to trait verbal aggressiveness. In T. A. Avtgis & A. S. Rancer (Eds.), *Arguments, aggression, and conflict: New directions in theory and research* (pp. 267–284). Routledge.

27 Ekman, P., Friesen, W. V., & Ellsworth, P. (1972). *Emotion in the human face: Guidelines for research and an integration of findings.* Pergamon.

28 Knapp, M. L., & Hall, J. A. (2010). *Nonverbal communication in human interaction* (7th Ed). Wadsworth/Cengage.

29 Linke, L., Saribay, S. A., & Kleisner, K. (2016). Perceived trustworthiness is associated with position in a corporate hierarchy. *Personality and Individual Differences, 99,* 22–27. https://doi.org/10.1016/j.paid.2016.04.076

30 Ekman, P. (2003). *Emotions revealed.* New York: Times Books.

31 Allyn, B. (2019, September 26). The "OK" hand gesture is now listed as a symbol of hate. *NPR.* https://www.npr.org/2019/09/26/764728163/the-ok-hand-gesture-is-now-listed-as-a-symbol-of-hate

32 Kita, S. (2009). Cross-cultural variation of speech-accompanying gesture: A review. *Language and Cognitive Processes, 24*(2), 145–167. https://doi.org/10.1080/01690960802586188

33 Sanchez-Burks, J., Bartel, C. A., & Blount, S. (2009). Performance in intercultural interactions at work: Cross-cultural differences in response to behavioral mirroring. *Journal of Applied Psychology, 94*(1), 216–223. https://doi.org/10.1037/a0012829

34 Martín-Santana, J. D., Reinares-Lara, E., & Reinares-Lara, P. (2017). How does the radio spokesperson's voice influence credibility? *Communications: The European Journal of Communication Research, 42*(2), 151–172. https://doi.org/10.1515/commun-2017-0015

35 Glenwright, M., Parackel, J. M., Cheung, K. R. J., & Nilsen, E. S. (2014). Intonation influences how children and adults interpret sarcasm. *Journal of Child Language, 41*(2), 472–484. https://doi.org/10.1017/S0305000912000773

36 Zuckerman, M., & Miyake, K. (1993). The attractive voice: What makes it so? *Journal of Nonverbal Behavior, 17*, 119–135. https://doi.org/10.1007/BF01001960

37 Hinkle, L. L. (2001). Perceptions of supervisor nonverbal immediacy, vocalics, and subordinate liking. *Communication Research Reports, 18*(2), 128–136. https://doi.org/10.1080/08824090109384790

38 Zuckerman, M., Hodgins, H. S., & Miyake, K. (1993). Precursors of interpersonal expectations: The vocal and physical attractiveness stereotypes. In P. D. Blanck (Ed.), *Interpersonal expectations: Theory, research, and applications* (pp. 194–217). Cambridge University Press.

39 Davis, M., Markus, K. A., & Walters, S. B. (2006). Judging the credibility of criminal suspect statements: Does mode of presentation matter? *Journal of Nonverbal Behavior, 30,* 181–198. https://doi.org/10.1007/s10919-006-0016-0; see also: Ozuru, Y., & Hirst, W. (2006). Surface features of utterances, credibility judgments, and memory. *Memory & Cognition, 34*(7), 1512–1526. https://doi.org/10.3758/BF03195915

40 Sommer, R. (1969). *Personal space: The behavioral basis of design.* Prentice-Hall.

41 Teven, J. J., & Comadena, M. E. (1996). The effects of office aesthetic quality on students' perceptions of teacher credibility and communicator style. *Communication Research Reports, 13,* 101–108. https://doi.org/10.1080/08824099609362076

42 Schauss, A. G. (1985). The physiological effect of color on the suppression of human aggression: Research on Baker-Miller pink. *International Journal of Biosocial Research, 7,* 55–64.

43 Gaby, J. M., & Zayas, V. (2017). Smelling is telling: Human olfactory cues influence social judgments in semi-realistic interactions. *Chemical Senses, 42*(5), 405–418. https://doi.org/10.1093/chemse/bjx012

44 Kadohisa, M. (2013, October 10). Effects of odor on emotion, with implications. *Frontiers in Systems Neuroscience, 7*(66). https://doi.org/10.3389/fnsys.2013.00066

45 Hall, E. T. (1963). A system for the notation of proxemic behavior. *American Anthropologist, 65*(5), 1003–1026. https://doi.org/10.1525/aa.1963.65.5.02a00020; see also: Hall, E. T. (1959). *The silent language.* Doubleday.

46 Hall, E. T. (1959). *The silent language.* Doubleday.

47 Burgoon, J. K., Buller, D. B., & Woodall, W. G. (1996). *Nonverbal communication: The unspoken dialogue* (2nd ed.). McGraw-Hill.

48 Burgoon, J. K., Guerrero, L. K., & Floyd, K. (2016). *Nonverbal communication.* New York: Routledge.

49 Rocque, R., & Leanza, Y. (2015). A systematic review of patients' experiences in communicating with primary care physicians: Intercultural encounters and a balance between vulnerability and integrity. *PLoS One, 10*(10), Article e0139577. https://doi.org/10.1371/journal.pone.0139577

50 Field, T., Lasko, D., Mundy, P., Henteleff, T., Kabat, S., Talpins, S., & Dowling, M. (1997). Brief report: Autistic children's attentiveness and responsivity improve after touch therapy. *Journal of Autism and Developmental Disorders, 27,* 333–338. https://doi.org/10.1023/A:1025858600220

51 Field, T., Figueiredo, B., Hernandez-Reif, M., Diego, M., Deeds, O., & Ascencio, A. (2008). Massage therapy reduces pain in pregnant women, alleviates prenatal depression in both parents and improves their relationships. *Journal of Bodywork and Movement Therapies, 12*(2), 146–150. https://doi.org/10.1016/j.jbmt.2007.06.003

52 Hertenstein, M. J., Holmes, R., McCullough, M., & Keltner, D. (2009). The communication of emotion via touch. *Emotion, 9*(4), 566–573. https://doi.org/10.1037/a0016108

53 Breuner, C. C., & Levine, D. A. (2017). Adolescent and young adult tattooing, piercing, and scarification. *Pediatrics, 140*(4), Article e20171962. https://doi.org/10.1542/peds.2017-1962

54 Seiter, J. S., & Hatch, S. (2005). Effect of tattoos on perceptions of credibility and attractiveness. *Psychological Reports, 96*(3), 1113–1120. https://doi.org/10.2466%2Fpr0.96.3c.1113-1120

55 Hickson, M. III, Stacks, D. W., & Moore, N. (2004). *Nonverbal communication: Studies and applications* (4th ed.). Roxbury Publishing.

56 Murphy, N. A., Mast, M. S., & Hall, J. A. (2016). Nonverbal self-accuracy: Individual differences in knowing one's own social interaction behavior. *Personality and Individual Differences, 101,* 30–34. https://doi.org/10.1016/j.paid.2016.05.023; see also: Friedman, H. S., & Miller-Herringer, T. (1991). Nonverbal display of emotion in public and in private: Self-monitoring, personality, and expressive cues. *Journal of Personality and Social Psychology, 61*(5), 766–775. https://doi.org/10.1037/0022-3514.61.5.766

57 Burgoon, J. K., Stern, L. A., & Dillman, L. (1995). *Interpersonal adaptation: Dyadic interaction patterns.* Cambridge University Press. https://doi.org/10.1017/CBO9780511720314; see also: Burgoon, J. K., & Dunbar, N. E. (2000). An interactionist perspective on dominance–submission: Interpersonal dominance as a dynamic, situationally contingent social skill. *Communication Monographs, 67*(1), 96–121. https://doi.org/10.1080/03637750009376497

58 Proctor, R. F. II, & Wilcox, J. R. (1993). An exploratory analysis of responses to owned messages in interpersonal communication. *ETC: A Review of General Semantics, 50*(2), 201–220.

59 Davis, M., Markus, K. A., & Walters, S. B. (2006). Judging the credibility of criminal suspect statements: Does mode of presentation matter? *Journal of Nonverbal Behavior, 30,* 181–198. https://doi.org/10.1007/s10919-006-0016-0; see also: Ozuru, Y., & Hirst, W. (2006). Surface features of utterances, credibility judgments, and memory. *Memory & Cognition, 34*(7), 1512–1526. https://doi.org/10.3758/BF03195915

60 Sabatelli, R. M., & Rubin, M. (1986). Nonverbal expressiveness and physical attractiveness as mediators of interpersonal perceptions. *Journal of Nonverbal Behavior, 10,* 120–133. https://doi.org/10.1007/BF01000008

61 Riggio, R. E. (2006). Nonverbal skills and abilities. In V. Manusov & M. L. Patterson (Eds.), *The SAGE handbook of nonverbal communication* (pp. 79–96). Sage; see also: Riggio, R. E., & Feldman, R. S. (2005). *Applications of nonverbal communication.* Erlbaum.

Chapter Seven

1 Young, S. N. (2007, Nov.). How to increase serotonin in the human brain without drugs. *Journal of Psychiatry and Neuroscience, 32*(6), 394–399; see also: Marazziti, D., Akiskal, H. S., Rossi, A.,

& Cassano, G. B. (1999). Alteration of the platelet serotonin transporter in romantic love. *Psychological Medicine, 29*(3), 741–745. https://doi.org/10.1017/S0033291798007946

2 Lorber, M. F., Erlanger, A. C. E., Heyman, R. E., & O'Leary, K. D. (2015). The honeymoon effect: Does it exist and can it be predicted? *Prevention Science, 16,* 550–559. https://doi.org/10.1007/s11121-014-0480-4

3 Gross, J. J., Richards, J. M., & John, O. P. (2006). Emotion regulation in everyday life. In D. K. Snyder, J. A. Simpson, & J. N. Hughes (Eds.). *Emotion regulation in couples and families: Pathways to dysfunction and health* (pp. 13–35). American Psychological Association; see also: Prinz, J. (2005). Are emotions feelings? *Journal of Consciousness Studies, 12*(8–10), 9–25.

4 Rolls, E. T. (2005). *Emotion explained.* Oxford University Press.

5 Maglione-Garves, C. A., Kravitz, L., & Schneider, S. (2005). Cortisol connection: Tips on managing stress and weight. *ACSM's Health and Fitness Journal, 9*(5), 20–23; see also: Berscheid, E., & Regan, P. (2005). *The psychology of interpersonal relationships.* Pearson.

6 Gottman, J. M., Katz, L. F., & Hooven, C. (1997). *Meta-emotion: How families communicate emotionally.* Erlbaum.

7 Albert Ellis Institute. *Rational Emotive Behavior Therapy.* https://albertellis.org/rebt-cbt-therapy/

8 Wang, T. R., & Schrodt, P. (2010). Are emotional intelligence and contagion moderators of the association between students' perceptions of instructors' nonverbal immediacy cues and students' affect? *Communication Reports, 23*(1), 26–38. https://doi.org/10.1080/08934211003598775

9 Negari, G. M., & Rezaabadi, O. T. (2012). Too nervous to write? The relationship between anxiety and EFL writing. *Theory and Practice in Language Studies, 2*(12), 2578–2586. https://doi.org/10.4304/tpls.2.12.2578-2586

10 Goleman, D. (2005). *Emotional intelligence: Why it can matter more than IQ.* Random House.

11 Schutte, N. S., Malouff, J. M., Bobik, C., Coston, T. D., Greeson, C., Jedlicka, C., Rhodes, E., & Wendorf, G. (2001). Emotional intelligence and interpersonal relations. *The Journal of Social Psychology, 141*(4), 523–536. https://doi.org/10.1080/00224540109600569

12 Peña-Sarrionandia, A., Mikolajczak, M., & Gross, J. J. (2015). Integrating emotion regulation and emotional intelligence traditions: A meta-analysis. *Frontiers in Psychology, 6,*(160). https://doi.org/10.3389/fpsyg.2015.00160; see also: Salovey, P., & Grewal, D. (2005). The science of emotional intelligence. *Current Directions in Psychological Science, 14*(6), 281–285. https://doi.org/10.1111/j.0963-7214.2005.00381.x

13 Ciarrochi, J., Chan, A. Y. C., & Caputi, P. (2000). A critical evaluation of the emotional intelligence construct. *Personality and Individual Differences, 28*(3), 539–561. https://doi.org/10.1016/S0191-8869(99)00119-1

14 Greenberg, D. M., Warrier, V., Allison, C., & Baron-Cohen, S. (2018). Testing the Empathizing–Systemizing theory of sex differences and the Extreme Male Brain theory of autism in half a million people. *Proceedings of the National Academy of Sciences, 115*(48), 12152–12157. https://doi.org/10.1073/pnas.1811032115

15 Morris, A. S., Silk, J. S., Steinberg, L., Myers, S. S., & Robinson, L. R. (2007). The role of the family context in the development of emotion regulation. *Social Development, 16*(2), 361–388. https://doi.org/10.1111/j.1467-9507.2007.00389.x

16 Hoge, C. W., Castro, C. A., Messer, S. C., McGurk, D., Cotting, D. I., & Koffman, R. L. (2004). Combat duty in Iraq and Afghanistan, mental health problems, and barriers to care. *New England Journal of Medicine, 351,* 13–22. https://doi.org/10.1056/NEJMoa040603

17 Worrall, H., Schweizer, R., Marks, E., Yuan, L., Lloyd, C., & Ramjan, R. (2018). The effectiveness of support groups: A literature review. *Mental Health and Social Inclusion, 22*(2), 85–93. https://doi.org/10.1108/MHSI-12-2017-0055

18 Yuki, M., Maddux, W. W., & Masuda, T. (2007). Are the windows to the soul the same in the East and West? Cultural differences in using the eyes and mouth as cues to recognize emotions in Japan and the United States. *Journal of Experimental Social Psychology, 43*(2), 303–311. https://doi.org/10.1016/j.jesp.2006.02.004

19 Soto, J. A., Levenson, R. W., & Ebling, R. (2005). Cultures of moderation and expression: Emotional experience, behavior, and physiology in Chinese Americans and Mexican Americans. *Emotion, 5*(2), 154–165. https://doi.org/10.1037/1528-3542.5.2.154

20 Chaplin, T. M. (2015). Gender and emotion expression: A developmental contextual perspective. *Emotion Review, 7*(1), 14–21. https://doi.org/10.1177/1754073914544408

21 Chaplin, T. M. (2015). Gender and emotion expression: A developmental contextual perspective. *Emotion Review, 7*(1), 14–21. https://doi.org/10.1177/1754073914544408

22 Andreano, J. M., & Cahill, L. (2010). Menstrual cycle modulation of medial temporal activity evoked by negative emotion. *NeuroImage, 53*(4), 1286–1293. https://doi.org/10.1016/j.neuroimage.2010.07.011; see also: Altemus, M. (2006). Sex differences in depression and anxiety disorders: Potential biological determinants. *Hormones and Behavior, 50*(4), 534–538. https://doi.org/10.1016/j.yhbeh.2006.06.031

23 Van Wingen, G. A., Ossewaarde, L., Bäckström, T., Hermans, E. J., & Fernández, G. (2011). Gonadal hormone regulation of the emotion circuitry in humans. *Neuroscience, 191,* 38–45. https://doi.org/10.1016/j.neuroscience.2011.04.042

24 Kilpatrick, L. A., Zald, D. H., Pardo, J. V., & Cahill, L. F. (2006). Sex-related differences in amygdala functional connectivity during resting conditions. *NeuroImage, 30*(2), 452-461. https://doi.org/10.1016/j.neuroimage.2005.09.065

25 Scott, C., & Myers, K. K. (2005). The socialization of emotion: Learning emotion management at the fire station. *Journal of Applied Communication Research, 33*(1), 67–92. https://doi.org/10.1080/0090988042000318521; see also: Tracy, S. J. (2005). Locking up emotion: Moving beyond dissonance for understanding emotion labor discomfort. *Communication Monographs, 72*(3), 261–283. https://doi.org/10.1080/03637750500206474

26 Knobloch, L. K., & Carpenter-Theune, K. E. (2004). Topic avoidance in developing romantic relationships: Associations with intimacy and relational uncertainty. *Communication Research, 31*(2), 173–205. https://doi.org/10.1177/0093650203261516

27 Johnson, N. J., & Klee, T. (2007). Passive-aggressive behavior and leadership styles in organizations. *Journal of Leadership & Organizational Studies, 14*(2), 130–142. https://doi.org/10.1177/1071791907308044

28 Wang, Q., Fink, E. L., & Cai, D. A. (2012). The effect of conflict goals on avoidance strategies: What does not communicating communicate? *Human Communication Research, 38*(2), 222–252. https://doi.org/10.1111/j.1468-2958.2011.01421.x

29 Sargent, J. (2002). Topic avoidance: Is this the way to a more satisfying relationship? *Communication Research Reports, 19*(2), 175–182. https://doi.org/10.1080/08824090209384845

30 McCabe, D. (1995). *To teach a dyslexic.* AVKO Dyslexia Research Foundation.

31 Tepfenhart, O. M. (2017). What is emotional withholding? *Vocal Media: Humans.* https://vocal.media/humans/what-is-emotional-withholding

32 Samar, S. M., Walton, K. E., & McDermut, W. (2013). Personality traits predict irrational beliefs. *Journal of Rational-Emotive & Cognitive-Behavior Therapy, 31,* 231–242. https://doi.org/10.1007/s10942-013-0172-1; see also: Samovar, L. A., Porter, R. E., McDaniel, E. R., & Roy, C. S. (2013). *Communication between cultures* (8th ed.). Wadsworth, Cengage Learning.

33 Salovey, P., & Grewal, D. (2005). The science of emotional intelligence. *Current Directions in Psychological Science, 14*(6), 281–285. https://doi.org/10.1111/j.0963-7214.2005.00381.x

34 Andrade, E. B., & Ariely, D. (2009). The enduring impact of transient emotions on decision making. *Organizational Behavior and Human Decision Processes, 109*(1), 1–8. https://doi.org/10.1016/j.obhdp.2009.02.003

35 Lazarus, R. S. (1991). *Emotion and adaptation.* Oxford University Press.

36 Holtgraves, T. M. (2002). *Language as social action: Social psychology and language use.* Erlbaum.

37 Pennebaker, J. W. (1997). *Opening up: The healing power of expressing emotions* (Rev. ed.). Guilford Press; see also: Pennebaker, J. W. (1997). Writing about emotional experiences as a therapeutic process. *Psychological Science, 8*(3), 162–166. https://doi.org/10.1111/j.1467-9280.1997.tb00403.x

38 Rosenberg, M. B. (2015). *Nonviolent communication: A language of life.* (3rd ed.). PuddleDancer Press; see also: Rosenberg, M. (2012). *Living nonviolent communication: Practical tools to connect and communicate skillfully in every situation.* Sounds True; Hargie, O. (2011). *Skilled interpersonal communication: Research, theory, and practice* (5th ed.). Routledge.

39 Yoshimura, S. M., & Berzins, K. (2017). Grateful experiences and expressions: The role of gratitude expressions in the link between gratitude experiences and well-being. *Review of Communication, 17*(2), 106–118. https://doi.org/10.1080/15358593.2017.1293836

40 Smith, E. E. (2014, June 12). Masters of love. *The Atlantic.* https://www.theatlantic.com/health/archive/2014/06/happily-ever-after/372573; see also: Gottman, J. M., & Levenson, R. W. (2002). A two-factor model for predicting when a couple will divorce: Exploratory analyses using 14-year longitudinal data. *Family Process, 41*(1), 83–96. https://doi.org/10.1111/j.1545-5300.2002.40102000083.x

41 Toussaint, L. L., Owen, A. D., & Cheadle, A. (2012). Forgive to live: Forgiveness, health, and longevity. *Journal of Behavioral Medicine, 35,* 375–386. https://doi.org/10.1007/s10865-011-9362-4

42 Witvliet, C. V. O., Worthington, E. L., Root, L. M., Sato, A. F., Ludwig, T. E., & Exline, J. J. (2008). Retributive justice, restorative justice, and forgiveness: An experimental psychophysiology analysis. *Journal of Experimental Social Psychology, 44*(1), 10–25. https://doi.org/10.1016/j.jesp.2007.01.009

43 Merolla, A. J. (2008). Communicating forgiveness in friendships and dating relationships. *Communication Studies, 59*(2), 114–131. https://doi.org/10.1080/10510970802062428

44 Waldron, V. R., & Kelley, D. L. (2005). Forgiving communication as a response to relational transgressions. *Journal of Social and Personal Relationships, 22*(6), 723–742. https://doi.org/10.1177%2F0265407505056445

45 Acevedo B. P., Aron, A., Fisher, H. E., & Brown, L. L. (2012). Neural correlates of long-term intense romantic love. *Social Cognition and Affective Neuroscience, 7*(2), 145–159. https://doi.org/10.1093/scan/nsq092

46 Slater, L. (2006, February). Love: The chemical reaction. *National Geographic, 209*(2), 32–49; see also: Aron, A., Fisher, H., Mashek, D. J., Strong, G., Li, H., & Brown, L. L. (2005). Reward, motivation, and emotion systems associated with early-stage intense romantic love. *Journal of Neurophysiology, 94*(1), 327–337. https://doi.org/10.1152/jn.00838.2004

47 Mohapel, P. (n.d.). *The Quick Emotional Intelligence Self-Assessment.* Retrieved July 1, 2020, from https://benefits.cat.com/content/dam/benefits/eap/EQ-Self-Assessment.pdf

Chapter Eight

1 Episcopal Church. (1979). *The book of common prayer and administration of the sacraments and other rites and ceremonies of the church: Together with the psalter or psalms of David according to the use of the Episcopal Church.* Seabury Press.

2 Richtel, M. (2012, September 28). Till death, or 20 years, do us part. *The New York Times.* https://www.nytimes.com/2012/09/30/fashion/marriage-seen-through-a-contract-lens.html; see also: Romo, R. (2011, October 4). *Mexican legislator proposes 2-year marriage dissolution option.* CNN. https://www.cnn.com/2011/10/03/world/americas/mexico-2-year-marriages/index.html

3 Lodge, H. (2007, June 17). Why emotion keeps you well. *Parade Magazine,* 12.

4 Holt-Lunstad, J., Smith, T. B., & Layton, J. B. (2010). Social relationships and mortality risk: A meta-analytic review. *PLOS Medicine, 7*(7), Article e1000316. https://doi.org/10.1371/journal.pmed.1000316; see also: Trowbridge, L. (2010, August 7). *Study: Lack of friends is like smoking 15 cigs a day health wise.* Digital Journal. http://www.digitaljournal.com/article/295653

5 Christakis, N. A., & Fowler, J. H. (2009). *Connected: The surprising power of our social networks and how they shape our lives.* Little, Brown; see also: Granovetter, M. S. (1973). The strength of weak ties. *American Journal of Sociology, 78*(6), 1360–1380. https://doi.org/10.1086/225469

6 Gil de Zúñiga, H., & Valenzuela, S. (2011). The mediating path to a stronger citizenship: Online and offline networks, weak ties, and civic engagement. *Communication Research, 38*(3), 397–421. https://doi.org/10.1177/0093650210384984

7 Ray, G. B., & Floyd, K. (2006). Nonverbal expressions of liking and disliking in initial interaction: Encoding and decoding perspectives. *Southern Communication Journal, 71*(1), 45–65. https://doi.org/10.1080/10417940500503506

8 Hecht, M. L., Marston, P. J., & Larkey, L. K. (1994). Love ways and relationship quality in heterosexual relationships. *Journal of Social and Personal Relationships, 11*(1), 25–43. https://doi.org/10.1177%2F0265407594111002.

9 Richmond, V. P., McCroskey, J. C., & Hickson, M. L. (2012). *Nonverbal behavior in interpersonal relations* (7th ed.). Allyn & Bacon; see also: Bell, R. A., & Daly, J. A. (1984). The affinity-seeking

function of communication. *Communication Monographs, 51*(2), 91–115. https://doi.org/10.1080/03637758409390188

10 Steuber, K. R., & McLaren, R. M. (2015). Privacy recalibration in personal relationships: Rule usage before and after an incident of privacy turbulence. *Communication Quarterly, 63*(3), 345–364. https://doi.org/10.1080/01463373.2015.1039717; see also: Shimanoff, S. B. (1980). *Communication rules: Theory and research.* Sage.

11 Galvin, K. M., Bylund, C. L., & Brommel, B. J. (2007). *Family communication: Cohesion and change* (7th ed.). Allyn & Bacon.

12 High, A. C., & Solomon, D. H. (2011). Locating computer-mediated social support within online communication environments. In K. B. Wright & L. M. Webb (Eds.), *Computer-mediated communication in personal relationships* (pp. 119–136). Peter Lang; see also: Bleske-Rechek, A., Remiker, M. W., & Baker, J. P. (2009). Similar from the start: Assortment in young adult dating couples and its link to relationship stability over time. *Individual Differences Research, 7*(3), 142–158.

13 Markey, P. M., & Markey, C. N. (2007). Romantic ideals, romantic obtainment, and relationship experiences: The complementarity of interpersonal traits among romantic partners. *Journal of Social and Personal Relationships, 24*(4), 517–533. https://doi.org/10.1177/0265407507079241

14 Amodio, D. M., & Showers, C. J. (2005). 'Similarity breeds liking' revisited: The moderating role of commitment. *Journal of Social and Personal Relationships, 22*(6), 817–836. https://doi.org/10.1177/0265407505058701

15 Sprecher, S. (2014). Effects of actual (manipulated) and perceived similarity on liking in get-acquainted interactions: The role of communication. *Communication Monographs, 81*(1), 4–27. https://doi.org/10.1080/03637751.2013.839884

16 Cropanzano, R., & Mitchell, M. S. (2005). Social exchange theory: An interdisciplinary review. *Journal of Management, 31*(6), 874–900. https://doi.org/10.1177/0149206305279602; see also: Thibaut, J. W., & Kelley, H. H. (1959). *The social psychology of groups.* John Wiley & Sons.

17 Molm, L. D., Peterson, G., & Takahashi, N. (2001). The value of exchange. *Social Forces, 80*(1), 159–184. https://doi.org/10.1353/sof.2001.0081

18 Dibble, J. L., Punyanunt-Carter, N. M., & Drouin, M. (2018). Maintaining relationship alternatives electronically: Positive relationship maintenance in back burner relationships. *Communication Research Reports, 35*(3), 200–209. https://doi.org/10.1080/08824096.2018.1425985

19 Guerrero, L. K., Andersen, P. A., & Afifi, W. A. (2014). *Close encounters: Communication in relationships* (4th ed.). Sage; see also: Stafford, L., & Canary, D. J. (2009). Equity and interdependence as predictors of relational maintenance strategies. *Journal of Family Communication, 6*(4), 227–254. https://doi.org/10.1207/s15327698jfc0604_1

20 Schneider, F. W., Gruman, J. A., & Coutts, L. M. (Eds.). (2012). *Applied social psychology: Understanding and addressing social and practical problems.* Sage.

21 Easley, D., & Kleinberg, J. (2010). *Networks, crowds, and markets: Reasoning about a highly connected world.* Cambridge University Press.

22 Aron, A., Melinat, E., Aron, E. N., Vallone, R. D., & Bator, R. J. (1997). The experimental generation of interpersonal closeness: A procedure and some preliminary findings. *Personality and Social Psychology Bulletin, 23*(4), 363–377. https://doi.org/10.1177/0146167297234003

23 Berger, C. R. (2005). Interpersonal communication: Theoretical perspectives, future prospects. *Journal of Communication, 55*(3), 415–447. https://doi.org/10.1111/j.1460-2466.2005.tb02680.x

24 Berger, C. R., & Calabrese, R. J. (1975). Some explorations in initial interaction and beyond: Toward a developmental theory of interpersonal communication. *Human Communication Research, 1*(2), 99–112. https://doi.org/10.1111/j.1468-2958.1975.tb00258.x

25 Walther, J. B., Kashian, N., Jang, J.-W., Shin, S. Y., Dai, Y., & Koutamanis, M. (2018). The effect of message persistence and disclosure on liking in computer-mediated communication. *Media Psychology, 21*(2), 308–327. https://doi.org/10.1080/15213269.2016.1247718; see also: Altman, I., & Taylor, D. A. (1973). *Social penetration: The development of interpersonal relationships.* Holt, Rinehart, & Winston.

26 Sunnafrank, M. (1988). Predicted outcome value in initial conversations. *Communication Research Reports, 5*(2), 169–172. https://doi.org/10.1080/08824098809359819

27 Cole, T., & Teboul, Jc. B. (2004). Non-zero-sum collaboration, reciprocity, and the preference for similarity: Developing an adaptive model of close relational functioning. *Personal Relationships, 11*(2), 135–160. https://doi.org/10.1111/j.1475-6811.2004.00075.x

28 Seiter, J. S., & Bruschke, J. (2007). Deception and emotion: The effects of motivation, relationship type, and sex on expected feelings of guilt and shame following acts of deception in United States and Chinese samples. *Communication Studies, 58*(1), 1–16. https://doi.org/10.1080/10510970601168624

29 Schmidt, T. O., &. Cornelius, R. R. (1987). Self-disclosure in everyday life. *Journal of Social and Personal Relationships, 4*(3), 365–373. https://doi.org/10.1177/026540758700400307

30 Coffelt, T. A., & Hess, J. A. (2014). Sexual disclosures: Connections to relational satisfaction and closeness. *Journal of Sex & Marital Therapy, 40*(6), 577–591. https://doi.org/10.1080/0092623X.2013.811449

31 Bareket-Bojmel, L., & Shahar, G. (2011). Emotional and interpersonal consequences of self-disclosure in a lived, online interaction. *Journal of Social and Clinical Psychology, 30*(7), 732–759. https://doi.org/10.1521/jscp.2011.30.7.732

32 Knapp, M. L., & Vangelisti, A. L. (2005). *Interpersonal communication and human relationships* (5th ed.). Allyn & Bacon.

33 West, R., & Turner, L. H. (2012). *IPC.* Cengage Learning; see also: Lane, S. D. (2010). *Interpersonal communication: Competence and contexts.* Pearson.

34 Gouran, D. S., Wiethoff, W. E., & Doelger, J. A. (1994). *Mastering communication* (2nd ed.). Allyn & Bacon.

35 Aron, A., Melinat, E., Aron, E. N., Vallone, R. D., & Bator, R. J. (1997). The experimental generation of interpersonal closeness: A procedure and some preliminary findings. *Personality and Social Psychology Bulletin, 23*(4), 363–377. https://doi.org/10.1177/0146167297234003

36 Kellermann, K., Reynolds, R., & Chen, J. B. (1991). Strategies of conversational retreat: When parting is not sweet sorrow. *Communication Monographs, 58*(4), 362–383. https://doi.org/10.1080/03637759109376236

37 Johnson, A. J., Wittenberg, E., Haigh, M., Wigley, S., Becker, J., Brown, K., & Craig, E. (2004). The process of relationship development and deterioration: Turning points in friendships that have terminated. *Communication Quarterly*, 52(1), 54–67. https://doi.org/10.1080/01463370409370178

38 Baxter, L. A., & Scharp, K. M. (2015). Dialectical tensions in relationships. In C. R. Berger & M. E. Roloff (Eds.), *The international encyclopedia of interpersonal communication*. https://doi.org/10.1002/9781118540190.wbeic017; see also: Baxter, L. A., & Braithwaite, D. O. (2010). Relational dialectics theory, applied. In S. W. Smith & S. R. Wilson (Eds.), *New directions in interpersonal communication research* (pp. 48–66). Sage.

39 Sahlstein, E., & Dun, T. (2008). "I wanted time to myself and he wanted to be together all the time": Constructing breakups as managing autonomy-connection. *Qualitative Research Reports in Communication*, 9, 37–45. https://doi.org/10.1080/17459430802400340

40 Morris, D. (1997). *Intimate behaviour: A zoologist's classic study of human intimacy*. Kodansha International.

41 Baxter, L. A., & Scharp, K. M. (2015). Dialectical tensions in relationships. In C. R. Berger & M. E. Roloff (Eds.), *The international encyclopedia of interpersonal communication*. https://doi.org/10.1002/9781118540190.wbeic017; see also: Baxter, L. A., & Montgomery, B. M. (1996). *Relating: Dialogues and dialectics*. Guilford.

42 Pornpitakpan, C. (2003). The effect of personality traits and perceived cultural similarity on attraction. *Journal of International Consumer Marketing*, 15, 5–30. https://doi.org/10.1300/J046v15n03_02; see also: Burleson, B. R., Kunkel, A. W., & Birch, J. D. (1994). Thoughts about talk in romantic relationships: Similarity makes for attraction (and happiness too). *Communication Quarterly*, 42 (summer), 259–273. https://doi.org/10.1080/01463379409369933; Burleson, B. R., Santer, W. and Lucchetti A. E. (1992). Similarity in communication values as a predictor of friendship choices: Studies of friends and best friends. *Southern Communication Journal*, 57, 260–276. https://doi.org/10.1080/10417949209372873

Chapter Nine

1 Akhtar, O. (2013, March 22). The hatred and bitterness behind two of the world's most popular brands. *Fortune*. http://fortune.com/2013/03/22/the-hatred-and-bitterness-behind-two-of-the-worlds-most-popular-brands; see also: Hall, A. (2009, September 21). Adidas and Puma bury the hatchet after 60 years of brothers' feud. *The Telegraph*. https://www.telegraph.co.uk/news/worldnews/europe/germany/6215542/Adidas-and-Puma-bury-the-hatchet-after-60-years-of-brothers-feud.html

2 Gross, M. A., Guerrero, L. K., & Alberts, J. K. (2007). Perceptions of conflict strategies and communication competence in task-oriented dyads. *Journal of Applied Communication Research*, 32(3), 249–270. https://doi.org/10.1080/0090988042000240176

3 Gunlicks-Stoessel, M. L., & Powers, S. I. (2009). Romantic partners' coping strategies and patterns of cortisol reactivity and recovery in response to relationship conflict. *Journal of Social and Clinical Psychology*, 28(5), 630–649. https://doi.org/10.1521/jscp.2009.28.5.630

4 Bach, G. R., & Wyden, P. (1968). *The intimate enemy: How to fight fair in love and marriage*. Avon.

5 Guerrero, L. K., Andersen, P. A., & Afifi, W. A. (2011). *Close encounters: Communication in relationships* (3rd ed.). Sage.

6 Powers, S. I., Pietromonaco, P. R., Gunlicks, M., & Sayer, A. (2006). Dating couples' attachment styles and patterns of cortisol reactivity and recovery in response to a relationship conflict. *Journal of Personality and Social Psychology*, 90(4), 613–628. https://doi.org/10.1037/0022-3514.90.4.613

7 Lucas-Thompson, R. G., Lunkenheimer, E. S., & Dumitrache, A. (2017). Associations between marital conflict and adolescent conflict appraisals, stress physiology, and mental health. *Journal of Clinical Child and Adolescent Psychology*, 46(3), 379–393. https://doi.org/10.1080/15374416.2015.1046179

8 American Institute of Stress. (2020). How can stress affect your body? The latest research shows it can vary. https://www.stress.org/how-does-stress-affect-your-body-the-latest-research-shows-it-can-vary; see also: El-Sheikh, M., Kelly, R. J., Koss, K. J., & Rauer, A. J. (2015). Longitudinal relations between constructive and destructive conflict and couples' sleep. *Journal of Family Psychology*, 29(3), 349–359. https://doi.org/10.1037/fam0000083; El-Sheikh, M., Kelly, R., & Rauer, A. (2013). Quick to berate, slow to sleep: Interpartner psychological conflict, mental health, and sleep. *Health Psychology*, 32(10), 1057–1066. https://doi.org/10.1037/a0031786; McEwen, B., & Sapolsky, R. (2006). Stress and your health. *The Journal of Clinical Endocrinology and Metabolism*, 91(2), p. E2. https://doi.org/10.1210/jcem.91.2.9994

9 Ilies, R., Johnson, M. D., Judge, T. A., & Keeney, J. (2011). A within-individual study of interpersonal conflict as a work stressor: Dispositional and situational moderators. *Journal of Organizational Behavior*, 32(1), 44–64. https://doi.org/10.1002/job.677; see also: Greenhaus, J. H., Allen, T. D., & Spector, P. E. (2006). Health consequences of work-family conflict: The dark side of the work-family interface. In P. L. Perrewé & D. C. Ganster (Eds.), *Research in occupational stress and well being: Vol. 5: Employee health, coping and methodologies* (pp. 61–98). JAI Press. https://doi.org/10.1016/S1479-3555(05)05002-X; Caughlin, J. P., & Vangelisti, A. L. (2006). Conflict in dating and marital relationships. In J. G. Oetzel & S. Ting-Toomey (Eds.), *The Sage handbook of conflict communication: Integrating theory, research, and practice* (pp. 129–158). Sage.

10 Hicks, A. M., & Diamond, L. M. (2011). Don't go to bed angry: Attachment, conflict, and affective and physiological reactivity. *Personal Relationships*, 18(2), 266–284. https://doi.org/10.1111/j.1475-6811.2011.01355.x

11 Vanhee, G., Lemmens, G. M. D., Stas, L., Loeys, T., & Verhofstadt, L. L. (2018). Why are couples fighting? A need frustration perspective on relationship conflict and dissatisfaction. *Journal of Family Therapy*, 40(S1), S4–S23. https://doi.org/10.1111/1467-6427.12126

12 Samter, W., & Cupach, W. R. (1998). Friendly fire: Topical variations in conflict among same- and cross-sex friends. *Communication Studies*, 49(2), 121–138. https://doi.org/10.1080/10510979809368524

13 LEESA. (2020). Coupled up and crowded: Exploring couples' sleep habits and relationship satisfaction. LEESA Sleep Partner Survey. https://www.leesa.com/pages/married-couples-separate-beds

14 Ward, B. (2012, October 9). A separate sleep keeps the peace. *Grand Rapids Press*, B1; see also: BBC News. (2009, September 9).

Bed sharing 'bad for your health.' http://news.bbc.co.uk/2/hi/8245578.stm

15 Gordon, A. M., & Chen, S. (2013). The role of sleep in interpersonal conflict: Do sleepless nights mean worse fights? *Social Psychological and Personality Science, 5*(2), 168–175. https://doi.org/10.1177/1948550613488952

16 Merrill, A. F., & Afifi, T. D. (2017). Couple identity gaps, the management of conflict, and biological and self-reported stress in romantic relationships. *Human Communication Research, 43*(3), 363–396. https://doi.org/10.1111/hcre.12110

17 Luchies, L. B., Wieselquist, J., Rusbult, C. E., Kumashiro, M., Eastwick, P. W., Coolsen, M. K., & Finkel, E. J. (2013). Trust and biased memory of transgressions in romantic relationships. *Journal of Personality and Social Psychology, 104*(4), 673–694. https://doi.org/10.1037/a0031054

18 Thomas, K. W., & Kilmann, R. H. (2020). An overview of the TKI assessment tool. http://www.kilmanndiagnostics.com/overview-thomas-kilmann-conflict-mode-instrument-tki; see also: Kilmann, R. H., & Thomas, K. W. (1977). Developing a forced-choice measure of conflict-handling behavior: The MODE instrument. *Educational and Psychological Measurement, 37*(2), 309–325. https://doi.org/10.1177/001316447703700204

19 Kuster, M., Bernecker, K., Backes, S., Brandstätter, V., Nussbeck, F. W., Bradbury, T. N., Martin, M., Sutter-Stickel, D., & Bodenmann, G. (2015). Avoidance orientation and the escalation of negative communication in intimate relationships. *Journal of Personality and Social Psychology, 109*(2), 262–275. https://doi.org/10.1037/pspi0000025

20 Roloff, M. E., Reznik, R. M., Miller, C. W., & Johnson, K. L. (2015). "I thought we settled this?!" Antecedents and consequences of resolution of an initial episode in a serial argument. *Argumentation and Advocacy, 52*(1), 8–31. https://doi.org/10.1080/00028533.2015.11821858

21 McCornack, S. (2013). *Reflect & relate: An introduction to interpersonal communication* (3rd ed.). Bedford/St. Martin's.

22 Ayenew, E. (2016). Association of conflict resolution style and relationship satisfaction between couples. *The International Journal of Indian Psychology, 3*(2), 166–181. doi: 10.25215/0302.111, dip: 18.01.111/20160302; see also: La Valley, A. G. & Guerrero, L. K. (2012). Perceptions of conflict behavior and relational satisfaction in adult parent-child relationships: A dyadic analysis from an attachment perspective. *Communication Research, 39*(1),48–78. https://doi.org/10.1177/0093650210391655

23 Thomas, K. W., & Kilmann, R. H. (2017). An overview of the Thomas-Kilmann Conflict Mode Instrument. http://www.kilmanndiagnostics.com/overview-thomas-kilmann-conflict-mode-instrument-tki; see also: Womack, D. F. (1988). Assessing the Thomas-Kilmann Conflict Mode Survey. *Management Communication Quarterly. 1*(3), 321–349. https//doi.org/10.1177/0893318988001003004

24 Aloia, L. S. (2018). Verbal aggression in romantic relationships: The influence of family history, destructive beliefs about conflict, and conflict goals. *Communication Quarterly, 66*(3), 308–324. https://doi.org/10.1080/01463373.2017.1381626

25 Taylor, M. (2010). Does locus of control predict young adult conflict strategies with superiors? An examination of control orientation and the organizational communication conflict instrument. *North American Journal of Psychology, 12*(3), 445–458.

26 Bevan, J. L., Tidgewell, K. D., Bagley, K. C., Cusanelli, L., Hartstern, M., Holbeck, D., & Hale, J. L. (2007). Serial argumentation goals and their relationships to perceived resolvability and choice of conflict tactics. *Communication Quarterly, 55*(1), 61–77. https://doi.org/10.1080/01463370600998640

27 Schutz, W. C. (1966). *The interpersonal underworld.* Science & Behavior Books; see also: Schutz, W. C. (1958). *FIRO: A three-dimensional theory of interpersonal behavior.* Rinehart.

28 Sturm, R. E., & Antonakis, J. (2014). Interpersonal power: A review, critique, and research agenda. *Journal of Management, 41*(1), 136–163. https://doi.org/10.1177/0149206314555769

29 Wilmot, W. W., & Hocker, J. L. (2007). *Interpersonal conflict* (7th ed.). McGraw-Hill; see also: Rancer, A. S., & Avtgis, T. A. (2006). *Argumentative and aggressive communication: Theory, research, and application.* Sage; Littlejohn, S. W., & Domenici, K. (2001). *Engaging communication in conflict: Systemic practice.* Sage.

30 Wildermuth, S. M., Vogl-Bauer, S., & Rivera, J. (2006). Practically perfect in every way: Communication strategies of ideal relational partners. *Communication Studies, 57*(3), 239–257. https://doi.org/10.1080/10510970600845891; see also: Sprecher, S., Schmeeckle, M., & Felmlee, D. (2006). The principle of least interest: Inequality in emotional involvement in romantic relationships. *Journal of Family Issues, 27*(9), 1255–1280. https://doi.org/10.1177/0192513X06289215

31 Frost, D. E., & Stahelski, A. J. (2006). The systematic measurement of French and Raven's bases of social power in work groups. *Journal of Applied Social Psychology, 18*(5), 375–389. https://doi.org/10.1111/j.1559-1816.1988.tb00023.x

32 Sprecher, S. (2005). Sex differences in bases of power in dating relationships. In W. Dragon & S. Duck (Eds.), *Understanding research in personal relationships: A text with readings* (pp. 114–121). Sage.

33 Checton, M. G., & Greene, K. (2010). College students' use of compliance-gaining strategies to obtain prescription stimulant medications for illicit use. *Health Education Journal, 70*(3), 260–273. https://doi.org/10.1177/0017896910375879

34 Steiner, C. M. (1981). *The other side of power: How to become powerful without being power-hungry.* Grove.

35 Kellermann, K., & Cole, T. (1994). Classifying compliance gaining messages: Taxonomic disorder and strategic confusion. *Communication Theory, 4*(1), 3–60. https://doi.org/10.1111/j.1468-2885.1994.tb00081.x

36 O'Connell, B. (2012). *Solution-focused therapy* (3rd ed.). Sage.

37 Smith, S., Adam, D., Kirkpatrick, P., & McRobie, G. (2011). Using solution-focused communication to support patients. *Nursing Standards, 25*(52), 42–47. https://pubmed.ncbi.nlm.nih.gov/21941806/

38 Reps, P. (1967). Pillow education in rural Japan. In *Square sun, square moon* (pp. 17–19). Tuttle.

39 Medvene, L., Grosch, K., & Swink, N. (2006). Interpersonal complexity: A cognitive component of person-centered care. *The Gerontologist, 46*(2), 220–226. https://doi.org/10.1093/geront/46.2.220; see also: Joireman, J. (2004). Relationships between attributional complexity and empathy. *Individual Differences Research, 2*(3), 197–202.

40 Wilmot, W. W., & Hocker, J. L. (2007). *Interpersonal conflict* (7th ed.). McGraw-Hill; see also: Raider, E., Coleman, S., & Gerson, J.

(2006). Teaching conflict resolution skills in a workshop. In M. Deutsch, P. T. Coleman, & E. C. Marcus (Eds.), *The handbook of conflict resolution: Theory and practice* (2nd ed., pp. 695–725); Weider-Hatfield, D. (1981). A unit in conflict management communication skills. *Communication Education, 30*(3), 265–273. https://doi.org/10.1080/03634528109378478

Chapter Ten

1 Tsao, G. (2016, February 21). Guest blog post: Growing up Asian American with a disability. *Disability Visibility Project.* https://disabilityvisibilityproject.com/2016/02/21/guest-blog-post-growing-up-asian-american-with-a-disability-by-grace-tsao

2 Tsao, G. (2016, February 21). Guest blog post: Growing up Asian American with a disability. *Disability Visibility Project.* https://disabilityvisibilityproject.com/2016/02/21/guest-blog-post-growing-up-asian-american-with-a-disability-by-grace-tsao

3 Orbe, M. P., & Spellers, R. E. (2004). From the margins to the center: Utilizing co-cultural theory in diverse contexts. In W. B. Gudykunst (Ed.), *Theorizing about intercultural communication* (pp. 173–192). Sage.

4 Clark, J. (2016, October 7). *Life on a submarine: Raunchy, cramped and occasionally smells like sh*t.* Task and Purpose. https://taskandpurpose.com/mandatory-fun/life-submarine-raunchy-cramped-occasionally-smells-like-sht/

5 Penn State (2020). *Guide to American culture and etiquette.* https://harrisburg.psu.edu/international-student-support-services/guide-american-culture-etiquette; see also: Nelson, B. (2019). 10 rude manners that are actually polite in other countries. *Reader's Digest.* https://www.readersdigest.ca/travel/world/rude-manners-polite-countries

6 Durkee, M. I., & Williams, J. L. (2015). Accusations of acting White: Links to Black students' racial identity and mental health. *Journal of Black Psychology, 41*(1), 26–48. https://doi.org/10.1177/0095798413505323

7 Crenshaw, K. (2019). *On intersectionality: The essential writings of Kimberlé Crenshaw.* New Press.

8 Lustig, M. W., & Koester, J. (2012). *Intercultural competence: Interpersonal communication across cultures.* (7th ed.). Pearson; see also: Hall, B. J. (2005). *Among cultures: The challenge of communication.* Harcourt.

9 Okoro, E. (2012). Cross-cultural etiquette and communication in global business: Toward a strategic framework for managing corporate expansion. *International Journal of Business and Management, 7*(16), 130–138. https://doi.org/10.5539/ijbm.v7n16p130

10 Akechi, H., Senju, A., Uibo, H., Kikuchi, Y., Hasegawa, T., & Hietanen, J. K. (2013, March 13). Attention to eye contact in the West and East: Autonomic responses and evaluative ratings. *PLoS One, 8*(3), Article e59312. https://doi.org/10.1371/journal.pone.0059312

11 Ferraro, G. (2008). *Cultural anthropology: An applied perspective* (7th ed.). Wadsworth.

12 Merkin, R. S. (2009). Cross-cultural differences in approach-avoidance communication in South Korea and the US. *Human Communication, 12*(2), 199–213; see also: Merkin, R. S. (2009). Cross-cultural communication patterns: Korean and American communication. *Journal of Intercultural Communication, 20*, 5–15.

13 Iverson, J. M., Capirci, O., Volterra, V., & Goldin-Meadow, S. (2008, Jan 1). Learning to talk in a gesture-rich world: Early communication in Italian vs. American children. *First Language, 28*(2), 164–181. https://doi.org/10.1177/0142723707087736

14 Pflug, J. (2011). Contextuality and computer-mediated communication: A cross cultural comparison. *Computers in Human Behavior, 27*(1), 131–137. https://doi.org/10.1016/j.chb.2009.10.008

15 Governors State. (2015, March 27). *Roberto Garcia—Understanding and managing Latin American culture* [Video]. YouTube. https://www.youtube.com/watch?v=LS5it4HuBXo; see also: Gelbtuch, J. (2012, July 3). *Latin American cultural differences: A survey.* Sounds and Colours. https://soundsandcolours.com/articles/brazil/latin-american-cultural-differences-a-survey-14666

16 Murthy, D. (2011). Twitter: Microphone for the masses? *Media, Culture, and Society, 33*(5), 779–789. https://doi.org/10.1177/0163443711404744

17 Chung, A., & Rimal, R. N. (2016). Social norms: A review. *Review of Communication Research, 4*, 1–28. https://rcommunicationr.org/index.php/rcr/article/view/18; see also: Hofstede, G., Hofstede, G. J., & Minkov, M. (2010). *Cultures and organizations: Software of the mind* (3rd ed.). McGraw-Hill.

18 Hofstede Insights. (2020). *Cultural compass survey.* https://www.hofstede-insights.com/country/the-usa; see also: The Hofstede Centre. (2016). *What about the USA?* https://www.hofstede-insights.com/country/the-usa/. Saenz, M. G., McGregor, T., & Nguyen, M. (2017). A cross-cultural examination of the United States, Argentina, and Mexico using Hofstede's dimensions and the World Values Survey. *Humanities and Social Sciences Review, 7*(20), 227–236.

19 Liu, S. S., Morris, M. W., Talhelm, T., & Yang, Q. (2019). Ingroup vigilance in collectivistic cultures. *PNAS: Proceedings of the National Academy of Sciences of the United States of America, 116*(29), 14538–14546. https://doi.org/10.1073/pnas.1817588116

20 Tili, T. R., & Barker, G. G. (2015). Communication in intercultural marriages: Managing cultural differences and conflicts. *Southern Communication Journal, 80*(3), 189–210. https://doi.org/10.1080/1041794X.2015.1023826

21 Ting-Toomey, S., & Chung, L. C. (2012). *Understanding intercultural communication.* Oxford University Press.

22 Zerfass, A., Verčič, D., & Wiesenberg, M. (2016). Managing CEO communication and positioning: A cross-national study among corporate communication leaders. *Journal of Communication Management, 20*(1), 37–55. https://doi.org/10.1108/JCOM-11-2014-0066; see also: Santilli, V., & Miller, A. N. (2011). The effects of gender and power distance on nonverbal immediacy in symmetrical and asymmetrical power conditions: A cross-cultural study of classrooms and friendships. *Journal of International and Intercultural Communication, 4*(1), 3–22. https://doi.org/10.1080/17513057.2010.533787; Hofstede, G., Hofstede, G. J., & Minkov, M. (2010). *Cultures and organizations: Software of the mind* (3rd ed.). McGraw-Hill.

23 Hofstede Insights. (2020). *Cultural compass survey.* https://www.hofstede-insights.com/country/the-usa; see also: The Hofstede Centre. (2016). *What about the USA?* https://www.hofstede-insights.com/country/the-usa/.

24 Ekberg, J., Eriksson, R., & Friebel, G. (2013). Parental leave—A policy evaluation of the Swedish "Daddy-Month" reform.

Journal of Public Economics, 97, 131–143. https://doi.org/10.1016/j.jpubeco.2012.09.001

25 Hofstede Insights. (2020). *Cultural compass survey.* https://www.hofstede-insights.com/country/the-usa; see also: The Hofstede Centre. (2016). *What about the USA?* https://www.hofstede-insights.com/country/the-usa/.

26 Duranti, G., & Di Prata, O. (2009). *Everything is about time: Does it have the same meaning all over the world?* [Conference session]. PMI® Global Congress 2009—EMEA, Amsterdam, North Holland, The Netherlands; see also: Hall, E. T., & Hall, M. R. (1990). *Understanding cultural differences: Germans, French, and Americans.* Intercultural Press.

27 Beaulieu, M. C. (2004). Intercultural study of personal space: A case study. *Journal of Applied Social Psychology, 34*(4), 794–805. https://doi.org/10.1111/j.1559-1816.2004.tb02571.x

28 Onnela, J.-P., Waber, B. N., Pentland, A., Schnorf, S., & Lazer, D. (2014, July 15). Using sociometers to quantify social interaction patterns. *Scientific Reports, 4,* Article 5604. https://doi.org/10.1038/srep05604

29 Planned Parenthood. (2017). *What's intersex?* https://www.plannedparenthood.org/learn/sexual-orientation-gender/gender-gender-identity/whats-intersex

30 Intersex Society of North America. (2017). *How common is intersex?* https://isna.org/faq/frequency/

31 National Center for Transgender Equality. (2017). *About transgender people.* https://www.transequality.org/about-transgender

32 Lee, E.-J. (2007). Effects of gendered language on gender stereotyping in computer-mediated communication: The moderating role of depersonalization and gender-role orientation. *Human Communication Research, 33*(4), 515–535. https://doi.org/10.1111/j.1468-2958.2007.00310.x; see also: Holmes, J. (1997). Women, language and identity. *Journal of Sociolinguistics, 1*(2). https://doi.org/10.1111/1467-9481.00012

33 Wood, J. T. (2005). *Gendered lives: Communication, gender, and culture* (6th ed.). Wadsworth.

34 Weinberg, F. J., Treviño, L. L., & Cleveland, A. O. (2019). Gendered communication and career outcomes: A construct validation and prediction of hierarchical advancement and non-hierarchical rewards. *Communication Research, 46*(4), 456–502. https://doi.org/10.1177/0093650215590605

35 Keegan, L. C., Togher, L., Murdock, M., & Hendry, E. (2017). Expression of masculine identity in individuals with a traumatic brain injury. *Brain Injury, 31*(12), 1632–1641. https://doi.org/10.1080/02699052.2017.1332389; see also: Murnen, S. K. (2015). A social constructivist approach to understanding the relationship between masculinity and sexual aggression. *Psychology of Men & Masculinities, 16*(4), 370–373. https://doi.org/10.1037/a0039693

36 Woodhill, B. M., & Samuels, C. A. (2004). Desirable and undesirable androgyny: A prescription for the twenty-first century. *Journal of Gender Studies, 13*(1), 15–28. https://doi.org/10.1080/09589236.2004.10599911

37 Hirokawa, K., Yagi, A., & Miyata, Y. (2004). An examination of masculinity-femininity traits and their relationships to communication skills and stress-coping skills. *Social Behavior & Personality: An International Journal, 32*(8), 731–740. https://doi.org/10.2224/sbp.2004.32.8.731

38 Prakash, J., Kotwal, A. S. M., Ryali, V., Srivastava, K., Bhat, P. S., & Shashikumar, R. (2010). Does androgyny have psychoprotective attributes? A cross-sectional community-based study. *Indian Psychiatry Journal, 19*(2), 119–124. https://doi.org/10.4103/0972-6748.90343

39 Norlander, T., Erixon, A., & Archer, T. (2000). Psychological androgyny and creativity: Dynamics of gender-role and personality trait. *Social Behavior & Personality: An International Journal, 28*(5), 423–435. https://doi.org/10.2224/sbp.2000.28.5.423

40 Srivastava, N., & Nair, S. K. (2011). Androgyny and rational emotive behaviour as antecedents of managerial effectiveness. *Vision: The Journal of Business Perspective, 15*(4), 303–314. https://doi.org/10.1177/097226291101500401

41 GLAAD. (2016). *GLAAD media reference guide-lesbian/gay/bisexual glossary of terms.* www.glaad.org/reference/lgbtq

42 Dindia, K. (2006). Men are from North Dakota, women are from South Dakota. In K. Dindia & D. J. Canary (Eds.), *Sex differences and similarities in communication* (2nd ed., pp. 3–18). Erlbaum.

43 Carothers, B. J., & Reis, H. T. (2013). Men and women are from Earth: Examining the latent structure of gender. *Journal of Personality and Social Psychology, 104*(2), 385–407. https://doi.org/10.1037/a0030437

44 Fullwood, C., Orchard, L. J., & Floyd, S. A. (2013). Emoticon convergence in Internet chat rooms. *Social Semiotics, 23*(5), 648–662. https://doi.org/10.1080/10350330.2012.739000

45 Palomares, N. A. (2008). Explaining gender-based language use: Effects of gender identity salience on references to emotion and tentative language in intra- and intergroup contexts. *Human Communication Research, 34*(2), 263–286. https://doi.org/10.1111/j.1468-2958.2008.00321.x; see also: Hall, J. A. (2006). Women's and men's nonverbal communication: Similarities, differences, stereotypes, and origins. In V. Manusov & M. L. Patterson (Eds.), *The Sage handbook of nonverbal communication* (pp. 201–218). Sage. https://doi.org/10.4135/9781412976152.n11

46 Mulac, A. (2006). The gender-linked language effect: Do language differences really make a difference? In K. Dindia & D. J. Canary (Eds.), *Sex differences and similarities in communication* (2nd ed., pp. 211–231). Erlbaum.

47 Horne, R. M., & Johnson, M. D. (2018). Gender role attitudes, relationship efficacy, and self-disclosure in intimate relationships. *The Journal of Social Psychology, 158*(1), 37–50. https://doi.org/10.1080/00224545.2017.1297288

48 Tezer, E., & Demir, A. (2001). Conflict behaviors toward same-sex and opposite-sex peers among male and female late adolescents. *Adolescence, 36*(143), 525–533. https://eric.ed.gov/?id=EJ642640

49 Holt, J. L., & DeVore, C. J. (2005). Culture, gender, organizational role, and styles of conflict resolution: A meta-analysis. *International Journal of Intercultural Relations, 29*(2), 165–196. https://doi.org/10.1016/j.ijintrel.2005.06.002

50 Hancock, A. B., & Rubin, B. A. (2014). Influence of communication partner's gender on language. *Journal of Language and Social Psychology, 34*(1), 46–64. https://doi.org/10.1177/0261927X14533197

51 Schumann, K., & Ross, M. (2010). Why women apologize more than men: Gender differences in thresholds for perceiving offensive behavior. *Psychological Science, 21*(11), 1649–1655. https://doi.org/10.1177/0956797610384150

52 Kay, K., & Shipman, C. (2014, April 14). The confidence gap. *The Atlantic.* https://www.theatlantic.com/magazine/archive /2014/05/the-confidence-gap/359815; see also: Babcock, L., & Laschever, S. (2009). *Women don't ask: The high cost of avoiding negotiation—and positive strategies for change.* Princeton University Press.

53 Burgoon, J. K., & Bacue, A. E. (2003). Nonverbal communication skills. In J. O. Greene & B. R. Burleson (Eds.), *Handbook of communication and social interaction skills* (pp. 179–220). Erlbaum.

54 Vrugt, A., & Luyerink, M. (2000). The contribution of bodily posture to gender stereotypical impressions. *Social Behavior and Personality, 28*(1), 91–103. https://doi.org/10.2224/sbp .2000.28.1.91; see also: Hall, J. A. (2006). Women and men's nonverbal communication: Similarities, differences, stereotypes, and origins. In V. Manusov & M. L. Patterson (Eds.), *The Sage handbook of nonverbal communication* (pp. 201–218). Sage.

55 Tezer, E., & Demir, A. (2001). Conflict behaviors toward same-sex and opposite-sex peers among male and female late adolescents. *Adolescence, 36*(143), 525–533. https://eric.ed .gov/?id=EJ642640

56 Rosip, J. C., & Hall, J. A. (2004). Knowledge of nonverbal cues, gender, and nonverbal decoding accuracy. *Journal of Nonverbal Behavior, 28*(4), 267–286. https://doi.org/10.1007/s10919-004-4159-6; see also: Weisfeld, C. C., & Stack, M. A. (2002). When I look into your eyes: An ethological analysis of gender differences in married couples' nonverbal behaviors. *Psychology, Evolution & Gender, 4*(2), 125–147. https://doi.org/10.1080/1461666031000063656

57 Rosman, K. (2011). Read it and weep, crybabies. *The Wall Street Journal.* https://www.wsj.com/articles/SB1000142405274870392 2804576300903183512350; see also: Peter, M., Vingerhoets, A. J. J. M., & Van Heck, G. L. (2001). Personality, gender, and crying. *European Journal of Personality, 15*(1), 19–28. https://doi .org/10.1002/per.386

58 Major, B., Schmidlin, A. M., & Williams, L. (1990). Gesture patterns in social touch: The impact of setting and age. *Journal of Personality and Social Psychology, 58*(4), 634–643. https://doi .org/10.1037/0022-3514.58.4.634

59 Berenbaum, S. A., & Beltz, A. M. (2016). How early hormones shape gender development. *Current Opinion in Behavioral Sciences, 7,* 53–60. https://doi.org/10.1016/j.cobeha.2015.11.011

60 Mayo Clinic. (2017). *Test ID: ESFT estrogens, estrone (E1) and estradiol (E2), fractionated, serum.* https://www.mayocliniclabs. com/test-catalog/Clinical+and+Interpretive/84230; see also: Mayo Clinic. (2017). *Test ID: TTFB testosterone, total, bioavailable and free, serum.* https://www.mayomedicallaboratories.com /test-catalog/Clinical+and+Interpretive/83686.

61 O'Connor, D. B., Archer, J., & Wu, F. C. W. (2004). Effects of testosterone on mood, aggression, and sexual behavior in young men: A double-blind, placebo-controlled, cross-over study. *The Journal of Clinical Endocrinology & Metabolism, 89*(6), 2837–2845. https://doi.org/10.1210/jc.2003-031354

62 Wu, M., Liang, Y., Wang, Q., Zhao, Y., & Zhou, R. (2016). Emotion dysregulation of women with premenstrual syndrome. *Scientific Reports, 6,* Article 38501. https://doi.org/10.1038/srep38501

63 Ingalhalikar, M., Smith, A., Parker, D., Satterthwaite, T. D., Elliott, M. A., . . . Verma, R. (2014). Sex differences in the structural connectome of the human brain. *PNAS: Proceedings of the National Academy of Sciences of the United States, 111*(2), 823–828. https://doi.org/10.1073/pnas.1316909110

64 Mulac, A. (2006). The gender-linked language effect: Do language differences really make a difference? In K. Dindia & D. J. Canary (Eds.), *Sex differences and similarities in communication* (2nd ed., pp. 211–231). Erlbaum.

65 Fivush, R., Haden, C. A., & Reese, E. (2006). Elaborating on elaborations: Role of maternal reminiscing style in cognitive and socioemotional development. *Child Development, 77*(6), 1568–1588. https://doi.org/10.1111/j.1467-8624.2006.00960.x

66 Advocate.com Editors. (2010, June 2). China launches school for "sissies." *The Advocate.* https://www.advocate.com/news /daily-news/2010/06/02/china-launches-school-sissies

67 Baculinao, E. (2017, January 9). *China tackles 'masculinity crisis,' tries to stop 'effeminate' boys.* NBC News. https://www .nbcnews.com/news/china/china-tackles-masculinity -crisis-tries-stop-effeminate-boys-n703461

68 Diam, L. M. (2006). The intimate same-sex relationships of sexual minorities. In A. L. Vangelisti & D. Perman. (Eds.), *The Cambridge handbook of personal relationships* (pp. 293–312). New York: Cambridge University Press; see also: Peplau, L. A., & Spalding, L. R. (2000). The close relationships of lesbians, gay men, and bisexuals. In C. Hendrick and & S. S. Hendrick (Eds.), *Close relationships: A sourcebook* (pp. 111–123). Thousand Oaks, CA: Sage.

69 Gillig, T. K., & Bighash, L. (2019). Gendered spaces, gendered friendship networks? Exploring the organizing patterns of LGBTQ youth. *International Journal of Communication, 13,* 4895–4916; see also: Boyer, C. R., & Galupo, M. P. (2018). Transgender friendship profiles: Patterns across gender identity and LGBT affiliation. *Gender Issues, 35,* 236–253. https://doi .org/10.1007/s12147-017-9199-4

70 Kurdek, L. A. (2006). Differences between partners from heterosexual, gay, and lesbian cohabiting couples. *Journal of Marriage and Family, 68,* 509–528. https://doi.org/10.1111 /j.1741-3737.2006.00268.x

71 Gottman, J. M., Levenson, R. W., Swanson, C., Swanson, K., Tyson, R., & Yoshimoto, D. (2003). Observing gay, lesbian and heterosexual couples' relationships: Mathematical modeling of conflict interaction. *Journal of Homosexuality, 45*(1), 65–91. https://doi.org/10.1300/J082v45n01_04

72 Metz, M. E., Rosser, B. R. S., & Strapko, N. (1994). Differences in conflict-resolution styles among heterosexual, gay, and lesbian couples. *The Journal of Sex Research, 31*(4), 293–308. https://doi.org/10.1080/00224499409551764

73 Cornell University. (2021). *What does the scholarly research say about the wellbeing of children with gay or lesbian parents?* Cornell University Public Policy Research Portal. https:// whatweknow.inequality.cornell.edu/topics/lgbt-equality/what -does-the-scholarly-research-say-about-the-wellbeing-of -children-with-gay-or-lesbian-parents

74 Gartrell, N., & Bos, H. (2010). US national longitudinal lesbian family study: Psychological adjustment of 17-year-old adolescents. *Pediatrics, 126*(1), 28–36. https://doi.org/10.1542/peds.2009-3153

75 Reczek, C., & Umberson, D. (2016). Greedy spouse, needy parent: The marital dynamics of gay, lesbian, and heterosexual intergenerational caregivers. *Journal of Marriage & Family, 78*(4), 957–974. https://doi.org/10.1111/jomf/12318

76 Keppelman, K. L., & Goodhart, R. L. (2011). *Understanding human differences: Multicultural education for a diverse America.* Allyn & Bacon.

77 Edwards, F., Lee, H., & Esposito, M. (2019). Risk of being killed by police use of force in the United States by age, race–ethnicity, and sex. *Proceedings of the National Academy of Sciences*, 116(34), 16793–16798, https://doi:10.1073/pnas.1821204116

78 Bilefsky, D. (2015, June 11). Women respond to Nobel laureate's 'trouble with girls.' *The New York Times*. https://www.nytimes.com/2015/06/12/world/europe/tim-hunt-nobel-laureate-resigns-sexist-women-female-scientists.html

79 Pica-Smith, C., & Poynton, T. A. (2014). Supporting inter-ethnic and interracial friendships among youth to reduce prejudice and racism in schools: The role of the school counselor. *Professional School Counseling*, 18(1), 82–89. https://doi.org/10.1177/2156759X0001800115; see also: Žeželj, I. L., Ioannou, M., Franc, R., Psaltis, C., & Martinovic, B. (2017). The role of inter-ethnic online friendships in prejudice reduction in post-conflict societies: Evidence from Serbia, Croatia and Cyprus. *Computers in Human Behavior*, 76, 386–395. https://doi.org/10.1016/j.chb.2017.07.041

80 Pew Research Center. (2013, June 13). *A survey of LGBT Americans*. https://www.pewresearch.org/social-trends/2013/06/13/a-survey-of-lgbt-americans/

81 Chen, G. M., & Starosta, W. J. (2000). The development and validation of the Intercultural Sensitivity Scale. *Human Communication*, 3, 1–14; see also: Fritz, W., Mollenberg, A., & Chen, G. M. (2001). Measuring intercultural sensitivity in different cultural contexts. *Intercultural Communication Studies*, XI(2). https://digitalcommons.uri.edu/cgi/viewcontent.cgi?article=1019&context=com_facpubs

Chapter Eleven

1 Wood, M. (2015, Feb 4). Led by Tinder, a surge in mobile dating apps. *The New York Times*. https://www.nytimes.com/2015/02/05/technology/personaltech/led-by-tinder-the-mobile-dating-game-surges.html

2 Strate, L. (2008). Studying media as media: McLuhan and the media ecology approach. *Media Tropes*, 1, 127–142.

3 Sharpsteen, A. (2012, May 6). Unplug yourself. Leave the electronics behind and aim for a healthier lifestyle. *The Grand Rapids Press*, K1.

4 Kluger, J. (2012, August 16). We never talk anymore: The problem with text messaging. *Time*. https://techland.time.com/2012/08/16/we-never-talk-anymore-the-problem-with-text-messaging; see also: Pinchot, J. L., Douglas, D., Paullet, K. L., & Rota, D. R. (2011). Talk to text: Changing communication patterns. *Conference for Information Systems Applied Research Proceedings*, 4, Article n1830. http://proc.conisar.org/2011/pdf/1830.pdf

5 Turkle, S. (2012, February). *Connected, but alone?* [Video]. TED Conferences. https://www.ted.com/talks/sherry_turkle_alone_together; see also: Turkle, S. (2011). The tethered self: Technology reinvents intimacy and solitude. *Continuing Higher Education Review*, 75, 28–31.

6 Turkle, S. (2011). The tethered self: Technology reinvents intimacy and solitude. *Continuing Higher Education Review*, 75, 28–31.

7 Turkle, S. (2012, February). *Connected, but alone?* [Video]. TED Conferences. https://www.ted.com/talks/sherry_turkle_alone_together.

8 Przybylski, A. K., & Weinstein, N. (2013). Can you connect with me now? How the presence of mobile communication technology influences face-to-face conversation quality. *Journal of Social and Personal Relationships*, 30(3), 237–246. https://doi.org/10.1177/0265407512453827

9 Gaudin, S. (2009, August 10). *Study: Facebook use fuels jealousy, hurts relationships*. Computerworld. https://www.computerworld.com/article/2526986/study—facebook-use-fuels-jealousy—hurts-relationships.html

10 Muise, A., Christofides, E., & Desmarais, S. (2009). More information than you ever wanted: Does Facebook bring out the green-eyed monster of jealousy? *CyberPsychology & Behavior*, 12(4), 441–444. https://doi.org/10.1089/cpb.2008.0263

11 Iqbal, M. (2020, October 30). *Tinder revenue and usage statistics (2020)*. Business of Apps. https://www.businessofapps.com/data/tinder-statistics; see also: Dredge, S. (2015, May 7). 42% of people using dating app Tinder already have a partner, claims report. *The Guardian*. https://www.theguardian.com/technology/2015/may/07/dating-app-tinder-married-relationship

12 Dibble, J. L., Punyanunt-Carter, N. M., & Drouin, M. (2018). Maintaining relationship alternatives electronically: Positive relationship maintenance in back burner relationships. *Communication Research Reports*, 35(3), 200–209. https://doi.org/10.1080/08824096.2018.1425985

13 Dibble, J. L., & Drouin, M. (2014, May). Using modern technology to keep in touch with back burners: An investment model analysis. *Computers in Human Behavior*, 34, 96–100. https://doi.org/10.1016/j.chb.2014.01.042

14 Clayton, R. B., Nagurney, A., & Smith, J. R. (2013). Cheating, breakup, and divorce: Is Facebook use to blame? *Cyberpsychology, Behavior, and Social Networking*, 16(10), 717–720. https://doi.org/10.1089/cyber.2012.0424

15 Lenhart, A., & Duggan, M. (2014, February 11). *Couples, the Internet, and social media: How American couples use digital technology to manage life, logistics, and emotional intimacy within their relationships*. Pew Research Center. https://www.pewresearch.org/internet/2014/02/11/couples-the-internet-and-social-media/

16 Bevan, J. L. (2017). Romantic jealousy in face-to-face and technologically-mediated interactions: A communicative interdependence perspective. *Western Journal of Communication*, 81(4), 466–482. https://doi.org/10.1080/10570314.2017.1283048

17 Bevan, J. L. (2017). Romantic jealousy in face-to-face and technologically-mediated interactions: A communicative interdependence perspective. *Western Journal of Communication*, 81(4), 466–482. https://doi.org/10.1080/10570314.2017.1283048; see also: Moyano, N., Sánchez-Fuentes, M., Chiriboga, A., & Flórez-Donado, J. (2017). Factors associated with Facebook jealousy in three Spanish-speaking countries. *Sexual and Relationship Therapy*, 32(3–4), 309–322. https://doi.org/10.1080/14681994.2017.1397946

18 Roberts, J. A., & David, M. E. (2016, January). My life has become a major distraction from my cell phone: Partner phubbing and relationship satisfaction among romantic partners. *Computers in Human Behavior*, 54, 134–141. https://doi.org/10.1016/j.chb.2015.07.058

19 Moeller, S. D. (2010). *The world unplugged: A global media study*. International Center for Media & the Public Agenda (ICMPA), University of Maryland and Salzburg Academy on Media & Global Change. https://theworldunplugged.wordpress.com

20 Liu, M., & Luo, J. (2015). Relationship between peripheral blood dopamine level and Internet addiction disorder in adolescents: A pilot study. *International Journal of Clinical and Experimental Medicine*, 8(6), 9943–9948; see also: Krach, S., Paulus, F. M., Bodden, M., & Kircher, T. (2010). The rewarding nature of social interactions. *Frontiers in Behavioral Neuroscience*, 4, Article 22. https://doi.org/10.3389/fnbeh.2010.00022

21 Stern, J. (2013, May 29). *Cellphone users check phones 150x/day and other Internet fun facts*. ABC News. https://abcnews.go.com/blogs/technology/2013/05/cellphone-users-check-phones-150xday-and-other-internet-fun-facts

22 GlobalWebIndex. (2018). *Flagship report 2018: Social media*. https://www.globalwebindex.com/hubfs/Downloads/Social-H2-2018-report.pdf

23 Limelight Networks. (2019). *The state of online gaming - 2019*. https://www.limelight.com/resources/white-paper/state-of-online-gaming-2019

24 Hunt, M. G., Marx, R., Lipson, C., & Young, J. (2018). No more FOMO: Limiting social media decreases loneliness and depression. *Journal of Social and Clinical Pyschology*, 37(10), 751–768. https://doi.org/10.1521/jscp.2018.37.10.751; see also: Tandoc, E. C., Ferrucci, P., & Duffy, M. (2015). Facebook use, envy, and depression among college students: Is facebooking depressing? *Computers in Human Behavior*, 43, 139–146. https://doi.org/10.1016/j.chb.2014.10.053; Hertlein, K. M., & Hawkins, B. P. (2012). Online gaming issues in offline couple relationships: A primer for marriage and family therapists (MFTs). *The Qualitative Report*, 17(8), 1–48. https://nsuworks.nova.edu/tqr/vol17/iss8/1

25 S. (2008, November 24). WoW-widows and widowers. *World of Warcraft Widows and Orphans Club*. https://wow-widows.blogspot.com/2008/11/wow-widows-and-widowers.html

26 Li, J., Theng, Y.-L., & Foo, S. (2014). Game-based digital interventions for depression therapy: A systematic review and meta-analysis. *Cyberpsychology, Behavior, and Social Networking*, 17(8), 519–527. https://doi.org/10.1089/cyber.2013.0481

27 Kühn, S., Berna, F., Lüdtke, T., Gallinat, J., & Moritz, S. (2018). Fighting depression: Action video game play may reduce rumination and increase subjective and objective cognition in depressed patients. *Frontiers in Psychology*, 9, Article 129. https://doi.org/10.3389/fpsyg.2018.00129

28 Kowert, R., Domahidi, E., & Quandt, T. (2014). The relationship between online video game involvement and gaming-related friendships among emotionally sensitive individuals. *Cyberpsychology, Behavior, and Social Networking*, 17(7), 447–453. https://doi.org/10.1089/cyber.2013.0656

29 Ho, S. S., & McLeod, D. M. (2008). Social-psychological influences on opinion expression in face-to-face and computer-mediated communication. *Communication Research*, 35(2), 190–207. https://doi.org/10.1177/0093650207313159; see also: Suler, J. (2004). The online disinhibition effect. *CyberPsychology & Behavior*, 7(3), 321–326. https://doi.org/10.1089/1094931041291295

30 Panopoulos, A. P., & Sarri, K. (2013). E-mentoring: The adoption process and innovation challenge. *International Journal of Information Management*, 33(1), 217–226. https://doi.org/10.1016/j.ijinfomgt.2012.10.003

31 Bastiaensens, S., Vandebosch, H., Poels, K., Van Cleemput, K., DeSmet, A., & De Bourdeaudhuij, I. (2014). Cyberbullying on social network sites: An experimental study into bystanders' behavioural intentions to help the victim or reinforce the bully. *Computers in Human Behavior*, 31, 259–271. https://doi.org/10.1016/j.chb.2013.10.036

32 Magsamen-Conrad, K., Billotte-Verhoff, C., & Greene, K. (2014). Technology addiction's contribution to mental wellbeing: The positive effect of online social capital. *Computers in Human Behavior*, 40, 23–30. https://doi.org/10.1016/j.chb.2014.07.014

33 Walther, J. B. (1996). Computer-mediated communication: Impersonal, interpersonal, and hyperpersonal interaction. *Communication Research*, 23(1), 3–43. https://doi.org/10.1177/009365096023001001

34 Jiang, L. C., Bazarova, N. N., & Hancock, J. T. (2013). From perception to behavior: Disclosure reciprocity and the intensification of intimacy in computer-mediated communication. *Communication Research*, 40(1), 125–143. https://doi.org/10.1177/0093650211405313

35 Hammick, J. K., & Lee, M. J. (2014). Do shy people feel less communication apprehension online? The effects of virtual reality on the relationship between personality characteristics and communication outcomes. *Computers in Human Behavior*, 33, 302–310. https://doi.org/10.1016/j.chb.2013.01.046; see also: Baker, L. R., & Oswald, D. L. (2010). Shyness and online social networking services. *Journal of Social and Personal Relationships*, 27(7), 873–889. https://doi.org/10.1177/0265407510375261; Brunet, P. M., & Schmidt, L. A. (2007). Is shyness context specific? Relation between shyness and online self-disclosure with and without a live webcam in young adults. *Journal of Research in Personality*, 41(4), 938–945. https://doi.org/10.1016/j.jrp.2006.09.001

36 Vondráčková, P., & Šmahel, D. (2015). Internet addiction. In L. D. Rosen, N. Cheever, & L. M. Carrier (Eds.), *The Wiley handbook of psychology, technology, and society* (pp. 469–485). John Wiley & Sons.

37 Lapidot-Lefler, N., & Barak, A. (2012). Effects of anonymity, invisibility, and lack of eye-contact on toxic online disinhibition. *Computers in Human Behavior*, 28(2), 434–443. https://doi.org/10.1016/j.chb.2011.10.014; see also: Caspi, A., & Gorsky, P. (2006). Online deception: Prevalence, motivation, and emotion. *CyberPsychology & Behavior*, 9(1), 54–59. https://doi.org/10.1089/cpb.2006.9.54

38 American Psychological Association. (2015, August 8). *How common is sexting?* [Press release]. https://www.apa.org/news/press/releases/2015/08/common-sexting

39 Hertlein, K. M., & Ancheta, K. (2014). Advantages and disadvantages of technology in relationships: Findings from an open-ended survey. *The Qualitative Report*, 19(11), Article 2. https://nsuworks.nova.edu/tqr/vol19/iss11/2

40 Drouin, M., & Landgraff, C. (2012). Texting, sexting, and attachment in college students' romantic relationships. *Computers in Human Behavior*, 28(2), 444–449. https://doi.org/10.1016/j.chb.2011.10.015

41 Cyberbullying Research Center. (2015, May 1). *Cyberbullying facts*. https://cyberbullying.org/facts/

42 Shamus, K. J. (2015, July 13). Why shaming your child on YouTube is a terrible idea. *Detroit Free Press*. https://www.freep.com/story/life/2015/07/13/online-child-shaming-videos-discipline/29583005

43 Shamus, K. J. (2015, July 13). Why shaming your child on You-Tube is a terrible idea. *Detroit Free Press*. https://www.freep.com/story/life/2015/07/13/online-child-shaming-videos-discipline/29583005

44 Berman, T., & Deutsch, G. (2010, October 6). *Inside 'Catfish': A tale of twisted cyber-romance*. ABC News. https://abcnews.go.com/2020/catfish-movie-tale-twisted-cyber-romance/story?id=11817470

45 Yahoo Sports. (2013, January 17). *Legend of Manti Te'o's girlfriend: A tall tale everyone wanted to believe*. https://sports.yahoo.com/news/ncaaf—legend-of-manti-te-o-s-girlfriend-a-tall-tale-everyone-wanted-to-believe-052534925.html

46 Wojciechowski, G., Fortuna, M., Miller, T., & Fish, M. (2013, January 16). Story of Manti Te'o girlfriend a hoax. ESPN. https://www.espn.com/college-football/story/_/id/8851033/story-manti-teo-girlfriend-death-apparently-hoax; see also: Curry, C., James, M. S., & Harris, D. (2013, January 16). *Notre Dame: Football star Manti Te'o was 'catfished' in girlfriend hoax*. ABC News. https://abcnews.go.com/US/notre-dame-football-star-manti-teo-dead-girlfriend/story?id=18232374

47 Armour, S. (2011, August 14). Twitter bombing the boss. *Grand Rapids Press*, B4.

48 Italie, L. (2010, July 4). Divorce lies get caught in web. *Grand Rapids Press*, A6.

49 White, C., Vanc, A., & Stafford, G. (2010). Internal communication, information satisfaction, and sense of community: The effect of personal influence. *Journal of Public Relations Research*, 22(1), 65–84. https://doi.org/10.1080/10627260903170985

50 Derks, D., & Bakker, A. B. (2010). The impact of e-mail communication on organizational life. *Cyberpsychology: Journal of Psychosocial Research on Cyberspace*, 4(1), Article 4. https://cyberpsychology.eu/article/view/4233/3277; see also: Rainey, V. P. (2000). The potential for miscommunication using e-mail as a source of communication. *Journal of Integrated Design & Process Science*, 4(4), 21–43.

51 David, A. (2009, March 4). *Catholics are urged to give up texting for lent*. The Sydney Morning Herald. https://www.smh.com.au/technology/catholics-are-urged-to-give-up-texting-for-lent-20090305-8onj.html

52 Sharpsteen, A. (2012, May 6). Unplug yourself. Leave the electronics behind and aim for a healthier lifestyle. *The Grand Rapids Press*, K1.

53 Turkle, S. (2012, February). *Connected, but alone?* [Video]. TED Conferences. https://www.ted.com/talks/sherry_turkle_alone_together

54 Kaufman, S. B. (2013). *Ungifted: Intelligence redefined*. Basic Books; see also: Gregoire, C. (2013, October 3). *How daydreaming can actually make you smarter*. The Huffington Post. https://www.huffpost.com/entry/mind-wandering_n_4024852

55 National Sleep Foundation. (2011, March 7). *Sleep in America poll—Communication technology in the bedroom*. https://www.sleepfoundation.org/professionals/sleep-americar-polls/2011-poll-technology-and-sleep

56 Harvard Health Publishing. (2020, July 7). *Blue light has a dark side*. Harvard Health Medical School. https://www.health.harvard.edu/staying-healthy/blue-light-has-a-dark-side; see also: Stevens, R. G., Brainard, G. C., Blask, D. E., Lockley, S. W., & Motta, M. E. (2013). Adverse health effects of nighttime lighting: Comments on American Medical Association policy statement. *American Journal of Preventive Medicine*, 45(3), 343–346. https://doi.org/10.1016/j.amepre.2013.04.011

57 Colten, H. R., & Altevogt, B. M. (Eds.). (2006). *Sleep disorders and sleep deprivation: An unmet public health problem*. National Academies Press. https://doi.org/10.17226/11617

58 Holding, B. C., Sundelin, T., Lekander, M., & Axelsson, J. (2019). Sleep deprivation and its effects on communication during individual and collaborative tasks. *Scientific Reports*, 9, Article 3131. https://doi.org/10.1038/s41598-019-39271-6

59 Liu, C.-C., & Wissow, L. (2011). How post-call resident doctors perform, feel and are perceived in out-patient clinics. *Medical Education*, 45(7), 669–677. https://doi.org/10.1111/j.1365-2923.2010.03912.x

60 Peterson, S. M. (2016, December 8). *5 ways to sleep more soundly*. Mayo Clinic. https://www.mayoclinic.org/healthy-lifestyle/adult-health/in-depth/five-ways-sleep-soundly/art-20267152; see also: Singh, A., & Suni, E. (2020, November 3). *Technology in the bedroom*. Sleep Foundation. https://www.sleepfoundation.org/bedroom-environment/technology-in-the-bedroom

Chapter Twelve

1 Paul, T., & Charboneau, M. (2015, June 11). MSU softball player: Coaches purposely pitched at head. *The Detroit News*. https://www.detroitnews.com/story/sports/college/michigan-stateuniversity/2015/06/11/police-msu-investigate-softball-coaches/71104834; see also: Paul, T., & Charboneau, M. (2015, August 11). Investigation clears MSU softball coaches of wrongdoing. *The Detroit News*. https://www.detroitnews.com/story/sports/college/michigan-state-university/2015/08/11/investigation-clears-msu-softball-coaches-wrongdoing/31456461

2 The Detroit News Staff. (2015, June 16). Texts reveal animosity between MSU softball coaches, player allegedly hit on purpose. *The Detroit News*. https://www.detroitnews.com/story/sports/college/michigan-state-university/2015/06/15/msu-softball/28793475/

3 Arnett, R. C., Fritze, J. H., & Bell, R. M. (2009). *Communication ethics literacy: Dialogue and difference*. Thousand Oaks, CA: Sage; Pfeiffer, R.S. & Forsberg, R.I. (2005). *Ethics on the job: Cases and strategies*. Belmont, CA: Wadsworth; NCA (1999, November). Ethical statements platform. National Communication Association. http://www.natcom.org/Tertiary.aspx?id=2119

4 Roggensack, K. E., & Sillars, A. (2014). Agreement and understanding about honesty and deception rules in romantic relationships. *Journal of Social and Personal Relationships*, 31(2), 178–199. https://doi.org/10.1177/0265407513489914

5 Colb, S. F. (2015, June 18). *Is there a moral duty to disclose that you're transgender to a potential partner?* Justia Verdict. https://verdict.justia.com/2015/06/18/is-there-a-moral-duty-to-disclose-that-youre-transgender-to-a-potential-partner; see also: Epstein, R. (2003). Please don't say anything: Partner notification and the patient-physician relationship, Commentary 1. *Virtual Mentor*, 5(11), 366–368. https://doi.org/10.1001/virtualmentor.2003.5.11.ccas2-0311

6 Sohn, A. (2005, October 27). Before we go any further. *New York Magazine*. http://nymag.com/nymetro/nightlife/sex/columns/mating/14917/

7 Wickline, M., & Sellnow, T. L. (2013). Expanding the concept of significant choice through consideration of health literacy during crises. *Health Promotion Practice, 14*(6), 809–815. https://doi.org/10.1177/1524839913498752; see also: Arnett, R. C. (1988). A choice-making ethic for organizational communication: The work of Ian I. Mitroff. *Journal of Business Ethics, 7*(3), 151–161. https://doi.org/10.1007/BF00381862

8 Guerrero, L. K., & Bachman, G. F. (2010). Forgiveness and forgiving communication in dating relationships: An expectancy-investment explanation. *Journal of Social and Personal Relationships, 27*(6), 801–823. https://doi.org/10.1177/0265407510373258; see also: Merolla, A. J. (2008). Communicating forgiveness in friendships and dating relationships. *Communication Studies, 59*(2), 114–131. https://doi.org/10.1080/10510970802062428; Bachman, G. F., & Guerrero, L. K. (2006). Forgiveness, apology, and communicative responses to hurtful events. *Communication Reports, 19*(1), 45–56. https://doi.org/10.1080/08934210600586357

9 Govorun, O., Fuegen, K., & Payne, B. K. (2006). Stereotypes focus defensive projection. *Personality and Social Psychology Bulletin, 32*(6), 781–793. https://doi.org/10.1177/0146167205285556; see also: Schimel, J., Greenberg, J., & Martens, A. (2003). Evidence that projection of a feared trait can serve a defensive function. *Personality and Social Psychology Bulletin, 29*(8), 969–979. https://doi.org/10.1177/0146167203252969

10 Tyler, J. M., Feldman, R. S., & Reichert, A. (2006). The price of deceptive behavior: Disliking and lying to people who lie to us. *Journal of Experimental Social Psychology, 42*(1), 69–77. https://doi.org/10.1016/j.jesp.2005.02.003; see also: Wheeless, L. R. (1978). A follow-up study of the relationships among trust, disclosure, and interpersonal solidarity. *Human Communication Research, 4*(2), 143–157. https://doi.org/10.1111/j.1468-2958.1978.tb00604.x

11 Roland, C. E., & Foxx, R. M. (2003). Self-respect: A neglected concept. *Philosophical Psychology, 16*(2), 247–288. https://doi.org/10.1080/09515080307764

12 Costa, A. C., Roe, R. A., & Taillieu, T. (2001). Trust within teams: The relation with performance effectiveness. *European Journal of Work and Organizational Psychology, 10*(3), 225–244. https://doi.org/10.1080/13594320143000654

13 Feldblum, C. R., & Lipnic, V. A. (2016, June). *Select Task Force on the Study of Harassment in the Workplace: Report of co-chairs Chai R. Feldblum and Victoria A. Lipnic.* U.S. Equal Employment Opportunity Commission. https://www.eeoc.gov/eeoc/task_force/harassment/report.cfm

14 Farrar, D. (2014, February 14). Report on Richie Incognito-Jonathan Martin saga: History of "persistent bullying, harassment and ridicule" within Dolphins. *Sports Illustrated.* https://www.si.com/nfl/2014/02/14/richie-incognito-jonathan-martin-report

15 People Staff. (2003, April 28). Snow job: How did David Hempleman-Adams get away with his latest trip? *People, 59*(16), 103. https://people.com/archive/snow-job-vol-59-no-16/

16 Buller, D. B., & Burgoon, J. K. (1996). Interpersonal deception theory. *Communication Theory, 6*(3), 203–242. https://doi.org/10.1111/j.1468-2885.1996.tb00127.x

17 Feldman, R. (2009). *The liar in your life: The way to truthful relationships.* Hachette.

18 Ekman, P. (2001). *Telling lies: Clues to deceit in the marketplace, politics, and marriage* (3rd ed.). W. W. Norton & Company.

19 Horan, S. M., & Booth-Butterfield, M. (2013). Understanding the routine expression of deceptive affection in romantic relationships. *Communication Quarterly, 61*(2), 195–216. https://doi.org/10.1080/01463373.2012.751435

20 Day, A. M., James, I. A., Meyer, T. D., & Lee, D. R. (2011). Do people with dementia find lies and deception in dementia care acceptable? *Aging & Mental Health, 15*(7), 822–829. https://doi.org/10.1080/13607863.2011.569489; see also: Schermer, M. (2007). Nothing but the truth? On truth and deception in dementia care. *Bioethics, 21*(1), 13–22. https://doi.org/10.1111/j.1467-8519.2007.00519.x

21 Carton, S. T., & Horan, S. M. (2014). A diary examination of romantic and sexual partners withholding affectionate messages. *Journal of Social and Personal Relationships, 31*(2), 221–246. https://doi.org/10.1177/0265407513490587; see also: Floyd, K. (2006). *Communicating affection: Interpersonal behavior and social context.* Cambridge University Press. https://doi.org/10.1017/CBO9780511606649

22 Porter, S., & ten Brinke, L. (2010). The truth about lies: What works in detecting high-stakes deception? *Legal and Criminological Psychology, 15*(1), 57–75. https://doi.org/10.1348/135532509X433151

23 ten Brinke, L., & Porter, S. (2012). Cry me a river: Identifying the behavioral consequences of extremely high-stakes interpersonal deception. *Law and Human Behavior, 36*(6), 469–477. https://doi.org/10.1037/h0093929

24 Zimmerman, L. (2016). Deception detection. *Monitor on Psychology, 47*(3), 46. https://www.apa.org/monitor/2016/03/deception; Burgoon, J. K., & Qin, T. (2006). The dynamic nature of deceptive verbal communication. *Journal of Language and Social Psychology, 25*(1), 76–96. https://doi.org/10.1177/0261927X05284482

25 Levine, T. R. (2018). Scientific evidence and cue theories in deception research: Reconciling findings from meta-analyses and primary experiments. *International Journal of Communication, 12*, 2461–2479; see also: Levine, T. R., Serota, K. B., Shulman, H., Clare, D. D., . . . Lee, J. H. (2011). Sender demeanor: Individual differences in sender believability have a powerful impact on deception detection judgments. *Human Communication Research, 37*(3), 377–403. https://doi.org/10.1111/j.1468-2958.2011.01407.x; Burgoon, J. K., & Qin, T. (2006). The dynamic nature of deceptive verbal communication. *Journal of Language and Social Psychology, 25*(1), 76–96. https://doi.org/10.1177/0261927X05284482

26 Bond, C. F., Jr., & DePaulo, B. M. (2006). Accuracy of deception judgments. *Personality and Social Psychology Review, 10*(3), 214–234. https://doi.org/10.1207/s15327957pspr1003_2

27 Dunbar, N. E., Jensen, M. L., Burgoon, J. K., Kelley, K. M., Harrison, K. J., . . . Bernard, D. R. (2015). Effects of veracity, modality, and sanctioning on credibility assessment during mediated and unmediated interviews. *Communication Research, 42*(5), 649–674. https://doi.org/10.1177/0093650213480175

28 Dunbar, N. E., Bernhold, Q. S., Jensen, M. L., & Burgoon, J. K. (2019). The anatomy of a confession: An examination of verbal and nonverbal cues surrounding a confession. *Western Journal of Communication, 83*(4), 423–443. https://doi.org/10.1080/10570314.2018.1539760

glossary

abdicratic The power orientation characterized by a tendency to let others take charge or make decisions. *See also* autocratic *and* democratic.

ableism Negative beliefs and feelings toward people with disabilities. *See also* prejudice.

abstract language Language that refers to intangible concepts and ideas; generally more open to interpretation than concrete language. *See also* concrete language.

accent A distinct way of speaking a language. You may have an accent if you are speaking a language you were not taught at birth. *See also* dialect.

accommodating A conflict approach that prioritizes maintaining harmony at all costs. *See also* avoiding, collaborating, competing, *and* compromising.

acculturation The process of learning about and adopting the norms and values of a new or different culture. *See also* enculturation.

accusation A statement or question that implies that someone has done something bad or failed to do something important.

active listening Listening with a lot of mental focus and engagement. *See also* passive listening.

adaptors Nonverbal behaviors which satisfy a physical or emotional need or help you manage physical and emotional sensations better.

affectionate language (AL) The language you use to express the positive feelings you have toward someone.

ageism Negative beliefs and feelings toward people based on their age. *See also* prejudice.

androgynous expression A gender presentation that mixes masculine and feminine interests, behaviors, and communication styles. *See also* feminine expression *and* masculine expression.

asexual A sexual orientation characterized by an enduring lack of sexual attraction to others and/or a disinterest in sex. *See also* sexual orientation.

asynchronous communication Sending and receiving messages back and forth with a delay in feedback. *See also* synchronous communication.

attending The second stage of the listening process, in which you focus your attention on a particular message or conversation.

attraction The feeling of being drawn to someone; it's what you find appealing about a person. *See also* short-term attraction *and* long-term attraction.

attribution A reason you create to explain someone's communication behavior. *See also* perception.

autocratic The power orientation characterized by a tendency to take charge and make decisions. *See also* abdicratic *and* democratic.

avoidance The act of evading a person, interaction, or conversational topic.

avoiding A conflict approach that steers clear of all overt conflict. *See also* accommodating, collaborating, competing, *and* compromising.

back-channel cues Verbal and nonverbal listening responses. These cues can demonstrate that you are actively listening (positive back-channel cues) or that you are passively listening (negative back-channel cues). *See also* verbal back-channel cues *and* nonverbal back-channel cues.

beltlining The act of taking something a relational partner has disclosed to you in confidence and using it against this person in a future conversation. *See also* past-digging *and* gunny-sacking.

benefit-of-the-doubt message A statement that conveys that you believe a person's intentions or behaviors are or were good, understandable, or innocent.

benevolent deception Misleading or dishonest communication behavior meant to help the receiver.

biological sex A biological distinction determined at birth and characterized by genetics and physical attributes. *See also* intersex.

bisexual A sexual orientation characterized by attraction to individuals of both sexes. *See also* sexual orientation.

blended emotions Two or more emotions that you feel simultaneously, such as excitement and anxiousness.

brainstorming The process of generating as many ideas as possible without initial critiques.

catfishing The act of pretending to be someone you're not online, usually for monetary gain or romantic attention.

catharsis The release of negative emotions such as stress, fear, or guilt as a result of divulging personal struggles and secrets.

channel The medium through which a message passes from sender to receiver. *See also* lean channel *and* rich channel.

chronic sleep deprivation (CSD) A cumulative reduction in the length and quality of sleep.

cisgender A gender identity whereby a person's gender and biological sex match. *See also* gender identity, nonbinary, *and* transgender.

cisgenderism Negative beliefs and feelings toward people who do not identify with the biological sex they were given at birth. *See also* prejudice.

civility The level of politeness and courtesy you extend to a conversational partner.

classism Negative beliefs and feelings toward people of a different socioeconomic background. *See also* prejudice.

close-mindedness When you are unwilling to appreciate or consider another person's thoughts, feelings, or needs.

co-culture A smaller culture within a larger culture. Also called *subculture*. *See also* culture.

code-switching The effort to assimilate into a different culture while maintaining roots in your own culture. This often occurs when members of one culture change their speech patterns, dress, and other behaviors to temporarily fit in with an another culture.

cognitive valence theory The idea that a relationship is influenced by how relational partners perceive each other's nonverbal behaviors.

collaborating A conflict approach that prioritizes finding an outcome that is ideal for everyone. *See also* accommodating, avoiding, competing, *and* compromising.

collectivistic culture A cultural orientation characterized by an emphasis on interdependence and teamwork. *See also* individualistic culture.

communication accommodation theory (CAT) The idea that a relational partner may perceive your communication as effective and appropriate when you alter your communication to reflect your partner's communication style and emotional state.

communication apprehension (CA) The anxiety you feel in a social situation.

comparison level of alternatives The idea that you compare the costs and rewards of an existing relationship with those of a potential relationship; a cognitive assessment that may lead you to believe that an alternative relationship has more to offer than your current relationship.

competing A conflict approach where you prioritize getting what you want above all else; you must "win" at the expense of others. *See also* accommodating, avoiding, collaborating, *and* compromising.

compliance-gaining strategy A communication tactic that you use to get a relational partner to do what you want. *See also* power play.

compromising A conflict approach in which you make some concessions that are less than ideal but acceptable to everyone. *See also* accommodating, avoiding, competing, *and* collaborating.

concrete language Language that refers to things in the physical world that are easily identifiable or measurable using one or more of the five senses—what you can see, hear, smell, taste, and touch. *See also* abstract language.

confirmation bias When your first impressions cause you to focus your perception on communication behaviors that confirm what you've perceived in the past.

conflict ritual A reoccurring pattern of communication that sparks and inflames conflict.

conflict spiral A situation that occurs when relational partners address conflict in ways that are increasingly hostile and mean-spirited. *See also* de-escalation.

conflicting emotions Contradictory emotions that you feel at the same time, such as sadness and happiness.

congruence The degree to which two or more people share similar perceptions, expectations, or opinions about a communication experience. *See also* incongruence.

connotation The subjective or personal meaning attached to a word. *See also* denotation.

constructive conflict Conflict that results in positive relational outcomes. *See also* deconstructive conflict.

context The environment or setting in which communication takes place, including the people involved.

conversational turn-taking The behaviors you use to alternate between being a speaker and a listener. *See also* turn-denying signals, turn-requesting signals, *and* turn-yielding signals.

convoluted language Complex words or phrases that are rarely used in everyday life.

covert conflict Conflict that relational partners mask or do not acknowledge directly or openly. *See also* overt conflict.

cultural idiom A word or phrase whose meaning is unique to people who live in a certain geographic region or society. Also called *colloquialism*. *See also* interpersonal idiom.

culture The shared language, beliefs, interests, values, and customs of an interpersonal system or society.

cyberbullying The act of repeatedly posting disparaging remarks or photos about another person online. It may include taunts, negative comparisons, put-downs, gossip, and threats. *See also* cyberstalking.

cyberstalking The act of ongoing surveillance paired with the malicious use of technology. It can include identity theft, threats, coercion, and slander. *See also* cyberbullying.

dating information Information that specifies when something took place or will take place.

debilitative emotion An emotion that interferes with your ability to communicate and produces negative relational outcomes. *See also* facilitative emotion.

deception Communication behavior that is meant to deliberately mislead another person. Deception includes any communication behavior that is not completely honest or forthcoming. *See also* high-stakes deception *and* low-stakes deception.

deceptive affection (DA) Communication that does not express your true feelings.

decoding The mental process of interpreting or attaching meaning to a message. *See also* encoding.

deconstructive conflict Conflict that damages or hurts a relationship. *See also* constructive conflict.

de-escalation Using your communication to power down or decrease the intensity and scope of a conflict. *See also* conflict spiral.

defensive listening Listening for the purpose of winning an argument or proving that your conversational partner is wrong.

democratic The power orientation characterized by a fluctuating need for power; between abdicratic and autocratic. *See also* abdicratic *and* autocratic.

denotation The literal or dictionary meaning assigned to a word. *See also* connotation.

dialect A distinct way of speaking your first language. Dialects often indicate the class or region in which a person has grown up. *See also* accent.

dialectical tension The strain created between relational partners when their needs or motivations clash.

dichotomous thinking A way of thinking in which you see things as strictly one way or another; something is either good or bad, right or wrong.

digital infidelity The act of secretly exchanging sexual, romantic, or flirtatious messages online with someone who is not your current romantic partner.

direct language Language that communicates a message in a very straightforward and obvious way. *See also* indirect language.

discrimination The act of treating a person in a hurtful or unfair manner because of prejudice. *See also* prejudice.

disinhibition effect The tendency to express yourself more candidly and less guardedly when using asynchronous channels.

displacement The act of lashing out at someone who is not the cause of your negative emotions.

dopamine loop The cycle of pleasure-seeking behavior caused by the brain chemical dopamine.

dual perspective The ability to understand your own and your relational partner's thoughts, feelings, and needs.

duping delight The feeling of gratification you get the moment you realize your deception succeeded.

duty to disclose The ethical obligation to share information in a timely manner when it may involve or affect another person in some way. *See also* significant choice.

emotion A psychological and physiological response to an activating event. Also called a *feeling*.

emotional contagion The transfer of feelings from one person to another, e.g., the joy expressed at a wedding or sadness at a funeral.

emotional display rules The social dos and don'ts of emotional expression. These are influenced by culture and gender.

emotional experience The internal sensation and identification of your own emotions. *See also* emotional expression.

emotional expression How you communicate your emotions to others. *See also* emotional experience.

emotional intelligence (EI) The ability to identify, manage, and express your emotions effectively, including the ability to read and respond to the emotions of others.

emotional labor The effort it takes to generate, manage, and mask your emotions.

emotive language Language that describes something and also reveals the speaker's attitude about what is being described.

empathetic listening Listening in order to identify with and share the feelings of another person.

empathy The ability to understand, appreciate, and value what someone else is feeling. Empathy goes beyond acknowledging another person's emotions; it involves experiencing what someone feels.

encoding The mental process of creating and sending a message. *See also* decoding.

enculturation The process of learning about and adopting the norms and values of your own culture. *See also* acculturation.

enunciation The act of vocalizing a word clearly so others can understand what you're saying. *See also* pronunciation.

equity theory The idea that your relationship satisfaction is higher when you and a relational partner share equally in the costs and benefits of your relationship.

equivocation The intentional use of vague language in order to avoid saying what you really think or feel. Also called *doublespeak*.

ethnocentrism The tendency to view the beliefs and practices of one's own culture or co-culture as superior to others.

euphemism A kinder word or phrase that a speaker uses in place of a less agreeable one. Also called *kind speech*.

expectancy violations theory A communication theory that explains your reactions to behaviors that are unanticipated or contradict social expectations.

explicit rule A rule that is communicated in a clear, direct, and obvious manner. *See also* implicit rule.

external noise Noise that occurs in the environment (outside your mind and body). *See also* internal noise *and* semantic noise.

facial management techniques The expressions you make to either convey or mask your thoughts and feelings.

facilitative emotion An emotion that helps you improve the quality of your communication and enhance relational outcomes. *See also* debilitative emotion.

fairness The quality of your communication that demonstrates that you play by the same rules and ensure that everyone has equal access to resources, information, and opportunities.

fallacy An irrational belief that feeds into negative, debilitative emotions. *See also* fallacy of approval, fallacy of causation, fallacy of overgeneralization, fallacy of perfection, *and* fallacy of should.

fallacy of approval The belief that it's essential to seek and win everyone's acceptance and admiration. *See also* fallacy.

fallacy of causation The belief that a communication choice will definitely result in a certain outcome. *See also* fallacy.

fallacy of overgeneralization The belief that a single instance (or an isolated occurrence) signifies an enduring absolute. *See also* fallacy.

fallacy of perfection The belief that it's essential to communicate exceptionally well all the time. *See also* fallacy.

fallacy of should The belief that others ought to think and behave just as you do. *See also* fallacy.

feedback A verbal and/or nonverbal response to a message.

feminine culture A cultural orientation characterized by less distinct gender roles and a relatively egalitarian status for men and women. *See also* masculine culture.

feminine expression A gender presentation consistent with the interests, behaviors, and communication

style traditionally associated with femininity. *See also* masculine expression *and* androgynous expression.

flaming The hostile exchange of online messages, often in the form of insults.

frame of reference The perspective you bring to a conversation or interaction, including your past experiences and background.

fundamental attribution error When you attribute a person's behavior to internal factors without considering external factors.

gap-filling Interrupting to finish a person's thoughts or story or add details to a story.

gay A sexual orientation characterized by attraction to individuals of the same sex. The clinical term is *homosexual*. *See also* sexual orientation.

gaze aversion The act of avoiding or limiting eye contact.

gender expression The way in which a person prefers to express their gender, typically through interests, behaviors, and communication style. *See also* feminine expression, masculine expression, *and* androgynous expression.

gender identity Your sense of being a man, woman, neither, or both. *See also* cisgender, nonbinary, *and* transgender.

gender schemas Pervasive cultural beliefs about what it means to be male or female. *See also* gender socialization.

gender socialization The process of teaching children how to act in ways that align with the cultural expectations of their biological sex. *See also* gender schemas.

gesticulation The use of your arms and hands to communicate meaning.

ghosting The act of cutting off all communication with no explanation.

golden rule A moral decision-making approach in which you strive to treat others the way you wish to be treated. *See also* platinum rule.

gunny-sacking The act of bringing up a bunch of past, unexpressed grievances in the heat of an argument. *See also* past-digging *and* beltlining.

harassment Any behavior that makes a person feel uncomfortable, threatened, or unsafe. Such behaviors include intimidation, unwanted sexual attention or pressure, harsh criticism, unwelcome humor, false accusations, gossiping, name-calling, teasing, and interfering in a person's ability to do one's job. *See also* hostile work environment.

hearing The physiological process of receiving and recognizing sounds. *See also* listening.

heterosexism Negative beliefs and feelings toward non-heterosexual individuals. This term is often used interchangeably with the word *homophobia*, the fear of non-heterosexual individuals. *See also* prejudice.

high conversation orientation Family communication in which members interact frequently, speak more candidly, and talk spontaneously about a wide range of topics. *See also* low conversation orientation.

high power distance (HPD) culture A cultural orientation characterized by rigid social hierarchy and deference to power and authority. *See also* low power distance (LPD) culture.

high-context culture A cultural orientation characterized by the high value placed on indirect and informal communication as well as in-group harmony. *See also* low-context culture.

high-stakes deception Misleading or dishonest communication behavior that is significant in nature and likely to harm a relationship if discovered. Its repercussions are severe. *See also* deception *and* low-stakes deception.

hostile work environment A workplace in which employees engage in harassment without facing corrective or disciplinary action and the behaviors interfere with another employee's ability to perform a job. *See also* harassment.

hyperpersonal communication A form of online communication in which self-disclosure becomes intimate and revealing more quickly than it would likely occur in F2F and V2V contexts.

"I feel . . . because . . . I need" statement A sentence structure that helps you focus on the behavior that affects you and what you'd like your relational partner to do, e.g., "**I feel** respected **because** you go out of your way to introduce me to your friends. **I need** (or like) that. Keep it up!"

I-language A statement or question that starts with the pronoun *I*. *See also* you-language.

immediacy The degree of closeness, liking, and connection in a relationship.

implicit rule A rule that is communicated in an indirect, subtle manner. *See also* explicit rule.

impression management What you say or do to influence how others perceive you. Also called *facework*. *See also* public face *and* saving face.

inclusion The process of promoting diversity and making all people feel welcomed, valued, and accepted.

incongruence The degree to which two or more people share dissimilar perceptions, expectations, or opinions about a communication experience. *See also* congruence.

indirect language Subtle or suggestive language that hints at the intended message. *See also* direct language.

individualistic culture A cultural orientation characterized by a heavy emphasis on individual success and self-determination. *See also* collectivistic culture.

in-group A social group you identify with. *See also* out-group, code-switching, *and* theory of intersectionality.

insulating Blocking out or ignoring what you're hearing.

integrity The quality of your communication that demonstrates that your behaviors mirror your convictions.

interactive adaptation theory The idea that competent communicators alter their nonverbal communication to interact successfully with others.

internal noise Noise that occurs within your mind (psychologically) or body (physically). *See also* external noise *and* semantic noise.

interpersonal behavior What you say and/or do to convey a message—e.g., patting a friend on the back in a congratulatory way or saying "I'm sorry" sincerely.

interpersonal communication (IPC) The process of assigning meaning to the messages you share with potential and established relational partners.

interpersonal communication competence The ability to communicate effectively and appropriately on a relational level—one-on-one and within small groups.

interpersonal communication ethics The beliefs, values, and principles that guide communication behaviors within a relationship.

interpersonal conflict A tension or struggle between two or more relational partners. Common sources include unmet needs, opposing goals, and strongly held differences of opinion.

interpersonal goal A specific objective you are striving to accomplish with your communication; three primary types are practical, relational, and self-presentational. What you are striving to accomplish with your communication.

interpersonal idiom A word or phrase whose meaning is unique to two or more individuals who share a relationship. *See also* cultural idiom.

interpersonal need An inner drive (or motivating force) that is essential to your well-being and relational in nature—e.g., feeling understood or gaining the respect of others.

interpersonal power The ability to influence the thoughts, feelings, and behaviors of a relational partner.

interpersonal system Two or more interdependent individuals who rely on each other to accomplish personal and shared goals.

interpersonal trust A firm belief in the ability, reliability, and honesty of another person.

interpreting The meaning you assign to a message using sensory information, relating it to what you know and your experiences. It is the third stage of the listening process and the perception process. *See also* perception *and* selective perception.

interrupting Saying something before someone has finished speaking.

intersex Possessing a combination of male and female biological traits and/or chromosomes. *See also* biological sex.

intrapersonal communication The communication you have with yourself. This form of communication includes the silent thoughts you have, the things you may write or type in private to yourself, or what you say when you talk to yourself out loud. Also called *self-talk*.

jargon Nonstandard language used by members of a particular profession, trade, or academic community. Also called *shop talk*. *See also* slang.

language A system of words that are collectively understood to have meaning. *See also* verbal communication.

leakage Sudden or spontaneous—often unconscious—nonverbal reactions. *See also* microexpression.

lean channel A communication medium that provides few sources of sensory information to convey meaning, such as an email or text. *See also* channel *and* rich channel.

linguistic determinism The idea that language determines people's ability to perceive and think. *See also* linguistic relativism.

linguistic relativism The idea that language doesn't determine one's reality (as linguistic determinism suggests), but it does influence it. *See also* linguistic determinism.

listening Hearing that is focused and intentional. It is a physiological and psychological process. *See also* hearing.

listening bias A set of preconceived ideas or beliefs that affect how you listen to others.

listening fatigue When listening becomes mentally tiresome.

listening style Your preferred way of making sense of messages as you listen. There are many different types of listening styles, including action-oriented, time-oriented, relational-oriented, content-oriented, and analysis-oriented.

long-term attraction The feeling that motivates you to maintain a relationship and, when necessary, repair or reconcile it. *See also* attraction *and* short-term attraction.

low conversation orientation Family communication in which members interact infrequently, speak less candidly, and with more restrictions on conversation topics. *See also* high conversation orientation.

low power distance (LPD) culture A cultural orientation that values equality and allows for greater socioeconomic mobility. *See also* high power distance (HPD) culture.

low-context culture A cultural orientation characterized by communication that is formal, direct, and focused on getting things done. *See also* high-context culture.

low-stakes deception Misleading or dishonest communication behavior perceived as harmless. Its consequences, if any, are minor or unsubstantial. *See also* deception *and* high-stakes deception.

masculine culture A cultural orientation characterized by distinct gender roles and a higher social status for men. *See also* feminine culture.

masculine expression A gender presentation consistent with the interests, behaviors, and communication style traditionally associated with masculinity. *See also* feminine expression *and* androgynous expression.

media ecology perspective (MEP) The idea that technology reshapes and reorganizes your interpersonal communication values, perceptions, and behaviors.

memory reconstruction When you alter aspects of a memory. You may reconstruct a memory to feel better about it; or remember it in a way that justifies or alters your feelings.

message The meaning communicators assign to a symbol.

metacommunication Communicating about communication; a type of feedback.

meta-conflict Conflict caused by the way you express conflict.

meta-emotion An emotion about an emotion—or a feeling about a feeling, e.g., feeling embarrassed by your angry outburst.

microexpression A form of nonverbal leakage specific to the face; sudden, involuntary facial expressions that communicate an instant message. *See also* leakage.

mindfulness The ability to notice new things in your surroundings, within yourself, and in others.

mirroring When you consciously and subconsciously imitate or reflect a speaker's emotional state and communication behaviors.

mixed message Communication in which verbal and nonverbal messages contradict each other in some way.

monochronic culture A cultural orientation characterized by a strict, scheduled approach to time. *See also* polychronic culture.

monopolizing Talking too much and not giving others a chance to speak.

monotone voice A tone of voice that is flat or unchanging.

mood An emotional state that lacks a clear cause or contextual stimulus, such as having the blues or just feeling cheerful for no apparent reason.

moral absolutism The belief that certain actions are right or wrong no matter the circumstances. *See also* moral relativism.

moral relativism The belief that a given action is more or less ethical depending on the circumstances. According to this view, not all ethical considerations are black or white nor are all ethical choices intrinsically right or wrong. *See also* moral absolutism.

narcissistic listening Characterized by self-absorption; listening primarily to meet your needs and stroke your ego.

negative blanket statement A statement or question that implies that a person's feelings or behavior occur all the time or are unchanging. Also called *static evaluation* or *overgeneralization*.

noise An influence that distorts messages and makes clear and effective communication challenging. *See also* external noise, internal noise, *and* semantic noise.

nonbinary A gender identity whereby a person identifies as both genders or neither one. Also called *gender nonconforming* or *genderqueer*. *See also* gender identity, cisgender, *and* transgender.

nonverbal back-channel cues Listening responses that do not involve language. *See also* back-channel cues *and* verbal back-channel cues.

nonverbal communication Sending and receiving messages without the use of language. *See also* verbal communication.

nonverbal symbol Anything that conveys meaning separate from a letter or word. *See also* symbol *and* verbal symbol.

norms Common ways of communicating and behaving in social settings.

observational I-statement A statement that focuses on a person's observed behavior, starting with the first-person pronoun *I*; a specific type of I-language.

one-upping Responding by saying how you have it better or worse.

ongoing negative affect The lingering negative feelings you have toward someone as a result of a relational transgression. *See also* relational transgression.

organizing The second stage of the perception process, organizing is arranging sensory information in a meaningful way. *See also* perception, schemas, *and* script.

other-centered communication When you consider your relational partner's needs and goals as much as your own. *See also* relationship-centered communication.

out-group A social group you do not identify with. *See also* in-group, codeswitching, *and* theory of intersectionality.

overt conflict Conflict that relational partners express to each other in a direct and straightforward manner. *See also* covert conflict.

pansexual A sexual orientation characterized by attraction to both sexes and all gender identities. *See also* sexual orientation.

paralanguage The qualities of your voice that convey meaning apart from language. *See also* vocal pitch, rate, *and* volume.

paraphrasing Briefly restating in your own words what you heard someone say.

passive listening Listening half-heartedly—tuning in and out with your listening. Your lack of mental engagement makes you very susceptible to distractions. *See also* active listening.

passive-aggressiveness A form of indirect hostility that allows the sender to appear outwardly noncombative.

past-digging The act of bringing up a negative memory you have of your relational partner to drive home a point. *See also* gunny-sacking *and* beltlining.

perception checking The way in which you test the accuracy of your perceptions.

perception The mental process of receiving and interpreting sensory information—what you taste, touch, smell, see, and hear. Perception helps you make sense of the messages you receive, and it can also help you understand how the messages you send affect other people. *See also* attribution, interpreting, organizing, *and* selective perception.

personality The stable psychological characteristics or traits unique to you, including how you prefer to think, behave, and relate to people.

perspective-taking The act of imagining that you are the other person in a given situation.

phone snubbing The act of making it seem like your time on your cell phone is more important than your time with a relational partner.

phonological rules Rules that establish how a word is said or pronounced. *See also* pragmatic rules, semantic rules, *and* syntactic rules.

physical proximity How near or accessible you are to someone.

platinum rule A moral decision-making approach in which you strive to treat others the way they wish to be treated. *See also* golden rule.

polychronic culture A cultural orientation characterized by a flexible approach to time. *See also* monochronic culture.

post-cyber-disclosure panic The dread, regret, or anxiety you feel after sending an online message, usually the moment you realize your message could affect you or someone you care about in a negative way.

postponement Delaying a conversation until you are able and ready to communicate effectively.

power currency A desired resource that confers interpersonal power on the person who possesses it.

power play When you use a compliance-gaining tactic on someone repeatedly because it gets you what you want. *See also* compliance-gaining strategy.

powerless language Speech that makes a speaker sound less confident, resolute, or assertive.

pragmatic rules Rules that influence word choice and interpretation based on social norms and expectations. *See also* phonological rules, semantic rules, *and* syntactic rules.

predicted value outcome theory The idea that you'll use various communication strategies in your initial interactions with others to assess whether it benefits you to have future interactions.

prejudice A negative belief or feeling toward a group of people or people perceived as belonging to a certain group. *See also* ableism, ageism, racism, sexism, *and* unconscious bias.

principle of least interest The idea that a relational partner who has the least interest in continuing the relationship may feel less inclined to yield or share power.

projection The mental process of assuming that another person is thinking, feeling, or behaving as you would in a given situation.

pronunciation The act of saying a word correctly based on dictionary or phonetic rules. *See also* enunciation.

proxemic theory The idea that people perceive space differently and use space to achieve their communication goals.

pseudolistening Pretending to listen or acting like you're listening when your attention is focused elsewhere.

public face How you want to appear to others. This includes what you want others to know or not know about you. Also called *public image* or *presenting self*. *See also* impression management *and* saving face.

put-down Language that is demeaning or hurtful. *See also* trigger words.

queer A non-straight sexual orientation. Individuals who identify as queer may find other terms too constricting or inexact. The term is also used to refer to the LGBTQ community as a whole.

racism Negative beliefs and feelings toward other races. *See also* prejudice.

rational-emotive theory (RET) The idea that your cognitive interpretation of an event has more to do with your emotion than the activating event does.

recall test Checking to see if you remember what you've been told.

recalling The last stage of the perception process where you retrieve or remember a message or sensory information.

receiver A person who decodes a message. *See also* sender.

receiving The first stage of the listening process, in which you gain a sensory awareness.

receptivity Your willingness to receive a message or engage in a conversation.

reciprocity appeal An attempt to persuade someone by implying that it is time to return a favor.

relational cost An aspect of a relationship that you don't like or want. *See also* relational reward *and* social exchange theory.

relational partner Someone you know and share a connection with on some level, such as a parent, sibling, relative, friend, coworker, or romantic partner.

relational reward Something you receive from a relationship that you like and value. *See also* relational cost *and* social exchange theory.

relational rule A rule that governs what you can or cannot do within the context of a relationship. *See also* rules theory.

relational stages model A model that describes how relationships start, grow, endure, and end. The model's first five stages are associated with a relationship that is coming together and the last five are associated with a relationship that is coming apart.

relational transgression An unethical action taken by a relational partner that hurts you or makes you feel betrayed. *See also* ongoing negative affect.

relationship-centered communication When you make communication choices that are good for a relationship and reflect how much you value it. *See also* other-centered communication.

respect The quality of your communication that demonstrates that you value someone's time, safety, health, possessions, feelings, and needs.

responding The fourth stage of the listening process, in which you react verbally and/or nonverbally to a message.

responsibility The quality of your communication that demonstrates that you own your actions, respond reliably, and act proactively to solve interpersonal problems.

rich channel A communication medium that provides many sources of sensory information to convey meaning, such as face-to-face communication. *See also* channel *and* lean channel.

role A specific pattern of behavior you are expected to perform within an interpersonal system.

rules Behavioral guidelines for communication within an interpersonal system. *See also* explicit rule *and* implicit rule.

rules theory The idea that relationships are held together and torn apart based on relational partners' adherence to certain rules. *See also* relational rule.

sanction A verbal and/or nonverbal reprimand for breaking an explicit or implicit communication rule.

sandwich approach Presenting a constructive suggestion between two positive or complimentary statements in order to deliver corrective information in a softer, gentler way.

saving face The effort you make to protect or repair your public face when it's threatened. Also called *corrective facework*. *See also* public face *and* impression management.

schemas The clustered knowledge or structured thoughts you have about certain events and experiences. *See also* organizing, perception, *and* script.

script The sequence or pattern of behaviors you associate with an event or experience. *See also* organizing, perception, *and* schemas.

selecting The first stage in the perception process, selecting is when you focus your attention on a particular stimulus using one or more of your five senses. *See also* selective attention.

selective attention The tendency to focus on what interests you the most at a given moment and tune out what doesn't. *See also* selecting.

selective listening When you focus most of your attention on the messages you find interesting, unique, or important and tune out those you don't. *See also* selective attention.

selective memory Remembering what you want to remember. This includes distorting or blocking uncomfortable memories. Also called *selective recall*.

selective perception Seeing what you want to see or hearing what you want to hear. It occurs when your wants, needs, or beliefs influence how you interpret sensory information. *See also* perception *and* interpreting.

self-concept How you perceive yourself; the relatively stable, multifaceted perceptions you have of yourself. *See also* self-esteem *and* self-confidence.

self-confidence The degree to which you believe in your abilities and judgment. *See also* self-concept *and* self-esteem.

self-delusion The act or state of deceiving oneself.

self-disclosure The act of revealing personal information about yourself to others. *See also* social penetration theory.

self-esteem How you feel about yourself as a result of how you perceive yourself. *See also* self-concept *and* self-confidence.

self-fulfilling prophecy A prediction or expectation that comes true because the prediction itself causes you to act in ways that make it come true.

self-monitoring Thinking about and analyzing your communication with others.

self-serving bias Attributing a positive outcome to your own inner qualities and attributing a negative outcome to outside factors.

semantic noise Noise that occurs when language affects your ability to understand someone. *See also* external noise *and* internal noise.

semantic rules Rules that establish what a word means in a certain language. *See also* phonological rules, pragmatic rules, *and* syntactic rules.

sender A person who encodes a message and transmits it. *See also* receiver.

sensory overload When sensory stimulation exceeds what your nervous system can handle. Also called *message overload*.

sexism Negative beliefs and feelings toward the opposite sex. *See also* prejudice.

sexting The exchange of nude or seminude photos, videos, and sexually suggestive language via text messaging.

sexual orientation The enduring romantic and sexual attraction you have to individuals of a certain sex or gender identity. *See also* gay, straight, bisexual, pansexual, *and* asexual.

short-term attraction The initial feeling that motivates you to begin and develop a relationship. *See also* attraction *and* long-term attraction.

significant choice The ethical obligation to give a relational partner the ability to make free and fully informed decisions. A choice is free if it is made voluntarily with no manipulation or coercion involved; it is fully informed if the person making the choice has all of the necessary and available information. *See also* duty to disclose.

similarity assumption An automatic and uninformed belief that others are like you in some way.

skirting The act of avoiding conflict by either joking about a problem or changing the topic of conversation.

slang Informal language or words whose meaning is understood by members of a particular social group or subculture. *See also* jargon.

small talk Communication in which you disclose general information about yourself in order to get acquainted with someone.

sniping The act of alluding to a conflict but then backing away from it.

social comparison When you use your perception to determine how you measure up to others.

social exchange theory The idea that your willingness to develop a relationship is based on cost-benefit analysis. *See also* relational reward *and* relational cost.

social penetration theory The idea that the breadth and depth of self-disclosure influences a relationship's development. *See also* self-disclosure.

social validation appeal A persuasive technique used to convince you to do something because other people you know and like are doing the same thing.

society A large grouping of individuals who share a common social identity.

solution-based communication Communication that is focused on potential solutions rather than the behaviors that started a conflict.

speech-thought differential The difference between the rate at which a person speaks and your ability to process spoken messages.

spillover effect Carrying feelings that originate at work to people and situations outside the workplace.

stage-hogging Making yourself the focus of conversation.

stereotype An overly simplistic, preconceived impression or assumption you have about a group of individuals. Stereotyping is assuming something about a person based solely on her or his group affiliation.

storing The fourth stage of the perception process, storing is the process of sorting sensory information—putting some into memory, and discarding the rest.

straight A sexual orientation characterized by attraction to individuals of the opposite sex. The clinical term is *heterosexual*. *See also* sexual orientation.

strong tie A relationship that is significant to you; it influences your thoughts, feelings, and behaviors more compared to the other relationships you have. *See also* weak tie.

subjective evaluation A judgment you make based on your own perceptions, feelings, tastes, and opinions.

symbol Anything that stands for a thought, person, object, feeling, or idea. *See also* nonverbal symbol *and* verbal symbol.

synchronous communication Sending and receiving messages simultaneously. *See also* asynchronous communication.

syntactic rules Rules that govern the order in which words appear in a sentence. *See also* phonological rules, pragmatic rules, *and* semantic rules.

technology-mediated communication (TMC) The process of exchanging and assigning meaning to messages that are facilitated by technology channels and applications.

territoriality The tendency to claim user's rights to a space that you don't own.

theory of intersectionality The idea that social identity markers (for example, being a woman and being Black) do not exist independently of each other. Together, they may make you feel similar to or different from others—and affect how others treat you. *See also* in-group, out-group, *and* code-switching.

transgender A gender identity whereby a person's gender and biological sex do not match. *See also* gender identity, cisgender, *and* nonbinary.

trapping The act of asking someone to communicate in a certain way and then making that person regret doing what you've asked.

trigger words Language that sparks negative emotional reactions and intensifies arguments. *See also* put-down.

truthfulness The quality of your communication that is accurate, sincere, and doesn't omit information deemed important to a relational partner.

turn-denying signals Verbal and nonverbal behaviors you use during a conversation to deny someone the opportunity to speak. *See also* conversational turn-taking, turn-requesting signals, *and* turn-yielding signals.

turn-requesting signals Verbal and nonverbal behaviors you use during a conversation to encourage someone to stop talking so you can speak. *See also* conversational turn-taking, turn-denying signals, *and* turn-yielding signals.

turn-yielding signals Verbal and nonverbal behaviors you use during a conversation to encourage someone to speak. *See also* conversational turn-taking, turn-denying signals, *and* turn-requesting signals.

turning point An event that causes or signals a significant change in a relationship.

two-step perception check A technique in which you vocalize what you are sensing using an observational I-statement followed by a question for clarification.

uncertainty reduction theory The idea that we tend to seek out information about relational partners or social situations to reduce any discomfort associated with uncertainties we have about them.

uncomplimentary comparison A statement or question that compares the receiver to someone else in an unflattering way.

unconscious bias A prejudicial belief you hold that you are not aware of. *See also* prejudice.

validation The act of recognizing or acknowledging another person's stated or unstated thoughts, feelings, and needs.

verbal back-channel cues Listening responses that use language. *See also* back-channel cues *and* nonverbal back-channel cues.

verbal communication The use of words to convey meaning—how someone uses language to speak, write, and send electronic messages. *See also* language *and* nonverbal communication.

verbal symbol Any of the letters and words of a particular language. *See also* symbol *and* nonverbal symbol.

vocal pitch The intonation or inflection in your voice ranging from high to low sounds. *See also* paralanguage, vocal rate, *and* vocal volume.

vocal rate The speed at which you speak. *See also* paralanguage, vocal pitch, *and* vocal volume.

vocal utterances The filler sounds you make between words or sentences—such as "uhm" or "and uh."

vocal volume How loudly or softly you speak. *See also* paralanguage, vocal pitch, *and* vocal rate.

weak tie A relationship that is less developed or influential compared to a strong tie; you usually give a weak tie less of your time or effort. *See also* strong tie.

withholding When you purposely deprive someone of something they want or need (for example, affection, interaction, or intimacy) in order to express your negative feelings and exert control. Often used as a compliance gaining strategy.

workplace engagement The degree to which you are happy with, committed to, and energized by your job.

you-language A statement or question that starts with the pronoun *you*. You-language often provokes a negative response if paired with an accusation, negative blanket statement, or uncomplimentary comparison. *See also* I-language.

subject index

name index

Index entries below are followed by the page number where the person's work is referenced, and by a superscript number that corresponds to the numbered note on that page. For example, "Smith, A., 47[5]" means that Alice Smith's research is referenced on page 47 and is cited in note 5 on that page.

credits

Text

Chapter 3

Page 86 (Table 3.3): Courtesy of William deDie; pp. 88–89 (Assessing Your IPC: Communication Apprehension): Copyright 2017. From *Introduction to Rhetorical Communication* by James C. McCroskey. Reproduced by permission of Taylor and Francis Group, LLC, a division of Informa plc.

Chapter 7

Pages 194–96 (Assessing Your IPC: Problematic Behaviors and Emotion): The Quick Emotional Intelligence Self-Assessment. Reprinted by permission of Mohapel Consulting Ltd.

Photos

Front matter

Pages ii–iii: Plume Creative / Getty Images; p. ix: Katarzyna Bialasiewicz / Alamy Stock Photo; p. x: eggeegg / Shutterstock; p. xi: Lucky Business / Shutterstock; p. xii: simonkr / Getty Images; p. xiii (top): AS photostudio / Shutterstock; p. xiii (bottom): Dean Drobot / Shutterstock; p. xiv: Rawpixel.com / Shutterstock; p. xv: Rawpixel.com / Shutterstock; p. xvi: ANN PATCHANAN / Shutterstock; p. xvii: Rawpixel.com / Shutterstock; p. xviii: Hector Pertuz / Shutterstock; p. xix: CREATISTA / Shutterstock; p. xxi (top): Bruce Punches; p. xxi (bottom): Rik Anderson, University Photographer, West Texas A&M University

Part I

Page 3: Jack Frog/Shutterstock

Chapter 1

Pages 4–5: Katarzyna Bialasiewicz / Alamy Stock Photo; p. 8: Warner Bros. Television; p. 10: MAKI STUDIO / Alamy Stock Photo; p. 11: USA Network; p. 14: brubearbaby; p. 15: Daria Chichkareva / Shutterstock; p. 17: NBC Universal Television Distribution; p. 19: M J Fry via CartoonStock; p. 23: Trifecta Entertainment & Media; p. 24: Ron Levine / Getty Images; p. 26: Jeff Stahler / Distributed by Universal Uclick for UFS via CartoonStock

Chapter 2

Page 30–31: eggeegg / Shutterstock; p. 33: Christos Georghiou / Shutterstock; p. 34: Warner Bros. Television; p. 35: Warner Bros. Television; p. 37: DimaBerlin / Shutterstock; p. 42: Focus Features; p. 44: Warner Bros. Pictures; p. 45: Hill Street Studios / Getty Images; p. 46: Tim Cordell via CartoonStock; p. 47: 20th Century

Fox Television; p. 50: m-gucci / Getty Images; p. 51: Mike Baldwin via CartoonStock; p. 53: Shondaland Productions / ABC Studios

Part II

Page 59: David Oldfield / Getty Images

Chapter 3

Pages 60–61: Lucky Business / Shutterstock; p. 65: Full Picture Productions / Lifetime Television; p. 67: Shiho Fukada / Getty Images; p. 69: Broadway Video / NBC; p. 74: Moodboard Stock Photography / Alamy Stock Photo; p. 75: Mark Stivers / stiverscartoons; p. 78: Universal Television / NBC; p. 80: HBO Entertainment; p. 83: Leo Cullum via Cartoon Collections; p. 87: Dragon Images / Shutterstock

Chapter 4

Pages 92–93: simonkr / Getty Images; p. 95: Tetra Images, LLC / Alamy Stock Photo; p. 96: ABC Studios; p. 98: Freeform Original Productions; p. 102: Cultura Creative RF / Alamy Stock Photo; p. 104: Castle Rock Entertainment; p. 106: Tim Oliphant via CartoonStock; p. 109: Image Source Plus / Alamy Stock Photo; p. 110: Mark Anderson / Andertoons; p. 112: ABC Studios; p. 114: Jason Headley

Chapter 5

Pages 118–19: AS photostudio / Shutterstock; p. 122: ABC News; p. 123: Neil McAllister / Alamy Stock Photo; p. 124: Crowden Satz via CartoonStock; p. 126: 20th Century Fox / Lightstorm / Entertainment / Dune Entertainment / Ingenious Film Partners; p. 130: Shondaland Productions / ABC Studios; p. 132: Valerii Honcharuk / Alamy Stock Photo; p. 135: Marc Tyler Nobleman via CartoonStock; p. 136: LightField Studios / Shutterstock; p. 140: Ryan Seacrest Productions and Bunim / Murray Productions

Chapter 6

Pages 144–45: Dean Drobot / Shutterstock; p. 147: Iakov Filimonov/ Shutterstock; p. 148: Paramount Vantage; p. 152: Isabella Bannerman; p. 153: Luna Vandoorne / Shutterstock; p. 156: Canadian Broadcasting Company; p. 160: HBO; p. 164: Manel Ponce Rodriguez / Shutterstock; p. 165: BRAVO

Chapter 7

Pages 170–71: Rawpixel.com / Shutterstock; p. 174: BRAVO; p. 175: AJR_photo / Shutterstock; p. 182: Tom Cheney / The New Yorker Collection / The Cartoon Bank; P. 183: MLB; p. 185: MTV; p. 188: Dean Drobot / Shutterstock; p. 190: David Sipress via Cartoon Collections; p. 191: Mosaic Media Group / Wild West Picture Show Productions

Chapter 8

Pages 198–99: Rawpixel.com / Shutterstock; p. 201: Gelpi / Shutterstock; p. 204: Talk WW Productions, Inc.; p. 208: Chuck Lorre Productions; p. 209: Hongqi Zhang / Alamy Stock Photo; p. 214: Jubilee Media; p. 216: Copyright 2004 by Randy Glasbergen; p. 218: Folio Images / Alamy Stock Photo; p. 220: Scott Rudin Productions

Chapter 9

Pages 226–27: ANN PATCHANAN / Shutterstock; p. 229: Prisma by Dukas Presseagentur GmbH / Alamy Stock Photo; p. 232: Pamplona Productions; p. 234: Jack Ziegler via CartoonStock; p. 236: Color Force; p. 239: Trip the Light; p. 244: Gelpi / Shutterstock; p. 246: September Films; p. 250 (top): P.C. Vey via CartoonStock; p. 250 (bottom): Jacob Lund / Shutterstock; p. 254: Deedle-Dee Productions

Part III

Page 257: Leo Patrizi/Getty Images

Chapter 10

Pages 258–59: Rawpixel.com / Shutterstock; p. 262: SisterLee Productions; p. 265: W.B. Park via CartoonStock; p. 268: Tyler Stableford / Getty Images; p. 271: Jaimie Wilson; p. 273: AS photostudio / Shutterstock; p. 275: Upworthy; p. 278: Leo Cullum via Cartoon Collections; p. 281: Judgemental Films; p. 282: Thomas Barwick / Getty Images; p. 283: Gay Rosenthal Productions

Chapter 11

Pages 286–87: Hector Pertuz/Shutterstock; p. 292: Sergey Novikov/ Alamy Stock Photo; p. 293: Lloyd-Levitan Productions: p. 294: Robert R. Morris; p. 297: Fox 2000 Pictures; p. 298: samuel wordley / Alamy Stock Photo; p. 304: dekazigzag/Shutterstock; p. 306: Camp-Grounded; p. 307: Steve Smeltzer via CartoonStock

Chapter 12

Page 310–11: CREATISTA / Shutterstock; p. 313: Randy Glasbergen; p. 316: Columbia Pictures; p. 317: Sergio Mendoza Hochmann / Getty Images; p. 318: Dorothy Parker Drank Here Productions; p. 324: 21 Laps Entertainment; p. 325: Monkey Business Images / Shutterstock; p. 332: PacoRomero / Getty Images; p. 333: Kinley India TV